“This is truly a great book. In fact, I have n[illegible] Wilder have brought together a team of very know[illegible] from various perspectives why they could no long[illegible] leave Mormonism simply fall off the grid, the goo[illegible]s that there is an intellectually and spiritually vibr[illegible]sm to historical evangelical Christianity. The book [illegible] first place to go for anyone who wants an honest, se[illegible] of Mormonism, along with an alternative to consider. I give it my top recommendation.”

—J. P. Moreland, Ph.D.
Distinguished Professor of Philosophy,
Talbot School of Theology, Biola University

“*Leaving Mormonism* is a new kind of book that gives the inside story of four former Mormons who are now Christian academics. Each tells how they came to understand the good news of God’s grace, what sort of questions and challenges—intellectual, emotional, personal and professional—they faced, and how they integrated their academic work with their new Christian faith. There is great wisdom for academics, young and old, who are also navigating this difficult transition.”

—Ken Mulholland, Ph.D.
President, Western Institute for Intercultural Studies,
Former President, Salt Lake Theological Seminary

“For anyone who has Mormon family or friends, or contact with the LDS movement, many questions arise. If you are from a traditional or conservative Christian background, you find yourself struggling to reconcile the claims made by those within Mormonism with what the Bible and historic Christianity both teach and claim. Despite the insistence that we are all talking about Christian thought and ideas, as soon as one explores, compares, and considers carefully the actual claims of Christ, they stand in stark contrast to LDS teaching and claims. We are compelled to ask what is the truth? This unique volume is not only written by former “insiders”, who were all in their respective ways committed, but also by a group of deep thinkers who have taken the time to investigate and compare truth claims. Their histories, experiences, and education are all brought to bear on whether or not Mormon teaching is true, accurate, and reliable. As a resource to individuals, churches, or study groups, who will have to read carefully and thoroughly, this is a great tool. I learned much already from the insider view and experience which is a vital part of this work, as the ideas and teachings are rooted in a very demanding culture. I believe it deserves to be widely read, especially by those impacted or influenced by LDS teachings. It makes the gospel clear by its amazing contrast. May that grace touch many as a result of this work.”

—Stuart McAllister, D.D.
Ravi Zacharias International Ministries

“‘Leaving Mormonism’ today all too often means rejecting Christianity entirely in the mistaken belief that if Mormonism isn’t true then no form of Christian faith is true. In *Leaving Mormonism*, four Christian scholars, each of whom also happens to be a former Mormon, show that faith in Jesus Christ as he is revealed in the Bible is intellectually and spiritually viable for disillusioned Latter-day Saints. The authors combine their authentic personal stories with scholarly analysis of critical issues and are not afraid to point out how evangelicals have sometimes failed to engage Mormons in a constructive manner. There is much for everyone to learn from this book.”

—Robert M. Bowman Jr., Ph.D.
Executive Director,
Institute for Religious Research

"*Leaving Mormonism* provides a charitable and critical analysis of Mormonism by former Mormons who each reflect on their own stories of leaving the LDS Church and their reasons for embracing the eternal gospel of Jesus Christ. The volume spans across the breadth of Mormon theology, plumbs into the depths of Mormon experience, and crosses through some of the murky waters that so many former Mormons have to navigate. Readers will be encouraged and challenged by the unique expressions of anecdote, testimony, and renewed faith."

—John Anthony Dunne, Ph.D.
Assistant Professor of New Testament,
Bethel Seminary

"This book makes a noteworthy contribution to the ongoing academic dialog between Latter-day Saints and evangelical Christians. Even though former Mormons offer a unique perspective to that dialog—as their life experience bridges the gap between both sides—their voice has been missing from that conversation from the start. But this is not just an academic work. It is a stirring combination of inspiring personal stories told by people with warm hearts and vibrant souls as well as sharp minds."

—Ross Anderson, D.Min.
Teaching Pastor,
Alpine Church, UT

"I've read and highly recommend *Leaving Mormonism: Why Four Scholars Changed their Minds*. As a pastor in Utah we have a shortage of reliable resources that we can recommend without hesitation to those who are leaving Mormonism and making their way into gospel Christianity. This is at the top of my list for that kind of resource. Because the greatest factor in ministering to former Mormons is trust, I'm grateful that we can partner with the authors in providing 'trustworthy' reading for our people."

—Paul Robie, D.Min.
Lead Pastor,
South Mountain Community Church, UT

"A one of a kind book blending powerful personal testimonies with persuasive reasons for the truth and goodness of Christianity and the falsity of the Mormon faith. Written with compassion, charity, and courage, this will be the go-to book for those interested in Christian-Mormon dialogue for years to come."

—Paul M. Gould, Ph.D.
Associate Professor of Philosophy and Christian Apologetics,
Southwestern Baptist Theological Seminary

"*Leaving Mormonism* is a unique book that combines both personal stories and first-rate scholarship. Regardless of where you are on your spiritual journey, you will be challenged and equipped by reading and studying this book."

—Sean McDowell, Ph.D.
Assistant Professor of Christian Apologetics,
Biola University

"Most who leave Mormonism leave faith altogether. With this understanding, *Leaving Mormonism* stands as a book like no other on this subject. Scholars formerly from within the ranks of the LDS community share not only their reasons for leaving Mormonism, but also the evidence for turning to the Christ of the New Testament."

—Steve Crane, D.Min.
Senior Minister,
Eagle Christian Church, ID

LEAVING MORMONISM

Why Four Scholars Changed their Minds

COREY MILLER, LYNN K. WILDER,
VINCE ECCLES, AND LATAYNE C. SCOTT

EDITED BY COREY MILLER AND LYNN K. WILDER

Leaving Mormonism: Why Four Scholars Changed their Minds

Published by Kregel Publications, a division of Kregel, Inc., 2450 Oak Industrial Dr. NE, Grand Rapids, MI 49505-6020.

ISBN 978-0-8254-4481-4

Printed in the United States of America

18 19 20 21 / 5 4 3 2

Non nobis, non nobis, Domine,
sed nomini tuo da gloriam.

CONTENTS

FOREWORD

Dr. Richard Land

PRESIDENT OF SOUTHERN EVANGELICAL SEMINARY

Leaving Mormonism is indeed a unique and valuable volume. As Dr. Corey Miller and Dr. Lynn Wilder, contributing authors and co-editors, explain, no other book on Mormonism is written by people who are former Mormons, are trained professional academics, and confessed followers and disciples of Jesus Christ as Savior and Lord.

Drs. Miller and Wilder explain the unique tenor of the book, which is not mean-spirited or hostile to Mormons as people. Speaking for the authors, Dr. Miller says, "As former insiders, we have a unique perspective. As scholars, we value truth. As Christians, our commitment to Christ compels us to genuine love without which we could not claim to be anything but mere critics . . . ."

Dr. Miller also states unequivocally that the spirit motivating *Leaving Mormonism* was one of "urgent concern for those we love about a future that goes well beyond this life."

Apologetics trends toward left-brained, linear thinking, and rational argumentation. That is really the inherent nature of much of the apologetic enterprise: building on impressive cognitive, rational defense of Christianity's compelling truth claims, based on evidence, logic, and argumentation.

However, it can sometimes feel rather aridly academic and sterile to those non-Christians that Christian apologists are seeking not only to convince intellectually, but to convert to personal allegiance to Jesus Christ as their Lord and Savior.

That is where the right-brained arguments of personal narratives and stories are important. That is one reason this book is so powerful. The intellectual fire-power is there in abundance, marshalling the intellectual and evidential arguments for the veracity of the Christian faith. However, you also have the personal stories of the spiritual journeys of these four individuals who found Mormonism insufficient in meeting both their spiritual journey and intellectual questions. The personal testimonies are far more than academic treatises. These are heart-felt stories, connecting heart-to-heart with readers, narrating their personal journeys out of Mormonism and into truth and personal fulfillment and contentment in surrendering their lives and eternal destinies into the safe-keeping of the resurrected, ascended, victorious, and returning Christ.

The transparency and honesty of the authors in telling their personal stories is touching and powerful. In reading their personal narratives, I was reminded of what one of my pastoral mentors told me many years ago: "Every Christian has at least one great sermon to preach—what Jesus did for them and how He changed their lives as He transformed them from death to life, from darkness to light, and from the bondage of sin to the freedom of salvation."

Drs. Corey Miller, Latayne C. Scott, Lynn K. Wilder, and Vince Eccles are to be commended for producing a compelling narrative that will be invaluable in sharing the Gospel with Mormons and former Mormons, and in inspiring , informing, and equipping those who are seeking to defend the gospel (especially in Miller and Wilder's chapter 6).

I will keep two copies of this book in my library, one for reference and one to lend to others.

INTRODUCTION

CONTEMPLATING MORMONISM LOVINGLY, CREDIBLY, AND TRUTHFULLY

Corey Miller

> *"If you look for truth, you may find comfort in the end; if you look for comfort you will not get either comfort or truth only soft soap and wishful thinking to begin, and in the end, despair."*
>
> —C. S. Lewis

There is no other book like this. No other multi-authored volume on Mormonism exists that satisfies the following three criteria of authorship: each author possesses an earned academic doctorate, is a former Mormon, and yet is a follower and apprentice of Jesus Christ. As such, the authors of this book possess a unique perspective in that we were all once LDS "insiders." But rather than reject God altogether, as is common among so many who leave the LDS faith, all contributing authors trust in Jesus Christ alone for salvation. What follows are the individual accounts from our personal testimonies contributing to our various reasons why we can no longer be members of the Church of Jesus Christ of Latter-day Saints (hereafter LDS). We are followers of Christ, and the love of Christ compels us. This constitutes a major impetus for writing this book.

There is much to appreciate about LDS people. They share many things in common with evangelical Christians, not the least of which is the fact that we make natural alliances in civil and societal matters related to the consequences of theology and ethics.[1] For many of the same reasons, both groups experience their share of hostile opposition in an increasingly secular society.[2] This alone suggests a reason for reluctance in writing this book. At a time when we need each other greatly, given the massive assault on people of faith in this country, we nonetheless have the conviction to proceed and hope to generate more light than heat. Why? Because as one evangelical leader put it in 2013 to a Brigham Young University audience, as reported in the *Deseret News*, "I do not believe that we are going to heaven together, but I do believe we may go to jail together," later adding, "only those with the deepest beliefs and even the deepest differences can help each other against the encroaching threat to religious liberty, marriage, and the family." The month prior, another evangelical guest lecturer said, "When it comes to religious freedom, we all hang together or we all hang separately. We are common targets in this."[3]

It is with that spirit that we write this volume as friends and, in a respect, allies, but with urgent concern for those we love about a future that goes well beyond this life. This is a book for Mormons. It is also a book for Christians who are in dialogue with Mormon friends and family.

Other volumes on Mormonism exist involving scholars with a connection to discussion between Mormonism and evangelical Christianity, but there has been a wall at times precluding dialogue which seems to be coming down over these last few decades, and which calls for a new look at the relationship between Mormonism and traditional Christianity. Some works are in the form of Mormon and evangelical dialogue while others are simply collections or individual evangelical or Mormon scholars treating a topic that was largely responsible for this new direction, in the work heralded by BYU scholar Stephen E. Robinson, *Are Mormons Christians?* (Salt Lake City: Deseret Book Co., 1991). Following this was the dialogue Robinson had with an evangelical New Testament scholar in a collaborative work: Craig L. Blomberg and Stephen E. Robinson, *How Wide the Divide? A Mormon and an Evangelical in Conversation* (Downers Grove, Ill: InterVarsity Press, 1997). Then came the first major multi-authored critique of Mormonism by evangelical scholars: Francis J. Beckwith, Carl Mosser, and Paul Owen, *The New Mormon Challenge* (Grand Rapids: Zondervan, 2002). All of this set the stage for interreligious scholarly dialogue over the last decade: Robert L. Millet and Gerald R. McDermott, *Claiming Christ: A Mormon-Evangelical Debate* (Grand Rapids: Brazos Press, 2007); Richard J. Mouw, *Talking with Mormons: An Invitation to Evangelicals* (Grand Rapids: Eerdmans, 2012); Robert L. Millet and Richard Mouw, *Talking Doctrine: Mormons and Evangelicals in Conversation* (Downers Grove, Ill: InterVarsity Press, 2015). Others exist within the genre but are from a Catholic perspective, including Stephen H. Webb, *Mormon Christianity: What Other Christians Can Learn from the Latter-day Saints* (Oxford: Oxford University Press, 2013); Stephen H. Webb and Alonzo L. Gaskill, *Catholic and Mormon: A Theological Conversation* (Oxford: Oxford University Press, 2015).

Chatter among evangelicals about the trajectory of this dialogue seems to be moving in one of two general directions: (1) interpreted pessimistically sometimes as naive evangelical concession in light of academic pleasantries by those who do not truly understand Mormonism, or (2) interpreted optimistically as charitable dialogue that paves the way for either (a) hope that LDS people will "see the light" from the top down and come to faith in the biblical Christ, or (b) the realization that the two faith communities really are not as far apart as previously thought given that there was never really an opportunity for serious conversation about this.

Absent from all of this in the discussion is the present book. There are many works with good understanding—some authors were former LDS and some were not—who do good scholarly work but do not possess a doctorate or are not evangelical (sometimes they are atheists, agnostics, or otherwise). But our volume alone has the unique perspective of being written by a multidisciplinary group of evangelical scholars, all of whom have an insider's perspective as former Mormons. This provides a unique aspect of credibility. Furthermore, we desire engaging in respectful dialogue, but for serious theological reasons we refuse to sugarcoat matters. Truth matters, truth sometimes hurts, but truth can also set free.

The title may be misunderstood by some. Not all of us were scholars while we were Mormon. Two of us were. Some of us were born and raised Mormon either inside or outside of Utah and left the LDS faith later in life. Others were converted to Mormonism later in life and departed only after learning certain truths about the teachings and practices of the LDS faith. None of us makes the claim to be better scholars than others doing research in the field, since there are plenty of good works out there both in print and online. We simply have a unique perspective as authors having been students or faculty at BYU, lived in Utah, and/or seen things from the inside as critical thinkers who used reasoning in our pursuit of truth. In any case—and this cannot be overemphasized—even though we are all anti-Mormonism, none of us are anti-Mormon because of our love for God and our love for Mormons. We enjoy our Mormon connections, families, and friends, and are thus taking a substantial risk that could compromise those relationships by writing a volume like this. It is a risk that we would otherwise like to avoid. But we believe that our stories need to be told. As former insiders, we have a unique perspective. As scholars, we value truth. As Christians, our commitment to Christ compels us to genuine love, without which we could not claim to be anything but mere critics in this volume. Indeed, we could not claim to love Mormons if we withheld our stories, our testimonies, and our reasons. In fact, it is precisely *because* we esteem our LDS friends that we are convicted to offer an alternative view of faith and of Christ to that of their own. Consider these comments by LDS prophets followed by an illustration supporting our claim to goodwill:

> Joseph Smith said, "One of the grand fundamental principles of 'Mormonism, is to receive truth, let it come from whence it may."[4]
>
> Brigham Young said, "Take up the Bible, compare the religion of the Latter-day Saints with it, and see if it will stand the test."[5]
>
> John Taylor said, "I want no association with things that cannot be talked about and will not bear investigation."[6]

Accepting the sanctioned invitation of these LDS authorities and pursuing the good life, we seek to generate more light than heat, to contend for the truth while not being contentious, to provide reasonable argument while not being argumentative, and to share our testimonies of the biblical Jesus depicted in traditional Christianity.[7]

We encourage LDS readers to take such statements by their leaders seriously and with care concerning our mutual intent to seek the light and truth of Christ. It is all too common to dismiss critical considerations such as ours as "anti-Mormon" as a means of poisoning the wells of the message otherwise well-intended by conjuring up an alleged validation that one belongs to the truth simply on the grounds that one feels "persecuted" purely by virtue of disagreement. We need to defuse the cry of persecution since it is not necessarily persecution to be critical of a particular perspective—at least no more critical than roughly 85,000 missionaries informing traditional Christian, non-Mormon people in their homes that all their Christian creeds are an abomination and in need of restoration rather than mere reformation.[8]

Not all Christians who maintain a critical view of Mormonism should be branded as hating rather than loving LDS people. Consider an illustration involving someone you love who behaves in a destructive manner—physical or spiritual—to themselves or to others. Presumably, the loving thing to do is to respectfully confront the one you love with the truth. Suppose you have younger siblings and one of them is addicted to cocaine. Further, suppose this one steals family heirlooms for drug money. Moreover, he persuades at least one other sibling to follow in his path. Which of these three options is the most loving response under the circumstances? You can (1) celebrate him by purchasing some cocaine for him because you know that he likes cocaine and is sure to appreciate the gesture, (2) say nothing so as to coexist in the spirit of "live and let live," or (3) speak lovingly, but sternly, warning him of his destructive beliefs and behavior. Clearly, one would not be chastised for the phenomenon we will call "cocaine-o-phobia"[9] by choosing option (3). On the contrary, one may be chastised for choosing either of the other two options that encourage destructive beliefs and lives or express indifference for the same. Likewise, being critical of Mormonism does not necessarily make one guilty of Mormon-a-phobia if done with the right motives. Remember, LDS prophets have admonished people to investigate the truth wherever it is found. And the apostle Paul has this to say, "Have I now become your enemy by telling you the truth?" (Gal. 4:16). So please read with an open mind and without judging the motives and intents of our hearts prematurely.

Dr. Corey Miller has a Ph.D. in philosophical theology and is coeditor of a work that includes multiple authors who are either Christian or atheist.[10] He teaches philosophy and comparative religions at Indiana University and is the president of Ratio Christi, a global campus ministry that is dedicated to equipping faculty and students with scientific, philosophical, and historical reasons for following Jesus Christ. Like all other chapters in this one-of-a-kind volume (although some chapters have titled them differently), chapter 2 consists of two distinct sections, "Testimonies" and "Reasons," where Dr. Miller provides his personal testimony and distinct reasons for moving away from the LDS faith to his faith in Jesus represented by biblical and historical Christianity. His chapter is aptly titled, "In Search of the Good Life," the life of happiness that we are all after and that is only found in the knowledge of God. After having covered his testimony of growing up in Utah as a sixth-generation Mormon with ancestors who personally interacted with Joseph Smith nearly 180 years ago, Dr. Miller turns to the Reasons section. He examines the nature and reliability of testimony, crediting Mormon ideas where appropriate while fairly assessing both the value and level of confidence one can justifiably have in such a testimony, especially in a competing marketplace of testimonies. He then explores the path toward the good life according to Mormonism, which includes two fundamental steps: moral perfectibility and eternal progression (the LDS concepts of salvation and deification). Emphasizing the relevant analysis of LDS scriptures and prophetic authority regarding these matters, he concludes that the LDS path to the good life appears to be unattainable.

In chapter 3, "I Was There. I Believed," Dr. Latayne C. Scott relates her time as a happy, faithful Mormon on scholarship at Brigham Young University, and describes the compelling attraction of Mormonism's lifestyle and doctrine. With a doctorate in biblical studies from Trinity Southwest University in Albuquerque, NM, she is the award-winning author of more than seventeen books, including one in print for nearly thirty years, *The Mormon Mirage*, now in its third edition. She has spoken on over sixty radio and television programs. In her chapter she not only shares what pulled her away from the life to which she was committed, but she goes on to examine the Mormon Church's historical, philosophical, and practical relationship to truth. Using principles from her dissertation on representational theology, the chapter examines the relationship between facts and representations and its implications for an understanding of the Trinity and also for ex-Mormons struggling with such things as false prophecy and "past issues." In the last section of her chapter, she utilizes principles from linguist Dr. John W. Oller Jr. to examine the difference between a true narrative representation (TNR) and its degenerate forms—error, fiction, and lie—and how such concepts can illuminate the relationship of Mormonism to biblical truth.

Chapter 4, "Social Consequences of Mormon Teachings: Finding Post-Mormon Mental Health," is by Lynn K. Wilder, author of the popular book *Unveiling Grace: The Story of How We Found Our Way Out of the Mormon Church*. She is a professor, scholar, speaker, and author with a doctorate in education.[11] Dr. Wilder is an executive associate editor for the journal *Multicultural Learning and Teaching*. Once tenured faculty at Brigham Young University, Dr. Wilder resigned in 2008 when she experienced a crisis of faith and accepted a professorial position at Florida Gulf Coast University. Indeed, teaching diversity at Brigham Young University was one in a series of catalysts that initiated her faith crisis. This chapter explains why she left the Mormon Church and her beloved job at BYU and how she came to faith in another, more powerful Jesus. Over the years, she has mentored thousands of students, chairing doctoral commitees, and has produced sixty scholarly publications. These publications span both her professional field and that of faith, with publications in *Christianity Today* and *Christian Post*. She has also appeared on Christian TV and radio, including interviews by Janet Parshall, Michael Brown, Terry Meeuwsen, a TV series with Sandra Tanner on the John Ankerberg show, and a monthly interview on Dove TV. Dr. Wilder and her husband of forty-two years, Michael, cofounded a Christian ministry, Ex-Mormon Christians United for Jesus. Among her reasons for leaving Mormonism are discussions relative to current LDS scriptures on dark skin and polygamy, LDS practices regarding the Jewish connection, and the many social consequences directly or indirectly related to LDS teachings, including depression, prescription drug abuse, sexual abuse, pornography, suicide, etc. However, the most important reason for her leaving the LDS Church was that the God of the Bible rocked her world and his teachings were not in the Mormon scriptures.

Chapter 5, "Wrestling with Nature and God," was authored by James Vincent Eccles. Vince is a research scientist with a doctorate in physics. After finishing his postdoctoral work at Max Planck Institute for Extraterrestrial Physics in Garching, Germany, Dr. Eccles worked in industry and university environments on topics of atmospheric and space science. As a young Mormon, Vince integrated his interest in science and history with his faith in God. His ideas about God and his desire for an honest approach to human knowledge came into conflict with the beliefs of his local Mormon leaders. Life events revealed a racist and judgmental quality within his inherited conservative Mormon culture. Vince drifted away from his Mormon heritage and eventually discovered a new faith within biblical Christianity. He and his wife have served in small evangelical churches for many years. After thirty years in evangelical Christian congregations, Vince succumbed to a deeper crisis of faith caused by converging difficulties in life as well as continuing conflicts with many biblical Christians over the integration of science and faith. Vince details his path from Mormonism to biblical Christianity to a deep crisis of faith and a cathartic return with what he sees as a healthy dose of epistemic humility. The Creator, Jesus the Son, and the Spirit of the New Testament continue to provide the ground for faith and life.

Chapter 6 marks the conclusion: "Why Believe in God? Objections to Faith by the New Atheism," written by Drs. Miller and Wilder. With a heart for those former LDS who have embraced atheism or agnosticism, we discuss the importance of sound thinking in matters of faith. We present logical fallacies we learned in Mormonism and why they do not represent sound thinking. This chapter raises three typical arguments that post-Mormon atheists make against belief in God and discusses each. Where we and post-Mormon atheists differ is that we *do* believe God exists and we believe there are rational, evidential reasons for that faith. The authors provide a vision for future dialogue and a foray into the path forward to experiencing the good life via the good news.

Our hope is that our words will be respectfully, honestly, and openly considered with both mind and heart.

NOTES

1. For the convergent and divergent relationship of the LDS and evangelical faith perspectives, see one LDS author's recent perspective: J. B. Haws, "Mormons and Evangelicals in the Public Square," in *Talking Doctrine: Mormons and Evangelicals in Conversation,* ed. Robert L. Millet and Richard Mouw (Downers Grove, Ill: InterVarsity Press, 2015), 90–99.
2. Sociology professor George Yancey dispels the myth that there exists no bias against certain conservative and religious people in academia. Indeed, the results of surveying faculty attitudes regarding the likelihood of hiring someone with an LDS or evangelical faith background is startling. Given that both are amongst the lowest in terms of favorability when compared with various demographics, it is clear that one stands a far better chance of being hired at a university if one were a Muslim, a communist, or an atheist. This opposition is not relegated to academia alone. George Yancey and David A. Williamson, *Compromising Scholarship: Religious and Political Bias in American Higher Education* (Waco, TX: Baylor University Press, 2011); *So Many Christians, So Few Lions: Is There Christianophobia in the United States?* (Lanham, Maryland: Rowman & Littlefield, 2014).
3. These lecturers, Albert Mohler and Richard Land, are both presidents of respected seminaries in the evangelical world. Tad Walch, "At BYU, Baptist Says Mormons and Evangelicals 'May Go to Jail Together,'" *Deseret News*, October 21, 2013, http://www.deseretnews.com/article/865588850/At-BYU-Baptist-says-Mormons-and-evangelicals-may-go-to-jail-together.html?pg=all.
4. Joseph Smith, *History of the Church*, 7 vols., ed. B. H. Roberts, 2nd ed. (Salt Lake City: Deseret Book Co., 1978), 5:499.
5. Brigham Young, *Discourses of Brigham Young,* comp. John Widtsoe (Salt Lake City, Deseret Book Company, 1925), 126.
6. John Taylor, *Journal of Discourses* Vol. 20, (March 2, 1879): 264. https://en.wikisource.org/wiki/Journal_of_Discourses/Volume_20/The_Interest_of_Humanity_Should_be_Observed.
7. The subtitle of the Book of Mormon makes clear that it is intended as "Another Testament of Jesus Christ." We believe, however, that it is a testament of *another* Jesus Christ, one that is not well-grounded in the biblical narrative. Traditional Christians, for example, do not believe that Jesus was polygamous, the spirit brother of Lucifer, sexually procreated via normal biological processes, and someone who at some point became a god himself. Some recent authors, however, seem to be unaware of the stark differences of the identity of the LDS Jesus compared with the traditional view of Jesus. Simply using the name "Jesus" for common reference fails to capture the breadth of differences. See Stephen H. Webb, "Mormonism Obsessed with Christ," February 2012, http://www.firstthings.com/article/2012/02/mormonism-obsessed-with-christ.
8. For statistics on full-time missionaries, see http://www.mormonnewsroom.org/article/2014-statistical-report-for-2015-april-general-conference. Last accessed August 28, 2015.
9. Literally, "phobia" connotes a sort of fear. But as used in contemporary vernacular like "homophobia," the term is used to include hatred.
10. Corey Miller and Paul Gould, eds. *Is Faith in God Reasonable? Debates in Philosophy, Science, and Rhetoric.* N.Y.: Routledge, 2014.
11. Find Dr. Wilder's academic curriculum vitae at: http://coe.fgcu.edu/1228.asp and ministry bio at: http://www.unveilingmormonism.com/bio/

2

IN SEARCH OF THE GOOD LIFE

Corey Miller

Many people have believed, and I agree, that the purpose of human life is some sort of happiness. Mormonism affirms this under the "plan of happiness" (or the "plan of salvation"), but the prospects for attaining it by their understanding seem doubtful as we will see. In this chapter, I will discuss what I think is the main goal of Mormonism as understood in my growing up LDS and later reflecting on that experience. I will then share my LDS background and why I left. Finally, I will provide a few thoughts for serious Mormons to consider about whether Mormonism is a plausible pathway toward achieving the good life by exploring the nature and value of testimony, the LDS and Christian views of salvation, and the concept(s) of God.

"The good life" here is synonymous with happiness in that it seems to be something—reflectively or not—everyone is seeking but without necessarily defining it in the same way. In this sense, it is generic. Unlike our present culture, I believe that happiness is an objective notion. It is not an emotionally fleeting subjective feeling that comes and goes. It is a way of life for which we were made. Mormonism understands this and, of course, has special meaning for happiness as will be shown.

Since you are reading this, it is probably because you are, like me, concerned about this issue and believe that there is a purpose for life. We are all searching for purpose, meaning, and significance. This is no accident. We are by nature purpose-driven beings. Whenever we act, we do so for the sake of some end we have in mind. There is a word in Greek that describes this: *telos*. It means "purpose," "end," or "goal". The Greek philosopher Aristotle observed human behavior and various philosophies of life, concluding by unaided reason that we are teleological or purpose-driven beings, and that the ultimate end for the sake of which we do all that we do is happiness. But even this pagan philosopher understood that happiness is an objective notion even if, like love, many people are looking for it in all the wrong places or in all the wrong ways.

Aristotle said, "Man, by nature, desires to know." This separates us from rocks, plants, and animals. But man desires to know what? Ultimately, man desires to know what is behind it all and, perhaps more personally relevant, what man's place is in the universe. Man's ultimate quest in exercising that one human feature which most distinguishes him from everything else under the sun—his capacity for rational thought—is to know ultimate reality. While there are various candidates for what constitutes "happiness" (e.g., wealth, health, power, etc.), Aristotle concluded that it is found in our knowledge of ultimate reality or, more accurately, the knowledge of God.[1]

Several centuries later another sage would come along as the central figure to the greatest movement on the planet, Christianity, declaring with much greater perspective, certainty, and authority that the purpose of life is to know God (John 17:3). It is in the knowledge of God that man finds true and everlasting happiness, the good life. Indeed, man finds the ultimate meaning of his existence in and through this knowledge, a relational knowledge to be sure with deep intellectual content and attending volitional (willing) consent. It is so deep in fact that it becomes a matter of participating in the divine nature. As the prominent fourth century philosopher-theologian, Augustine, once prayed, "Thou madest us for Thyself, and our heart is restless, until it repose in Thee."[2] It is in knowing God that we become most like God, living the god-like life, the good life. Happiness in the classical sense, therefore, cannot be divorced from holiness.

Mormonism affirms that the purpose of life is happiness. The late BYU philosophy and religion professor Truman Madsen said, "The only sense in which one can fail to *be* [italics original] is in not realizing his full potential. His fundamental existence is not, and never will be, in jeopardy."[3] For Madsen, man, like God, is eternal. Everything is about actualizing one's potential, which is why the question by Hamlet, "To be or not to be?" is the wrong question. The question is about becoming, about eternally progressing. For Madsen, "there is no beginning to our 'beginning.' Mind has no birthday and memory has no first. Age is relative only to stages, not existence. No one is older, or younger, than anyone else."[4] Everything hinges on becoming.

As Americans, we can appreciate the old army slogan, "Be all you can be." Of course, this becoming process has, at least for traditional Christians, a beginning. And it also has, for both Christians and Mormons alike, an end. But significantly, the "end" is understood in terms of one's natural *telos* rather than in terms of the termination of some time frame. There is a prerequisite to knowing what the good life is for man. We first need to know what sort of beings we are in order to know what sort of beings we can be (or become) in light of attaining the good life, our *telos*. If our *telos* consists in our knowing God, then we need to know something about us, God, and how we can acquire that good life constituted by knowing God. If it consists in becoming a god, that too requires knowing something about us and about God.[5] To give credit where credit is due,

Mormonism, like Aristotle and like Jesus, teaches that the purpose of life is happiness—a sort of happiness that involves knowledge of God. But the process by which we move from human nature to the good life on the LDS account is highly problematic—indeed it is fatal—on multiple levels, which will be discussed in Section II: Reasons.[6]

SECTION I: TESTIMONY

Uncommon Descent

Some of my Mormon family tell me that I descend "from healthy stock." I take it that what they mean by this is not that an ancestor of mine fathered dozens of children through plural marriage—though, of course, he did. He had five wives, following faithfully in Joseph Smith's new teachings that turned some Mormons away.[7] Rather, what they mean is that my LDS roots are historically early and significant. Genealogical records confirm that I descend from one who knew Joseph Smith intimately. He talked with, walked with, and was prepared to die for the founder of what is now known as the Church of Jesus Christ of Latter-day Saints (LDS or, more commonly, Mormons). Indeed, my ancestor was a colonel in an early Mormon militia known as the Nauvoo Legion. Unlike that of many converts, my historical connection with Mormonism goes back to its inception. In 1836, just six years after the publishing of the Book of Mormon, my family lineage would become Mormon through the baptism of the man John Scott (1811–1876). Of Scottish descent, Scott was born in Ireland, raised in Canada, and later moved to the United States of America. In 1839, three years after his conversion, he served as an LDS missionary to England before making the trek westward to Utah.

I have often wondered what it would have been like in that day to experience what John did, conversing with the visionary, Joseph Smith, who founded Mormonism. Certainly, it must have felt surreal being at the fountainhead of the "Restoration" of the Gospel. All other churches until that time allegedly were part of the Great Apostasy (as described later) lasting nearly two millennia. One man, Joseph Smith, would lead the LDS movement in what was for him a hostile but questioning environment. Serving directly under his leadership in those days was surely intense. Indeed, because Joseph Smith had sought to take to himself in marriage the wife of one of his own leaders, William Law (a member of Smith's First Presidency), he thereby broke confidence with Law who was also a family friend of the Scotts. At that point, John Scott turned away from all of his siblings and parents because they sided with Law, whereas Scott sided with Smith.

John Scott was one of Smith's personal bodyguards up until the time of Smith's death in 1844. He later carried Smith's body back to Nauvoo, Illinois, for burial and was present at the meeting when it was determined that the mantle of authority should fall on Brigham Young as Smith's successor (although consensus was lacking). Then, as dedicated as ever, he became one of the early Mormon pioneers to Utah, beginning his trek westward in 1846 and arriving in 1848 together with Heber C. Kimball, one of the original Quorum of the Twelve Apostles. Scott began taking instruction from Brigham Young (the second President of the LDS Church). He rose to the rank of colonel in the Mormon Battalion in the Mexican-American War. Testifying of his devotion and speaking at his death in 1876 were President John Taylor and future President Joseph F. Smith, as well as another LDS leader, George Q. Cannon.

This, then, is what they mean by "healthy stock." From the beginning of Mormonism and for six generations my family was Mormon until now. I offer a brief recounting of my faithful departure from Mormonism, for my departure was full of faith and was not in my view a falling away, at least not from Christ to whom I am eternally grateful.

Being Raised in the Community

The first half of my life was spent growing up in Salt Lake City, Utah, albeit being raised in a nontraditional, single-parent, Mormon home. My father and mother never married, and my father never wanted me for reasons that are unfathomable to me, a father of three children. Despite a rocky beginning, I nonetheless found my way while in search of the good life as a young child. My grandparents on both sides helped raise me. My grandfather on my mother's side, who lived next door to us, provided significant help. My mother loved me and was very dedicated to provide for me, often working at least two jobs to make ends meet. I grew up in an old garage with the furnace in my bedroom. My needs—at least my physical needs—were met.

While not herself what Utahns would call an "active member" of the LDS Church, my mother nonetheless encouraged my church attendance and related activities. I was all too happy to be engaged. Admittedly, I found an element of comfort going to church. It provided hope, and I desired it as a means of community. In regard to family, while my earthly father did not love me, I found solace in believing that my Heavenly Father did. I recall dressing up and walking to church each Sunday. Sometimes I would eagerly attend an occasional "cupcake day," a fundraising event, and like the other kids I was thrilled to buy the sweets. I spent my allowance for more cupcakes than a boy could possibly carry, probably dropping half of them by the time I arrived at home. I was a dedicated Cub Scout, even earning badges for church-related events (in Utah, scout involvement is often directly tied to church involvement). I participated in church activities like basketball and church dances which were intended to build community.

In terms of religious content, I believed what I was being taught. I was eager to learn, through the Book of Mormon and other means, about my faith. My grandmother on my father's side taught me about the need to tithe. I enjoyed Sunday school. I recall singing songs about the current prophet at that time, Spencer W. Kimball, an awe-inspiring figure whose picture was displayed on church walls and up front as we all extolled him in song. He was a man of wonder to me as a child, significant for his role in expanding the church, and I aspired to meet him one day. (However, sometime in the future, I would be greatly bothered by his teachings in matters of faith, which I will explain in due time.) I can never forget the day in primary school when I was given my anticipated CTR ("choose the right") ring and how sad I was upon losing it that same day in church.

I was eventually baptized (by my grandfather on my mother's side), and received the laying on of hands to receive the Holy Ghost. As an indicator of my early zeal to choose the right path, I actually hesitated to be baptized at age eight, the standard age at which young Mormons are typically baptized. My reluctance was not for lack of faith. Quite the opposite. The reason for my delay was that I so badly wanted to achieve Celestial Glory and spend eternity with my Heavenly Father. But even then I wrestled internally with conflicting Mormon theology.

Entering Celestial Glory entails a degree of perfection (i.e., no unclean thing can enter heaven). I was aware of this as a young boy. I recall being taught that baptism was an essential requirement for salvation. At baptism my sins were allegedly cleansed. When I inquired about what happens after baptism if and when we sin, I was informed that each additional sin becomes a black mark on what was previously a blank slate at baptism. Being aware that Celestial Glory precluded anything unclean from entering, I reasoned as an eight-year-old boy that I would find a way to "beat the system" by procrastinating my baptism until my deathbed, which I surmised would be around age eighty-eight. But there I stood, fearfully wondering what might happen if I were to die before the mature age of eighty-eight having failed to be baptized as I ought. And so at age nine I capitulated, finally succumbing to baptism. While I may not have understood the whole picture at the time, this thinking did demonstrate my sincerity and eagerness to press on for Celestial Glory. Further, it revealed an apparent conflict that I believe I am not mistaken about in Mormon theology, one that could explain the controversy over why Utah ranks so high among adults suffering from the mental illness of depression.[8] There is an extreme performance mentality in Utah which can place a high burden on people.

Over the next few years I began feeling ostracized from the community. My mother was poor, did not attend church herself, and her behavior elicited a definite frown in Mormonism. She smoked and drank coffee. Violating the Word of Wisdom is not something appreciated by the LDS faithful.[9] While ostracism may not represent common LDS behavior, it was nonetheless my experience that I was isolated in part because of this. In any event, I felt alone and did what many adolescents should not do and found a wayward crowd in which I was accepted. The rest is history, as they say, in that I embraced the lifestyle and standards of that crowd as my own.

While I stopped attending church it was not for a lack of belief in God or the end goal, heavenly happiness. Rejection by a certain community influenced my decision to move away from active church attendance. I decided that I did not need that particular church community in order to maintain my personal belief in God, including the LDS god. Even though I was not living the ideal life, time was on my side—or so I reasoned. I believed that I would one day get back on the straight and narrow path when I grew older.

Admittedly, the determination to follow through with this belief eroded over time. My life took a bad turn as I lived a life of pleasure and of not being very responsible, from robbery and drugs to sexual freedom, a life of complete self-governance including some pursuits which I dare not mention. My report card one quarter said it all: GPA 0.3. I was saved by one D-! I was a living failure even though I thought at the time that I was living the good life.

Turning Toward the Light

When I was sixteen years old, a friend invited me to spend the summer with him at his father's home in California. I was excited, thinking a beach life could go a long way to extending the road to pleasure. His father, however, conditioned my summer fun upon our attending a non-denominational Christian camp for one week; paid in full, of course. "What could that hurt," I reflected, "trading one week for an entire summer at the beach?" Besides, I still believed in God even though I was determined to delay serious pursuit until I grew older.

The speaker at the camp taught something almost foreign to me. I was informed about the real existence of hell and a robust notion of sin. I knew intimately the notion of sin because of the life I was living. What was new was the utter *sinfulness* of sin. The biblical model presented sin as something perilous, separating one in a state of utter corruption from an absolutely holy and righteous God, a God who never knew sin. This was not the same "exalted-man" conception of God that I had been raised with in Mormonism , a being who worked out his own salvation and perhaps even overcame sin himself (though that concept is somewhat disputed), eventually becoming worthy of exaltation. Against this backdrop of the holiness of God and my intuitive grasp of my own wretchedness was also a picture of God's love that I had never encountered before. The gospel of grace for the first time made perfect and penetrating sense in my mind. God in Christ loved me despite my wretched state and made gestures toward me that displayed real sacrifice and commitment, the kind of commitment that I could not help but respond with commitment myself. I embraced the biblical Jesus Christ and committed my life to him. I was found. I was home. Moreover, prior to this I had never experienced such a genuine display of community love that resided in the people around me at that camp, never in all my years of what was by contrast a religious veneer of behaviorism (even if practiced by many well-intentioned and sincere people). I received permission to accept an invitation to stay with that family in California for my junior year of high school. I was baptized, discipled, and loved. During that seminal year, I experienced genuine Christian community.

Testing the Truth

Things would change when I returned to Utah for my senior year. I was accused of committing apostasy by those in Utah whom I knew and loved. Whether properly interpreted or not, becoming a "son of perdition" and living an eternity apart from God in outer darkness sufficiently scared me into rereading the Book of Mormon for the sake of testing truth rather than merely taking for granted the sixth-generational family tradition that I inherited. Over time, after carefully investigating the evidence, I came to see that my inheritance was bankrupt—bankrupt not only existentially, but also theologically, philosophically, scientifically, and historically. More will be shared in greater detail later, but the LDS concept of god in the Book of Mormon did not seem consistent with itself, other LDS teachings, or the Bible. The history and science in the Book of Mormon seemed unquestionable only to those with a prior LDS commitment. I voluntarily requested my name be removed from the official membership roll of the LDS Church.

But the sense of frustration in feeling that I had been duped was not isolated to Mormonism. It made me wonder if, in the end, the biblical foundation of my new belief grounded in traditional Christianity could be justified and sustained or whether it, too, was intellectually bankrupt. To make a long story short, the biblical foundations can be justified as they are well-grounded in historical records that have been faithfully passed down from generation to generation. Further, what we have now in our hands is essentially what the early church had in its hands.[10] After limited but careful research, I became convinced of my faith and confidently fell into the arms of Jesus who enveloped me into a new Christian community. I was once lost, but had now been found with assurance. I testify that in Jesus Christ, and him alone, I have eternal life and will be blessed with the good life—happiness—with my heavenly Father. As it says in 1 John 5:9–13, this much is true about one who has the proper testimony:

> We accept human testimony, but God's testimony is greater because it is the testimony of God, which he has given about his Son. Whoever believes in the Son of God accepts this testimony. Whoever does not believe God has made him out to be a liar, because they have not believed the testimony God has given about his Son. And this is the testimony: God has given us eternal life, and this life is in his Son. Whoever has the Son has life; who-

> ever does not have the Son of God does not have life. I write these things to you who believe in the name of the Son of God so that you may know that you have eternal life.

That said, I *know* that I have eternal life because I trust God in Christ's saving work—nothing of my own merit contributes to this. I seek to do good works, but this is from a grateful response to the salvation that has been given to me. I know this both via the internal witness of the Holy Spirit and by the objective witness of Scripture and history. My response is to live for him.

Ironically, my serious pursuit of the knowledge of God and knowing God transformed my pursuit of knowledge more generally.[11] I now hold three graduate degrees (biblical studies, philosophy, and philosophy of religion and ethics), as well as a Ph.D. in philosophical theology. I teach university level philosophy and religion courses. I went from a total lack of interest in pursuing knowledge to an insatiable desire for knowledge. So what changed? It is simple. I met Jesus. Jesus said that the good life was about knowing God (John 17:3), the highest form of knowledge. That relationship has consequently changed my life and daily brings me into further desiring the things of God rather than the things of the world with all of its lusts.

While this story is my story, many will contend that it contains a good bit of mere autobiographical description concerning some negative experiences, but nothing said is sufficient in itself to render Mormonism false. Fair enough. Both my aversion to Mormonism and my conversion to Jesus is not without rational grounding. One needs to be careful not to commit the fallacy of reasoning known in logic as the *genetic fallacy* whereby the origins of a belief are confused with the rational grounds for that belief. Some will charge that I came to my new faith while in rebellion as an inactive LDS member and so my justification is lacking. But actually, in my case of repenting from my adolescent adventure, I came to see on both experiential and rational grounds that Mormonism is false and I was eventually compelled to live for Jesus alone (2 Cor. 5:14). I later voluntarily requested my name be removed from LDS membership records simply because I did not want LDS missionaries using my name to bolster already inflated membership numbers in conversations with prospects whom they are trying to persuade.

I testify that Jesus, the one called the Word or *logos* in Greek (from whence we derive our word *logic*), is the experiential and, in part, the rational grounding explanation for why I had to leave Mormonism and pursue the Christ accurately depicted in historic Christian thought. In what follows, I will address the issue of the nature of "testimony" and discern its capacity to know truth along with invariable pitfalls that might beset it, as well as some of the more seminal reasons for why I think Mormonism is false and, thus, why it cannot bring about the good life that so many desire.

SECTION II: REASONS

Introduction

This next section will focus on what are for me primary reasons why I cannot return to my Mormon roots, but also why I must share my thought processes with my Mormon loved ones. First, I examine the nature of testimony as a criterion for truth since testimony is the *sine qua non* of many people's authoritative foundational explanation for their sustained deep commitment to Mormonism. Second, I then focus on some of the essential doctrines which that testimony is supposed to underwrite, doctrines that sharply divide traditional Christian thought from Mormonism because they are so obviously contrary to one another. These are the doctrines of God and of salvation which seem to be problematic and yet are essential to the question of man's pursuit of the good life, the Godlike life.

Admittedly, Mormonism possesses considerable attraction for many in the Christian community. Like Christians, Mormons are people of faith and have similar family values. Faith is an essential ingredient to the good life. There is much to appreciate from the traditional Christian perspective about the faithful possessing strong testimonies. The overall LDS ethos of faith is juxtaposed in the cultural war of religion versus secularism. Conservative convictions forge common voting blocks on cultural issues. LDS people boast of and seek to create strong families. It seems to be a rather successful religion with many successful people in a worldly sense as many Mormons earn the honors of men.[12] Indeed, demonstrated by the number of LDS presidential candidates over the last few decades, it is not improbable that one day we may see a Mormon sitting in the Oval Office of the White House as president. The LDS Church utilizes marketing principles well and appreciates sustained growth. Given the increasing acceptability of Mormonism by those in mainstream Christian culture, many are ignorant of what lies under the veneer. This ignorant mass includes both LDS and non-LDS.

The Foundations

Mormonism makes two fundamental assumptions early on in its teaching to prospective converts that, while not necessarily hidden, nonetheless create obstacles for biblical Christians.

First, Mormonism assumes that there was a "Great Apostasy" or a complete falling away from the truth as it was originally revealed. Regarding all Christian creeds and churches, God revealed to Joseph Smith that he was to join none of them, "for they were all wrong; and the Personage who addressed me said that all their creeds were an abomination in his sight."[13] Furthermore, this requires that "Nothing less than a complete apostasy from the Christian religion would warrant the establishment of the Church of Jesus Christ of Latter-day Saints."[14]

Second, Mormonism assumes that it is the gospel restored after the Great Apostasy. Joseph Fielding Smith, tenth LDS prophet, said, "[There is] no salvation without accepting Joseph Smith. If Joseph Smith was verily a prophet, and if he told the truth. . . . No man can reject that testimony without incurring the most dreadful consequences, for they cannot enter the kingdom of God."[15] As one Mormon apostle, Bruce R. McConkie, writes, "If it had not been for Joseph Smith and the restoration, there would be no salvation."[16] This may seem audacious enough to a biblical Christian; that is, until one reads Smith's own words about himself: "I have more to boast of than ever any man had. I am the only man that has ever been able to keep a whole church together since the days of Adam. A large majority of the whole have stood by me. Neither Paul, John, Peter, nor Jesus ever did it. I boast that no man ever did such a work as I. The followers of Jesus ran away from Him; but the Latter-day Saints never ran away from me yet."[17] This is reminiscent of a hymn that was sung in church when I was a boy about Smith titled, "Praise to the Man." This is all quite audacious unless true.

These two non-negotiable assumptions need defending by sincere Latter-day Saints, but most simply bear their testimony and take the assumptions for granted. All of this suggests a steep burden resting on the Mormon testimony in favor of the LDS movement to show that for thousands of years, since the death of the last apostle, millions of bright Christian thinkers and committed devotees have been misinformed, misled, or otherwise severely lacking in their faith and theology. Were they misinformed until Joseph Smith came along, claiming to have seen and conversed with God and, thus ushering in the restoration of that which has been lost for eons? Consider what is more probable: One man's claim of literally seeing God who informed him that for thousands of years, millions of brilliant and godly Christians and Jews were lost and in the dark? Or that this one man himself was lost and in the dark? Let me put it this way: Suppose we were out in the wilderness together and I told you I just had a private experience with God in the wilderness akin to the Joseph Smith "First Vision." Would you believe me if I made the claim to have seen God, and then asked for you and all other people to leave their religions, begin tithing to my restored movement, and follow me as I took the lead in this new proposal? Hardly. If this sounds steep, and you would not believe me, then how is it any different from committing yourself to the words of Joseph Smith? This reveals the apparent heavy burden of proof the Mormon faces to place all one has on one man over and against thousands of years of Judeo-Christian history, especially in light of the arguably clear statements of Jesus who denies the occurrence of a total historical apostasy (Matthew chapters 16 and 28), even if small-scale apostasy is admitted elsewhere in the New Testament (1 Tim. 4).

Of course, a naturalist (i.e., a typical atheist who denies the existence of the supernatural) might consider someone making such claims as worthy of being institutionalized. But for one who believes in the supernatural, in God, one cannot automatically rule out the possibility of Smith's account even if it seems highly implausible. What's more important, however, is that the average prospect is asked to take this all on faith—a sort of faith that rests almost entirely on what is referred to as "the testimony." Indeed, LDS missionaries are emphatic in encouraging investigators to pray and receive a supernatural testimony. At the end of the Book of Mormon is a verse that LDS missionaries encourage investigators to read and which they say promises spiritual knowledge—a feeling really—for any who pray sincerely to see if the Book of Mormon is true (Moroni 10:4). It is believed that one can receive a spiritual confirmation that it and the LDS Church representing the restored gospel as a whole are true. But what are we to make of this sort of knowledge—a spiritualized epistemology? Don't traditional Christians also affirm a similar experience? Is such knowledge sufficient in and of itself? It is simple, but also complicated. In assessing these questions, we can both affirm testimonial knowledge and also find it to be highly problematic in certain respects.

"The Testimony"

First, the confidence expressed in a Mormon testimony is similar but relevantly different from the confidence possessed in a Christian testimony. For traditional Christians the meaning of a testimony (i.e., a sort of witness or experience) varies from, on the one hand, how God has moved or changed the individual's life to, on the other hand, denoting his or her conversion story in particular. But more weight is placed for the biblical Christian understanding on the objective nature of a testimony than merely on the subjective (more on that later). For the Mormon, it is difficult to draw a conclusion regarding which is more authoritative for the average devotee: Joseph Smith, living prophets, the Standard Works, or "the testimony." Surprisingly, for many Mormons it really comes down to "the testimony," even though LDS literature points to one of the other alternatives. For a Mormon, a testimony is a powerful experience and is encouraged even among LDS General Authorities (i.e., prophets and apostles.) How is someone supposed to attain this testimony?

One LDS apostle who recently passed away, Boyd K. Packer, said that "A testimony is to be *found* in the *bearing* of it. Somewhere in your quest for spiritual knowledge, there is that 'leap of faith,' as the philosophers call it."[18] Given that this supposed anchor of truth known as "the testimony" is all-guiding, it is most surprising that the way to discover it is simply by telling it over and over and over. But there is something spurious and dubious about that. Further, even though the expression "leap of faith" was coined by a disgruntled European Christian philosopher (Søren Kierkegaard) in the nineteenth century, it is not the view embraced by the majority of Christian thinkers in the history of Christian thought, because they have viewed faith as part of a knowledge tradition. Elsewhere, Packer reveals the nature of testimony: "Bear testimony of the things that you hope are true, as an act of faith."[19] He seems to be advocating a sort of faith here that is akin to wish-fulfillment, just the sort of notion ridiculed by atheistic thinkers such as Marx and Freud. LDS apostle Dallin Oaks identifies the testimony, the "'burning in the bosom' (see D&C 9:8–9) as that which signifies a feeling of comfort and serenity."[20]

One LDS leader encouraged the bearing of one's testimony in moments of evangelism, explaining that "sincere feelings conveyed from heart to heart by means of testimony convert people to the truth where weak, wishy-washy, argumentative statements will not."[21] Finally, in an official LDS Church manual, it says, "In order to know that the Book of Mormon is true, a person must read, ponder, and pray about it. The honest seeker of truth will soon come to feel that the Book of Mormon is the word of God."[22]

So we see that non-Mormons are challenged to experience this burning in the bosom, a feeling of ecstatic serenity, as the confirmation of the truth of the Book of Mormon. But Mormons are also encouraged to bear testimony in order to find testimony and in evangelistic encounters to help others find it. It is no surprise when an outsider finds this notion suspect. Further, failure to bear such a testimony regularly has negative consequences in one's pursuit of the good life according to one LDS apostle and (later) prophet who warned about loss of merit points toward the heavenly goal due to failure to bear testimony frequently.[23]

When a Mormon bears his or her testimony (and Mormons do it quite often and for various aforementioned purposes), it can become part of a process of self-induced indoctrination that began for them as children. LDS kids are groomed to frequently tell their testimonies and hear others bear their testimonies, too, hundreds or even thousands of times before adulthood. If you tell yourself something a thousand times, is it any wonder that you come to believe it? Testimony allegedly involves some sort of "knowledge" rather than mere belief. Something else that differentiates an LDS testimony from the rest of Christian witness concerning this notion is that it almost always sounds the same—sort of cookie-cut or made from a mold. Every LDS person reading this knows exactly what I am talking about. It may go like this: "I know that Joseph Smith is a prophet of God. I know that the Book of Mormon is the Word of God. And I know that the Church of Jesus Christ of Latter-day Saints is the one true church. I bear you my testimony!" Sometimes, whether in a testimony meeting or in an encounter with a prospective convert, the LDS person is brought to tears by their own expression of faith. Mormons often modify the order, but an essential testimony nearly always involves knowing that (1) Joseph Smith was a true prophet, (2) the Book of Mormon is true, (3) the Church of Jesus Christ of Latter-day Saints is the only true church and is guided by modern revelation. Lately, it has been more theologically focused to include statements about God and Jesus. There may be a few other items appended to the list, emotively expressed in a series of "I know" statements as the LDS person looks his audience in the eye with what appears to be and often is utter sincerity.[24] It is as though the more expressively a person tells it the more true it becomes, for all hearers involved. Mormons are under the impression that repeating the testimony will make everyone ecstatic with desire to join the church. Students will confound the wise and the learned. Testimony will trump any and all arguments that can ever be forged against it. It is that powerful.

If not already apparent, this comes along with significant problems. One of these is when a subjective personal testimony is taken as a sole criterion for truth. Consider the fact that there are dozens and dozens of Mormon splinter groups. The Salt Lake City church is doubtlessly the largest and usually the one people think of when hearing the term "Mormon." But it is not alone and most Mormons know this even if they are unware of just how many competing sects exist. Most of these sects come fully loaded with their own prophets and apostles claiming the title of the authentic restoration, which excludes the Salt Lake City-based sect. On numerous occasions I have personally spoken to leading members of the splinter groups and have seen them present stacks of papers they claim to be modern revelation. One group had sixteen volumes! Furthermore, they all have access to the same Mormon claim of the promise to receive a testimony about the truthfulness of the Book of Mormon and their particular authorized and restored version of Mormonism.

To illustrate the problem, suppose you inquire regarding which of the Mormon sects you should join, and request permission to get one representative from each (perhaps even the prophet of each) in a room to bear you his or her testimony. Whether lining up four or five or fifty of these representatives, they all sincerely bear much of the same content in their testimony and yet they all contradict each other at serious points—not to mention that each thinks that the other is apostate and false.[25] This is a familiar occurrence. The Joseph Smith account of the First Vision parallels in remarkable ways this presentation of various options regarding which church to join. In the vision, Smith claims to have received instructions from God concerning restoring the Church. He questioned which of the Christian sects he should join and the apparition told him to join none of them but to begin a restoration movement.

How might a prospective member of the LDS Church conclude, when confronted by all of these Mormon sects, which one is true? Logically, only one could be true since they are contraries or even contradictories of one another. At best, only one can be true and all else false. At worst, they are all false and the truth is to be found elsewhere. How does one decide? If you are reading this and are an LDS member of the Salt Lake City sect, do you judge the heart of all the others as insincere or lying? Or, standing your ground, do you simply claim that they were deceived by a lying spirit? The late apostle Boyd K. Packer warns, "Be ever on guard lest you be deceived by inspiration from an unworthy source. You can be given false spiritual messages. There are counterfeit spirits just as there are counterfeit angels."[26] How do you know it is not you who are deceived in your testimony? One is reminded of the apostle Paul's warning when speaking of the possibility of people being deceived by an angel of heaven (Gal. 1:6–9). Consider the angelic statue depicted atop most of the LDS temples. How do you know that you are not the one who was deceived when your contraries testify of an equally emotive feeling of peace and serenity?

The passage Mormons rely on is Moroni 10:4, which states, "And when ye shall receive these things, I would exhort you that ye would ask God, the Eternal Father, in the name of Christ, if these things are not true; and if ye shall ask with a sincere heart, with real intent, having faith in Christ, he will manifest the truth of it unto you, by the power of the Holy Ghost."

Further, there are more than a billion Muslims who might pray sincerely. Like Mormonism with its alleged relationship between the angelic messenger, Moroni, and the origin of Book of Mormon, Muslims have a connection between an angelic messenger, Gabriel, and the origin of the Quran. In addition, there is a similar promise in the Hindu *Bhagavad Gita* that resembles the promise invoked in the Book of Mormon. What about nearly one billion Hindus? And what of all the Christians who have sincere testimonies?

Moroni 10:4 is, of course, a passage that a traditional Christian would not accept because it is found in a book not considered Scripture. So LDS people, since they also accept the Bible, invoke James 1:5 for support, which reads: "If any of you lacks wisdom, you should ask God, who gives generously to all without finding fault, and it will be given to you." But in James, the context concerns wisdom acquired via trials, not knowledge *per se*—certainly not knowledge of some fact like whether a book is true or whether 2+2=4 is a true equation. There are other, perhaps better, ways of confirming truth.

One does not have to pray to test truth claims. For example, do I need to pray simply to know truths like "don't murder," "2+2=4," "gravity exists," or "God exists"? We have the Scriptures given to us so that if we come across a particular idea, we can test it against Scripture to see if it holds up (cf. 1 Thess. 5:21). Also in Scripture we are told to use our faculties of reason. If Mormonism is false, it stands or falls on the veracity of its teachings, not on the tenacity or strength of an adherent's belief. And more generally, Christianity itself is a religion that is flooded with evidence, not "blind faith," as atheists tend to claim. We are told by Jesus to "love the Lord your God with . . . all your mind." (Matt. 22:37) God told the Israelites, "Come now, let us reason together" (Is. 1:18, ESV). God is no fan of intellectual slackers any more than he is of any other slackers. The Christian life is one marked by reason and reflection. It is not solely based on feelings or emotion, which are not always accurate guides by themselves for determining truth. We read in Scripture that "the heart is deceitful above all things and beyond cure. Who can understand it?" (Jer. 17:9). Not only do we not need to pray about the Book of Mormon, we should *not* pray about it. There is no biblical basis for praying to know some fact like whether a book is true or not. There are many things we should not pray about (e.g., whether to love our spouse, whether we should follow foreign gods, or in order to evaluate certain promised roads to salvation that are not harmonious with the Bible.). Many of these relate to what we already know in Scripture. If Mormonism teaches a foreign god(s) or means of salvation, then biblical Christians should no more pray about this than whether we ought to murder. God has already spoken.

For these reasons, I'm inclined to think that LDS people overemphasize their testimonies. But overemphasis is no automatic basis for wholesale rejection. The assertion most Christians make when encountering Mormons is that we ought to give reasons, not testimonies. Many Christians who reject Mormonism claim that God reveals himself only in the Bible. That is not accurate. God also reveals himself, for example, in nature and in our conscience (Rom. 1–2) and of course ultimately revealed himself in Jesus Christ (John 1:18). The Bible, as God's Word written, is the final authoritative source for knowing how to understand what God has revealed. While revelation is necessary to know God in the appropriate way, there are other ways God has of revealing, both generally and specifically. For the most part, and on final analysis, I'm inclined to agree with those Christians asking for reasons, except for the fact that a testimony can also be a kind of reason, at least a reason for *knowing* something to be true even if not a reason used for *showing* something to be true. Suffice it to say the testimony should not be relied upon as a sole criterion for truth. But knowledge can be transmitted via testimony and we should admit this. I want to be honest and share that in a certain respect I am sympathetic with the invocation by Mormons of a spiritual kind of epistemology (theory of knowledge). I want to explore some thoughts, positive and negative, being both charitable and critical, about this in order to give a fair assessment of this issue of paramount importance to the Mormon.

Faith and the Transmission of Testimonial Knowledge

There is no greater motivation in life , for both good and for evil, than seriously held religious faith. For example, this motive accounts for the vast majority of hospitals and the rise of medicine in the Western world. It produces people like Mother Teresa with her compassion in Calcutta, India. It also produces mass destruction. One only need read virtually every day and on every continent about a Muslim suicide bomber's alleged calling in life. But faith, contrary to popular secularist opinion, is not necessarily blind. It can actually be quite reasonable and quite fruitful if it maps onto something that is true and rational. Biblical faith is often understood within a knowledge tradition. My dissertation involved an exploration of the virtue of faith taken as such by the most influential intellectual figures within the Judeo-Christian world.[27]

Faith, when properly understood, is not and should not be a problem for traditional Christians. It certainly is not a problem for me. It is a form of trust. But as a form of trust, it is not a virtue when it is blind or when one's trust is toward an object that is either untrustworthy or nonexistent. Mormons prize testimonial knowledge as an experiential phenomenon. One can experience direct testimonial knowledge, and sometimes that knowledge comes directly from God and sometimes indirectly. Given that Mormons understand the language of experience when it comes to religious truth claims, let me share a series of interrelated personal experiences underpinning some of my testimonial knowledge of God beyond my radical conversion experience. Mormons should be able to appreciate this, at least in principle.

During my adolescent stage, as I shared already, I became a corrupt person in my journey into the darkness and I took upon myself some bad habits and perspectives. One, for example, was my view of women. I understood them primarily in sexual ways. When I became a new creation in Christ—a Christian—I could not immediately or completely shed my past. I struggled deeply with images and habits in accordance with psychological and neural pathways that I had helped to create. Yet I wanted so badly to faithfully entrust myself to a God who is trustworthy. Three things happened to help me on this journey.

First, I had a dream. When I was around nineteen or twenty years old, I recall having a dream where I was in a gymnasium somewhere, sharing Christ's love with some young man, when suddenly three beautiful girls approached and began flirting from a distance. I made eye contact and darted toward them. Shortly after, the better part of me assumed my evangelistic connection to the young man and I returned to sharing God's love with him. But then the girls surrounded us and their images transformed into hellish creatures who chased us. I grabbed the young man and we ran into a closet. The women were clawing at the door when I insisted that the young man and I pray together.

I woke up in a sweat. We have all experienced dreams at times that seem so real that it takes time to transition from our dream state to being fully awake and cognizant. Upon realizing that my frightening experience was just a dream, I could not help but wonder, in light of Acts 2:17 which discusses God's people dreaming dreams and seeing visions, if this was not one of those sort of divinely spiritual dreams or just an ordinary dream. In any case, connecting the dots, I surmised that if it were a divinely spiritual dream, perhaps it was a message from God to me showing me that one day I would finally conquer my deep struggle and place God above girls; or, rather, that I would at long last, in light of Christ, have a pure perspective with respect to girls and would become an evangelist.

Second, not long after this dream, I was in California again, this time working at the same church that took me to the camp where I first met Christ. I was hired as an intern youth pastor. En route to my office early one morning, I felt a near inexplicable impression on my heart about a decision that I must make. Perplexed and fearful, I spent about ten minutes with my head down, alone in my dark office, contemplating the decision

I would make in committing myself to God in celibacy. This was not conjured up by me. This was not what I wanted or intended. I concluded that it was not a self-manufactured, psychologically induced thought. Sure, I wanted to put God over girls, but not to forsake them altogether. I merely wanted to have a God-honoring perspective. But it was the kind of feeling that I could not shake and could not explain without seriously considering that it might be from God.

So I bowed and I prayed somewhat of a compromise prayer. I say "compromise" because I was not yet willing to promise to God that I would never marry because I was not certain of the message being from God and I did actually hope to marry one day. Nevertheless, I was relatively confident of the importance of that experience, and I prayed to God and committed to live in celibacy for one year, avoiding any consideration of dating. Moreover, I told God that if my conviction remained the same at the end of the year, I would then commit myself to celibacy for my entire life. This was a huge expression of faith, or faithfulness, in response to what I took as a witness or testimony of God's Spirit to my spirit. During that year my conviction never waned and my perspective on girls largely changed. At the end of the year, my priorities were different. I had a pure motive and also a desire for a life companion.

Third, a pastor that I had only met once or twice before spoke a word of knowledge over me. I don't claim to be of the charismatic type, but I have always wanted to be open to God. After all, either I really believe in a God who intervened in history and continues to love and intervene in His creation or I do not. I am not a deist, someone who maintains belief in a God who created the world but has since remained indifferent to it. Midway through that California internship of six months, I was back in Utah for a break, and I recall being together one night with that pastor and his associate pastor sitting around discussing spiritual things. The pastor spoke directly to me and told me the commitment that I had recently made. Admittedly, I had a ring on my ring finger. I suppose he could have conjectured. But he also told me the very Scripture verse upon which I based my commitment. The astonishing thing was that he hardly knew me, I had never told him of my commitment, and it seems inexplicable that he would know my chosen verse: "He must become greater; I must become less" (John 3:30). Having both a B.A. and M.A. in biblical studies, I look back in embarrassment as that verse was completely ripped from its context to support my confident decision. I can recall that I probably invoked it in a distorted way, which again is remarkable: that out of all the verses in the Bible I should pick that one, and that he should connect it to my commitment.

Doubtless, I had a problem with my perspective on women. I also wanted deliverance in accordance with the revelation of the Bible and God's convicting me of that struggle. And God seems to have communicated to me through three unlikely methods the hope that I needed. First, the very real or surreal dream; then an unshakeable impression that was not naturally what I intended; and finally the word of knowledge from someone else whom I hardly knew, someone who could not have known my internal thoughts concerning my commitment outside of divine aid.

Can I use this triplex experience to persuade others? Maybe. But it involves an element of subjectivity that I cannot put on display in a laboratory to be examined in some sort of third-person description. People have no access to a person's private mental life; it is not even a possibility for neurosurgeons now or ever. But I know that which I may not be able to adequately show.

Fortunately, we do not need to be able to *show* that something is true in order to *know* that something is true. This is not inconceivable. Consider a case where someone is framed for murder. All the evidence is stacked against the man, yet he is in fact innocent. He knows that he is innocent, but does not know how to prove it. Can I be certain that God transmitted knowledge to me via testimony and that these things were not mere psychological inducements or lucky guesses? No. As a philosopher, I believe certainty can only be had this side of eternity in fields like mathematics, logic, and some areas of introspective philosophy. As a matter of fact, I do not believe that you, the reader, can know for certain that there are even symbols we call "words" appearing before you now. Your sense perceptions might not be reliable, and any argument for their reliability would be a circular argument invoking some sort of past track record that begs the question. One can never refute the perception skeptic, but one can rebut him. And, of course, it would be far more foolish to deny commonsense experiences like these that can be buttressed in other ways, even if one is incapable of knowing for certain.

So as a matter of reasonable faith rather than strictly so-called knowledge, it seems to me that it would take much more faith to disbelieve that God communicated to me than the faith or trust it takes to believe that God indeed communicated to me, transmitting knowledge via testimony. Testimonial knowledge is a form of knowledge; and testimonies by Mormons should be considered in principle even if their practical usage of testimonial knowledge here turns out to be an abject failure to acquire knowledge or even reasonable belief, since it appears not only to be conjoined with evidence but even held in the face of contrary evidence.

Faith and the Assessment of Testimonial Knowledge

Faith is a virtue; or at least it can be. It is required of both Mormons and traditional Christians. It can also be a vice if it fails to map on to reality or alleges a reality that brings about much harm. Biblically, faith is an expression of trust or confidence in a trustworthy God. Having a testimony about God is about having faith or trust in God. It is commonly agreed in the social sciences that testimony can transmit knowledge. But how confident can we be in our assessment of this? We seem to rely on it regularly. We rely on testimony in our grasp of science, history, geography, and a host of other areas. Which bus to catch, what to eat for a proper diet, etc., are all decided based on someone's testimony.

Memory beliefs parallel testimonial beliefs. Beliefs about the past are not infallible, and yet we have confidence in memory beliefs. Memory is a psychological mechanism that conveys beliefs across stages of a life, whereas testimony is social and conveys beliefs across lives at a time. Some testimony we can and do check for confirmation. But most testimony is not checkable (often due to a lack of time and resources). Thomas Reid spoke of God implanting in our natures two principles that tally with each other: (1) propensity to speak truth (principle of credulity), and (2) a disposition to have confidence in the veracity of others (principle of veracity).[28] Trust is an important element for the character of knowledge-transmitting testimony. The one communicating via testimony can invite trust, and the other one accepting the invitation voluntarily gives the trust. In this way knowledge can be transmitted from the testimonial sender to the testimonial receiver if done reliably and in a reliable context.[29] Some privilege interpersonal relations in their account of testimony. For example, in describing her position, one author says, "Certain features of this interpersonal relationship—such as the speaker offering her assurance to the hearer that her testimony is true, or the speaker inviting the hearer to trust her—are (at least sometimes) actually responsible for conferring epistemic value on the testimonial beliefs acquired."[30]

It is easy enough to understand how one person gives trust to another to gain, say, scientific knowledge via testimony when shared by an expert scientist in the relevant field, or to receive classroom directions on the first day of class from an older student in the hallway. In some such cases, perhaps the willingness of one to give trust to another relies on some evidence related to the credentials of the one providing testimony (e.g., expert scientist) or on the presumed likelihood of the other to give correct information (e.g., older student in the hallway), rather than something grounded in an ongoing and developing interpersonal relationship since the receiver of the testimony may never have met or seen the person prior to the deliverance of the testimony.

It is possible to will to believe something and that doing so is justifiable. Obviously, it would be problematic if one person were told by another that 2+2=5 and that person willed to believe this. Can one have any confidence in some beliefs one wills and not in others? If one cannot will to believe, then one also cannot will to trust. If some belief, and trust in particular, is such that there can be no voluntary component, then it follows that trust is not the sort of thing one can give or be invited to give as the expression "trust me" suggests. This would differ little, if at all, from belief generated by evidence. But it seems that there is such an element in that someone can withdraw trust as much as give it. For example, a child gives trust to the parent who teaches her about Santa Claus only to later withdraw trust in particular areas after having found out that her parent was not being truthful in this one area.

Admittedly many, or perhaps most, beliefs are of an involuntary sort. For example, I cannot just will to believe that an elephant rather than a computer screen is in front of me. But some beliefs do have a voluntary component; in other words, a will to believe.[31] Belief or trust comes in degrees of strength, even though decisions based on the belief necessarily require going beyond that degree. I do not know, for example, whether my car will get me to the airport. I do not know whether the airplane I am about to board will make it to its destination. But in both cases, I decide either to board the vehicle or not as if an all-or-nothing affair. The great medieval philosophical theologian, Thomas Aquinas, relates faith to wisdom, a process that begins with the will and results in an intellectual virtue. And living faith (as opposed to dead faith, faith with no action) is a case where the transmission of knowledge occurs through testimony. Indeed, one's spiritual formation develops, at least in part, via a pneumatically relational sort of epistemology whereby the Holy Spirit plays a central role in communicating God's love and will to us.[32]

Much literature is being produced in the social and neurosciences about the nature of knowledge that is grounded in second-personal experience, a shared sympathy or awareness of one another and our ability to be moved by what or who we know. It is an experience that can be somewhat analogical to our relationship with God.[33] Individuals suffering from cognitive abilities on some level seem to lack this experience, whereas those who are capable of experiencing it are able to experience triadic "joint attention" or "mind reading," wherein both individuals in the relationship can have their attention fixed on some third object such that their attitudes and responses can be shared in a manner that is intuitive and direct. This social insight can shed light on the sharing of minds between God and another person. People fail in terms of the ability to be "moved" affectively by God when they suffer from an analogical form of autism, spiritual autism. Second-personal dispositions involve the shared experience of embodied relationship, a mutual presence and shared stance. The person so identifies with the other that they take on something of the other's psychological disposition such that they come to a "shared evaluation" or sort of mind reading.[34] The Bible often speaks of walking by or being led by the Spirit (cf. Gal. 5 and Rom. 8).

The fact of God's revelation in Scripture and in the incarnation of Christ makes clear God's immanent presence and interest in the divine-human relationship. The doctrine of the Holy Spirit in the life of the believer is crucial in our understanding of spiritual formation. God's immanence even in evangelism in locations very hard for human missionaries to reach reveals the active role of God in the affairs of man. For example, many Muslims report having dreams of Christ which led to their conversion.[35] Hence, we might expect to experience God's presence in his immanence, not just God's otherness in his transcendence. One does not have to be a charismatic to see this. I am not. I am open, but cautious as a critical thinker who has experienced God multiple times.

It is important for biblical Christians, therefore, to be open to a spiritual epistemology and to appropriately credit and be considerate of Mormons for their openness in this regard.

This does not mean, however, that all claims to religious knowledge grounded on religious experience are veridical—or true—or even that all are equal with respect to the evidence confirming such knowledge claims. Something must arbitrate between competing experiential religious truth claims. Recall all of the Mormon sects competing for authentic grounding of their testimony based on the Moroni 10:4 promise. In a book I coedited, based on a debate I moderated with a live and live-stream audience of around 14,000, multiple Christian and atheist scholars representing fields of philosophy, science, and rhetoric debated the objective reasonableness of faith in God.[36] This sort of debate can also be objectively applied between competing theistic or religious groups like biblical Christianity and Mormonism.

Obviously, any meaningful discussion of the reasonableness of faith in God relies on some basic target concepts of "faith, "reasonableness," and "God." It is a matter of controversy whether the "God of the philosophers" is the same as the "God of the prophets." In other words, what hath Athens to do with Jerusalem? Do reason and religion dance in the same ballroom together? I believe they can and do. Over time, the dialectic in philosophy has provided us with a concept of God as the *greatest conceivable being*; a being whose supremacy is unassailable and matchless. Some Mormons demur at what is aptly called "perfect being theology" (a theology that emerges from considering what it means to be a supreme being).[37] But there are good reasons for affirming it. For example, if God exists, it would not be reasonable (or biblical) to conclude that God is less powerful, less moral, less knowledgeable than humans. He would be comparatively greater. Indeed, God would be the superlative, the greatest conceivable being, supreme in all divine attributes.[38]

As a supreme being, God exhibits certain great-making characteristics such as omnipotence (all-powerful), omnipresence (everywhere present), omniscience (all-knowing), and omnibenevolence (all-loving or all-good). This conception of the divine finds remarkable convergence with what we find in biblical revelation: the God of the Bible, likewise, is a being of unassailable and matchless greatness that exhibits the traditional great-making attributes. "Great is our Lord and mighty in power; his understanding has no limit," declares the psalmist (147:5).

By the nature of supremacy, there can only be one Supreme Being. If more, then it negates supremacy. God must be thought of in superlative terms (e.g. good, better, best, or power, more powerful, most powerful, etc.) In the debate among traditional Christians and atheists it is clear that the God in question is the God who at least approximates biblical revelation. The God of Mormonism is scarcely considered in mainstream discussions by philosophers. I suspect that one reason this is the case is because "Anselmian reasoning" (a plausible form of reasoning articulated by the twelfth-century philosophical theologian Anselm) is largely responsible for creating a point of dialogue about God for various philosophers of religion. Further, the finite God or gods of LDS theology complicate rather than simplify matters given polytheism and anthropomorphism (projecting human qualities onto God). Many would contend that if God exists, then the principle of "Ockham's razor" would shave off a multiplicity of gods in favor of a Supreme Being in order to best explain the existence of the world, etc.[39] Monotheism is a simpler hypothesis. Thus, we have a concept of God robust enough for the religious believer to recognize and for the scholar to analyze; a being such that if He exists, is worthy of worship.[40]

But the concept of God in Mormonism is foreign to Christian biblical and theological understanding. So foreign, in fact, that when I teach courses in comparative religions at a secular university, I often teach Mormonism in the train of thought following Hinduism. Its theology is much closer to popular Hindu notions of polytheistic views of divinity than it is to the monotheism found in Judeo-Christianity or even Islam, representatives of theism in the west. The large number of deities in Mormonism is simply foreign to western theism. If I taught mythology, I suppose I would liken it most closely to the Greco-Roman pantheon of gods who are virtual supermen and superwomen. Thus, Anselmian perfect being theology is important. More will be said on the concept of God below.

Biblically speaking, faith in God is cognitively grounded in humanly experienced evidence of its divine personal object. On the one hand, the question of the "reasonableness" of faith in God may seem to be subjective or relative to individuals and in some sense it is, but on the other hand, reason as universally understood ought to be to some extent objective. The notion "reasonableness" is itself controversial if for no other reason than that "reasonable" is to "reason" like "desirable" is to "desire," namely, the former of the couplets are normative instead of merely psychologically descriptive. That is, one may have a personal subjective desire for something, but that doesn't imply that it is in itself desir*able* in any objectively normative sense. For example, one may desire to eat nothing but candy, but one's body will soon notify him that it is not desirable for good health. One may not subjectively desire to eat spinach, but the consumption of spinach is objectively desirable for good health.

Likewise, reasonableness cannot be understood apart from its normative content. What is the basis for drawing conclusions as to who is reasonable or unreasonable? First, as the noted philosopher Alvin Plantinga argues, the dispute as to who is rational or irrational, culpable or inculpable, reasonable or unreasonable, cannot be settled simply by attending to bare epistemological considerations it is fundamentally not an epistemological, but a metaphysical or a theological, dispute (metaphysics is the branch of knowledge that concerns reality). For assuming that God does not exist, religious belief must then be explained naturalistically by some sort of epistemic or intellectual defect. Conversely, if God does exist, then the defect fits on the other foot. That is, unless and until one first presupposes or successfully argues for God's nonexistence, one cannot conclude religious belief is irrational or intellectually lacking. To continue, belief in God, if God exists, is *properly basic*, according to Plantinga.[41] The theist doesn't see himself as suffering from cognitive deficiency (contra objectors). Indeed, his inclination is that the nonbeliever is suffering, in this way, from some illusion, noetic defect, or from an unfortunate and unnatural condition with poor noetic consequences. The situation of epistemic health and sickness is reversed. It's the atheist who is somehow the victim of sin in the world—his own or others' sin (albeit culpable only for his own). So there may well be more underlying the reasonableness or unreasonableness of faith in God than reason alone. Nonetheless, subjective testimonial knowledge can reliably be apprehended through the experience of faith.

The Problem of Subjective Testimony as the Sole Criterion for Truth

Suppose, then, that the Holy Spirit confirms to us that Christianity is true, how might a Christian under Plantinga's understanding reply to a Mormon who, by contrast, claims that he felt the Spirit confirm that Mormonism is true? Isn't this a relativistic and subjective argument such that the Christian can have no critique of Mormonism and vice versa? Even the Bible talks about "a different spirit." How does a biblical Christian know that the spirit confirming to him or her is the Holy Spirit and not a different spirit? And how can one know whether a Mormon is listening to the wrong spirit or not?

Again, the way we know Christianity to be true is by the self-authenticating, authoritative witness of God's Holy Spirit. The inner witness of the Holy Spirit is veridical for the person who genuinely has it. It does not require supplementary arguments or evidence in order to know that he or she is in fact experiencing the Spirit of God (Rom. 8:16). The genuine religious experience does not function in this case as a premise in any argument from religious experience to God. It is the immediate experiencing of God Himself. In certain circumstances and contexts the experience of the Holy Spirit will imply certain truths of the Christian faith like "God exists," "I am being convicted of sin," "God loves me," "I am redeemed by God," etc. Such an experience provides an assurance of Christianity's truth, but also some objective knowledge of that truth. In this way, faith is based on authority. But this does not imply that it is not or should not be reasonably confirmed. From a traditional Christian perspective, reason confirms, explains, and supports faith. The believer, acknowledging the defeasibility of her beliefs, may need to address defeaters or objections when they arise in order to remain rational or to show that her faith is rational.

First John 4:1–3 admonishes us to test the spirits to see if they are from God. God's revelation will not contradict itself. Any spirit which claims to give knowledge that contradicts cannot be from God. The inner witness of God's Spirit is sufficient to assure us of the truths to which He testifies, but those truths are incompatible with their contradictories. So Paul tells Timothy to avoid contradictions (1 Tim. 6). In both Old and New Testament revelations we are told to avoid falsities that oppose known truths. Deuteronomy 13 and 18, as well as Galatians 1, provide some of the content for which to test, namely, foreign conceptions of god(s) and erroneous routes to salvation (both of which are major issues I discuss in this chapter). In order for subjective testimony to count as knowledge, it must be in harmony with the objective testimony of Scripture.

That brings us to the scenario with a Mormon who claims to know that Mormonism is true because he experiences a "burning in the bosom," an emotionally ecstatic experience, when he reads the Book of Mormon. Now we are no longer talking about subjectively *knowing* Christianity to be true; we are talking about objectively *showing* Christianity to be true. The difference is crucial. Once apologetics (a rational consideration of the faith) is allowed to enter the picture, the objective difference between competing situations becomes salient. For since the Mormon only thinks he has a self-authenticating experience of God, when in fact he may not, the power of the evidence and argument may, by God's grace, crack one's faulty assurance of the truth.

This view of the matter enables us to hold to a reasonable faith which is supported by argument and evidence without our making that argument and evidence the ground of our faith. Faith is based or grounded on authority, the authority of God. Even the great Christian thinkers like Augustine and Aquinas, some of whose major objectives involved demonstrating the rational grounds for faith, affirmed that faith is not based on reason but on authority. Reason can confirm faith, remove obstacles for faith, explain or clarify matters of faith, and even arbitrate between competing faith claims. But faith is based on authority. Faith can increase and decrease (like an ordinary belief) in plausibility when it can be confirmed or disconfirmed with further evidence or reasons.

A Christian can declare to an unbeliever that her faith is true without being dependent upon the vagaries of argument and evidence for the assurance that her faith is true; at the same time we know confidently and without embarrassment that Christian faith is true without falling into some sort of relativistic subjectivism (i.e., truth is perhaps based on how I might feel) because the apologetic enterprise allows us to combine our subjective testimonial experience with the objective reason found in history in and outside of Scripture. The Bible, for example, is amply confirmed from outside sources as a collection of documents reliably recorded and transmitted throughout history, something that cannot be said for the Book of Mormon. There is scant archaeological evidence and absolutely no manuscript evidence beyond the nineteenth century. Indeed, that aspect of the Book of Mormon that is historically grounded is precisely that large percentage that seems to be directly lifted or even plagiarized from sections of the (King James Version) Bible.[42] Indeed, *because* the traditional Christian perspective on faith is said to be grounded in authority rather than reason, it is equally true that it is a reasonable faith—arguably the most reasonable faith.[43]

The LDS view is also based on a testimony of authority. This must not be underestimated. These authorities are great in the LDS eye. Indeed, one former LDS prophet proclaimed such presidential authority by saying, "I say to Israel, the Lord will never permit me or any other man who stands as president of this Church to lead you astray. It is not in the program. It is not in the mind of God."[44] (Do not forget his word "never" as it will be vitally important for the remainder of this chapter.) Thus, even though I'm sympathetic to a "pneumatical" or spiritual theory of knowledge, the deadlock of subjective testimonial knowledge can be broken and the LDS testimonial knowledge shown false by objective standards. What do LDS authorities teach about the most important matters of faith: God and salvation? If what the LDS authorities say contradicts previous biblical revelation or reason, then we can know that the LDS testimony is bankrupt based upon their trusted authority being deemed, at best, untrustworthy or, at worst, false.

Troubles on the Road to Human Perfectibility: Salvation

For our purposes concerning Mormonism, the process or progression toward the good life, including human perfectibility, involves discussion about two core issues constituting a two-step approach: salvation and exaltation.[45] In order to ascertain the ultimate *telos* or purpose in life in Celestial Glory, we must first achieve moral perfection; in other words, have our sins forgiven and have cleared out the very desire or urge to sin. Second, we also must somehow make the transition from humanity to divinity, a transition that is a change in degree rather than kind as we shall see. This two-step process toward human perfectibility is not precisely clear, however, even though it is clear that Mormonism teaches this, it results in troubling conclusions.[46]

Since we should want nothing more than to know the truth of how we can spend eternity with our heavenly Father and also embrace our own possible destiny toward greatness—following in God's footsteps, in essence—we need to know exactly what is required to be a recipient of eternal life (i.e., Celestial Glory for the Mormon), the highest glory available in the heavens according to Mormon theology and the *only* way to live with God the Father in the next life. We will be immensely helped along the way by hearing from LDS authorities like prophets and scriptures on what they have to say on the matter. While it begins with some standard discussion that LDS missionaries will share such as faith, repentance, baptism, and the laying on of hands to receive the Holy Ghost, it is not as straightforward as one might expect. We need to get clear about precisely what is required and then know the deadline by when that job must be accomplished; in other words, how and when moral perfection must be achieved in order for grace to be received in accordance with LDS theology. It will be shown via LDS General Authorities (LDS apostles and prophets in particular) and the Book of Mormon teaching on salvation that attaining the good life in Mormonism seems to be mission impossible. Next, we will look at competing and contradictory versions by LDS General Authorities on ultimate perfection, otherwise known as exaltation, and demonstrate that the spiritual knowledge claimed is other than from the God of the Bible.[47]

How the gospel of historic Christianity differs dramatically from Mormonism is shown in the following LDS illustration. I recall a friend who told me that he learned this illustration from his LDS seminary lesson manual and taught it to his students. While I cannot verify the source, his account is nonetheless instructive. On the blackboard he drew a pit to represent where mankind had fallen as a result of sin. It suggested separation from God. To return again into His presence required a means of getting out of the pit of separation. Jesus Christ became that means. This much is biblical. Here's the difference: Jesus's atonement. It is represented as a ladder that is lowered down into the pit where humans are stranded because of sin. It becomes the only opportunity afforded mankind to escape the result of sin. The work necessary to be saved is up to the individual. Each step on the ladder represents the works to be performed by the individual to effect deliverance from the pit. In this illustration, the first step on the ladder represented faith in God; the next represented repentance; the third was baptism; the fourth, the receiving of the Holy Ghost by the laying-on of hands; the fifth was receipt of the priesthood for men; the sixth was receiving the endowment in the temple; etc. This process of earning a right standing with God is summarized in the Book of Mormon, "For we know that it is by grace that we are saved, after all we can do."[48]

The typical Mormon assumes these various notions of faith, grace, repentance, baptism, etc., and embraces the idea I learned while a child: "Try, try your best, and God will make up the rest." First, it is true that Mormons believe that salvation requires grace. No one questions that. BYU professor Stephen Robinson passionately claims, "One sometimes hears that Latter-day Saints are not Christians because all true Christians believe in salvation by grace, while the Mormon believes in salvation by works. . . . this idea of salvation by works . . . has nothing to do with LDS doctrine. . . . The charge that this is what Latter-day Saints believe badly misrepresents the LDS position."[49]

To be sure, grace is a big part of the process. Jesus's work in the atonement is essential. He goes on to clarify: "Some critics may object that the Latter-day Saints do not insist that we are saved by grace alone . . . but the fundamental LDS belief regarding grace and works is well within the spectrum of traditional Christianity, with strong affinities to the Wesleyan position. While not every Christian will agree with this specific LDS concept of grace, the Latter-day Saints have never believed in salvation by any other means—and especially not by individual works. . . . The LDS scriptures are clear—we are saved by grace."[50]

It cannot get much clearer according to Robinson, who asserts that the LDS faith teaches salvation by grace. While all Christians affirm that salvation is by God's grace, not all agree about whether one can lose one's salvation. Wesleyans believe we can, and Robinson claims the LDS position is somewhat like theirs. But this is not the problem which all biblical Christians (including Wesleyans) have with Mormon theology regarding salvation. Consider this claim by an LDS apostle and prophet Spencer W. Kimball: "One of the most fallacious doctrines originated by Satan and propounded by man is that man is saved alone by the grace of God; that belief in Jesus Christ alone is all that is needed for salvation."[51]

For Protestants, at any rate, this now brings greater clarification to the LDS view because the battle cry of the Protestant Reformation was "by faith alone," or *sola fide* in Latin. So if Mormons maintain that salvation is based on grace and involves faith, what can it mean to deny the alleged "false" doctrine of *sola fide* if not that it is by grace through faith plus works? This is the matter of contention. Another LDS apostle, Boyd K. Packer, beautifully illustrates this for us:

> Let me tell you a story—a parable. There once was a man who wanted something very much. It seemed more important than anything else in his life. In order for him to have his desire, he incurred a great debt. He had been warned about going into that much debt, and particularly about his creditor. But it seemed so important for him to do what he wanted to do and to have what he wanted right now. He was sure he could pay for it later. So he signed a contract. He would pay it off some time along the way. He didn't worry too much about it, for the due date seemed such a long time away. He had what he wanted now, and that was what seemed important. The creditor was always somewhere in the back of his mind, and he made token payments now and again, thinking somehow that the day of reckoning really would never come. But as it always does, the day came, and the contract fell due. The debt had not been fully paid. His creditor appeared and demanded payment in full. . . . The debtor had a friend [Jesus Christ]. He came to help. He knew the debtor well. . . . He wanted to help because he loved him. He stepped between them, faced the creditor, and made this offer. "I will pay the debt if you will free the debtor from his contract so that he may keep his possessions and not go to prison." As the creditor was pondering the offer, the mediator added, "You demanded justice. Though he cannot pay you. I will do so. You have been justly dealt with and can ask no more. It would not be just." And so the creditor agreed. The mediator turned then to the debtor. "If I pay your debt, will you accept me as your creditor?" "Oh yes, yes," cried the debtor. "You save me from prison and show mercy to me." "Then," said the

> benefactor, "you will pay the debt to me and I will set the terms. It will not be easy, but it will be possible. I will provide a way. You need not go to prison."[52]

I appreciate Packer's provisional parable. Jesus taught in parables. The problem is that this parable seems to clearly contradict Jesus's teachings and that of the whole New Testament. What is clear in this parable is that the person who owes the debt, the sinner, does not get his debt paid, cancelled, or otherwise forgiven. Rather, it seems more like his debt has been refinanced or simply transferred so that the debtor owes another creditor. Anyone who owns a home knows the difference between thirty years of constant month-after-month mortgage payments until the deed finally arrives one day in the mail with these glorious words: PAID IN FULL. More often, people have their mortgages transferred from bank to bank via refinancing the loan rather than paying it off. When this occurs, the home "owner" does not ever own the home. The banks own it until it is paid in full. The only time the homeowner comes to own the home is when the final payment is made. It is not simply when one bank pays off another. The debt remains for the homeowner until it is paid off. The standard LDS book of doctrinal instruction, *Gospel Principles*, has this to say about it: "Without Jesus Christ, who is our Savior and Mediator, we would all pay for our sins [which are our spiritual debts] by suffering spiritual death. But because of him, if we will keep his terms, which are to repent and keep his commandments, we may return to live with our Heavenly Father."[53]

"If we will keep his terms" is quite concerning. All mortgages come along with terms of agreement that two parties enter into via the mortgage contract. Since the terms here are to repent and keep his commandments in order to live with the Heavenly Father, it is important to know just what these terms are. More often than not people do not read the fine words in a contract, but these words must be read and understood because they are the terms of the agreement with reference to eternal life. Repentance is a large part of this contractual agreement. So just what does it mean to "repent"? The LDS definition of repentance is found in the same book of LDS doctrinal instruction: "Repentance means not only to convict yourselves of the horror of the sin, but to confess it, abandon it, and restore to all who have been damaged to the total extent possible; then spend the balance of your lives trying to live the commandments of the Lord so he can eventually pardon you and cleanse you."[54]

To bring it home more forcefully, the book goes on to invoke the authority of LDS scriptures, "We can hardly be too forceful in reminding people that they cannot sin and be forgiven and then sin again and again and expect repeated forgiveness.... Those who receive forgiveness and then repeat the sin are held accountable for their former sins" (D&C 82:7 and Ether 2:15).[55]

So repentance seems to involve horror of sin, confession, abandonment, and even some restoration, concluding with commandment-keeping so that

God can pardon and cleanse (i.e., forgive or pay the debt otherwise owed). Moreover, repeated sins have the added burden of bringing back the past sins and adding them back on to the principal balance of the debt owed. This is a heavy burden to bear. Perhaps it explains the tension that I experienced as a young Mormon between grace and works, and most profoundly in Stephen Robinson's own writings as depicted in his account of his wife's experiences in *Believing Christ*![56] His wife, Janet, explodes:

> All right. Do you want to know what's wrong? I'll tell you what's wrong—I can't do it anymore. I can't lift it. My load is just too heavy. I can't do all the things I'm supposed to. I can't get up at 5:30, and bake bread, and sew clothes, and help the kids with their homework, and do my own homework, and make their lunches, and do the housework, and do my Relief Society stuff, and have Scripture study, and do my genealogy, and write my congressman, and go to PTA meetings, and get our year's [food] supply organized, and go to my stake meetings, and write the missionaries. . . .[57]

His reflective and quiet response is brutally honest: "She just started naming, one after the other, all the things she couldn't do or couldn't do perfectly—all the individual bricks that has been laid on her back in the name of perfection until they had crushed the light out of her."[58]

But it did not stop there. She continues: "No matter how hard I try to love everyone, I fail. I don't have the talent Sister X has, and I'm just not as sweet as Sister Y. Steve, I'm just not perfect—I'm never going to be perfect, and I just can't pretend anymore that I am. I've finally admitted to myself that I can't make it to the Celestial Kingdom, so why should I break my back trying?"[59]

I do not believe that this is an isolated incident. Maybe this is the reason Utah is among the top states consuming antidepressants like Prozac and Zoloft, often known as the "stress drugs."[60] The social pressure based on LDS doctrine is overwhelming. Finally, Robinson writes:

> I asked Janet, "Do you have a testimony?" She responded, "Of course I do—that's what's so terrible. I know the gospel is true, I just can't live up to it." I asked her if she had kept her baptismal covenants, and she replied, "No. I've tried and I've tried, but I can't keep all the commandments all the time." I asked her if she had kept the covenants she had made in the temple, and a gain she said, "I try, but no matter how hard I try, I don't seem to be able to do all that's asked of me."[61]

Unsurprisingly, "the testimony" takes center stage here. Janet, the wife of a famous BYU professor with a Ph.D. from Duke University, and herself an individual who has interacted quite a bit with evangelical Christian theology, understands the gospel to mean something she cannot live up to. It seems to be mission impossible. But why is this the case if the gospel means "good news"? Is it because her understanding is that salvation is by grace, through faith, plus an enormous load of works involved in the terms of the contract via repentance and commandment-keeping?

We can move from mostly standard LDS instructional publications and BYU professors, to a more in-depth look at what those with more authority have to say: the General Authorities, including significant writings by LDS prophets, and the Standard Works (i.e., LDS scriptures) like the Book of Mormon and Doctrine and Covenants (D&C). For, as one BYU professor says, "For us, authority is everything."[62]

All active Mormons are aware of Spencer W. Kimball, a man I used to sing about in church as a little child. While he wrote only two books during his lifetime, one is of primary importance. Kimball, who was an LDS apostle for twenty years and a prophet for another ten, wrote a book on the most important topic he could think of, in order to leave his mark and message about the truth of Mormonism and the destiny of the faithful. Some may resist the following use of Kimball's book, *The Miracle of Forgiveness*, on the grounds that it is not canonical Scripture, that a prophet does not always speak as a prophet, or that prophets are entitled to their opinions.

I offer two responses to these common statements made by Mormons. First, LDS leaders have encouraged the faithful to read the book.[63] Second, we aren't expecting these prophets to advise or be correct on every matter. But if one cannot trust prophets with the word of the Lord on matters of eternal life and death or about the nature of God when they make pronouncements on these nonnegotiable and essential parts of the faith, then one really should not trust such living prophets at all. For then they fail to reliably communicate testimonial knowledge, or perhaps they even contradict known truth. This would mean that one should not trust the LDS religion since it stands or falls on such modern-day revelation. The whole structure collapses since it is built upon the absolute need of authoritative, living prophets. Further, in this case, Kimball (one of the few prophets whose words made it into the one of the Standard Works—namely, Doctrine and Covenants—in the twentieth century), who was an apostle for twenty years with the authority of the apostle Paul (who wrote one third of the New Testament), took many years to reflectively write the book. It was reprinted after he became the prophet (now with the authority of Moses). He could have easily clarified or modified the treatise he chose to leave as his legacy. No one since Kimball has refuted or disowned his perspective (although curiously, recently the LDS Church has decided to no longer print it). If an apostle-prophet of thirty years does not know how to instruct people on something as important and basic as how to get your sins forgiven, then he was not necessary and was probably a false prophet unworthy of our trust or faith.

Finally, I leave it to the LDS reader to assess whether he or she thinks an ordinary member's authority is decisive over and against an LDS prophet and apostle, especially when the prophets themselves think that their words amount to scripture even when not formally "canonized" as scripture.[64] For all Mormons know that "doctrinal finality rests with apostles and prophets, not theologians or scholars."[65] The day after a living prophet dies, he should not be less authoritative in his teachings on the most important matters of the faith, assuming they were authoritatively given by God in the first place.

Kimball's teaching as demonstrated by his lauded masterpiece, *The Miracle of Forgiveness,* was, according to his successors, the same teaching that is revealed in LDS scripture. His citations are plentiful and his teaching faithfully represents the official LDS position articulated in the Pearl of Great Price, Articles of Faith 1:3, which says, "We believe that through the atonement of Christ, all mankind may be saved, by obedience to the laws and ordinances of the gospel.'"[66] Once again, Mormonism asserts that salvation is by grace (the atonement of Christ). But it is also—and this is significant—by obeying the laws and ordinances of the gospel. This begs the question, how many laws and ordinances? Is this the same gospel that Janet Robinson was so stressed out about? Think about how many laws and ordinances must faithfully be observed in the four standard works. Another LDS scripture says, "And, if you keep my commandments and endure to the end you shall have eternal life, which gift is the greatest of all the gifts of God."[67] Now, it does not take long for an LDS person to think about what is the greatest of all the gifts. It is more than just living forever. It is the good life, the best life: eternal life in Celestial Glory as an eternal family. But again, note the emphasis on commandment-keeping throughout this life.

This religious stress is not something unique among LDS people. Martin Luther, the father of the Protestant Reformation, while a monk experienced the heavy burden of reliance on good deeds to appease God in order to gain the forgiveness of sins. Roland Bainton recounts an episode in his biography of Luther. Luther's confessor, Johann von Staupitz, became frustrated with the young Luther over his obsession with repentance. Luther would wake him at all hours of the night to confess in addition to daytime confessions to ensure that he kept a short account with God and have his sins forgiven so that he might enter the pearly gates of heaven.[68] In Luther's mind, to get your sins forgiven, you must first confess them. But his anxiety over the possibility of forgetting to confess a particular sin made him obsessive about this. It was not until he understood grace and the proper faithful response did his anxiety subside.

Returning to the LDS scriptures that have an affinity with Luther's own pre-conversion account concerning confession and repentance, Doctrine and Covenants states, "Behold, he who has repented of his sins, the same is forgiven, and I the Lord, remember them no more. By this ye may know if a man repenteth of his sins—behold, he will confess them and forsake them."[69] Note carefully that to know with confidence that one's sins will be forgiven in order to get into heaven, one must repent of them. But here is the catch. To repent here means confessing each and every sin and then forsaking it. That is, stop committing sin. This is in agreement with the statement discussed earlier from *Gospel Principles*. True repentance does not permit making the same mistake again.

In his masterpiece legacy, Kimball writes, "Repentance must involve an all-out, total surrender to the program of the Lord. That transgressor is not fully repentant who neglects his tithing, misses his meetings, breaks the Sabbath, fails in his family prayers, does not sustain the authorities of the Church, breaks the Word of Wisdom, does not love the Lord nor his fellowmen. . . . God cannot forgive unless the transgressor shows a true repentance which spreads to *all* areas of his life."[70]

Furthermore, Kimball speaks of "the repentance which *merits* forgiveness. It is that the former transgressor must have reached a 'point of no return' to sin wherein there is not merely a renunciation but also a deep abhorrence of the sin—where the sin becomes most distasteful to him and where the desire or urge to sin is cleared out of his life."[71]

Now let us pause for a moment. Kimball was not a mere BYU professor. He was not a mere Mormon bishop or ward member. He was none other than God's mouthpiece to the LDS Church and the world—the interpreter of scripture and the officiator of proper LDS thought on important matters and writings. Certainly, Kimball's authority, matching that of both the apostle Paul (as an apostle) and the prophet Moses (as a prophet), is unassailable in the Mormon mind and should be believed by the faithful. His book sold 1.6 million copies and is now fading out of print for interesting reasons. Could it be because, despite the praise it has received by LDS leaders over the decades, it has actually been a source of doubt for many and has become a useful tool in the hands of evangelists seeking to liberate LDS people from the bondage found in the LDS gospel and introduce those people to the immeasurable grace found in the New Testament?

To date, none of Kimball's prophetic successors have disagreed with Kimball's position of perfectionism achieved in this lifetime in order to receive the grace of Christ. Kimball doesn't address insignificant matters like how to bake cookies or play video games or even peripheral religious matters. Of all those things that a worthwhile prophet should know about, he should know the terms of the agreement with God, how to get your sins forgiven and get to heaven. Hence the title of his book. He defined repentance for us in no uncertain terms as moral perfection. He said that the genuine repentance that guarantees forgiveness is one where the sinner reaches a point of no return without having even the desire or urge for sin. He even claims that God himself cannot forgive the sinner unless the sinner shows a true repentance, which is nothing more than to stop sinning completely. This is the requirement in order to get one's sins forgiven and to receive eternal life according to Kimball. In agreement with the *Gospel Principles*, Kimball makes clear that all former sins—all former payments made on the mortgage—return if one does not reach moral perfection. He says, "To return to sin is most destructive to the morale of the individual and gives Satan another hand-hold on his victim. Those who feel that they can sin and be forgiven and then return to sin and be forgiven again and again must straighten out their thinking. Each previously forgiven sin is added to the new one and the whole gets to be a heavy load."[72]

Surely, Kimball takes justification for this idea of cancellation of one's forgiveness based on one's reversion to sin from Doctrine and Covenants 82:7 which states, "Unto that soul who sinneth shall the former sins return."

This is why my friend's illustration discussed above depicted the commandments as rungs on the ladder. As each step is made, one advances closer and closer toward the top of the pit where grace exists to cover one's past upon arrival. But grace is not granted, one is not secure, until one is finally and fully out of the pit. For any sin—any at all (including drinking a Starbucks coffee per the above quote about the Word of Wisdom)—will bring about a fall all the way back down to the bottom of the pit to start all over again, as though one were signing a 30-year mortgage for the very first time. Kimball has the Book of Mormon to guide him here:

> Come unto Christ, and be perfected in him, and deny yourselves of all ungodliness; and if ye shall deny yourselves of *all* ungodliness, and love God with *all* your might, mind and strength, *then* is his grace sufficient for you, that by his grace ye may be perfect in Christ; . . . And again, *if* ye by the grace of God are perfect in Christ, and deny not his power, *then* are ye sanctified in Christ by the grace of God, through the shedding of the blood of Christ, which is in the covenant of the Father unto *the remission of your sins*, that ye become holy, without spot.[73]

Some Mormons will be tempted to comment at this point that God does not really expect us to be perfect. He knows we will sin. I counsel Mormons to not lean on their own popularized understanding but instead to submit to their own scriptures which say, "The Lord giveth *no* commandments unto the children of men, save he shall prepare a way for *them* that *they* may *accomplish* the thing which he commandeth them."[74]

Which commandments does God consider optional for obedience? Which are unimportant to God? According to the Book of Mormon, there is no commandment that God gives which cannot and should not be obeyed (1 Nephi 3:7). Indeed, based on the tenth chapter of the book of Moroni and in the verses that follow in the same chapter about the challenge to pray over the Book of Mormon to receive a "testimony," we are given a clear conditional. Getting the remission of sins, having them forgiven by grace, requires that the sinner first enter into complete self-denial of all ungodliness and come to love God completely and wholeheartedly before the grace of the atonement can even apply to one's life. It is as though one must climb the entire ladder up from the pit to be fully repentant and must satisfactorily keep all the commandments all the time in order to reach the prize, grace. This seems to nullify the very meaning of grace. Grace is not depicted here as a gift, but as something earned after a long, toilsome, and near-impossible mission. Second Nephi 25:23 in the Book of Mormon affirms exactly that, and Mormons often do mental gymnastics to justify or explain away this problematic passage: "For we labor diligently to write, to persuade our children, and also our brethren, to believe in Christ, and to be reconciled to God; for we know that it is by grace that we are saved, *after all we can do*" (emphasis added).[75]

So then, according to LDS scriptures and prophetic authority of a living oracle in conjunction with standard manuals of instruction, is salvation by grace? Yes! But only after we have done all we can do. How much can we do? Clearly a relevant question that even interests BYU professor Robert Millet who says, "We must work to our limit and then rely upon the merits, mercy, and grace of the Holy One of Israel . . ." and "there are certain things that must be done in order for divine grace and mercy to be activated in the lives of individual followers of the Christ."[76] Fine. But what is our limit before we are able to rely upon the merits of Christ? According to 1 Nephi 3:7 in the Book of Mormon, "The Lord giveth no commandments unto the children of men, save he shall prepare a way for them that they may accomplish the thing which he commandeth them." We are never forced to sin. We choose to do it and thus do not in that instance do all that we can do to our limit. If we can keep every commandment according to God's provision, and only then rely on the merits of Christ, it follows that keeping all of the commands is the prerequisite to relying on grace. This does not seem to be very good news. To clarify, I remind you of Kimball's statement, quoted earlier: "One of the most fallacious doctrines originated by Satan and propounded by man is that man is saved alone by the grace of God; that belief in Jesus Christ alone is all that is needed for salvation."[77] Apparently, salvation is not by grace through faith—at least not unless one understands grace to be in some sense earned, which of course means that it is no longer grace.

While LDS salvation no doubt involves grace, there is an insurmountable obstacle of works that constitute the precondition to receiving it. The Book of Mormon categorically rejects the idea that someone can fail to endure to the end, can fail to stop sinning, and be forgiven because nothing unclean can enter heaven and the reason given is "the justice of the Father."

> And it shall come to pass that whoso repenteth [stops sinning] and is baptized in my name shall be filled; and if he endureth to the end [does not go back to sinning], behold, him will I hold guiltless before my Father at that day when I shall stand to judge the world. And he that endureth not unto the end [does not stop sinning permanently, but returns to sinning], the same is he that is also hewn down and cast into the fire, from whence they can no more return, because of the justice of the Father. . . . And no unclean thing can enter into his kingdom; therefore nothing entereth into his rest save it be those who have washed their garments in my blood, because of their faith, and the repentance of *all* their sins, and their faithfulness unto the end. . . . Therefore, what manner of men ought ye to be? Verily I say unto you, even as I am.[78]

For the Mormon who thinks that we have been misunderstanding this, Kimball forcefully concludes: "Eternal life hangs in the balance awaiting the works of men. This progress toward eternal life is a matter of achieving perfection. Living all the commandments guarantees total forgiveness of sins and assures one of exaltation through that perfection which comes by complying with the formula the Lord gave us. . . . 'Be ye therefore perfect, even as your Father which is in heaven is perfect.' . . . . Perfection therefore is an achievable goal."[79]

It cannot be made any clearer than that. "Perfection is an achievable goal." It is also quite obviously a necessary goal. What is also clear is why Stephen Robinson's wife was beside herself. She cannot live up to the standard teaching of the General Authorities behind Mormon scriptures and prophets. No "testimony" can do what is necessary to earn the "grace" required. Grace is not free in LDS theology. There are massive preconditions to its being offered. A "testimony" is only supposed to confirm the truth, not complete the job to be done. Kimball says, "There is no promise nor indication of forgiveness to any soul who does not totally repent."[80] At this point many LDS people I talk with will claim that we have time. But this brings up the next important point about the LDS concept of salvation, namely, the deadline according to LDS authorities.

Deadline for Having One's Sins Forgiven

The Book of Mormon is unmistakably clear about when the job must be completed. While some interpret Kimball's message as pertinent only for matters of exaltation, the Book of Mormon on which he stands is explicit. In Alma, we are told:

> For behold, this life is the time for men to prepare to meet God; yea, behold the day of this life is the day for men to perform their labors. And now, as I said unto you before, as ye have had so many witnesses, therefore, I beseech of you that ye do not procrastinate the day of your repentance until the end; for after this day of life, which is given us to prepare for eternity, behold, if we do not improve our time while in this life, then cometh the night of darkness wherein there can be no labor performed. Ye cannot say, when ye are brought to that awful crisis, that I will repent, that I will return to my God. Nay, ye cannot say this; for that same spirit which doth possess your bodies at the time that ye go out of this life, that same spirit will have power to possess your body in that eternal world. For behold, if ye have procrastinated the day of your repentance even until death, behold, ye have become subjected to the spirit of the devil, and he doth seal you his; therefore, the Spirit of the Lord hath withdrawn from you, and hath no place in you, and the devil hath all power over you; and this is the final state of the wicked.[81]

The notion that there are many opportunities and many different kingdoms of heaven to which a Mormon might progress after this life is just not a live option according to the Book of Mormon. Can any sincere Mormon really think that the final state of the wicked where the devil seals one as his and has all power over him is any kind of heaven? This "eternal world" exists for people who have failed to adequately repent in this life. Of course, this is why Kimball warns the faithful that even under the extra-scriptural doctrine about vicarious salvational work for the dead, any talk about "opportunities in the next life" is simply not an option for the Mormon person—perhaps the person reading this book right now.

> Christ became perfect through overcoming. Only as we overcome shall we become perfect and move toward godhood. As I have indicated previously, *the time to do this is now, in mortality*. . . . One cannot delay repentance until the next life, the spirit world, and there prepare properly for the day of judgment while the ordinance work is done for him vicariously on earth. It must be remembered that vicarious work for the dead is for those who could not do the work for themselves. Men and women who live in mortality and who have heard the gospel here have had their day, their seventy years to put their lives in harmony, to perform the ordinances, to repent and to *perfect* their lives.[82]

Kimball mentioned godhood here, but we will delay comment until a later section. Suffice it to say before exaltation to godhood is even remotely considered, one must achieve the first step: moral perfection in this life. Lest someone be tempted, as I was, to fall back on their childhood teaching concerning "Try, try your best, and God will make up the rest," Kimball cuts off that route. As a former member of the military myself, I can appreciate the illustration Kimball provides of an army officer who gives instructions to an army private concerning a mission the former wishes the latter to complete. After a series of inadequate replies from the private such as "I'll try," "I'll do my best," all of which the officer rebukes, Kimball concludes the illustration by stating that the messenger is able-bodied, it is a short distance, and the task is reasonable to complete. He forcefully states that "trying is not sufficient."[83]

The Testimony of the Gospel

The LDS authoritative view of salvation is clear. Salvation is by grace, through faith, after one has repented by terminating sin to the point where all thought, urge, or desire to sin is completely gone. This is bad news, not good news. It is not the gospel that Jesus and the apostles preached. Further, this calls into question the Mormon "testimony," because Scripture is clear what the "testimony" is concerning salvation.

In 1 John 5:9–13, we are told explicitly that the "testimony" has content relative to the doctrine of salvation. This passage puts the LDS testimony at odds with the objective witness of the Spirit. The "testimony" in 1 John 5:9-13 is also rendered "witness" in some translations. But it concerns the testimony of God to us via the Holy Spirit in us regarding the issue of salvation. One can know of one's eternal destiny on the basis of faith, or belief, in what the Son of God has accomplished and nothing else. It says here we can "know" this. It uses the present tense in the Greek that whoever has the Son has life. Any testimony that rejects the doctrine that salvation is by grace alone through faith alone makes God a liar and denies the genuine testimony of the Holy Spirit. Any people who reject this need to question the spirit living in or among them or what spirits they are trusting. For the Mormon, the plan of salvation involves a debt refinanced rather than a debt paid. But the biblical gospel with the biblical "testimony" involves God in Christ canceling the debt, paying it in full. "When you were dead in your transgressions and the uncircumcision of your flesh, He made you alive together with Him, having forgiven us all our transgressions, having canceled out the certificate of debt consisting of decrees against us, which was hostile to us; and He has taken it out of the way, having nailed it to the cross."[84] The apostle Paul says that the gospel effectively "canceled out the certificate of debt." Jesus's last words on the cross were "It is finished" (John 19:30).

There are only two kinds of people: the "do," and the "done." For the "do" they are still trying to perfect themselves, which is the standard according to the Book of Mormon as well as the Bible (Matt. 5:48). Consider the movie *Saving Private Ryan,* where Captain John Miller (played by Tom Hanks) sacrificed himself and many in his unit to save Private James Ryan (played by Matt Damon). Near the end of the movie, Captain Miller was dying from a fatal gunshot and spoke these last words to Private Ryan: "Earn this." Private Ryan carried that awful burden of trying to earn the sacrificial gift his whole life, which is why at the end of the movie Ryan, now transposed to the present time as an old man revisiting the gravesite of Captain Miller. After speaking to Captain Miller's grave, Ryan asks his wife, who was with him, if he was a good man. In anxiety, he then turned toward the grave telling Captain Miller that he hopes he has done enough.

But for Bible believers, only Jesus lived the sinless life that we can then count as our own via substitutionary atonement. For the "done," it is just a matter of trust or faith but one where faith is in accordance with the Hebrew understanding as faithfulness. God does not change his standard from complete righteousness. But rather than requiring we become perfect on our own before the grace is applied (LDS route), we get the privilege of counting Christ's sacrificial atonement to our credit as though it were our righteousness. It is a gift not preconditioned on works even though it inevitably eventuates in works. This notion, however, is in contradiction to the Book of Mormon claim that "it is by grace that we are saved, after all we can do."

This is why Paul says, "For it is by grace you have been saved, through faith—and this is not from yourselves, it is the gift of God—not by works, so that no one can boast" (Eph. 2:8–9). Salvation is by grace, through faith, as God's gift. Should we do works? Of course! But works are the fruit of salvation, not the root of salvation, according to the Bible.[85] God does not want us boasting. God in Christ is the hero of the story, which brings us to our next major issue: the LDS concept of God.

More Trouble on the Road to Human Perfectibility: Concept(s) of God

As said previously, when I teach comparative religions in the secular university I usually place Mormonism in the same category as Hinduism since it has more in common with Hindu theology than any of the major Abrahamic faiths: Judaism, Christianity, or Islam. Classical conceptions of God are monotheistic and denote a God who is supreme and supremely worship-worthy. He has properties, attributes, and characteristics often considered unique to God, such as omnipotence, omniscience, omnipresence and omnibenevolence, which mean having power, knowledge, and moral goodness to the maximum degree. God is understood to be an eternal (or everlasting) being of immense power, knowledge, and goodness, and who is worthy of worship. God's omniscience means that he is a being who has unlimited knowledge of all true propositions. God's knowledge is neither inferential nor dependent on causal processes, and is not something to which God arrived at some point.

Mormons sometimes, though not always, speak as though they and Christians worship the same God. But such worship must necessarily be in name only. Consider this. While we all have a mom and all of us can even spell 'mom' backwards and forwards, it doesn't follow that we have the same mom. In order to discern whether we do or not would simply require us to describe the characteristics or attributes of our mothers and we would quickly find that they are not the same at all. Likewise, the Christian and Mormon conceptions of "God" reveal that they are not the same.

Is God omnipresent? Is God omnipotent? Is God omnibenevolent? Is God omniscient? Is God eternal as God? Is there only one God in existence? For the Christian the answer to all of these is a resounding "yes," but for the Mormon it is an emphatic "no" because of their "law of eternal progression." For Mormons, there are many gods for other worlds, and each god is equal to the god of this world in terms of his nature as divine (even if each is progressively different in development or degree). There are countless many gods who create and rule over other worlds. It is sometimes said in Hinduism that there are 300,000,000 gods. In Mormonism, that number might well turn out to be small by comparison. And why shouldn't it be if eternal progression has been happening for eternity? Apostle Bruce McConkie states, "[A] plurality of gods exist. . . . There is an infinite number of holy personages, drawn from worlds without number, who have passed on to exaltation and are thus gods."[86] Further, on those other worlds where other gods exist and are worshipped, worship excludes the god of our world—a god who is worshipped only on our world and not worshipped by all those on other worlds. So there is only one god for our world according to LDS thinking, and this god is typically referred to as the Heavenly Father (this view is properly titled "henotheism"). Mormons may also use the term "god" in reference to "the godhead," which is a team of polytheistic separate gods.[87] Indeed, some LDS thinkers outright declare not only the existence of a plurality of gods on our world but that we are to worship a plurality of gods. The most prominent LDS scholar in the inter-religious dialogue, Robert Millet, says in reference to Jesus and our Heavenly Father, "Those holy beings are and forever will be the Gods we worship."[88]

For the God of Abrahamic religions (including Islam), there is only one God for all worlds who created and rules over all existence. Indeed, this God does not even know of another God.[89] These are not even remotely the same conception of God. Christians and Mormons do not worship the same God. One might as well be praying to a doorknob and calling it "God" in the same way Mormons and Christians use the same term for "mom" and "God" yet clearly without reference to the same concept or being.

Perhaps the most salient difference between the LDS and traditional Christian conceptions of God is the feature that makes the difference in all of the differences spelled out above in terms of divine attributes, namely, the LDS "law of eternal progression" itself. Basically, this involves the process of becoming a god or goddess. It is not uncommon to hear LDS defenders falsely invoke traditional theologians of the early church in the first few centuries in defense of this idea but called by a different name: *theosis*.[90] Such authors clearly misread the early theologians as can be shown by examining the teachings of the latter more carefully. Indeed, in my aforementioned dissertation work, I even considered this concept relative to Thomas Aquinas, most poignantly with respect to his doctrine of "participation." But contrary to the LDS claims, *theosis*, deification, divinization, or participation in the nature of God by man according to these early authors is not at all what is meant by Mormons. It is participating in the divine nature, not becoming divine by nature.[91] Indeed, there would be no point to the apostle Peter's discussion of such participation or, as is often translated, being "partakers" of the divine nature (2 Pet. 1:4) if in fact one were already divine in nature in embryo as LDS theology teaches. As one recent traditional Christian author specializing on just this topic contends, "Because the Christian understanding of deification ensures that we do not claim to become God by nature—we do not become God as God is God—then *all* accounts must speak in terms of analogy."[92] Eastern Orthodox scholar John McGuckin provides a summary statement of the eastern notion of deification (one that LDS thinkers like to say parallels their own): "In the Greek Christian understanding, the concept of deification is the process of the sanctification of Christians whereby they become progressively conformed to God; a conformation that is ultimately demonstrated in the glorious transfiguration of the 'just' in the heavenly kingdom, when immortality and a more perfect vision (and knowledge and experience) of God are clearly manifested in the glorification . . . of the faithful."[93]

Traditional Christians of all stripes can get on board with the expression "eternal progression" as noted here; namely, we will eternally, worlds without end, progress in conformity to godlikeness as we worship and experience God forever. But this speaks of an infinite God whose being or capacities are immeasurable so that we can progress forever and never attain such divine greatness. We are human. For traditional Christians, we will never become one with God in some blended pantheistic notion breaking down the barrier between Creator and creature, but neither will we ever be like God is today in all his glory, except by distant analogy at best. As one of the clearest thinking early theologians on the matter of deification makes known, "Nothing at all changes its nature by being deified."[94] But this is not quite what Mormons mean by the expression, the "law of eternal progression." They cannot therefore cite the early church fathers to support their peculiar view.

Interestingly, a few Christian scholars even creatively pretend that the LDS Church does not hold to this teaching, perhaps because LDS thinkers tell them so, whereas others who possess self-admitted "Mormon envy" pass over it as if unimportant.[95] But this is not without connection to what some contemporary LDS leaders assert and such authors simply allow.

I recall the astonishment I felt in 1997 when I first saw the cover article of *Time Magazine* where the prophet and president at that time, Gordon B. Hinckley, appeared to deny what was otherwise a main feature of Mormonism. The conversation between the journalist and Hinckley went like this:

> Interviewer: "God the Father was once a man as we were. This is something that Christian writers are always addressing. Is this the teaching of the church today, that God the Father was once a man like we are?"
>
> Hinckley: "I don't know that we teach it. I don't know that we emphasize it. I haven't heard it discussed for a long time in public discourse. I don't know. I don't know all the circumstances under which that statement was made. I understand the philosophical background behind it. But I don't know a lot about it and I don't know that others know a lot about it."[96]

This was nothing less than shocking. But what was even more shocking is that Hinckley gave a similar response during the same year to a different non-LDS journalist.

> Interviewer: "There are some significant differences in your beliefs. For instance, don't Mormons believe that God was once a man?"
>
> Hinckley: "I wouldn't say that. There was a little couplet coined, 'As man is, God once was. As God is, man may become.' Now that's more of a couplet than anything else. That gets into some pretty deep theology that we don't know very much about."[97]

Had Hinckley forgotten one of the central tenets separating Mormonism from historic Christianity? Not likely. In a five-month period Hinckley communicated that deification in Mormonism is not something taught or hardly even known about all the while admitting at least one source from whence the doctrine originated. Of course, he merely brushed off that doctrine as if it were no big deal. Suspiciously, this seems to be a public relations tactic when communicating with non-LDS people. In between those two interviews was his own published work communicating to the LDS faithful: "The whole design of the gospel is to lead us onward and upward to greater achievement, even, eventually, to godhood. . . . enunciated by the prophet Joseph Smith in the King Follet Sermon (see *Teachings of the Prophet Joseph Smith*, pp. 342–62) and emphasized by President Lorenzo Snow. It is this grand and incomparable concept: As God now is, man may become!"[98] So not only does Hinckley clearly know of the teaching, but he even goes beyond what he said to the non-LDS journalists in admitting the source of the teaching in Joseph Smith. While he admits that Snow emphasized it, the truth is that Snow claims to have received it via revelation even prior to the famous Smith Sermon where Smith excitedly confirmed to Snow his revelation concerning deification. So this seems to be either a bad case of Alzheimer's or obvious lying and/or deception, perhaps even self-deception. Perhaps it is just that Hinckley didn't know the doctrine thoroughly. Wrong again. At the semiannual LDS General Conference in October 1997, he spoke to a large LDS crowd alluding to the interviews and assuring the faithful that he knew the theology well. He said concerning these theological matters, "I think I understand them thoroughly."[99]

Some contemporary LDS thinkers go to great lengths in order to explain away or to render intelligible this aberrant teaching by Joseph Smith and other LDS prophets. But try as they may, what really matters is not what the LDS thinkers do with their intellectual gymnastics given problematic statements from their authoritative leaders, but what the LDS General Authorities have to say on the matter which, in their individual cases, seems clear—even if they cannot agree amongst themselves on specifics. (This is ironic given that LDS complain about disagreement amongst Christian thinkers as a rationale for why we all need to have living oracles). Can these leaders not clarify what they mean for themselves without invoking scholars to try to help the prophet understand God's revelation to the prophet? After all, one would think that God is more capable than the LDS scholar to help the prophet understand God's message.

Early LDS writings, which are even today still regarded as scripture, teach a plurality of gods: "Then shall they be gods, because they have no end; therefore shall they be from everlasting to everlasting, because they continue; then shall they be above all, because all things are subject unto them. Then shall they be gods, because they have all power, and the angels are subject unto them."[100]

LDS prophets have been largely united, at least in terms of the divinization of humanity. "Here, then, is eternal life—to know the only wise and true God; and you have got to learn how to be gods yourselves, and to be kings and priests to God, the same as all gods have done before you, namely, by going from one small degree to another, and from a small capacity to a great one; from grace to grace, from exaltation to exaltation, until you attain to the resurrection of the dead and are able to dwell in everlasting burnings, and to sit in glory, as do those who sit enthroned in everlasting power."[101] More will be said on this passage later, but Brigham Young, Joseph Smith's successor—at least for the Salt Lake City sect—affirmed his predecessor's teaching: "The Lord created you and me for the purpose of becoming Gods like Himself."[102]

Following Brigham Young in consecutive prophetic order for the Salt Lake City sect, prophet and third LDS President John Taylor stated, "Christ's service places Godhood within man's reach. As a man through the powers of his body he could attain to the dignity and completeness of manhood, but could go no further. As a man he is born, as a man he lives, and as a man he dies. But through the essence and power of the Godhead, which is in him . . . he is capable of eternal exaltation, eternal lives, and eternal progression."[103]

Without missing a beat, the fourth prophet and president reiterates, "There are a few individuals in this dispensation who will inherit celestial glory, and a few in other dispensations; but before they receive their exaltation they will have to pass through and submit to whatever dispensation God may decree. But for all this they will receive their reward, they will become Gods. . . ."[104]

We finally come upon the fifth prophet and president, the one to whom Hinckley was making reference, Lorenzo Snow. Now, Snow was both an apostle and a prophet for three decades, much like the credentials of Spencer W. Kimball who held offices for four decades. Snow, a contemporary of my ancestor John Scott, did not see this mere "couplet" as anything less than divine revelation.[105] Any LDS apologist must either accept it as such or claim that Snow did not hear it from God. By what standard does such an apologist defend his own hearing or testimony from God when he rejects that of the one who is supposed to have had that authority? For Snow said, "The Spirit of God fell upon me to a marked extent and the Lord revealed to me, just as plainly as the sun at noon-day, this principle, which I put in a couplet: 'As man now is, God once was; As God now is, man may be.'"[106] In referencing Joseph Smith's views on the matter, Snow said that he "taught that man by constantly progressing may eventually develop into a divine being, like unto his Father in Heaven."[107]

The Law of Eternal Progression

With respect to the "law of eternal progression," we seem to have a sharp divide about its nature. For instance, prophets Young and Woodruff, along with apostle Widstoe, affirm an ongoing progression of the divine beings, whereas Joseph Fielding Smith and apostles Pratt and McConkie claim that the progression stops upon arriving at the highest state of divinity. It is problematic that Mormons should even have disagreement at this level on this topic such that they must choose which of the General Authorities to believe and which to conclude are not following the Lord.

What precisely is this law of eternal progression? Is God responsible for it? One might think the answer to the second question is yes, but that would be false. God—or precisely gods—are governed by that law.[108] Let's look at two different interpretations and implications of this law on God the Father's progression. We need to distinguish between what we might call the "bound capacity" view and the "unbound capacity" view of eternal progression. The former emphasizes the omni-quality of the state in which one has finally arrived, a sort of upper limit, whereas the latter emphasizes the enumerative nature of progress throughout the state. Which of these does Mormonism actually affirm? Both and neither, depending on which Mormon is asked. The Book of Mormon does not engage in this sort of speculation, but the living prophets and apostles most certainly do. It seems that they are split and confused on the matter. I was always told that "Our Heavenly Father is not a God of confusion." Then what explains the confusion among his prophets assuming they are God's prophets?

The second president and prophet, Brigham Young, chided those who limited the progress of all the gods by saying, "They appear to be bounded in their capacity for acquiring knowledge, as [Apostle] Brother Orson Pratt, has in theory, bounded the capacity of God. According to his theory, God can progress no further in knowledge and power; but the God that I serve is progressing eternally, and so are his children: they will increase to all eternity, if they are faithful."[109] Perhaps, as Young intimates by separating out the God that he serves, these General Authorities serve different gods. This disunity is galactic in comparison to the modest list of disagreements between evangelicals on secondary and tertiary doctrines that scholars like Millet like to cite in order to support the need for a living oracle to guarantee consistent doctrine. Furthermore, "When we use the term perfection, it applies to man in his present condition, as well as to heavenly beings. We are now, or may be, as perfect in our sphere as God and angels are in theirs, but the greatest intelligence in existence can continually ascend to greater heights of perfection."[110]

For Christians, our eternal progression is always from depravity to ideal humanity; for LDS, it is from humanity to divinity (and even with the step of perhaps becoming angels along the way), where the evolution occurs only in degree, not in kind. In this respect, it exhibits micro-evolution (change within a species) rather than macro-evolution (change from one species to another species). For humanity and divinity are not different in species or kind according to Mormonism, but only in a gradation of degree (the same goes for angels considering LDS thinking that John the Baptist and Moroni were first men and then angels).[111]

Following Young's interpretation of eternal progression as unbound capacity is the fourth president, Wilford Woodruff, who writes, "God is increasing in knowledge. If there was a point where man in his progression could not proceed any further, the very idea would throw a gloom over every intelligent and reflecting mind. God Himself is increasing and progressing in knowledge, power, and dominion, and will do so, worlds without end."[112]

Finally, the Harvard-trained apostle John Widtsoe argues that this was the view of Joseph Smith. "Through the system of truth taught by Joseph Smith runs the doctrine of eternal progression."[113] Elsewhere he writes, "However, if the great law of progression be accepted, God must have been engaged from the beginning, and must now be engaged in progressive development, and infinite as God is, he must have been less powerful in the past than he is today."[114]

Lorenzo Snow has said, "We must advance through stages to godhood. As man now is, God once was—even the babe of Bethlehem, advancing to Childhood—thence to boyhood, manhood, then to the Godhead. This then is the 'mark of the prize of man's high calling in Christ Jesus.'"[115] He was a man who became a superman.

In assessing this unbound-capacity interpretation of eternal progression we find it highly problematic. If the individual Mormon affirms this view, as some LDS prophets and apostles have, where gods literally progress in all attributes or characteristics of deity throughout eternity rather than at some point arriving at omniscience, omnipotence, etc., then we can assume that the god who just began the transition into divinity (wherever that line begins is unclear since it is only a difference in degree) is far behind in terms of progress to the god that he was worshipping before he became a god himself (and would presumably continue worshipping as his god, which is curious). And that god that he worshipped was likewise far behind in progression compared to the god before him, *ad infinitum*. In other words, if the process has been going on for all eternity, then the god that we worship in this world as God has a near infinite number of gods greater than him in knowledge, power, dominion, etc. By comparison, he would seem to be a flea.

So why worship a 'god' who is of the lowest rank amongst the infinite number of gods that must exist on that account? Is this not scraping from the bottom of the barrel in contrast to responding to a genuinely Supreme Being worthy of worship? This does not seem like a god, but a superman whose current powers you and I can potentially surpass one day regardless of how long it takes. Of course, he will be more powerful and knowledgeable by that time as will his god, and his god's god, *ad infinitum*, etc. But the knowledge and power he has today can potentially be surpassed by you and me tomorrow. Perhaps this is why Spencer W. Kimball wittingly or not referred to "superman" in speaking of the goal of our perfection: " 'Doesn't that take superman?' 'Yes,' I said, 'but we are commanded to be supermen. . . . We are gods in embryo . . . .' "[116] So the first five prophets affirm this view.

The other interpretation, bound capacity, likewise enjoys LDS prophetic and apostolic support. The tenth president, Joseph Fielding Smith, noted that not all in Celestial Glory will be made equal in power and in might and in dominion. But some will become equal.[117] He embraced the idea that God does not eternally progress but at some point can be said to have arrived. His capacity is bound by some upper limit: "It seems very strange to me that members of the Church will hold to the doctrine, 'God increases in knowledge as time goes on.' . . . Where has the Lord ever revealed to us that he is lacking in knowledge? That he is still learning new truth; discovering new laws that are unknown to him? I think this kind of doctrine is very dangerous."[118] So the unbounded view, held by a number of prophets—not just "members"—is now considered dangerous? Spencer W. Kimball concurs with the bounded view. He said, "To this end God created man . . . to become as God, omniscient and omnipotent."[119] He arrived at his final destination.

One of the more philosophically inclined LDS apostles, Orson Pratt, remarked, "They are all equal in knowledge, and in wisdom, and in the possession of all truth. None of these Gods are progressing in knowledge, neither can they progress in the acquirement of any truth."[120] Further,

> Some have gone so far as to say that all the Gods were progressing in truth, and would continue to progress to all eternity, and that some were far in advance of others: but let us examine, for a moment, the absurdity of such a conjecture. If all the Gods will be eternally progressing, then it follows, that there must be a boundless infinity of knowledge that no God ever has attained to, or ever can attain to, throughout infinite ages to come: this boundless infinity of knowledge would be entirely out of the reach and control of all the Gods; therefore it would either not be governed at all, or else be governed by something that was infinitely Superior to all the Gods—a something that had all knowledge, and consequently that could not acquire more. . . . This is the great absurdity, resulting from the vague conjecture that there will be an endless progression in knowledge among all the Gods. Such a conjecture is not only extremely absurd, but it is in direct opposition to what is revealed.[121]

So the unbounded view is not only dangerous, but is also rationally absurd and contradicts revelation. This is matched by the recent late great LDS apostle of our time and son-in-law of Joseph Fielding Smith, whose words indicate that many of the other General Authorities were just clueless: "There are those who say that God is progressing in knowledge and is learning new truths. This is false—utterly, totally, and completely. There is not one sliver of truth in it. It grows out of a wholly twisted and incorrect view of the King Follett Sermon and of what is mean by eternal progression."[122]

Apparently, the current status (which may change tomorrow) affirms the bounded view but it is not clear. What's more, ask five different Mormons and you will get six different opinions. The fact is that the LDS prophets themselves, who are supposed to know, really have no clue and each asserts his contrary views so confidently even to the point of claiming that the other position is irrationally condemned and dangerous. One wonders whether these prophets ever read their predecessors' works. Can we really have a testimony that gives trust or has faith in such living "prophets" who are irrational and dangerous? It seems to me that we cannot. What is the point of having living prophets if they cannot agree on important and essential spiritual matters? Knowledge of how to make Jell-O or live out the basic morals consonant of religion is something that does not require the perpetual existence of living prophets, especially those who offer nothing more than contradiction to prophetic utterance already provided in the Bible. The Book of Mormon is no different from the LDS prophets in terms of internal conflict. While utterly silent or agnostic about the notion of eternal progression, it has its own theological inconsistencies.[123]

If the individual Mormon affirms this bounded interpretation of "eternal progression" such that divine perfection in all God's attributes (omniscience, omnipotence, etc.) is arrived at over time through a successive addition of discrete finite events, then we may inquire about the plausibility or even possibility of such a feat. How, for instance, is this even logically possible for a being to have acquired his last bit of knowledge in the process such that he now has infinite knowledge (i.e., he is now omniscient)? Suppose God is omniscient and the set of all God's knowledge is infinite. It is disputable even in mathematics whether an infinite actually exists or whether it is just in one's mind. But suppose it exists and God knows an infinite number of things. To arrive at an infinite number of things by successive addition is impossible. This would exhibit what we call an asymptotic property where arrival seems just around the corner but one never actually arrives. Just as I cannot reach infinity if I begin counting 1 . . . 2 . . . 3 . . . 4 . . . , so I cannot ever reach the status of infinite knowledge by acquiring one bit at a time no matter how many seconds or even centuries that might take. Progressing through successive addition will never bring about one's arrival.

The Bible describes God as the one "who has perfect knowledge" (Job 37:16) and "knows everything" (1 John 3:20), things actual and possible (Ps. 139:1–4); indeed, "his understanding has no limit." Theologians speak of God as being "omniscient," or all-knowing. This is understood to mean that God knows every true proposition and believes no false proposition. When Christians say that God knows an infinite number of true propositions, they are speaking of the extent of his knowledge, not the mode of his knowledge. Consider numbers as abstract objects where the set of all numbers correspond to the set of all true propositions. What God knows is that, according to standard number theory, there is an actually infinite number of numbers. Moreover, God knows that an actually infinite number of arithmetic truths follow from the axioms of standard arithmetic, like 1+1=2, 2+1=3, 3+1=4 . . . . But he does not know these truths propositionally in the same way that we come to know such truths, through discursive reasoning. He knows them nonpropositionally, nondiscursively. God does not need to make inferences from premises to conclusions. He knows all things conceptually like a mind's knowledge of innate ideas. So if God began knowing with a finite pool of knowledge as a man, say, knowledge of six bits to pick a random finite number, then by successive addition en route to deification, it would be 6+1=7, 7+1=8, 8+1=9 . . . . Since one more can always be added, it is clear that inasmuch as one cannot begin counting from a finite number and ever reach the infinite, so likewise, one cannot begin as a man with finite knowledge and ever hope to acquire omniscience. It seems dubious that one can ever possess infinite knowledge by acquiring bits of knowledge via successive addition. One must either be all-knowing from eternity or else merely eternally progress exhibiting an asymptotic property.

But this is precisely what this bounded interpretation seems to entail. As apostle McConkie explains (citing Joseph Fielding Smith), the God of this world (Elohim) went through the same process until he reached a point at which he was "not progressing in knowledge, truth, virtue, wisdom, or any of the attributes of godliness."[124] Beginning with a finite number, it is impossible to reach infinity by successive addition. The Mormon concept of God here entails a being who began with a finite number of propositions known and reached infinite knowledge by successive addition. Therefore, this Mormon concept of God is incoherent. Some modern LDS apologists offer an even different view, namely, that there is a head god who was never a man.[125] But this too is contradicted by the prophets whose views are really the ones that matter anyhow, given their roles relative to authority and modern revelation.[126]

Thus, we are either faced with a Mormon God who is vastly inferior to all other gods who each possess far more power, knowledge, etc., than himself, and whose present qualities we can surpass in time even while he is ever progressing; or with a Mormon God whose nature seems to be incoherent and nonexistent. Either way, these options are untenable for biblical Christians and are not revelations of God's nature. The LDS prophets themselves—the only ones outside of LDS scripture who should really matter for Mormon doctrine and theology—demonstrate remarkable and utter confusion on the matter, which is especially significant given that they are supposed to be God's mouthpieces concerning spiritual truth and the basis for much ado about the need for living oracles for doctrinal consistency. Remember, as LDS people like to say, "Our God is not a God of confusion." Unfortunately, the same cannot be said of LDS "prophets" and "apostles." Perhaps the LDS prophets need to read their predecessors more carefully. Better yet, perhaps they should all read the Bible more carefully.

In LDS theology there are two steps to ultimate human perfectibility—first moral perfection and then godhood—neither of which is plausible.

Both are fraught with serious problems rendering the LDS "testimony" highly problematic. We have seen that while testimonial knowledge is quite valuable, it can also be a poor source to invoke in the marketplace of competitive religious ideas if standing by itself. The LDS testimony based on the notion of salvation emerging from LDS teachings in the Book of Mormon and living prophets offers a different gospel than that in the New Testament (Gal. 1:6–9) such that it makes the biblical God a liar (1 John 5:9–13). This gospel is antithetical to the central tenet of grace and culminates in what seems to be mission impossible. Grace is the single most salient feature that separates biblical Christianity from every other world religion, including those non-biblical religions under the banner of Christendom. Finally, while the "Christian concept of God"? in Mormonism has defenders in the LDS scholastic world, the LDS apostolic and canonical authorities—the ones who really matter—vary significantly in their understanding of the nature of God (and godhood) and advocate non-biblical, theologically and philosophically inferior, or otherwise incoherent perspectives.

The apostle Paul's heartfelt words in Romans 10 toward his fellow Israelites are relevant here, but in place of "Israelites" we might substitute "Mormons": "Brothers and sisters, my heart's desire and prayer to God for the Mormons is that they may be saved. For I can testify about them that they are zealous for God, but their zeal is not based on knowledge. Since they did not know the righteousness of God and sought to establish their own, they did not submit to God's righteousness. Christ is the culmination of the law so that there may be righteousness for everyone who believes."

Mormonism has produced some great people, some fine citizens, neighbors, and productive members of society, and often makes for a productive cultural alliance in the face of secularism. But although I love Mormon people (including many in my own family who remain LDS), I must conclude that Mormonism is not genuinely Christian. While it shares much in common with those who affirm biblical Christianity, it is found lacking in essential matters. One can be wrong on every other nonessential Christian doctrine and still go to heaven. But no matter how sincere one is, if one is wrong on the doctrines of God and salvation, one could be sufficiently wrong to lose one's soul. In this, Mormonism does not provide a path to the reality of the good life, eternal happiness in the knowledge of God.

NOTES

1. Interestingly, "God" serves as an important premise in the writings on the good life by the pagan philosopher, Aristotle. "God" is mentioned twice as often as "happiness" in a book where happiness is the central purpose of life (e.g., Aristotle's *Nicomachean Ethics*). See John Hare, *God and Morality: A Philosphical History* (Oxford: Oxford University Press, 1996), 7–74.
2. Augustine of Hippo, *The Confessions*, trans. Edward Pusey (New York: Pocket Books, 1952), 1.
3. Truman G. Madsen, *Eternal Man* (Salt Lake City: Deseret Book Company, 1966), 16.

4. Ibid., 26.
5. Capital "G" will signify the God we generally speaking of in terms of the one we worship. For traditional Christians, this is straightforward. For Mormonism it can be a bit complicated. So we will use lowercase "g" when denoting any god that is not the one we take ourselves to worship.
6. While there are differences in nuance between the Greek words used by Aristotle for "happiness" (*eudaimonia*) and by Jesus in his teachings on the beatitudes (*makarios*), some have sought to merge them. See the first chapter discussion on Aristotle in Corey Miller, "Moses Maimonides and Thomas Aquinas on the Good Life: From the Fall to Human Perfectibility" (Ph.D. dissertation, University of Aberdeen, 2014).
7. Polygamy is presently prominent for tens of thousands of practicing Mormons who are divided into dozens of Mormon sects together with their own self-proclaimed prophets and apostles. These "fundamentalists" believe that the Salt Lake Church has abandoned the truth in apostasy for political expediency. Consider, for example, the 1890 temporary ban on polygamy that the Salt Lake City-based movement claims was revelation but that curiously emerged coincidentally with the desire for Utah to acquire statehood but for this inhibition (Utah was finally granted statehood in 1896). This is similar to the curious connection of the "revelation" that blacks could finally ascend to the priesthood, coincidentally taking place during the latter part of the Civil Rights Movement.
8. Recent research by Mental Health America, the oldest independent mental health advocacy organization in America, ranked Utah the most depressed state in the country. (2017). *Ranking the States*. Retrieved from http://www.mentalhealthamerica.net/issues/ranking-statesGoldman, Russell. (2008, March 7). *Two Studies Find Depression Widespread in Utah*. Retrieved from http://abcnews.go.com/Health/MindMoodNews.
9. The Doctrine and Covenants (D&C) 89.
10. For readers interested in considering the basis for this, see the popular series by Lee Strobel—*The Case for a Creator*, *The Case for Christ*, and *The Case for Faith*—which deals with scientific, philosophical, and historical reasons for following Jesus. For an intermediate reader, see Norman Geisler and Paul K. Hoffman, *Why I Am a Christian: Leading Thinkers Explain Why They Believe* (Grand Rapids: Baker Books, 2006).
11. I make a distinction here because knowing that God exists or that God is present is different from knowing God's existence or God's presence *per se*. The former requires only intellectual assent, whereas the latter requires an existential encounter with the Divine.
12. Brandon S. Plewe, editor, *Mapping Mormonism: An Atlas of Latter-day Saint History* (Provo, UT: BYU Press, 2012).
13. Joseph Smith, *History of the Church*, 7 vols., ed. B. H. Roberts, 2nd ed. (Salt Lake City: Deseret Book Co., 1978), 1:19.
14. Ibid., 1:40–41.
15. Joseph Smith, *Doctrines of Salvation: Sermons and Writings of Joseph Fielding Smith*, 3 vols., ed. and comp. Bruce R. McConkie (Salt Lake City: Bookcraft, 1955), 1:190.
16. Bruce R. McConkie, *Mormon Doctrine* (Salt Lake City: Bookcraft, 1966), 670.
17. Roberts, *History of the Church*, 6:408–09.
18. Boyd K. Packer, *That All May Be Edified* (Salt Lake City: Bookcraft, 1982), 340; italics in original.
19. Boyd K. Packer, "The Candle of the Lord," *Ensign* (January 1983): 55.
20. Dallin Oaks, "Teaching and Learning by the Spirit," *Ensign* (March 1997): 13.
21. Gene R. Cook, "Are You a Member Missionary?" *Ensign* (Conference Edition) (May 1976): 103.
22. Church of Jesus Christ of Latter-day Saints, *Preach My Gospel: A Guide to Missionary Service* (2004), 38.
23. Spencer W. Kimball writes, "Monthly there are testimony meetings held where each one has the opportunity to bear witness. To by-pass such opportunities is to fail to that extent to pile up

credits against the accumulated errors and transgressions." See his *The Miracle of Forgiveness* (Salt Lake City: Bookcraft, 1969), 204–6.

24. Sometimes it is said that there are five spiritual truths to include: Our heavenly father lives, Jesus is the savior, Joseph Smith was a prophet who restored the gospel, the Book of Mormon is the word of God, and the church is led by living prophets and apostles. See http://www.lds.org/friend/2008/10/testimony-glove.

25. For example, the FLDS (fundamentalists) think that the Salt Lake church went apostate over polygamy for the sake of political expediency and its denial of the Adam-God doctrine taught by Brigham Young, etc. The formerly RLDS (Reorganized and now named Community of Christ) denies that Brigham Young was a legitimate prophet since prior to Joseph Smith's death, they argue, his choice was to pass it on to his son, Joseph Smith III, who eventually became the prophet of the nearly 300,000 member congregation based primarily in the Midwest where Joseph Smith's first wife, Emma, and their son remained. The Salt Lake Church has its own idiosyncratic points at which it contradicts many of the other sects as well.

26. Packer, "The Candle of the Lord," *Ensign* (January 1983): 55.

27. The term for "faith" (Hebrew, *emunah*; Greek, *pistis*; Latin, *fides*) connotes belief, loyalty, faithfulness, or trust with attending intellectual content and volitional consent, usually in the context of committing trust in a trustworthy object. Moses Maimonides (the greatest Jewish legal scholar and philosopher in the last three millennia) held that faith is a virtue, a moral virtue with intellectual content. Thomas Aquinas, perhaps the most influential Christian philosopher and theologian, held that faith is an intellectual virtue, apart from which none of the other virtues can be virtuous. Faith for Maimonides and Aquinas was the functional equivalent of what Aristotle believed to be the master virtue, *phronesis* (often translated as "prudence" or taken as "practical reasoning"). Corey Miller, "Moses Maimonides and Thomas Aquinas on the Good Life: From the Fall to Human Perfectibility," (Ph.D. dissertation, University of Aberdeen, 2014).

28. Reid says, "It is evident that in the matter of testimony, the balance of human judgment is by nature inclined to the side of belief; and turns to that side of itself, when there is nothing put into opposite scale. If it was not so, no proposition that is uttered in discourse would be believed, until it was examined and tried by reason; and most men would be unable to find reason for believing the thousandth part of what is told them." Thomas Reid, "An Inquiry into the Human Mind" (1764) in his *Inquiry and Essays*, ed. R.E. Beanblossom and Keith Lehrer (Dordrecht: Reidel, 1975), 93–95; cited in Ernest Sosa, "Testimony," in *A Companion to Epistemology*, ed. Jonathan Dancy and Ernest Sosa (Oxford: Blackwell, 1998), 503–5. See this article for comparison of testimony with memory and perception. Testimony can be seen as a basic source of knowledge in addition to perception, memory, etc.

29. Indeed, in some cases knowledge can be transmitted because of the testimony and not just through it, where the receiver and not the sender possesses knowledge because of it (e.g., when the sender contributes a portion to the receiver's whole that adds up to other portions previously possessed to result in knowledge by the receiver).

30. Jennifer Lackey, "Testimony: Acquiring Knowledge from Others," in *Social Epistemology: Essential Readings*, ed. Alvin Goldman and Dennis Whitcomb (Oxford: Oxford University Press, 2011), 78.

31. For example, moral responsibility (which entails moral beliefs) seems to imply that we are responsible for at least some of our actions. Philosopher Robert Adams claims that we are sometimes blamed for desires, states of mind, and morally defective beliefs that are involuntary. For example, some beliefs and attitudes we form, like being raised in the corrupt environment of the Ku Klux Klan (KKK) and coming to form beliefs consistent with the KKK, are still culpable regardless of how they were acquired. See Adams, "Involuntary Sins," *The Philosophical Review* 94 (January 1985). See also, Ian DeWeese-Boyd, "Self-Deception and Moral Responsibility," Ph.D. dissertation, St. Louis University, 2001). And this is true whether we go about this process of belief formation self-deceptively or not. There are clear and numerous cases of deciding to believe both with and without self-deception. For such arguments see J. Thomas Cook, "Deciding to

Believe Without Self-Deception," *The Journal of Philosophy* 84 (August 1987): 441–46; William James, "The Will to Believe," in *Philosophy of Religion: An Anthology*, ed. Louis Pojman, (Belmont, CA: Wadsworth, 1998): 404–12. To further illustrate, the atheist Thomas Nagel exhibits a cosmic authority problem revealing a will not to believe when he says, "I hope there is no God! I don't want there to be a God; I don't want the universe to be like that." Thomas Nagel, *The Last Word* (Oxford: Oxford University Press, 1997), 130.

32. I use "pneumatically" with respect to the Greek word for "spirit," or *pneuma*. In the act of faith in receiving God's love and goodness a mutual second-personal relation emerges which is characterized by trust in God, and further openness to God grows in the individual. Consequently, the person develops a kind of "sympathy with God." When the person is in this second-personal relation with God, his or her mind is attuned to God's, thereby forming a resonance or sympathy. Such sympathy enables the development of particular dispositions of intellect in the person. A person understands things and has insight into things in ways he or she otherwise would not have apart from that new openness to the mind of God. For more, see Eleonore Stump, "Faith, Wisdom, and the Transmission of Knowledge through Testimony," ed. Laura Frances Callahan and Timothy O'Connor in *Religious Faith and Intellectual Virtue* (Oxford: Oxford University Press, 2014), 210.

33. There are certain necessary conditions for second-personal experience: (1) Some person A is aware of some other person B (a relation of personal interaction), (2) A's personal interaction with B is of a direct and immediate sort, and (3) B is conscious. Note that (1) does not entail the requirement of seeing, hearing, smelling, touching, or tasting, another person. It could, frankly, be a conversation via email, etc. Physical perception is not required here. For more on this interpersonal communication relative to what some social scientists and philosophers are now calling "mind reading," see Eleonore Stump, *Wandering in Darkness* (Oxford: Oxford University Press, 2010), 75–76.

34. Andrew Pinsent, *The Second-Person Perspective in Aquinas's Ethics: Virtues and Gifts* (New York: Routledge, 2011), 62. Pinsent, a physicist and Thomistic philosopher, argues for a major revision in our understanding of Aquinas's virtue ethics. See my review of *The Second-Person Perspective in Aquinas' Ethics: Virtues and Gifts*, by Andrew Pinsent, in *American Catholic Philosophical Quarterly* 87 (Winter 2013): 207–11. Wisdom is a matter of comprehending the highest (or the deepest) causes of things, Aristotle says. For Christians, this cause is God, who is goodness itself. So here is one way of understanding true human wisdom. When a person comes to faith, a person also comes to understand that certain things are truly good and worth desiring and other things are not. The indwelling Holy Spirit and attendant gifts are second-personal in character. When Ananias goes to relieve Saul of his blindness, in Acts chapter 9, he does so because in dialogue with the Holy Spirit he has come to understand that this act at this time is good to do. There is connaturality or sympathy where a human person has an understanding more like God's than he would have otherwise.

35. Tom Doyle, *Dreams and Visions: Is Jesus Awakening the Muslim World?* (Nashville, TN: Thomas Nelson, 2012).

36. Corey Miller and Paul Gould, *Is Faith in God Reasonable? Debates in Philosophy, Science, and Rhetoric* (New York: Routledge, 2014). To see the debate between William Lane Craig and Alex Rosenberg on which the book is based, see https://www.youtube.com/watch?v=1d2X9rrzgso.

37. One reason for objecting might be that it is grounded in philosophy rather than Scripture. But I fail to see this as problematic if the philosophy is well-reasoned and is consistent with Scripture. For a Mormon philosopher's objection, see Blake T. Ostler, *Exploring Mormon Thought: The Attributes of God* (Salt Lake City: Greg Kofford Books, 2001); *Exploring Mormon Thought: Of God and Gods* (Salt Lake City: Greg Kofford Books, 2008).

38. For an understanding of the contemporary Christian perspectives on God's attributes or those discussed in more detail with some common ground for conversation between theists and atheists, see Stephen T. Davis, "Three Conceptions of God in Contemporary Christian Philosophy," in *Readings in the Philosophy of Religion*, 2nd edition, ed. Kelly James Clark (New York: Broadview, 2008), 491–508; Joshua Hoffman and Gary Rosenkrantz, *The Divine Attributes* (Malden, MA: Blackwell Publishers, 2002). For a critique of the Mormon conception, see several essays in the volume edited

by Francis J. Beckwith, Carl Mosser, and Paul Owen, *The New Mormon Challenge* (Grand Rapids: Zondervan, 2002). For an anthology of Mormon and Christian reflections, see Jacob Baker, *Mormonism at the Crossroads of Philosophy and Theology* (Salt Lake City: Greg Kofford Books, 2002).

39. Ockham's razor was developed initially by the fourteenth-century philosopher and theologian but is used by modern philosophers and scientists. The principle states that among competing hypotheses that predict equally well, the one with the fewest assumptions should be selected. The simplest explanation is usually the best explanation rather than multiplying entities to explain a particular phenomenon. Usually, this shifts the burden of explanation onto the one proposing multiple entities (in this case gods). It is also referred to as the "law of parsimony." Monotheism is a simpler explanation with greater explanatory power than polytheism. Granted, there are some LDS apologists who seek to argue that Mormonism affirms a head God. But even in such cases it is readily admitted that, according to Blake Ostler, "until recently almost all Mormons believed that Joseph Smith taught that God progressed to become fully divine from a lower state of non-divinity . . . I believe that such a view has been widely reassessed . . . . It seems to me that the view is now widely accepted among Mormon scholars and writers that the Father was fully divine before becoming mortal, just as the Son was." Ostler goes on to assert that it is his own writings that have largely accounted for the change of opinion among Mormon thinkers. That's nice for him to think so highly of his influence, but Mormon scholars and authors need to know their place in Mormon ecclesiological hierarchy of authority and God's economy of revelation in Mormonism. It is the LDS prophetic voice that carries authority, not the scholars or apologists. Somehow, as we'll see later in this chapter, scores of prophets and apostles never received Ostler's memo and, well, it is either him or the General Authorities. The LDS testimony mentions living prophets, not LDS apologists and scholars. See Ostler, *Exploring Mormon Thought: Of God and Gods*, 17–18.

40. For an excellent work by Christian philosophers providing up-to-date arguments for the Christian God, including the God of Perfect Being Theology from natural reasoning, see William Lane Craig and J. P. Moreland, *The Blackwell Companion to Natural Theology* (Malden, MA: Blackwell, 2009).

41. Since Plantinga's views are widely known among philosophers but perhaps fairly complex for others it will be helpful for the unfamiliar reader to simply see the lengthy note here for a summary, or to reference Alvin Plantinga's monumental work in religious epistemology, *Warranted Christian Belief* (Oxford: Oxford University Press, 2000), for details. Essentially, he responds to both *de jure* and *de facto* objections to belief in God. The *de facto* objection says that Christianity is false; the truth claims espoused are factually in error. It is a truth-dependent objection. A *de jure* objection is not that it is necessarily false, but that it is unjustified, irrational, or unwarranted, regardless of its veracity. It is a truth- independent objection. That is, it is irrational, unjustified, or unwarranted to believe in God whether or not it is true. Plantinga is trying to refute *de jure* objections to Christian belief. He is not claiming that his model is true, instead he argues (1) it is epistemically possible, and (2) if Christian belief is true, then something like his model is very likely to be true. He shows that there is no reason to think that Christian belief lacks justification, rationality, or warrant, apart from, and unless one presupposes, the falsity of Christianity. It shows that there is no successful *de jure* objection. For any objection to be successful, it is going to have to be a *de facto* objection. In order to show Christianity is unjustified, unwarranted, or irrational, one would have to show it to be false. Thus, if God exists, then one's properly basic belief in God is certainly rational; it is warranted. Properly basic beliefs entail a normative notion respecting the proper functioning of the one holding them. And this is relevant to assigning culpability to nonbelief. If God exists, it seems quite reasonable that God could create us such that our noetic structure is adequately pointed at truth, rather than merely survival, when we are properly functioning the way we were designed to function as image bearers.

42. For one recent discussion, see Robert M. Bowman, Jr., "The Sermon at the Temple in the Book of Mormon: A Critical Examination of Its Authenticity through a Comparison with the Sermon on the Mount in the Gospel of Matthew." (Ph.D. Dissertation, 2014).

43. It is beyond the scope of this chapter to display the great depth of historical, scientific, and philosophical evidence and reason in support of the traditional Christian faith, but the resources are readily available for the genuine seeker. Some examples for readers at the popular or intermediate level would include Norman Geisler, *Baker's Encyclopedia of Christian Apologetics* (Grand Rapids: Baker, 1999); Josh McDowell, *New Evidence that Demands a Verdict* (Nashville, TN: Thomas Nelson, 1999); William Lane Craig, *Reasonable Faith: Christian Truth and Apologetics*, 3rd ed., (Wheaton, Ill: Crossway Books, 2008). Gary Habermas, The Historical Jesus: *Ancient Evidence for the Life of Christ* (Joplin, Missouri: College Press, 1996); Lee Strobel, *The Case for Faith* (Grand Rapids: Zondervan, 2000).

44. Wilford Woodruff, *The Discourses of Wilford Woodruff*, selected by G. Homer Durham. (Salt Lake City: Bookcraft, 1946), 212–13.

45. Salvation is understood both generally and specifically. Generally speaking, the LDS faith teaches that all people will be resurrected from the dead and live forever. But personal salvation is up to the individual and it can lead toward exaltation, the highest calling for man according to Mormonism.

46. Spencer W. Kimball speaks of the two-step process in *The Miracle of Forgiveness*, 6. This is not unlike some ancient and medieval models of human perfectibility and the good life. Aristotle and Maimonides likewise had a two-step process.

47. The notion "eternal life" has been used to connote pre-mortal and post-mortal existence in Mormonism; it has denoted salvation, but it has most predominantly been referred to as exaltation per Celestial Glory.

    Joseph Smith affirmed this two-step process, the first being resurrection into a particular glory; the second an advancement within Celestial Glory to the highest point. See *Teachings of the Prophet Joseph Smith*, 348; *Gospel Principles*, 1997, 305. Exaltation is only pertinent to Celestial Glory.

48. 2 Nephi 25:23.

49. Stephen E. Robinson, *Are Mormons Christians?* (Salt Lake City, Utah: Deseret Publishing Co., 1998), 104–105.

50. Ibid., 108.

51. The full list of the Articles of Faith, a segment of LDS scriptures found within the larger text, The Pearl of Great Price, is available on the LDS website www.lds.org/scriptures/pgp

52. Boyd K. Packer, "The Atonement" *Ensign* (May 1977): 54–55.

53. *Gospel Principles* (Salt Lake City: The Church of Jesus Christ of Latter-day Saints, 1981), 69–71.

54. Ibid., 122.

55. Ibid., 244. After citing D&C 82:7, "Unto that soul who sinneth shall the former sins return, saith the Lord your God," Kimball goes on to say, "Those who feel that they can sin and be forgiven and then return to sin and be forgiven again and again must straighten out their thinking. Each previously forgiven sin is added to the new one and the whole gets to be a heavy load. . . . When one quits, he must quit." *Miracle of Forgiveness*, 170.

56. Stephen Robinson, *Believing Christ: The Parable of the Bicycle and Other Good News* (Salt Lake City: Deseret Book, 1992), 15–16.

57. Ibid.

58. Ibid.

59. Ibid.

60. In fairness, one cannot draw a conclusion about Utah's depression and stress relative to religious motifs since correlation is not identical to causation. But neither can one deny the plausible view that the stress is brought about due to an extreme performance mentality. From an LDS perspective, see: http://en.fairmormon.org/Utah/Statistical_claims/LDS_use_of_antidepressants. What is also of note, however, is the fact that such an extreme performance mentality not only induces high levels of stress, but also seems to drive people to private sin more than usual. LDS missionaries are

often pointing to the fruits of Mormonism to confirm their message. Yet, Utah is also known for its secret sins like being the porn-consumer capital of the country. I doubt one can attribute this to all and only non-Mormons in a Mormon-dominated state. See Elaine Jarvik, "Utah No. 1 in Online Porn Subscriptions, Report Says," *Deseret News*, March 3, 2009, http://www.deseretnews.com/article/705288350/Utah-No-1-in-online-porn-subscriptions-report-says.html.

61. Robinson, *Believing Christ*, 15–16.

62. Robert Millet, "Authority is Everything," in *Talking Doctrine: Mormons and Evangelicals in Conversation*, ed. Robert L. Millet and Richard Mouw (Downers Grove, Ill: InterVarsity Press, 2015), 176.

63. The current LDS prophet and president, Thomas S. Monson, said, "President Spencer W. Kimball has always been a prolific worker. He spent several summers working on a book which he later entitled *The Miracle of Forgiveness*. As one reads the book, particularly the first portion, one wonders if anyone will make it to the Celestial Kingdom. However, in reading the final portion, it is apparent that, with effort, all can qualify." Thomas S. Monson, *On the Lord's Errand: Memoirs of Thomas S. Monson* (self-published, 1985), 342.

64. Consider, as examples, statements by LDS prophets of what they think about their own statements in regard to them being scripture. "I have never yet preached a sermon and sent it out to the children of men, that they may not call Scripture. Let me have the privilege of correcting a sermon, and it is as good Scripture as they deserve. The people have the oracles of God continually." (Brigham Young, January 2, 1870, *Journal of Discourses* 13:95). "When a man speaks as he is moved upon by the Holy Spirit what he says is the word of the Lord; it is the mind of the Lord, it is scripture, it is the will of the Lord, it is the power of God until salvation to everyone that believes." (Wilford Woodruff, September 1, 1899, *Collected Discourses* 1:340–1). "What is Scripture? When one of the brethren stands before a congregation of the people today, and the inspiration of the Lord is upon him, he speaks that which the Lord would have him speak. It is just as much scripture as anything you will find written in any of these records, and yet we call these the standard works of the Church" (Joseph Fielding Smith, *Doctrines of Salvation* 1:186) "There is scripture other than the standard works. Some people get the idea that the only scripture we have in the Church today is that which is contained in the four standard Church works." (The *Teachings of Harold B. Lee*, Edited by Clyde J. Williams. (Salt Lake City: Bookcraft, 1996), 148.

65. Robert Millet, *A Different Jesus? The Christ of the Latter-day Saints* (Grand Rapids: Eerdmans, 2005), 50.

66. Kimball, *The Miracle of Forgiveness*.

67. The Doctrine and Covenants (D&C) 14:7.

68. Roland Bainton, *Here I Stand: A Life of Martin Luther* (NY: Penguin, 1950).

69. D&C 58:42–43.

70. Kimball, *The Miracle of Forgiveness*, 203; emphasis mine.

71. Ibid., 354–55; emphasis mine.

72. Ibid., 170.

73. Book of Mormon, Moroni 10:32–33; emphasis mine.

74. Ibid., 1 Nephi 3:7; emphasis mine.

75. Mormon scholars have sought to work around this passage's apparent contradiction with the Bible's Ephesians 2:8–9. Robert Millet says, "No matter how much we do, it simply will not be enough to guarantee salvation without Christ's intervention. . . . there is a very real sense in which, "all we can do, is come before the Lord in reverent humility, confess our weaknesses, and plead for his forgiveness, for his mercy, and grace." Robert L. Millet, *Grace Works*, (Salt Lake City: Deseret Book, 2003), 131–2. But it is not always viewed in that way as he records on pages 6–7. Shortly before leaving on his two-year mission, Millet inquired of his father, "'Dad, what does it mean to be saved by grace?' He stared at me for a moment and then said firmly, 'We don't believe in that!'" When he asked why not, his father responded, "Because the Baptists do!"

Obviously, Millet's father didn't see it the way Millet articulates LDS belief. But Millet insists on page 13, "The great plan of happiness is a gift. Salvation, which is exaltation, which is eternal life, is free. It is not something for which we can barter, nor is it something that may be purchased with money. Neither is it, in the strictest sense, something that can be earned." Whether attempting to assuage the Bible-believing Christians here via traditional rhetoric or not, what he really believes contradicts his leaders whose voices trump his own in matters of authority. Recall Kimball who referred to repentance which "merits" forgiveness (p. 355). Millet even contradicts himself. On page 18 while insisting that "grace is unmerited favor" (a classical Protestant definition of grace), he goes on to explicate it as "an enabling power that allows men and women to lay hold on eternal life and exaltation after they have expended their own best efforts." Some Christian scholars likewise have not seen this verse as seriously problematic. Gerald McDermott goes on to quote Stephen Robinson and concludes, "So let's put some old staples of evangelical anti-Mormon apologetics to rest." (171) McDermott has about as much as a problem as Richard Mouw and perhaps for some of the same reasons. His problem, as a Calvinist, is more about who makes the first move, God or man, and construes Mormonism much like Arminianism in the Calvinist-Arminian debates. See Robert L. Millet and Gerald R. McDermott, *Claiming Christ: A Mormon-Evangelical Debate* (Grand Rapids: Brazos Press, 2007).

76. Millet, *A Different Jesus?*, 69, 95.

77. Kimball, *The Miracle of Forgiveness*, 206. Often times LDS people misconstrue Christian thinking about salvation as if faith is necessary but faith need not be accompanied by works. In truth, genuine salvation must eventuate in works even though the works are not a precondition to receiving grace as is taught in Mormonism.

78. Book of Mormon, 3 Nephi 27:16, 17, 19, 27; emphasis added.

79. Kimball, *The Miracle of Forgiveness*, 208–9.

80. Ibid., 353.

81. Book of Mormon, Alma 34:32–35.

82. Kimball, *The Miracle of Forgiveness*, 209–10, 213–4; emphasis mine.

83. Ibid., 164.

84. *NASB*. Colossians 2:13–14.

85. Some seek to show an inconsistency between James in James 2:24 and Paul in Romans 3:28. But a closer examination reveals that James is teaching on what saving faith looks like while Paul is focusing in on what constitutes saving faith. Both authors reference the story of Abraham. Abraham was justified by his faith, a functional faith.

86. While McConkie is now dead, his words, like other dead General Authorities, should still be respected by LDS people. If they were true at that time, then they are equally true now. Otherwise, perhaps today's truth can become tomorrow's lie and no "truth" taught by a General Authority today should be believed. Bruce R. McConkie, *Mormon Doctrine*, 2nd edition (Salt Lake City: Bookcraft, 1991), 576–77.

87. McConkie, *Mormon Doctrine*, 576–77; Joseph Fielding Smith, ed., *The Teachings of the Prophet Joseph Smith*, 346–47 [pre-2002 edition]; Abraham 4:1, *Pearl of Great Price*; and "God," *LDS Bible Dictionary*.

88. Millet, *A Different Jesus?*, 117.

89. See Genesis 1:1; Deuteronomy 4:39; 10:14; Nehemiah 9:6; Psalm 96:5; Isa. 40:12–26; 43:10; 44:6, 8, and 24; 45:5; John 1:1–3; and 17:3.

90. Robinson, *Are Mormons Christians?*, 60–61. Millet, *A Different Jesus?*, 115.

91. While primarily talked about among members of the early Greek Eastern Church, there have been quite a number of authors writing in recent times about members of the Latin Western Church having a concept of *theosis*, perhaps sometimes exaggerated in these Western treatments at the expense of diminishing the ideas of the Eastern concept. These include: David Vincent Meconi, *The*

One Christ: St. Augustine's Theology of Deification (Washington, DC: Catholic University of America Press, 2013); Jordan Cooper, *Christification: A Lutheran Approach to Theosis* (Eugene, OR: Wipf & Stock, 2014); Carl Moser, "An Exotic Flower? Calvin and the Patristic Doctrine of Deification," in Michael Parsons, ed., *Reformation Faith: Exegesis and Theology in the Protestant Reformations* (Milton Keynes: Paternoster Press, 2014), 33–56; Daria Spezzano, *The Glory of God's Grace: Deification According to St. Thomas Aquinas* (Washington, DC: Sapientia Press, 2015); Andrew Hofer, ed., *Divinization: Becoming Icons of Christ Through the Liturgy* (Chicago and Mundelein: Hillenbrand Books, 2015); David Vincent Meconi and Carl Olson, eds., *Called to Be the Children of God: The Catholic Theology of Human Deification* (San Francisco: Ignatius Press, 2016).

92. Daniel A. Keating, "Typologies of Deification," 5–6, in *International Journal of Systematic Theology* (2015): 11–17.

93. John McGuckin, "The Strategic Adaptation of Deification in the Cappadocians," in Christensen and Wittung, eds., *Partakers of the Divine Nature* (Grand Rapids: Baker, 2008), 95.

94. Maximus' view reflects that of Athanasius, Augustine, Cyril and others whose notions retain the distinction between the divine and the human in the activity of human participation in the divine. Maximus the Confessor, *Opus*. 7, trans. Adam G. Cooper, in Adam G. Cooper, *The Body in St. Maximus the Confessor: Holy Flesh, Wholly Deified* (Oxford: Oxford University Press, 2005), 157.

95. Such authors would be Richard Mouw and Stephen Webb. Neither of these authors say anything in terms of this being a substantial problem rendering Mormonism as an aberrant cult or pseudo-Christian movement but instead seem to readily embrace the words of LDS scholars or other well-prepared public statements by General Authorities to the effect that Mormonism isn't importantly related to such speculative theology. Richard Mouw, the former president of Fuller Seminary, and others sometimes make apology for evangelical critics of Mormonism on account of what some modern LDS scholars assert about deification in LDS theology having no present-day import. This is simply academic pleasantries gone awry. For one, even if Mouw's most recent work finally reflects the actual research rather than mere acceptance of some contemporary LDS scholars' words, it is irrelevant. Mormonism is based on modern-day revelation and all confidence is placed is the living prophets, not the LDS scholars. If living prophets taught it, and taught it as revelation, what non-prophets of the LDS faith say is simply irrelevant. That prophet claims to have received it from God and is thus either a false prophet or not. See response to Richard Mouw in Ronald Huggins, "Lorenzen Snow's Couplet: 'As Man Now Is, God Once Was; As God Now Is, Man May Be': 'No Functioning Place in Present-Day Mormon Doctrine?' A Response to Richard Mouw," *Journal of the Evangelical Society* 49 (2006): 549–68. See Richard Mouw, *Talking with Mormons: An Invitation to Evangelicals* (Grand Rapids: Eerdmans, 2012); Mouw and Millet, eds., *Talking Doctrine: Mormons and Evangelicals in Conversation*. In the first line of his chapter on "Mormon Envy," Catholic (former Protestant) author, Stephen Webb, says, "I'm not a Mormon, but sometimes I wish I were one." Stephen H. Webb, *Mormon Christianity: What Other Christians Can Learn from the Latter-day Saints* (Oxford: Oxford University Press, 2013), 11.

96. Richard Ostling, *Time Magazine* (August 4, 1997), 56. To see discussion and correspondence on the LDS response concerning the authenticity of the reporting by *Time* see: http://mit.irr.org/dodging-and-dissembling-prophet.

97. Don Lattin, "Musings of the Main Morman/Gordon B. Hinckley, 'President, Prophet, Seer, and Revelator' of the Church of Jesus Christ of Latter-day Saints, Sits at the Top of One of the World's Fastest-Growing Religions," *San Francisco Chronicle* (April 13, 1997). Lattin provided this rejoinder to Hinckley's statement, "So you're saying the church is still struggling to understand this?" And Hinckley replied, "Well, as God is, man may become. We believe in eternal progression. Very strongly." I'm not sure what to make of this other than perhaps Hinckley is admitting ignorance as to the depth of the doctrine or that he's talking one way to non-LDS people and another way to LDS people.

98. Gordon B. Hinckley, *Teachings of Gordon B. Hinckley*, (Salt Lake City: Deseret Book, 1997), 179.

99. Richard N. and Joan K. Ostling, *Mormon America: The Power and the Promise* (New York: HarperCollins, 1999), 296.

100. D&C 132:20.

101. Joseph Smith, *Teachings of the Prophet Joseph Smith*, selected by Joseph Fielding Smith, (Salt Lake City: Deseret Book, 1976), 346–347.

102. Brigham Young, August 8, 1852, *Journal of Discourses* 3:93.

103. John Taylor, *The Gospel Kingdom* (Salt Lake City: Bookcraft, 1964. 4th edition), 58.

104. Wilford Woodruff, June 27, 1875, *Journal of Discourses* 18:39.

105. Lorenzo Snow was baptized in 1836, the same year that my ancestor, John Scott, was baptized. Snow reflected on a statement made to him two weeks prior to his baptism by the founder of Mormonism's father, Joseph Smith senior (the same man who laid hands of prayer on John Scott since Scott abandoned his family to follow Joseph Smith). It was a sort of prediction that Snow would have a great future, namely, "Become as great as you can possibly wish—even as great as God." By Snow's own account, just prior to his 1840 mission to England he listened to one Mormon Elder teach and suddenly received revelation on which he formed the famous couplet. In 1843 Snow mentioned it to Joseph Smith who said to him, "Brother Snow, that is true gospel doctrine, and it is a revelation from God to you." He then had a vision. In 1894 he described the couplet "as a star continually before me." Throughout his life he continued to refer to it as a "vision" and write poetry about it. Even five days after his 1898 inauguration to the office of Prophet, he preached on it, calling it a most complete and perfect "direct revelation." He went on to say, "If ever there was a thing revealed to man perfectly, clearly, so that there could be no doubt or dubiety, this was revealed to me, and it came in these words: 'As man now is, God once was; as God now is, man may be.'" See "Unchangeable Love of God" (Sept. 18, 1898) in *Collected Discourses* 5.453. And about three months before his death in 1901 Snow alluded to the first moment he had thought of the doctrine: "That fulfilled Father [the father of the founder of Mormonism] Smith's declaration. Nothing was ever revealed more distinctly than that was to me." Lorenzo Snow, *Journal History* (July 20, 1901) 4, as cited in Huggins, "Lorenzo Snow's Couplet." Since the moment of that first revelation, the apostle and prophet Lorenzo Snow, held tenaciously to its veracity for sixty-five years of his life and claimed that nothing was more of a revelation to him than that couplet.

106. Lorenzo Snow, *The Teachings of Lorenzo Snow*, ed. Clyde Williams (Salt Lake City: Bookcraft, 1984), 2. On the same page Snow maintains that gods will be "increasing eternally."

107. Ibid., 27. Other more recent prophets have affirmed the view of deification entailed by the law of eternal progression. For example, the tenth prophet said Mormons believe that we will have the privilege of being made equal in power, might and dominion (D&C 76:95), and to possess all that the Father hath (D&C 84:38)…." (Joseph Fielding Smith, Jr., *The Way to Perfection*, 9). He went on to say that "Joseph Smith taught a plurality of gods, and that man by obeying the commandments of God and keeping the whole law will eventually reach the power and exaltation by which he also will become a god." (Joseph Fielding Smith, *Doctrines of Salvation* 1:98). Kimball, the prophet discussed here at length in the section on salvation, said, "To this end God created man…to perfect himself and to become as God, omniscient and omnipotent." (Kimball, *The Miracle of Forgiveness*, 2).

108. To repeat from an earlier note, "God" is referred to with a capital "G" when denoting the God of our world generally understood as the God whom we worship. For Christians there is only one God, so that is simple; for Mormons it is usually intended to be God the Father. But the confusion is often evident among Mormons because their authorities and scholars are not clear. For example, one of the premier LDS scholars of our age, Robert Millet, mentioned in his glossary of important terms, "God and Christ will always be the object of our devotion and our worship." As is well known, Mormonism denies the orthodox view of the godhead being three persons in one nature. Instead, it affirms three persons who are three separate gods whose "oneness" is only a oneness in purpose. For further elaboration, see the entry in the Encyclopedia of Mormonism. http://eom.byu.edu/index.php/Godhead. Millet evidently is no "henotheist" because these

makes clear his polytheist belief not only in terms of believing in the existence of many Gods/gods, but even worshipping many (in this case at least two). Of course, this must have escaped the notice of Richard Mouw, LDS defender and former president of Fuller Seminary, who apparently claims to have a better understanding of Mormonism than most of his evangelical colleagues critical of Mormonism. He says on page ix in the Foreword, "The fact is that many of my Christian friends think they know what the LDS believe, even though they have never seriously attempted to understand those beliefs from the LDS perspective." This doesn't get him off the hook. He wrote the Afterword after having read the manuscript and did not even comment on this important admission by Millet. See Millet, *A Different Jesus?*, 194. In the Afterword, Mouw's understanding of Millet's view of salvation by grace is little different from Arminian perspectives in Protestantism and he is convinced that Millet is trusting in the Jesus of the Bible for his salvation. If these two things were correct, then Millet is no more a Mormon than am I and should likewise have his name stricken from the LDS roster because such views do not comport with the likes of the Book of Mormon and Spencer W. Kimball, whose epistemic authority as prophet is a whole lot greater than Millet's as scholar. Millet knows this, which is why he and other Mormon scholars keep reminding us that their books are not very significant comparatively. Millet's stated purpose in writing the book is to offer what he thinks LDS Christianity is, but then in the preface page xiii offers this disclaimer heard all too often, "This book is a private endeavor and is thus without imprimatur or authorization of The Church of Jesus Christ of Latter-Day Saints . . .

109. Brigham Young, January 13, 1867, *Journal of Discourses* 11:286.

110. Young, *Discourses of Brigham Young*, 89.

111. See Doctrine and Covenants section 13 and for elaborate descriptions on both John the Baptist and Moroni see entries in the Encyclopedia of Mormonism owned by the LDS church. http://eom.byu.edu.

112. Woodruff, *The Discourses of Wilford Woodruff*, 3.

113. John A. Widtsoe, "The Divine Mission of Joseph Smith," *Handbook of the Restoration: A Selection of Gospel Themes Discussed by Various Authors* (Kessinger Publishing), 35–36.

114. John A. Widtsoe, *Rational Theology*, 1915, 23.

115. Snow, *The Teachings of Lorenzo Snow*, 5.

116. Spencer W. Kimball, *The Miracle of Forgiveness*, 286.

117. Joseph Fielding Smith, *Church History and Modern Revelation*, (Salt Lake City: Deseret Book Company, 1953), 1:287.

118. Joseph Fielding Smith, *Doctrines of Salvation* (Salt Lake City: Bookcraft 1954–56), 1:7–8.

119. Kimball, *The Miracle of Forgiveness*, 2.

120. Orson Pratt, *The Seer*, 117, as cited in *In Their Own Words: A Collection of Mormon Quotations*, comp. Bill McKeever (Kearncy, NE: Morris Publishing 2010), 104.

121. Ibid.

122. Bruce R. McConkie, "The Seven Deadly Heresies," an address given at BYU on June 1, 1980. Transcribed from actual speech.

123. The LDS concept of God depicted in the Standard Works (e.g., Book of Mormon, Doctrine and Covenants, etc.), on the one hand, appears to deny classical theism and affirm polytheism (D&C 132), but on the other hand is also close to classical theism in affirming a monotheistic supreme being. God is described as "omnipotent" (Mosiah 3:5, 17–18; D&C 61:1), infinitely good (2 Nephi 1:10; Moroni 8:3), all-knowing (Alma 40:8; D&C 130:7). Actually, with respect to the Trinity, it seems that in the Book of Mormon, one can find trinitarianism and modalism, but not the radical doctrines flowing from the living prophets, approach which favors the concept of exaltation grounded in the law of eternal progression. The Book of Mormon appears to teach the Trinity in that there is only one God and three persons. The redeemed will sing praises "unto the Father, and unto the Son, and unto the Holy Ghost, which are one God" (Mormon 7:7; see also 2 Nephi

31:21; Alma 11:44). And again, Trinitarian monotheism seems affirmed in Alma 11:28–29 and 44 that say, "Is there more than one God? And he answered, No. . . . be arraigned before the bar of Christ the Son, and God the Father, and the Holy Spirit, which is one Eternal God." Then the Book of Mormon appears to teach modalism (Ether 3:14 cross references Mosiah 15:2 where one person self identifies as both Father and Son, being one person manifesting in two modes). There it appears that Jesus is the Father rather than being distinct from the Father. The Book of Mormon seems to offer little more by way of clarity about God than the LDS prophets.

124. McConkie, *Mormon Doctrine*, 221.

125. While there is some LDS textual evidence for this polytheistic view with a monarch atop the pantheon, it isn't the final word and isn't backed up by any more prophetic force than the other views. See Chapter 12 in Blake Ostler, *Exploring Mormon Thought: The Problems of Theism and the Love of God* (Salt Lake City: Greg Kofford Books, 2006).

126. The sixth LDS president and Prophet following Snow reaffirmed the view that God was once a man when he said, "I know that God is a being with body, parts and passions. . . . Man was born of woman; Christ, the Savior, was born of woman; and God, the Father was born of woman." (*Church News*, Sept 19, 1936) as quoted in *Search These Commandments: Melchizedek Priesthood Personal Study Guide* (Salt Lake City: The Church of Jesus Christ of Latter-day Saints, 1984), 152. This continued to be believed. The tenth LDS president and Prophet Joseph Fielding Smith said, "Our Father in heaven, according to the Prophet [Joseph Smith], had a Father; and since there has been a condition of this kind through all eternity, each Father had a Father" (*Doctrines of Salvation* 2:42).

3

I WAS THERE. I BELIEVED.

Latayne C. Scott

Each participant in this book addresses issues from a very unique perspective. And just as each of us will address the reasons for leaving the Church of Jesus Christ of Latter-day Saints, each will tell his or her history as it intersected with that church.

"I would be remiss if I didn't stand up here and bear my testimony," to echo the phrase used millions of times in fast and testimony meetings; we would be remiss.

But let me begin by asserting something of which I am quite sure: I was the happiest Mormon who ever lived, completely satisfied, nourished, rescued, and ennobled by being a Mormon.

HOW I BECAME A MORMON

I became a Mormon the way many do: Mormon missionaries came to our door when I was eleven years old. We lived in Albuquerque, and they were invited in by my father who had encountered them on the other end of his regular run as a railroad fireman in the little town of Las Vegas, New Mexico. There he was baptized and became a Mormon.

(My mother said he was attracted to Mormonism because its teaching on polygamy could justify his adultery. For his part, he proudly told me that he knew Mormon children could go to the church-sponsored Brigham Young University for a fraction of what it would cost others. And then there was his fascination with Masonry—he was Worshipful Master of the Masonic lodge in Las Vegas at one time—and there are obvious connections between Masonic rites and temple Mormonism.)

But I didn't know any of that at the time.

I was a young girl with an unusually active spiritual sensitivity and hunger for God. Some of my earliest memories are of a picture of Jesus that hung on my bedroom wall, a close-up detail of His face from a famous old painting of Him as a young boy teaching in Herod's temple. I looked into His eyes and wondered what He thought, what He knew. I heard a story when

I was very young, telling of how Jesus never had a place to lay His head. I wondered if He still walked the earth, and many nights as a little girl I would press myself against the wall of my bunk bed so as to leave room for Him to sleep there, if He wandered at night, if He came to New Mexico.

My home was filled with instability, violence, and mental illness, since even before my birth as the firstborn. My mother had run away from home at age seventeen to marry my dad, and he'd taken her from her home in Tennessee, where her mother was a society lady and her dad the chairman of the school board, all the way to the wilds of life in post-WWII rural New Mexico where my father worked, off and on, on the railroad. My dad insisted she finish high school, school she hated, school she thought she'd run away from.

He was sometimes in trouble with the law for brawling and barely escaped jail time for stealing (from strangers and friends alike) anything that wasn't nailed down, as the saying goes: unrefined "drip" gasoline from his employer, deer out of season, his neighbor's cattle, a widow lady's antique souvenirs of her childhood, a stock-trailer full of his vacationing friends' household goods.

My mother's parents, good Baptists, told her there'd never been a divorce in their family, she'd made her bed, and she'd sleep in it. She once told me that when she became pregnant, if any such thing as a legal abortion had been within her reach, she would have done that. She was not perfect, but she was young, and over a thousand miles away from everyone she knew, married to an intelligent, arrogant, charismatic man that everyone called—ticking time bomb.

He had a scar that became visible as he aged: a curving reminder of the time, as a child, that a horse-drawn wagon's metal-rimmed wheel had run over his head. He would say that it was the defoliants sprayed by the military sprayed in his last months of service as a Marine in the Pacific that made him the way he was, that started the abscesses in his brain.

My mother said he was peculiar and came from a peculiar line of people, those Colvetts of Crockett County, Tennessee.

My earliest memories are of my parents fighting, wrestling, screaming, threatening to kill each other with the butcher knife; my mother telling him that she prayed every night for a train wreck; his open-handed slaps to her face; the whisp-whine of his leather belt as it slid out of the belt loops of his Levis; my mother whispering bitter, confrontational conversations when she was alone.

Both were Baptists, and apparently when I was very young they would attend church and my mother would play the piano. But then my father took the spark plugs out of the family car on Sunday mornings; he didn't want other men looking at his wife, even in church. And so their outward spiritual life withered away in despair, and during most of my first eleven years I learned of God from going to church with a babysitter, looking at the pictures in our family Bible, and sometimes going to a Vacation Bible School.

For much of my earliest life we lived near Navajo people. I became very interested in Indian life and read all I could about it. I would strip yucca leaves and try to weave with them. I trained my feet to walk straight forward and not splayed out like a white woman. I jabbered in what I hoped was Navajo. And many times as we drove across the reservation I would beg my parents to stop, to let me run to a hogan in the distance, to let me go live with the Navajos.

We moved to Albuquerque when I was ten years old. My mother was pregnant with her third child, Frank (my other brother Ben had been born nineteen months after me). A family friend had promised my mother that he would fly her to El Paso for an abortion because she had just saved up enough money to leave my father when she found out she was pregnant. But she decided that maybe moving to Albuquerque would change things, maybe the baby would change things. . . .

I remember my father standing next to the old upright piano in that new house, asking my mother to play "Sweet Hour of Prayer," as he cried (and I wondered at the complexity of a man who could do that, and then an hour later beat my brother until his screams stopped). Our house was only a few blocks from a little Baptist church, and Ben and I would walk to it. For me, it was like heaven: a place where people would talk to me about Jesus, a place where nobody yelled, ever.

And then, when I was eleven, everything changed.

On the one hand, my father's behavior continued to become more extreme for years, causing the red-faced shame, the palpable unhappiness of a house stuccoed with misery, of running out of food and using newspapers for sanitary pads when he would disappear with the paycheck and my mother would sell or hock furniture until he came back.

But with the arrival of the Mormon missionaries, everything else changed. Not just that house, not just the neighborhood where Albuquerque First Ward was located, not just New Mexico, not just the Southwest where Brigham Young University was, not just the country of America I learned had been chosen by the Mormon God and where a latter-day prophet would arise, not just a hemisphere where no one had suspected that Jesus would have not forgotten about but actually come to visit, not just the history of a world that suddenly became re-ordered by Mormonism, not just a cosmos created by a father-god who had once been a human person like me and knew how humans felt—but the entire universe, all that could be known and would be known, changed into a kindly, blessing place where there was hope for me.

There were answers. Somebody could tell me things, people in a glorious chain of command and communication that ended right at the feet of a tangible, flesh and bone Heavenly Father. (And, aha! as I suspected, as every unhappy child imagines, Mormonism assured me my real, original parents were somewhere else, perfect people who loved me and wanted me to come back to them.)

My father insisted my mother sit through the Mormon missionary lessons. From the beginning, though, she said she "just couldn't swallow the Joseph Smith story."

But for Ben and me—as soon as the missionaries asked us to set a baptismal date, we both did. (In defense of nine-year-old Ben who was a rough and tumble little boy more interested in lizards than theology, I say that he went along with it, but loved as much as I did the kindness of the people at the LDS ward where we began attending.)

I remember the two earnest young men: Elder Cronin and Elder Barfuss, slowly turning the pages of the flip chart with the beautiful pictures of Jesus, right here in America, just as I had always hoped. The Indians were our brothers!

Yes! I would read the Book of Mormon. Yes! I would live the Word of Wisdom. Yes, I would tithe! Yes! Yes! Yes!

I never looked back. The one, single time in the ten years that I was a Mormon that someone gave me a green and white pamphlet that said archaeology and other things proved Mormonism false, I got sick enough to vomit, and then I threw the pamphlet away.

But from the beginning, it was full steam ahead for an eleven-year-old who read voraciously and who craved culture and refinement and literature and nice, normal people. I couldn't have been happier. I stayed happy for ten years. Mormonism was a rich, delicious banquet for a starving little girl, and I feasted, savoring every morsel.

When I was thirteen years old, I went to the home of our Stake Patriarch, Garland Bushman, to have him put his hands on my head and harness the mysterious power of Mormon prophecy for me personally. The blessing he pronounced was recorded and transcribed. It became one of my most treasured possessions—I even made a satin embroidered cover for the three-page document. I read it over and over. It meant that the meaning of "home" and "family" could be redeemed from my own desolate experience of those things. It meant that I didn't have to wait until I got to heaven to have what I saw that other, regular people had. It meant that this replete joy I felt would go on, literally forever, getting better and better.

Here is some of what he said:

> In the pre-existence, you were one of the choice souls of heaven noted by Father Abraham. Your ancestors were noble people, of the tribe of Ephraim. You yourself have a great destiny—to become a leader of women in the church and in the state where you will reside. You will meet a fine young man, be married in a temple of our Lord, and raise up righteous children. Finally, you will arise in the morning of the first resurrection, surrounded by your family.

And with that thought, I felt the stirrings of future godhood in my breast, and I did everything I could to live within that. There were warnings in the patriarchal blessing, too, that Lucifer would try to derail my love for the church. Not me, I thought. Not me.

One day in a neighborhood grocery store, I saw the preacher from the little Baptist church we'd attended. I wondered if he remembered the two little kids who walked across a dusty mesa to come to his church. I thought he'd be delighted to hear I'd found a place where people would come and pick me up and take me to hear about "Christ." (Already I had absorbed the fact that we didn't call Him by His first name. Too "familiar," I was later told.)

The preacher looked busy, distracted. But when he heard the word "Mormon," his eyes widened and he muttered something about "false prophets deceive many," and then in frustration or anger or I don't know what, he walked away. I never heard from him again.

Whenever I could, whenever the doors opened, I was at church. LDS members kindly provided transportation for me (my mother wouldn't come and my father often couldn't). The Mormon Church knows how to keep youngsters busy with track meets, road shows, supervised dances, cookouts, camps, sports activities, firesides, work and service projects.

It was glorious in the fifth and sixth grades. It was glorious in junior high school. I couldn't get enough. I couldn't love it enough.

When I was fifteen, my mother served my father with divorce papers and a few hours later he had a seizure. Emergency surgery removed brain abscesses, one nearly the size of an orange and later another the size of an egg from his skull. He was left paralyzed on one side.

All the time I'd been a Mormon, I struggled with the contradiction that the man who'd introduced me to the religion I loved was also the most amoral man I had ever met, both volatile and sometimes maudlin when he spoke of religion or family or patriotism.

We dared to hope this precipitous medical event was the explanation for his behavior. But his behavior became worse. He raged in his illness. After months of trying, my mother went through with the divorce. She hadn't worked for years, and she was left with staggering debt.

In the midst of operations and hospitalizations, we had little income but the Mormon Church's local leadership just showed up at our house with armfuls of bags of groceries. They offered money. They offered help.

These were my people, I remember thinking, more family than family to me. I began wearing a silver charm around my neck. Where Christians wore a crucifix (which the Mormon Church despised—who would wear a torture instrument around her neck?), I had a little replica of the Salt Lake City Temple, the constant reminder that I would someday go to the place where I would learn the hidden mysteries of Mormonism, the secret things, the final explanations.

In high school, almost all my friends were either Jewish or Mormon. We knew we were the outsiders, the ones with the strange rituals that no one understood. I ate Passover, attended Bar Mizvahs, memorized the *Shemah*. But this was fellowship with other underdogs, not sisterhood.

As far as religion went, we couldn't truly speak each others' languages (and Mormonism's redefinition of English qualifies it as its own esoteric language, I knew even then).

I always had a temple recommend. I always deserved a temple recommend. I tithed, I was pure to the point of ignorance, I kept the Word of Wisdom, I supported the prophet, I fasted, I attended, I loved.

New Mexico had no LDS temple at the time, but when I was about fourteen, the church shipped us all in buses to Manti, Utah, for proxy baptisms. I could not wait! To be inside a temple!

I held my breath, not only for the fifteen sequential immersions, but figuratively as I peered respectfully over the edge of the giant baptismal font, which rested on the backs of life-sized statues of oxen. Where might an ancestor be? Would some of the women whose names I appropriated before gasping submersions appear to me? Would they nod their heads in approval, as I had heard happen to others?

No matter that I saw no apparitions. I didn't need visions to prove the Mormon Church was true. I said it to anyone who would listen. I bore my testimony in church. I told my friends. I tried to explain it to my grandmother who shook her head in disapproval, her lips held pinched together. She had no words for me.

I pitied her. She had no hope of visions, of revelations, of veils that would make everything plain.

But I'd learned a principle that kept me from speaking further. Don't say too much. If she didn't know enough about Mormonism to reject it on earth, someone could teach her about it in the spirit world. (Mormons don't teach second-chance salvation. You get one chance. If you blow off Mormonism on earth, you don't get another flip chart in eternity.)

If my grandmother waited to hear all about Mormonism in eternity, then, I thought, she'd have to see the wisdom, the glory of it. She'd accept it, and I or someone else would do a proxy baptism for her, and then some day I'd see her (married? or single, serving others?) when I toured lower kingdoms from my home in the highest level of the Celestial Kingdom. When I was a goddess. When my husband and I had our new world, perhaps I'd invite her to come and visit and watch what it's like, creating worlds without number (The Pearl of Great Price, Moses 1:33), the best of all situations for someone with no math skills.

I kept busy. Over the time I was a Mormon, I served in Sunday school as a teacher, Relief Society (ladies' organization), and Primary (children's organization). I was active as a speaker in regular weekly sacrament meetings and often prepared programs for the youths' "Mutual Improvement Association" and for special occasions. For a while, I worked as my ward's media-aids supervisor, and in various other church "jobs."

Through my senior year of high school I became very close to an extraordinary young man. He was unusually devoted to the LDS Church and was preparing to go on a mission after his first year of college. I had dreamed since the first time I heard of it about going to "the Y," Brigham Young University. He had a full scholarship as a David O. McKay Scholar.

Since the third grade when I won an essay contest on fire prevention, I have always been a writer. I entered a writing contest whose prizes were for scholarships and I won a partial scholarship to the Y. When I arrived on its campus (a place, I noted with wonder, that had more red-headed men in one place than I had seen in all my eighteen years of life), I felt I had come home, to the place that satisfied my soul.

The next three years at BYU were productive. I took English and Spanish classes, learned to play the clarinet (very badly), immersed myself in campus life and the life of my BYU ward. I wrote on staff for the university's weekly campus magazines, worked for the Latin American Studies Department, babysat, cleaned houses, worked as a resident assistant in the dorms. I returned home to Albuquerque each summer to work (driving an ice cream truck or waitressing) and counted the days until I could get back to the Y.

My high school boyfriend, Bruce Porter (now deceased, at the time of his death in 2016 had risen to the rank of General Authority of the church), was called on a mission to Germany, and during the time he was gone I dated casually a variety of Mormon young men: a Native American from Taos, another David O. McKay Scholar, a musician. But I was anxious for Bruce to return, and unbeknownst to him, I took enough German classes to nearly secure a minor in that language. When he returned, I planned to surprise him, by speaking Deutsch.

I took the required religion classes. I read daily on my own the Standard Works—the Book of Mormon, the Pearl of Great Price, and the Doctrine and Covenants, as well as the King James Bible. I did baptisms for the dead in the Provo temple, fasted five times a month, and prayed devotedly.

Though I acknowledge I was not perfect (the sin of pride comes to mind), I made every attempt to work on my character, using as an example Ben Franklin's method of charting character traits[1] (both desirable and undesirable) daily.

I truly wanted become perfect like God. I wanted to be a goddess, and I felt myself progressing toward that goal every day.

One story in the Book of Mormon intrigued me. It was the account of the brother of Jared, in the third chapter of the Book of Ether, a man whose faith was so great that the pre-mortal Jesus (who called himself both "the Father and the Son" in verse 14) couldn't withhold showing himself to this mortal man. I thought and thought about that kind of faith, a kind of faith I wanted to have. I began during my weekly fasts to ask Christ to let me see him, too.

I've never written about this before, for several reasons. Only the closest of my friends know of this. But I write about it now so that a reader can understand the depth of my devotion and belief in this Book of Mormon story. I realize that Mormons may have one explanation for what happened, Christians another, and agnostics another. But I know what transpired, and I know what I concluded and believe to this day.

After at least two years of begging Heavenly Father to see the face of Christ, one day as I knelt in prayer, I saw it. It was like seeing a video of the head and shoulders of a person—not pale like in Renaissance paintings, not narrow-visaged and gaunt; nor was it of the broad-smiled and earthy man like in many modern paintings.

It was a three-quarter-view of a swarthy young Middle Eastern man who looked off into the distance. I was startled by the fervor and smoldering determination in his eyes, the unblinking resolve and focus.

The living image stunned me, literally took away my breath. The image hovered in front of my sight and I couldn't take my eyes off it. But then a realization struck me with horrible force. I reached toward it. I knew with a sinking knowledge that seeing Him wasn't enough, I wanted to hear what He said. I wanted to know His words.

But the image faded away in the utter silence of the room. I pulled myself up to sit and remained there unmoving for a long, long while. I didn't feel the exhilaration of the fulfillment of months of prayers. I felt rebuked. Seeing the Lord Jesus would never be enough. It was a sinfully short-sighted goal. He'd granted my request but I'd passed up a greater and more enduring blessing. Hearing was far, far more important than seeing. I realized that I was being directed to seek and treasure His words.

This was my spiritual condition in May of 1973. I was humbled, devoted, determined, and completely in love with Mormonism. I repeat: I was the happiest, most sold-out Mormon I knew.

My boyfriend, Bruce, would return from his German mission in September. I went home to Albuquerque to work to earn the money for my last two semesters at the Y. Everything was good, satisfying, with a trajectory of joys to come.

I would have said at the time that Mormonism had saved my life, had saved my soul.

Except it hadn't. Except it didn't.

Except it couldn't.

MEETING DAN[2]

I was annoyed when my mother, who played ragtime piano at a local pizza parlor, suggested that I date non-Mormons the summer before my senior year at BYU. I was waiting for my missionary and I just wasn't interested in a non-LDS "gentile." But she introduced me to Dan Scott, the object of her praises, who started off our introductory conversation by saying, "So you're a Mormon. I've read the Book of Mormon. It was, uh, interesting." Immediately I thought to myself, "Maybe he could be converted."

Then, more cautious, I stalled, searching for a reply. Everyone I'd ever known who'd read the whole Book of Mormon had become a Mormon.

In fact, I reflected, I'd known plenty of faithful Mormons who had never read the whole thing unless and until required to do so in a religion class or while on a mission. Perhaps, I thought, this would be a good time to terminate this discussion, and I left quickly.

A few weeks later, a voice on the phone said, "Hi! Bet you don't know who this is!" His Tennessee accent had betrayed him. I said, "Yes—Dan Scott." He was crushed, his surprise foiled, but not crushed enough to forget to ask me out. I accepted against my better judgment.

Our first date was a disaster. He took me to midweek services at his church where he announced, "She's a Mormon." I was stared at as if I were from another planet. (Mormons get accustomed, to a degree, to such treatment from curious non-Mormons. Once when I was in junior high, a sincere classmate asked me if something her mother told her was true: that Mormons didn't have navels. We quickly went into the girls' room, and I dispelled that myth with a tug of my blouse!)

Nonetheless, I was attracted by Dan's openness and decided to date him again if he asked, and he did.

I soon found Dan to be a true and warm friend with a sense of humor he could aim at himself as well as at others. Our only disagreements came when we discussed religion. He was so transparently shocked when I answered his questions about baptism for the dead, polygamy, and why the LDS Church didn't give its priesthood to African Americans, that we made an agreement. He would study the Book of Mormon and other LDS scripture with me if I would study the Bible with him. I felt this to be a personal triumph, because I'd never studied Mormonism with anyone (except my mother) who did not join the LDS Church.

Soon Dan and I had to admit to ourselves the love that was growing between us. One thing we both agreed on: we could not take the chance of becoming more deeply involved with our hearts so near and our souls so far apart. We both acknowledged that our respective religions weren't just "versions" of each other. They were not just different, they were oppositional.

Our discussions usually put me on the defensive. I was knowledgeable about my religion, and what was more, I was stubborn. Add to that a strong dose of love for the doctrines and people of Mormonism, and you have an idea of the battle Dan had to fight. He didn't fight it alone, though; he had several powerful weapons.

One was his brother-in-law, Charles Williamson, a preacher of great intelligence and patience. One day Charles and I agreed to sit down and talk about religion. We sat on opposite sides of a table, me with my Bible, Book of Mormon, Doctrine and Covenants, Pearl of Great Price, and Gospel Principles; he with his Bible. Dan left the room, a scene he described as a "verbal ping-pong game." Both Charles and I were exhausted after two hours of table-slamming debate. I was on the verge of anger. I learned later that Charles told Dan in confidence that I knew more than any Mormon elder he'd ever spoken with, and frankly he didn't know if there was any hope for me.

My recurring headaches signaled tension that had begun to grow as my doubts had. Dan and Charles didn't think their talks had served any purpose. I was filled with a sick dread that I then thought was a godly sorrow for the lost souls of people like Dan and Charles. Actually, I was beginning to fear that *my* soul might be lost, and I dared not voice this fear—not even to myself.

Another of the mighty weapons used by Dan in the battle for my soul was the literature he somehow managed to find. These books dealt objectively and factually with Mormonism, from the view of non-Mormons. I was blessed by the fact that Dan chose the books he did for me to read. Most writings that criticized LDS doctrine that I had previously read had had very little lasting effect on me.

There are many books and magazine articles written to convince Mormons of their doctrinal errors. Many of these, however, make at least one of two major mistakes. One is underestimating the intelligence, integrity, or character of the LDS people. Many times when I was a Mormon, I had read some otherwise factual literature against Mormonism which by its bitter or berating tone "turned me off." The doctrinal point the writer was making never sank in. Such literature implies that Mormons believe as they do because they are stupid, narrow-minded, or satanic. Since I considered other Mormon friends and myself to be intelligent, open-minded children of God seeking to do His will, I would toss such offensive literature into the nearest trash can. Then I would offer a prayer to God for the soul of anyone who would tell such lies in print where they might be accepted as fact by someone who'd never met a good Latter-day Saint.

The other great error committed by many writers on Mormonism is that of not checking their facts. Like the mother of the girl who asked me about my navel, such writers discredit themselves with inaccuracies. Some writers, carried away in their enthusiasm, embellish facts—it's easy to do—but when I would run into such stretching or bending of the truth in writings critical of Mormonism, I would dismiss as also erroneous anything else I read there that didn't agree with LDS doctrines I had been taught.

When you confront many Mormons with, for example, copies of the original 1830 edition of the Book of Mormon, or strange prophecies made by Joseph Smith which never came true, some will be dumbfounded. Often such things are unavailable to them through regular Church channels. If, therefore, a book errs when covering things Mormons *do* know about, how can they trust new information on things they have never heard of?

The most effective weapon of all in Dan's armory was three-pronged. First was his overwhelming faith and confidence in the Word of God, the Bible. Second was the prayer that he continually offered for my soul's enlightenment. Third, and most penetrating, was the love he had for me. Had we not loved each other, I don't believe I would have had the courage to leave the comfortable LDS way of life. Had he ceased loving me before my conversion was completed, I fear I would have returned to the womb of Mormonism and lived ever an infant, frightened and dependent, but secure in my deliberate ignorance.

I finally came to an impasse in my spiritual progress. I was struggling against the bonds of Mormonism—tradition and heritage, doctrinal comfort and love. Yet I felt that something was terribly wrong there—why did my teachings and background in Mormonism conflict so sharply with my new knowledge of the Bible? Why the inconsistencies in LDS historical accounts and early documents?

One final acid test remained at the end of the summer. Since I had a scholarship and a writing job waiting for me at BYU, I decided to return, promising Dan that we would marry—if I came back in December feeling about Mormonism as I did then in August. As I was packing, I felt as if the summer had been a dream. Or was it the real part, and the rest of my past life the illusion? I was unhappy about leaving Dan, but I knew I must make my decision alone. No matter how much I loved him, my eternal soul and my relationship with God were more important to me.

I was putting my books into boxes when, tired, I sat down with my Doctrine and Covenants. Always, it had been my favorite book of scripture because of its practical commandments, like the Word of Wisdom, which had purified and uplifted the lives of millions of Latter-day Saints. Also commonly bound in the same volume with the Doctrine and Covenants is another book of scripture called the Pearl of Great Price, which includes two books that Mormons believe were written by Moses and Abraham. These scriptures are unique in that they have what purport to be illustrations by Abraham himself. These illustrations, reproduced by woodcuts, are in the ancient Egyptian style. I have always loved Egyptology, though I have no more than an avid layperson's knowledge of the subject.

I was looking idly through these familiar woodcuts when I was struck by an incongruity that upset me. Two of the women in the woodcut known as "Facsimile Number Three" had been labeled by Joseph Smith as men! Egyptian women are easily recognized in ancient documents by their distinctive strapped, ankle-length dresses.

Why I had never noticed this before, I do not know. I had looked at these woodcuts for years. I knew from reading authoritative experts on Egyptology that Egyptian women in history had dressed as men and acted as Pharaoh (Queen Hatshepsut, for example); but no Egyptian man would have been caught dead in a woman's clothing, especially to be preserved for posterity on a papyrus roll!

It was with this discovery that my most concrete doubts about Mormonism began to multiply. No "anti-Mormon" writer had pointed this out; no hater of the LDS Church could have falsified or altered these prints; they were in my own personal copy of scripture. I found myself crushed and exultant, all at the same time. . . .

When I arrived in Provo, I set about making myself as busy as possible. Soon old friends began to arrive for the new school year, and I fooled myself by thinking they wouldn't notice the difference in me. I registered for classes, reported for work, and caught up on all the news of who had married whom, who had gone on missions, and whose missionaries had returned.

But I have never been a good deceiver, and soon my feelings about the church began to surface. Close friends made no secret of the fact that they thought I'd gone crazy. Some attributed my change of heart about Mormonism to a broken relationship with a missionary. Many of my LDS friends, to this day, assume that I wanted to leave the LDS Church because of that missionary. An unhappy bargain that would be—to trade my soul's salvation for revenge!

I became even more upset each time I attended church services. My branch (congregation) hadn't really changed. There were new faces, but the same back-to-school jokes about snoring roommates and the excitement of worshipping together with maybe-your-future-spouse. Nothing had changed as much as I had, and I was sick at heart. In a letter to Dan in late September, I said,

> I can't explain the feelings I had in church today. I was looking at Mormonism through new eyes. In Sunday school class I listened to a discussion on the Holy Ghost and silently refuted almost everything that was said—by looking in the Bible. Things I've accepted for years seem suddenly strange. I experienced in part the pity that you felt for Mormons. Dan, I don't know what I'm going to do when they call me to a church position—and they surely will. I simply cannot stand up in front of people and teach from the Book of Mormon the way I feel now.

The dreaded call came late one afternoon when I was asked to meet with my branch president. Newly appointed to this job, he was nervous and unsure of himself. Everyone in his BYU student branch was to be interviewed and assigned a church job—teaching, visitation, social activity planning—and he seemed anxious to get these assignments over.

He began by congratulating me on my past service in the church (he had my records before him) and asked me about the kind of job I'd be willing to do.

"I'd like to work on an activities committee," I said, "or work on cleanups—I'm really good at that, and honestly, I don't mind. In fact, I'd love it."

He looked at me, confused. What did someone with teaching and leadership experience want with a cleanup job? Then a smile broke across his face. He had solved the puzzle—I was trying to be modest! He laughed, relieved, and then asked a question he thought would put us on common ground.

"Well, Latayne," he said, leaning back in his chair, "how do you feel about the prophet?"

Just that week, Harold B. Lee, the "Prophet, Seer, and Revelator of the Church," had come to BYU. When I had seen 20,000 students rise to their feet and sing through tear-choked throats the song "We Thank Thee, O God, for a Prophet," I had felt faint and ill.

How could I now tell this branch president of my feelings?

I looked away and said, "I don't think he *is* a prophet."

The young president sat up so suddenly that the back of his chair snapped forward. He acted as if he had had a bad day and I was pulling a very, very poor joke on him. I tried to explain that I hadn't come to a decision about the church, that I wanted to avoid talking about it publicly, but still wanted to attend services and work in the church.

He only shook his head, his disbelief turning to anger. "How can you think such things?" he asked. "Don't you know that if you leave the church, you'll never be able to reach the Celestial kingdom? You *will never be happy again!*"

Never to be happy again! What a load to put upon a young mind already troubled with uncertainty and fear of displeasing God! I left that interview with a dread in my soul. I went back to my apartment. That night I called Dan, and the next day disenrolled from Brigham Young University, telling only a few of my decision. My roommates were incredulous, my landlady tearful and reproachful, and all but one school official unsympathetic. A similar conflict, this registrar told me, had faced him when he was young. He had taken the part of Mormonism with few regrets, but his experience made him understanding, and concerned with my best interests.

When I arrived back in Albuquerque, little of the pressure was relieved. I received many letters, most anonymous and many cruel, which persuaded and threatened, pleaded and rejected. All had one object in mind—my return to Mormonism. Many pleaded, saying that my leaving would affect those I had taught and helped to convert, or those weak in the faith. (I pray to God it may be so!) Some of the letters told of the punishments awaiting apostates, and one ended by saying, "Don't you realize that you'll *never see the inside of a temple again?*"

Phone calls, too, didn't diminish for several months. Most were from friends who had "heard and just couldn't believe it." Close friends called one night and said several dozen other friends would be fasting and praying together the next day for me. On that day, I, too, fasted and prayed for my soul; for though I felt that I should leave Mormonism, I wasn't sure that Dan's teachings were any more reliable. Once you've found the tenets you most trusted and believed in to be false, you are not anxious to embrace a substitute.

Of only one thing was I certain: However I might begin to comprehend God, I knew that He loved me and knew my anguish, and would show me the way through His Son. This—and no more—could I be sure of.

Even Dan, much as I loved him, could not be the basis of my faith. I knew that if a group of people as dedicated and as sincere as most Mormons are could be so very wrong, then so could Dan, and his teachings. I have never felt more alone in my life.

I labored in agony with the great questions that left me sick at heart, and spiritually weakened. I pulled this burden along behind me, pushed it before me, and tried to take it upon my shoulders. When I found that I *could not* move it alone—it was too heavy—I gave up and did what I should have done long before. I put it in God's hands, and wondered why I had taken so long to make that wisest of decisions in my life.

I spent a lot of time reading everything I could get my hands on that dealt objectively with Mormonism, especially the densely-printed double-columned books first published by Jerald and Sandra Tanner, which included reprints of early Mormon documents. They, like I, had tried to prove Joseph Smith and the Book of Mormon true, and finally were so overwhelmed with the information that they decided to print for others.

I was both fascinated and repelled the more I realized my errors. A near-physical sickness would engulf me when I stopped to realize how I had flirted with hell while thinking I was courting heaven. Only a few doubts (those last barriers to real repentance) remained, and I took my questions to Lon Elkins, Dan's minister. I had grown to admire this man's vast knowledge of the Scriptures and of archaeology.

How simply he answered those questions I had been hiding so deep in my heart for so many months! I hadn't dared to ask anyone who it was Christ spoke of when He said, "I have other sheep that are not of this sheep pen. I must bring them also. They too will listen to my voice, and there shall be one flock and one shepherd" (John 10:16). The Mormons identify those "other sheep" as the Nephites, that is, the people the Book of Mormon teaches were the ancient inhabitants of the Americas who lived at the same time Christ did. The LDS Church teaches that Christ spent part of the time between His death and resurrection—here in America, teaching those Nephites. Could a Christian offer as reasonable an explanation?

Thank God, Lon both could and did. After he had explained this and answered many other questions, I realized how it is that any religious group teaching false doctrine can so easily misrepresent the Scriptures to someone who is unfamiliar with them. The greatest battles a cult can wage over the soul of the ignorant man, I believe, are already won when the proselyte is too lazy, or afraid, or unwilling to seek a more correct interpretation of a Scripture passage that is presented to teach a supposedly "new" doctrine. We have nothing to fear *but ourselves* when we ignore the admonition to "search the Scriptures."

I had realized this too late to undo my years in the Church of Jesus Christ of Latter-day Saints. I cannot say that I wish I had never been a Mormon. God richly blessed me during those years. Perhaps they were a preparation for my Christian life. I do not question or doubt the wisdom of God, even though I still sorrow for the wrong things I did and taught.

I knew then as now that I must recommit myself to God—I must become a new creature, as different from my LDS self as a butterfly is from a caterpillar. I had so many doubts—not knowing for certain what to trust, or what doctrine was true. I decided on a course of action that included two things: I would be baptized for the remission of my many sins, and I would depend wholly on the Bible as my spiritual guide.

Dan was a little apprehensive as we prepared for my baptism. He was anxious and happy to baptize me, as I had requested. But he was afraid because he'd never baptized anyone before, and he feared he would let me slip into the water or choke. I could only laugh—I knew I could take care of myself in that situation, because I once had been baptized thirty consecutive times (all within a matter of minutes) while doing proxy ordinances for the dead in the Manti, Utah, LDS temple!

This baptism was different, though. From that still September night to this very day, I feel a great sense of the majesty of God, and of His mercy so undeserved by me, a sinner.

RETROSPECTIVE

It's been decades since I was reborn. Someone might say that my story of loving and leaving Mormonism doesn't compare with the stories of those who had multigenerational roots in Mormonism and left it as adults—that only ten years as an adolescent and young adult in Mormonism doesn't have the force that multiple decades would have. I see their point. And I freely acknowledge that having few family ties to Mormonism, and certainly no threats to business and social status (unlike those who exit Mormonism in Utah have painfully learned) made my leaving in some senses "easier."

But do multiplied years of adulthood always trump ten years of youth? I recently read of the research of the French psychologist Pierre Janet who developed the "ratio theory" of how we as humans view the passage of time. Janet said we constantly evaluate chunks of time in our lives by comparing them with the total of time we've lived. For me, leaving the LDS Church at age twenty-one after ten years in (discounting the first six years of my life in which I had no knowledge of church) left me with what I'd known about 75 percent of my years on earth at that time.

When I decided to leave Mormonism and be born again, so to speak, it seemed a very long stretch of time (but actually only about three years) until I began writing *The Mormon Mirage*. But Mormonism has undergone a dramatic transformation during the years I have left it, often as imperceptibly-moving and yet as startling in its outcome as the swiftly-changing American culture that has incubated it.

I saw this in the blank stare of a Mormon college student recently when I mentioned something about the times when African Americans couldn't have the priesthood of the Mormon Church. She had absolutely no idea what I was talking about.

At the close of World War II, General Eisenhower toured the Nazi death camps and insisted that photojournalists record the piles of emaciated bodies. He knew that the day would come when people would deny such things ever happened. As Mormon archeologist Hugh Nibley said in quite a different context, "people underestimate the capacity of things to disappear."[3] My experience with the LDS college student demonstrated that less than one generation can change history. First-person histories, after all, are the representations of individuals who experienced events; and if those representations are edited, amended, or deleted, history changes. When "history" changes, our perceptions of reality itself change.

The Mormonism of my experience, I learned with jarring shock in 1973, bore little resemblance to the Mormonism of Joseph and Brigham; and now, the Mormonism of my own early adulthood resembles less and less the Mormonism of today. It is not just because my representations have changed but also that the religion itself has changed. Mormonism, I believe, aspires to be the greatest editor of reality in the religious world today.

Thus it was with greatest personal reluctance that I resumed this role of straddler of histories and testifier of changes. I am not your typical "anti-Mormon writer" caricatured by Mormon apologists. I wrote several books decades ago on Mormonism and a couple of articles some years ago, and have been interviewed here and there. I'm hardly the rabid dog snapping at the heels of Mormons and their doctrine. And, true to all the suspicions of Mormons, I lead the wild life of the apostate—except I never drank or smoked or used drugs, and I've only slept with one man in my life. I have attended the same church for forty-two years and my husband and children are likewise responsible members of our community and its churches.

When people ask me why I became a Mormon, I tell them that I wanted to please God, and I believed that I could do that in Mormonism. No ulterior motives, no grand plan, just simplicity and the literal faith of a child. I (like the Baptist I was) had a great respect for Scripture and a love for my Creator, and Mormonism gave me the chance to expand and act on that love while learning more about God and His mysteries than I'd ever dreamed.

I found it incomprehensible then that everyone would not want this expanded, updated, self-correcting and plenary version of Christianity. It seemed all very black and white to me. In my senior year of high school, an English teacher had all her students write themselves letters, which she then would mail to each of us after five years. I, with eighteen-year-old sobriety, spent the entire letter scolding my twenty-three-year-old future self for any minor infraction or distraction that would take me away from my wholehearted devotion to the Mormon Church. I congratulated her for staying faithful, for either going on a mission or being married in the temple, for beginning to fulfill the patriarchal blessing which promised her influence in the church and in her community.

The next fall I went away to BYU, where I was gloriously happy. I took religion classes on the Book of Mormon, the Doctrine and Covenants,

"Teachings of the Living Prophets," and "The Gospel in Principle and Practice." I studied, believed and lived Mormonism *as it wanted to be understood.*

My yearbooks show pictures of a relaxed, smiling, clear-eyed young woman, across the pages from Mitt Romney and my friends Deborah Legler and Paul Toscano.

When the Provo LDS temple was dedicated, I was in the crowd with a white handkerchief, waving it with the solemn "Hosanna shout." I honored the prophet and my leaders as personal heroes. I was there. I believed.

Of everything I read or studied at BYU, one work stands out in my memory above all others. In a literature class I was required to read Nathaniel Hawthorne's short story "Young Goodman Brown." It is a highly symbolic story about a man who has a traumatic experience that causes him to lose what I would have then called "his testimony." The closing lines of the story read:

> Often, waking suddenly at midnight, he shrank from the bosom of [his wife] Faith; and at morning or eventide, when the family knelt down at prayer, he scowled and muttered to himself, and gazed sternly at his wife, and turned away. And when he had lived long, and was borne to his grave a hoary corpse, followed by Faith, an aged woman, and children and grandchildren, a goodly procession, besides neighbors not a few, *they carved no hopeful verse upon his tombstone, for his dying hour was gloom.*[4]

Why was that story so terrifying? Because I could not think of anything more dreadful than the loss of beloved belief. I do not believe that Christians understand the concept of perdition—utter loss—as it is taught in Mormonism. Our children grow up with such persuasive teachings about the grace and forgiveness of God that many do not truly fear Him, I believe. In the evangelical world, children go from a pre-accountable state to cured culpability within the blink of an eye—whether by invocation or immersion—and from that moment trust in a last moment of reversal if necessary, when all can be forgiven. We have successfully assured them that a God of love will remember His Son's blood, or reward good intentions. Thus lostness as a heartfelt conviction is often at most momentary; something that exists only as a remote and, we assure them, nearly impossible, possibility.

But for a Mormon, you're either in or out. You're either a child or potential-Mormon gentile; or a post-baptism "confirmed" Mormon; or a member of a third class too horrible to contemplate. Consciously and permanently leaving the Mormon Church takes one beyond any hope. Apostasy from Mormonism—the idea of becoming what is called a son of perdition—is that of the sealed fate of a creature past redemption, a being of utter loss, beyond any spiritual lifeline or resuscitation, dead to God yet still living, a walking corpse of dismay to anyone who sees his or her spiritual condition.

Someone with no hopeful verse on his tombstone, someone for whom her dying hour would be gloom, such were the rushing fears of the person who in May of 1975, two years after leaving Mormonism, read the letter she'd written herself five years before in high school, saying that Mormonism was the only source of happiness, that it was worth dying for.

"Never be happy again. . . ."

I had been there. I believed.

The process of coming back to faith—in anything—was a difficult one, yet one whose steps I can recount. Though it sounds simple, this process was agonizing.

First of all, I looked around me at the beauty and diversity of nature, and concluded that such order and creativity indicated the existence of a Creator. But power and ability to create do not necessarily imply goodness—look at the bloodthirsty Hindu goddess Kali, for example. I looked again at nature and decided that whoever made all that was both complicated and good. If He created all of nature, and I was part of nature, He had created me. If He created me and all mankind, I concluded that surely He would want to communicate with us. Since I had seen the danger of unfettered "personal revelation," I supposed that there would have to be a type of communication that would be beyond human contrivances, something truly reliable.

And that's where the true leap of faith was—to believe the Bible was the inviolate communication of this good, relationship-seeking, Creator God. I couldn't trust anyone or anything else on earth but that Book. But sometimes it was almost too painful to read, and I shrank from His touch.

Fellowship was not enough. Here is a truth my Christian friends probably don't want to hear. In spite of having the Bible, and in the presence of a loving husband and a congregation of accepting and nurturing people, for years I felt desiccated inside. I wept in secret for what I had lost in Mormonism. My Christian friends had put me to work teaching "cradle roll" and children's worship and running a church bus program but no one knew how to teach me. In fact, they couldn't know how empty I felt even as they invited us over for dinner or hugged me with genuine affection and shared their lives with me. I responded the best way I knew: I was there every time the church doors opened and first on the list to take food to the sick, babysit, help at church camp, clean up.

But the Sunday school classes and devotional books and even the Bible seemed strangely colorless beside the exciting old stories of handcart pioneers and the prospect of living the United Order. Regardless of its truthfulness, nothing Christianity has to offer, after all, can top the possibility of being a god-in-progress, participating in a religious revolution. Around me, the big issues seemed to be squabbles over dancing or divorce or the Holy Spirit. Nobody talked (to me, at least) about fasting or spiritual disciplines or direct guidance from God in personal decisions. I guess they assumed that I knew what I was doing.

My church took egalitarianism, the one-level priesthood of believers, and the practical aspects of the Christian life of service and good citizenship and Bible knowledge to such a level that it seemed impolite to intrude with anything that might be construed as portraying oneself as holier than the thous of them.

And yet I knew God had put me in this group of people.

I began *The Mormon Mirage* in 1976 to explain to myself as much as to anyone why I had made the decision to abandon the single most satisfying and soul-healing thing in my life. Of course, the head-decision was reaffirmed constantly. I was startled over and over by the contrast between what I'd been taught in my BYU classes and what Mormon history really was like. The Book of Mormon continued to crumble before my eyes, unredeemed even by its quaintness and platitudes. Again and again the glaring difference between Bible doctrine and LDS doctrine disquieted me as if I'd never seen it before, new, like God's distant mercies, every morning.

But still I wanted to believe the best about Mormons themselves and was genuinely, continuously surprised by their actions as well. I didn't want to believe that people would lie about an apostate who left for doctrinal reasons, until another woman who left the Church learned that it had been announced in Relief Society meeting that she—who had always been faithful to her husband—was excommunicated for adultery.

I didn't want to believe that my own local LDS leadership could be deceptive until I asked to be excommunicated from the LDS Church several months before *The Mormon Mirage* was to be published. (Unbeknownst to me, a Mormon who was a self-appointed mole in ex-Mormon organizations was corresponding with me under the pretext that he had left the Church too and apparently had been reporting my research to Church leaders.) When the new bishop of my hometown ward told me that I couldn't be excommunicated because they had no record I had ever been a Mormon, only the existence of my baptismal certificate and temple recommend made the procedure go forward. (And the legitimacy of writing this book thus was rescued.)

A similar situation happened when I requested repeatedly that my official college transcript be sent from BYU to UNM so I could finish my degree. Until a UNM registrar intervened with the documentation I had in my possession, I did not officially exist. I could hardly believe that Mormons would lie about me.

Why, knowing that Mormonism could not possibly be "the true church," did I not at first feel satisfaction in a Bible-believing, faithful, and generous group of people? Nobody knew how to address the needs of a heart broken by a church.

The unarticulated and untargeted sense of betrayal I felt became the permanent inner garment of my soul. Charles Spurgeon articulated it best: "If God be thy portion, then there is no loss in all the world that lies so hard and so heavy upon thee as the loss of thy God."[5] I have tried to describe the state in which I lived for years after leaving Mormonism by comparing it to the aftermath of the discovery that your "forever" lover has left you and will never come back.

When Christians ask me how it felt, I ask them to consider how it would feel to wake up tomorrow morning and know beyond a shadow of a doubt that the God of the Bible did not exist. And never did; was a beloved fiction that just might closely resemble the truth, but with enough of lies as to be untrustworthy). How, I ask, would one assess all the hours of church attendance, all the vulnerabilities of prayer and fasting and secret sacrifice, all the people whose lives changed because of persuasion and diligence and risking of relationships just to get them lovingly wrangled into serving that God?[6] How utter the sense of loss, how unrecoverable the hours and years, how foolishly squandered the hopes.

Who do you blame when you have been duped by a church?

For me, I couldn't find anyone to blame. Not my Mormon friends. I knew their good hearts. Not church leadership; at that time I found it incomprehensible that people I knew—my bishops, stake presidents, regional representatives—could be aware of what I had found out. But how far up the chain of command would I look to find the ones who did know these things and had hidden them? Could it be possible they were unaware too? I had no way of knowing where the line of inner-sanctum complicity began.

I couldn't blame myself, though the responsibility surely lay there. I wanted to reproach myself for being suckered—but how could I hold responsible the trusting eleven-year-old? The trusting teenager? The trusting college student?

If there is no loss as great as the loss of one's god, there are few tasks to compare with setting out to learn to serve another One. If you've been burned by a god, how do you learn to trust another One? Make no mistake about it, I knew I needed what only He could provide: forgiveness of sins, eternal life, church and community based on truth, not beloved fictions.

I knew I had been bested by a superior, One who held all the cards; and I wrote this poem to describe the type of almost-daily battle I fought.

THE MATCH
Like Jacob and the angel
We face each other warily
Our eyes never releasing their vision-lock
What soundless circling,
Sliding of bared feet
Upon the mat of my life
I have heard the bell
For the opening of the match:
It rings even now in my brain
Insistent, insistent,

Sounded by
My divine Opponent
And I sigh
Because I do not know if I have the strength
I do not know the outcome
(For He with whom I joust
Is also judge)
My crowded consciousness chants:
"Though He slay me
Yet will I hope in Him"

The wrestling match
Begins

I knew from the beginning that I would walk with a spiritual limp the rest of my life, the price I paid for being there and believing. From this I have learned a truth that those who hope to bring faithful Mormons out of Mormonism must acknowledge and somehow negotiate: The power of its sociology—its cultures, its traditions, its people—is of such intensity and persistent power for those who love it, that doctrine can pale in significance unless truth is more important than any other thing.

I came to a time when I hung on only by my fingernails and Scripture passages. The summer of 1983 I hungered so desperately for the ability to trust and be vulnerable to God that I asked Him to take my life if I could not experience that. In 1984, in spiritual beggary, I read completely through the Bible eight times, fasted, prayed, learned every synonym in English, Spanish and German for the verb "plead." And then God brought extraordinary friendship, spiritual companionship, into my life. Ten years after leaving Mormonism, I began to recover from it.

In my writing I explored biblical themes in book-length projects on hospitality, agape love, stewardship, crisis, Bible marriage customs. I earned a Master's degree from Trinity Theological Seminary and School of the Bible (Newburgh, Indiana and Liverpool, Great Britain) and my Ph.D. from Trinity Southwest University, a small, onsite and distance-education university in Albuquerque.[7] In addition, I wrote *Why We Left Mormonism*, interviewing seven other ex-Mormons including Sandra Tanner, to show that there is no single factor that causes someone to begin to wrench free from LDS lifestyle, teachings, and community. Everywhere I go, fraught people come to me and ask what they can do to help their beloved Mormon child, spouse, friend, neighbor, coworker. If there were a single answer and it could be sold, its originator would be the wealthiest person on earth, for I know people who would sell all they have for that one solution. But there is no magic bullet to get someone out of Mormonism.

I knew that my ministry is writing, not one-on-one ministry, yet I also saw an enormous need to minister to ex-Mormons. The mad-as-hell-and-not-going-to-take-it-anymore hurt apostate has very different emotional needs than someone who had loved Mormonism, yet all need a way to think about truth and find a way to set pylons for the building of faith.[8] So I set out to provide a resource to help Christians teach ex-Mormons so that they would not have the same kind of experience I had as a new Christian, and wrote another book, *After Mormonism, What? Reclaiming the Ex-Mormon's Worldview for Christ.* In it, I used the "worldview" categories of James W. Sire[9] to help a Christian assess and deal with the usually unarticulated assumptions of someone who has left the LDS Church.

I have often compared the holding of doctrines in one's mind to filling up a bucket with water. One builds on what's already there, and the liquid conforms to all the space inside. If a bubble forms, its surroundings rush in to fill the holes. When one leaves an all-encompassing and comprehensive doctrinal system such as Mormonism, one does not just dump out the contents of the bucket. Only when resilient solids of biblical doctrine and understanding are placed in the bucket are some of the contents displaced; and only after a settling into order of those solids can the last vestiges of old ways be identified and dealt with. (All in all, if my experience is any indicator, it can take a long, long time and much of one's spiritual and emotional resources for the task. Perhaps it never ends; recently I found myself, over thirty years out of Mormonism, admonishing a flagging colleague to "magnify his calling.")[10]

But as years passed and my writing interests turned away from the Mormon Church to the Bible, people continued to write to me mostly about Mormonism. People I didn't know wrote reviews of my out-of-print book, using superlatives and urging that it be reprinted.

I began to revise it, thinking that just updating sources and statistics would be the biggest task. But the LDS Church had made changes I thought I'd never see—the retreat from doctrines about blacks, the retreat from doctrines about American Indians as Lamanites, the retreat from traditional pan-American *Book of Mormon* geography into a tiny slice of Mesoamerica, and most incomprehensible of all, the retreat from the distinctively Mormon doctrines about God Himself. Mormonism had morphed before my eyes into syncretism and assimilation. With it, an entire well-financed culture of Mormon apologetics arose to muddy once-clear distinctives. My book updates took years, not months.

In a way, *The Mormon Mirage* was my last will and testament about Mormonism. The first part of the book describes what factors caused me to make a decision to leave Mormonism. The second part describes why the rest of my life ratifies that decision. It can be quite simply stated: Mormonism is not biblical Christianity.

LDS apologists such as Robert Millet say those who critique Mormonism usually use a straw-man approach, characterizing Mormonism in terms of obscure statements by long-dead men and using disputed or fringe teachings to describe LDS doctrines. Even some Christian writers have made the same accusation.[11] Eric Johnson of Mormonism Research

Ministry, however, has formulated a simple list of beliefs to which the vast majority of Mormons of the twenty-first century would agree:

> 1) The idea that "As man is, God once was; as God is, man may become"; 2) the idea that temple work is essential to reaching the highest level of the celestial kingdom; 3) the idea that ultimate truth is to be found in the Standard Works[12] as well as the LDS prophet and apostles; 4) the idea that a person must be baptized in the Mormon Church in order to have an authentic baptismal experience; 5) the idea that Joseph Smith and succeeding church leaders were given complete authority on earth; and 6) the idea that the Mormon Church is the most trustworthy and authoritative church in the world.[13]

To Johnson's list I would add the following:

> 7) The idea that a complete apostasy from Christ's teachings and Church began in the second century A.D. and necessitated a restoration instead of a reform; and 8) the assertion that a personal, feelings-based "testimony" of events and doctrines outside of one's own personal experience (Joseph Smith's First Vision, for instance) is a reliable arbiter and authenticator of truth claims.

This is the Mormonism of real Mormons today. And there's not a single statement there with which an evangelical Christian could agree, no matter how many friendly fireside chats are held between us. Just as they make Mormonism distinctive from traditional Christianity, these elements are also significant enough and powerful enough to disqualify Mormonism from categorization as Christianity.

They are the reasons I left. These are the factors that have made my life after Mormonism bittersweet.

They are the reasons I won't go back.

THE TRUTH ISSUE

The vetting of truth and truth claims is a difficult issue, as old as Pilate who asked, "What is truth?" (John 18:38.)

There have been three useful conceptual frameworks that have allowed me to grapple with the concept of truth as it relates to my relationship with Mormonism. They are:

1. A straightforward examination of the way I as a faithful Mormon (and, as evidenced by what contemporary Mormons say about their religion, Mormons as a whole) once looked and now look at truth that is different from the way Christians would understand it. Mormons' concept of truth can be repletely illustrated with historical examples to show that the two groups do not define and appraise the concept of truth in the same way.

2. An in-depth look at the subject matter of my dissertation, representational research, and how that can provide layman-friendly language to assess the overall concept of facts and representations, which is foundational, before looking at true narrative representations (TNRs).

3. With the concept of the relationship of facts and representations firmly established, a discussion of the idea of a TNR as defined by Dr. John W. Oller Jr. and others, and how the representational cases of fictions, errors, and lies can be applied to Mormon doctrine and practice.

Mormonism and the Concept of Truth[14]

After leaving Mormonism, I struggled with its relationship to truth first by contrasting the Mormon concept of truth to the biblical concept of truth. In short, the Mormon concept of, and approach to, the subject of truth is radically different from that of the Bible in at least nine ways. A Mormon sees truth (1) as constantly changing, (2) as going, in culture and practice, far beyond written doctrine, (3) as determined by subjective feelings, and (4) as often divorced from its history. (5) The Mormon approach to truth is compromised by a heritage of deception as practiced by leaders from founder Joseph Smith until today. In addition, (6) truth to a Mormon is "layered" in the way that it is presented to prospective converts. And (7) the Church itself routinely edits both its own history and doctrine to make it seem consistent and palatable. In practice, therefore, (8) truth often yields to what the Church views as expedient. In the final analysis, (9) the Mormon concept of truth depends upon the character of its god, who as defined by LDS doctrine is constantly changing and himself ultimately human in nature.

The most basic Mormon statement of faith, known as "bearing your testimony," is taught to young children to repeat from their first chance to speak in a "fast and testimony meeting" until their dying day. It consists of a very simple yet psychologically potent affirmation: "I know the Church is true."

I believe from my own past experience as a Latter-day Saint that for most Mormons this statement encompasses two elements. First, to be a member of the only "true" church implies that all other churches are "false." Second, I believed (as wholeheartedly faithful Mormons do) that this emotional confirmation of the Church's truthfulness was supported by continuing revelation.

Now, after decades of distance from the Mormon Church—years in which I have matured as a Christian—I see that the biblical concept of truth is diametrically opposed to the Mormon one. This is borne out in nine major areas which involve not only the Mormon Church's view of history and veracity, but its worldview and theology as a whole.

Changing and Exceeding Written Doctrine

As a faithful Mormon I was confident that, because of continuing revelation from God to the prophet of the church, whatever my leaders told me took into account new developments in human history. I reasoned, for example, that since the birth control pill hadn't been invented until the twentieth century, it was useless to look for clues about its rightness or wrongness in a flawed, 2,000-year-old book (the Bible) when I had a direct line to God through His prophet on such issues. I was proud that Mormon doctrine is flexible, believing that although it can conform to contemporary situations, all new revelation dovetails with previous doctrines without contradiction.

Of course, even the most unbiased and cursory study of Mormonism reveals that the church's doctrine has undergone major changes in the past 187 years (with polygamy being the most obvious example). The official explanation of doctrines which conflict with prior teachings is that the church's "prophet, seer and revelator"—its president—is authorized as the only one who "writes something or speaks something that goes beyond anything that you can find in the standard church works" (i.e., its scriptures).[15]

Mormons have told me that such changes are really no different from those Jesus made when He came to earth and dramatically altered the way we are to worship. Indeed, Hebrews 7:12 emphasizes that a change in covenant necessitates a change in law. But the cataclysmic, one-time change in law that Jesus—Himself the fulfillment of the law (Matt. 5:17)—instituted can hardly be equated with the way that Mormon doctrine, as formulated by its various prophets, has waffled on major issues throughout its history. (Bible students will note that one's perception of truth is often progressive. In 1 Corinthians 3:2, Paul scolded his readers for letting their worldliness keep them on a diet of doctrinal milk when they should have matured in their understanding. However, there is a vast difference between one's own changing perception of truth and the Mormon belief that doctrinal truth itself is subject to ongoing revision.)

I have a small pink card that was given to me when I first joined the Mormon Church. It had all the characteristics of the "true" church. In the 1960s, according to the card, a characteristic was a church that practices divine healing. Yet nobody in the LDS Church would claim that today. When did that stop being important?

Or more important, when did it stop being true?

Mormon doctrine has backed itself into a corner with the idea of continuing revelation. You see, when Mormon leaders told their people that God withheld Mormon priesthood from people of black ancestry (and I and every Mormon of the '70s knew it was because they'd been "unvaliant" in the pre-existence) and then allowed them to have that priesthood, it caused many Mormons to wonder. As I explored in *The Mormon Mirage*, Brigham Young had said many times that God would never allow a black to rule over a white in government or religion. (I wonder what he would have had to say about a black president of the United States.) He also said that the seed of Cain (who had supposedly rejected the priesthood in the first place) wouldn't have the priesthood until after death[16] and after *all* of Adam's other children's seed (that is, all non-blacks) "had the privilege of receiving the Priesthood . . . . and have received their resurrection from the dead . . ."[17] The tenth president of the Church, the late Joseph Fielding Smith, explored the implications of Young's teachings on when Negroes could receive the priesthood and concluded that Abel, Adam's son, must be resurrected, achieve godhood, and raise up posterity "on some other world" before any faithful descendants of his murderer could receive the priesthood.[18]

The implications of this for a Mormon knowledgeable about his own history and doctrine, who believed in continuing revelation, on June 8, 1978—when it was announced that LDS priesthood would be granted to blacks —could be faith-shaking.

So what happened? Had the last "unvaliant" fence-sitter from the preexistence lived out his black-skinned earth life and died?

Or did Abel take cuts in the resurrection line ahead of all of us (including Joseph Smith, who was supposed to be resurrected first, you know) and become a daddy on his own earth?

And when the LDS prophet said on national television that he wasn't sure about the identity of God, saying that he didn't "know a lot about it,"[19] was he saying something as basic as the essential characteristics of his god had become opaque to him when Joseph Smith had been so specific about them?

Truth as Written on the Mormon Heart

As any sociologist can attest, the practices and beliefs of a people are determined by their worldview. This refers to the way they process information about the world and life based on their preconceptions and past experiences. These preconceptions and experiences often influence attitudes and behavior more than any formulated doctrine.

This is especially true in Mormonism, which as a subculture (and not merely a religion) structures a worldview that is often beyond an outsider's understanding.

For example, while there is very little written doctrine about the function of the special undergarments to be worn at all times by Mormons who have received their temple "endowments," there is a rich heritage of folklore describing how these sacred garments have saved soldiers from bullets, fire victims from burns, and others from death. Virtually all Mormon children learn such stories and grow up with them as a part of their world view.

In *Early Mormonism and the Magic World View*, excommunicated Mormon historian D. Michael Quinn notes that "the magic world view and practice of magic rarely substitute for religion, but do manifest a personal, rather than institutional, religious focus. Although one may label magic and religion in various ways, it is more difficult to differentiate between external manifestations of the two."[20]

For this reason, the Christian trying to communicate biblical truth to a Latter-day Saint must never forget that the Mormon's substructure of faith often extends far beneath the level of formal, written doctrine. When I began to write the first edition of *The Mormon Mirage*, which tells of how and why I left the Mormon Church after ten happy years, I was especially grateful that I had extensive written notes of meetings I'd attended as well as the journal I'd kept. These still illustrate to me that there is often a considerable difference between the way a system of thought is taught and the way in which it is believed and practiced.

Truth as Determined by Subjective Testimony

If one asks any Latter-day Saint for the primary proof that the Book of Mormon is true, he or she will assuredly point to the promise it gives in Moroni 10:4: "And when ye shall receive these things, I would exhort you that ye would ask God, the Eternal Father, in the name of Christ, if these things are not true; and if ye shall ask with a sincere heart, with real intent, having faith in Christ, he will manifest the truth of it unto you, by the power of the Holy Ghost." A physical sensation called a "burning in the bosom" is the spiritual confirmation from the Holy Ghost often said to accompany the conviction that a given thing is "true."

Not only written scripture is subject to such subjective confirmation. J. Reuben Clark, Jr., who was a counselor in the church's First Presidency to three of its prophets, once advised members that "we can tell when the [General Authorities] are 'moved upon by the Holy Ghost,' only when we, ourselves, are 'moved on by the Holy Ghost.' In a way, this completely shifts the responsibility from them to us to determine when they so speak."[21]

Mormon truth, then, is in one sense the domain of the heart and its perceptions. This is in distinct contrast to biblical teachings (which nowhere invite the reader to subjectively "test" them) and in direct opposition to the Bible's repeated warnings that the heart is deceitful and unreliable (e.g., Jer. 17:9; Prov. 19:21).

The introduction of new doctrine is a touchy subject for Mormons, showing that there are limits to this subjective approach. As noted earlier, only the church's president can "go beyond" previous doctrine in giving the church new revelation. Mormon doctrine also states that one can only receive revelation—personal communication from God—for oneself and for those of inferior rank in the church.[22] For a woman (or a man low in the priesthood echelons), recourse to "revelation" to determine truth is severely limited—and, consequently, so are viable criticism and reform. This is quite unlike the biblical profile of prophets like Jeremiah who were called by God to challenge and rebuke their priesthood leaders.

Truth as Divorced from History

When I was a Mormon I knew that the original printing of the Book of Mormon had some errors in it, but that Joseph Smith had nonetheless declared it "the most correct of any book on earth."[23] I later learned that there were over four thousand "errors." Most were errors in grammar and punctuation, but some that were later "corrected" represented significant doctrinal changes.[24] This process has continued for over 187 years, and includes the 1981 change of the Book of Mormon prophecy that "Lamanites" (Indians) who become Mormons would become "white and delightsome" (which now reads "pure and delightsome").[25] Along with other observers of Mormonism, I predict that the Book of Abraham in the Pearl of Great Price, supposedly translated from Egyptian papyri, will sometime soon be entirely removed as "scripture" for the LDS Church because its provenance and doctrinal issues (specifically as related to people of color) make it increasingly more embarrassing to Mormons.

The Mormon Church has been peerlessly cavalier in changing not only its own scriptures, but even its history, as Mormon scholars themselves repeatedly and publicly lament.[26] Historical events such as the Mountain Meadows Massacre; doctrinally inspired practices such as "blood atonement" (the taking of life as an atonement for a person's sins), administered by the church's "Avenging Angels," the Danites;[27] and teachings like Brigham Young's repeated identification of Adam as God the Father between 1852 and 1877[28] are conspicuously absent from many Mormon historical and doctrinal books.

Such alterations and omissions accompany the astounding doctrinal changes of Mormonism. A member of Joseph Smith's 1831 flock, Book of Mormon in hand, would be aghast at a church which teaches that God has a physical body and once lived on another earth; that man can himself progress to godhood; or that temple worship, eternal marriage, and genealogical research are essential for "exaltation" or eternal life. All of these are, of course, basic twenty-first century Mormon doctrine, but they appear in neither the Bible nor the Book of Mormon.

Truth as Betrayed by History

Many Mormons were shocked and ashamed when it came to light in 1991 that one of the church's most sought-after inspirational speakers, Elder Paul H. Dunn of the First Quorum of the Seventy, had blatantly lied for years about having played baseball for the St. Louis Cardinals and being the only uninjured survivor of his thousand-man combat group in World War II. Dunn's best-selling books and tapes inspired generations (and I was among them) with their dramatic, eyewitness stories of professional athletics, miraculous rescues, and divine protection.

The trouble is, not one of his best-known stories was completely true; they were—according to Dunn's own admission—fabrications and combinations of events that he felt were necessary to "illustrate points that would create interest."[29] Unfortunately, this tendency to exaggerate and fabricate—and, in some cases, to lie outright—is one that Dunn inherited, at least in spirit, from his predecessors in the church's leadership.

This has become so pervasive that even in the day of anyone's ability to check facts on the Internet, Mormonism has created an entire culture of verbal misrepresentation in an attempt to "protect" its members—and its reputation. This church-wide practice has continued, claims former BYU professor David Knowlton, who spoke publicly about what he called the "institutional lying" of church officials.[30]

Joseph Smith concealed his youthful occultic pursuits as a peep-stone-gazer and treasure-digger.[31] After introducing the doctrine of polygamy, he practiced it while denying that he was doing so. Later, when polygamy was renounced, Mormon prophets such as Joseph F. Smith continued to practice it in secret and to solemnize plural marriages.[32] Even today, faithful Mormons in Utah and other places turn a blind eye to the activities of friends and neighbors who illegally practice polygamy.

Sometimes such disregard for truth is displayed in deliberate cover-up tactics, as when high church leaders "stonewalled" the investigation of the connection of the Mark Hofmann forged-documents scam (a scam for which prominent church leaders had fallen) to the nationally publicized bombings in Salt Lake City in October of 1985.[33]

Years ago I would have said that such deceptive practices were an aberration for both the church and its adherents. However, I have found too much evidence to the contrary. As a further example, Robert Lindsey, the respected investigative reporter who covered the Hofmann case in his best-selling book, *A Gathering of Saints* (Simon and Schuster, 1988), characterized spying in the Mormon Church as "commonplace." I have corresponded with at least one individual, Steven L. Mayfield (a.k.a. Stan Fields), who wrote me claiming that he had left the church and needed my emotional support. Later I learned from Jerald and Sandra Tanner's book *Unmasking a Mormon Spy* (Modern Microfilm, 1980) that this man was in the employ of a church official and infiltrated ex-Mormon groups to dig up information to impugn the character of ex-Mormons. More recently, the church's "Strengthening Church Members Committee" (which disaffected Mormons have compared to the United States' government's CIA) has been seen as a constantly monitoring entity wherein members who question LDS teachings (in personal situations as well as on media) are identified with the aim of reconciling them to their church and its doctrine.

Truth as a Layered Reality

Truth, as presented to a prospective convert to Mormonism, is layered much like plywood: the outer surface is attractive, but, like the inner layers, is incapable of sustaining much weight until bonded with the others. Missionaries are trained to present carefully structured "lessons" that are designed to force conclusions based on incorrect premises. For instance, an "investigator," or prospective member, will conclude that there was a need for the true church to be divinely restored if he or she first accepts the faulty premise that it was utterly lost from the earth in the second century A.D. The investigator is carefully guided down a specific doctrinal path and urged to commit to a baptismal date, while missionaries postpone answering questions about "hot" issues like polygamy.

Other basic Mormon tenets are skimmed over—issues like the Heavenly Father's prior existence as a mortal man—while the Book of Mormon, priesthood authority, and the church's ecclesiastical structure are stressed. The most overtly unbiblical issues are not covered until much later, after the convert is less inclined to dispute them.

What an enormous contrast with the Christian life, which has no hidden doctrines or ceremonies and where access to the "mysteries" is determined only by one's personal relationship with the Mystery-Giver and His Word.

Perhaps this is most overtly illustrated by the biblical view of a temple—with explicit descriptions of ceremonies, furnishings, even clothing items—as compared to the LDS ideal of temple secrecy.

However, much of what was once opaquely secret about Mormonism is now, because of the Internet, transparent. A microcosm of what happens to Mormons who have only known the official, sanitized version of LDS history and then learn the truth was seen in the church in Japan, which suffered crippling losses with the advent of the Internet.[34]

The Church as the Guardian of the Truth

In Mormonism, as in other pseudo-Christian cults, the organization's leadership sets itself up as a shield to protect its members from factual information it regards as potentially harmful. Thus, instead of defending its members from outside attack, it must concentrate its efforts on guarding them from their own past; not only defining truth, but regulating how and when it will be disseminated.

As a young Latter-day Saint I was continually admonished not to read anything critical of the Mormon Church, and I obeyed without question. Apostle Boyd K. Packer offered a definition of "faithful history" as "history that bolsters belief and avoids awkward or embarrassing detail."[35] Thus, in the Mormon mind, to read anything unsupportive of Mormonism, far from reflecting openmindedness, is actually an act of faithlessness.

And how does the church deal with people or facts that include "awkward or embarrassing detail"? Consider the case of BYU professor Lynn Packer. Packer publicly revealed the glaring discrepancies in Elder Dunn's stories. He found, for instance, that Dunn's legendary tale of how his closest wartime buddy, Harold Lester Brown, died in his arms in Okinawa couldn't be true because Brown is very much alive in Odessa, Missouri. When these and many other lies and embellishments came to light, the church gave Dunn "emeritus" status due to "factors of age and health."[36] But "shortly afterwards . . . [Dunn] was traveling and speaking, and . . . took young men around the nation on a baseball tour."[37]

Packer, on the other hand, was sternly warned not to publish his findings about Dunn's stories; when he did, he was terminated from his BYU teaching position "in part because [he] was violating church and university policies that prohibit public criticism of church leaders, even if the criticism is true."[38]

One of the more recent LDS presidents, Ezra Taft Benson, like his predecessor Joseph Fielding Smith, became so mentally incapacitated as to be unable to carry on tasks of daily life, much less running a church. However, Benson's grandson Steve, a Pulitzer-prize winning journalist who left the LDS Church, was disgusted about the way the church covered up his grandfather's condition with the fiction that the Lord wouldn't allow a mentally incompetent man to keep the title of prophet. Benson says:

> In the name of maintaining faith, church leaders peddled the myth that the Mormon prophet was actively at the helm when, in fact, he was incapacitated. Propping him up for photo sessions as if he were some sort of storefront mannequin was a calculated, conspiring abuse of power, not to mention disrespectful and undignified for a man we love.[39]

Most unfortunately, it appears from my observations that the president of the LDS Church at this writing, Thomas Monson, is similarly incapacitated.

Truth as What Is Practical

The Mormon concept of truth often has little to do with what is historically verifiable, nor with how a concept fits with prior Mormon "revelation." In many cases, it is more closely identified with expediency: if it works, it's right.

LDS history is rife with examples. The "eternal doctrine" of plural marriage was rescinded as an earthly practice (Mormons believe it will be enjoyed in the next life) by means of a revelation known as the Manifesto, given by Mormon president Wilford Woodruff. This "revelation" came to Woodruff after the Supreme Court's landmark 1879 decision *Reynolds v. the United States* upheld the prohibition of polygamy in the Utah territory. Woodruff realized that Utah would never achieve statehood unless plural marriages were dropped.

In June of 1978 the church's leadership found itself in similar circumstances as it faced two difficult situations. First, missionary efforts in places like Brazil had reaped large numbers of converts, most of whom had at least some African ancestry (disqualifying them for the priesthood, thereby making it difficult to cultivate indigenous Mormon leadership). LDS leaders also perceived threats in both the outcome of a recent court case on racial discrimination and in the possibility of an IRS review of the church's tax-exempt status. So, in a tersely-worded statement (a far cry from earlier revelations, which began with "Thus saith the Lord") the church announced that blacks were suddenly eligible for the priesthood it had denied them for almost 150 years.

The Mormon Church is most anxious to present itself to the Christian world as "one of us." Its slick magazine advertisements, its polished television spots stressing moral values, and its desire to air television programs on Christian stations all reflect a concerted effort to be accepted. "We believe just like you do," I've heard many a Mormon say; "We're Christians too."

Quite a different picture, though, was presented in *Are Mormons Christians*? (Bookcraft, 1991) by BYU professor Stephen E. Robinson. Not only did he call Mormonism the only "true Christianity," he also identified all other groups bearing Christ's name as practitioners of the bastardized offspring of Greek philosophy and a supposed "original Christian" (i.e., Mormon) doctrine. However offensive a Christian may find this idea, at least Robinson told the truth—the real truth—about where honest Mormons of the 1990s placed their religion in relation to orthodox Christianity.

Perhaps that book was the crest of the wave that has broken on the shore of political correctness. From that point on, the LDS Church and its apologists began softening their stance to appear more mainstream Christian, gaining advocates such as evangelical Christian leader Richard Mouw, president of Fuller Theological Seminary, who in 2005 called for apologies from Christians who he said had "sinned against" Latter-day Saints by misrepresenting LDS doctrine and practices, and for more understanding and bridges between the two groups.

For a Mormon, a deep conviction that he or she is a Christian trumps any objections that an evangelical, for instance, might have, based on what the evangelical would see as irreconcilable differences. It is enough for the Mormon to "feel" Christian, and in a culture where a man can believe he is a woman or a Caucasian can "identify as" black, has increasing social validity.

Truth as a Reflection of the Mormon God

The ultimate key to understanding how Mormons view and treat truth is not found only in looking at the way they deal with history, or doctrinal issues, or even integrity in stating facts. We make a crucial mistake when we look at any cultic group and try to ascertain its motives by examining only its teachings or earthly leaders. People make mistakes, tell lies, and go to great lengths to uphold and protect individuals and ideals they believe in.

Historical, orthodox Christianity has always focused on truth as absolute and unchanging precisely because its God is absolute and unchanging. In the words of Hebrews 13:8, "Jesus Christ is the same yesterday and today and forever."

Similarly, the key to Mormon truth is found in its ultimate truth-giver: its god. Traditionally Mormons have believed that the being who made this earth was himself once a mortal human. The cherished doctrine generations of Mormons have believed, the doctrine of eternal progression—that their god is changing, becoming more perfect each day—necessarily implies that this being was less perfect each day we look backward into his past.

Thus, if one accepts the untenable premise that such a being exists, then one must also accept the logical implication that Mormon truth is also like its creator—constantly changing and ultimately human in origin.

BULWARKS

A concept which has been significant to my development as a Christian has been that found in 1 Timothy 3:15 which speaks of "how people ought to conduct themselves in God's household, which is the church of the living God, the pillar and foundation of the truth."

The first principle in this Scripture is the idea that one's conduct should be ordered by and predicated upon association with others, which the apostle Paul called "God's household," a lovely image of a place of safety, stability, and love. I know that many people who feel "burned" by Mormonism similarly reject all institutional religion, but those who want to continue with Jesus Christ cannot do it successfully without the fellowship, help, and support of others.

I myself have been a member of the same local church for forty-three years (except for a three-year period when we moved out of state and worshipped with a local group). I can say with no exaggeration that I would have been lost without the Mountainside Church of Christ who accepted and loved a strange young woman with strange residual ideas and an excessive amount of self-protection and soul-hurt; supplied a haven and undergirding as my husband and I raised two children to adulthood and faithful status before God; and have provided openheartedly and unflinchingly for my husband and me through his catastrophic illnesses.

But according to the 1 Timothy passage, a church body, both as local congregation and global entity, has another important function: that of holding up and sustaining truth itself. It is supposed to be the incubator and guardian of this abstract. However, "truth" is far from abstract here, but its meaning is specifically set out by the Bible.

We shouldn't be surprised when a group such as Mormonism devalues the Bible by placing other written works in authority over it. However, for almost as long as Mormonism has been in existence, Christians have ceded over the Bible's authority by giving preference to the manifestations of independent human intelligence in its manifestations in such areas as archaeology, sociology, linguistics, psychology, and the constantly revised field of history.

Watch any cable network show about biblical subjects, and a series of talking heads will speak patronizingly of the historical accounts of the Bible, saying that "we now know" such things as the "fact" that the Bible (particularly the Old Testament) is composed of strongly held myths, legends, homilies and embellished record keeping. An example of this is a PBS episode of *Empires*, "The Kingdom of David."[40] The program provides comments from Jewish Rabbi David Wolpe, who stated, "What is central about the story [of the Exodus] is not that it is factual but that it is true," and later said such accounts can be considered valid because they embody truth about the human condition.[41]

This perspective is echoed in the same PBS program by archaeologist William Dever, who said, "The Bible does not have to be literally true in every detail to be true in other senses."[42]

It should be no surprise to me, but I am nonetheless taken aback by the same tack taken now by Mormons. In particular, the church as a whole seems to be distancing itself from the Book of Abraham in the Pearl of Great Price. A recent essay published by the LDS Church entitled "Translation and Historicity of the Book of Abraham"[43] was groundbreaking because the church was officially admitting that the scrolls were not from the time of Abraham and that Joseph Smith (despite his attempts to write a grammar of ancient Egyptian) did not know that source language on the scrolls. Instead, the article concludes, "The book's status as scripture lies in the eternal truths it teaches and the powerful spirit it conveys."[44]

A Christendom which has been "softened up" to accept that the Bible could be true but not necessarily factual would therefore be much more tolerant of another religious group that now begs the same consideration of its own holy writ.

I live on an assertion about the Bible. By that I mean that I put my full weight, spiritually and intellectually speaking, on it and this truth about it: It is not like any other book. All other books—indeed, all other linguistic accounts of any sort—reflect not just culture and context but also the priorities and preferences of the writers. Nowhere can this more clearly be seen, for instance, than in the last forty years of textbooks of American history.

In fact, any "history" reflects the psychology of the writer or writers as he, she, or they make decisions about which details to include, what information to emphasize, and what sources are deemed to be reliable.

The Bible similarly depicts culture and context, but does it in a unique way: from the vantage point of a truly omniscient Author who has access to all aspects of every event, known and unknown, visible and hidden. The Bible reflects the psychology of this Author, breathing the essentials and the emphases into the minds of those who penned the stories. I realize this is not the "popular" view of Scripture; in fact, my insistence on this marks me in the minds of many as ignorant or at the very least unsophisticated. But it is the view the Bible presents of itself.

THE BASICS OF REPRESENTATIONAL RESEARCH

Seeing the Bible as the only true and complete representation of all reality is not something I figured out on my own. In fact, an emerging area of theology on which my dissertation is based, representational research, has been most edifying and clarifying to me in my post-Mormon years.[45]

One thing that characterizes true Christianity—quite in contrast to Mormonism and non-Christian religions—is the identification of our God, the eternal Being whom we worship, as an entity who is triadic in nature, a Trinity. (Some people, Mormons among them, object to the term "Trinity" because it does not appear in Scripture, but the concept is certainly there.)

Admittedly, this is hard to understand, how Someone can be completely One, as the *Shema*—"Hear, O Israel, the Lord our God, the Lord is one" (Deut 6:4)—asserts, and yet be comprised of three Personalities so clearly depicted in the New Testament. Jesus Himself dealt with this theological issue directly, in a way that completely refutes Mormonism's compartmentalized god, in John chapter 14. Over and over, Jesus asserts that He is *in* the Father and the Father is *in* Him. Furthermore, each of them can be in a believer, and most amazing of all—and completely precluded by LDS doctrine—they will make their home with the believer. *All* believers. That is impossible if they are body-bound, both now and in eternity.

Perhaps in no other area of thinking is there so much confusion as in discussion of that aspect of God that we call the Trinity. A book entitled *Knowing the Name of God: A Trinitarian Tapestry of Grace, Faith and Community* (Downers Grove, Ill.: InterVarsity Press,, 1996) by Roderick T. Leupp makes this observation:

> For most people and, sadly, for most Christians also, the Trinity is the great unknown. The Trinity, to use a familiar equation, is viewed as a riddle wrapped up inside a puzzle and buried in an enigma. A riddle, for how can any entity be at the same time multiple (three) yet singular (one)? A puzzle, for the Trinity is so clearly contrary to any rational thought as not to warrant a second thought from sensible people. An enigma, for even if the Trinity could be understood, of what practical value, even what religious value, would it have for ordinary people?[46]

Part of our problem is that we Christians actually misuse the name of God. Though we as a group would not use His name in vain nor curse using it, Christians are prone to misuse the name of God by having it refer only to the Father.

When I came out of Mormonism, I left a system of thought that called the Father "God" and referred to Jesus as the Christ or as the Savior but never as God. The Holy Spirit (or Holy Ghost, as Mormons say) was never referred to as God. I see shades of this among Christians who, when using the name God, are referring only to the Father. But Jesus and the Holy

Spirit are equally God. Here is a simple little diagram that might help with this dilemma. (This is a version of "the Shield of the Trinity," that Christians for over a thousand years have used to try to understand the nature of the Godhead.)

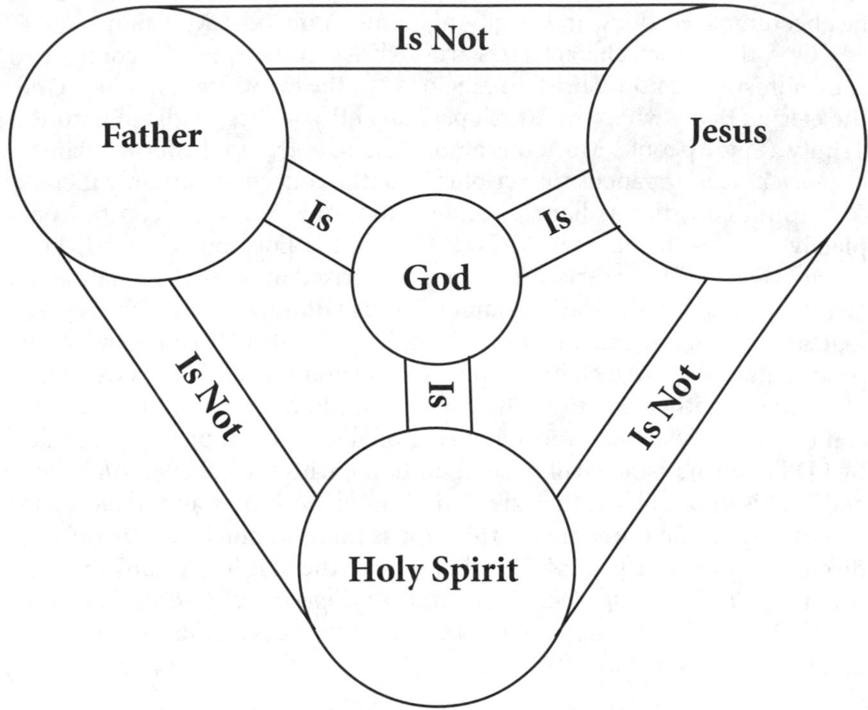

However, Jesus is not the Holy Spirit; the Father is not Jesus, and the Father is not the Holy Spirit.[47]

Thus, properly when we speak of God, we should have in mind that Highest One who encompasses our understanding of Him as Father, and as Son, and as Holy Spirit. And Scripture lets us see that God at times demonstrated a distinctiveness of the Father, the Son, and Holy Spirit. In each case that such a distinction is illustrated, it is always for the benefit of humans to observe, so that they can understand something about each.

These Scriptural facts demonstrate a foundational principle upon which representational research is founded. *Just as God Himself is triadic in nature, we can expect to see that all He created—reality, language, the physical objects of creation that surround us—reflect a triadic or trinitarian structure too.*

Looking for a tri-partite or triadic construction in the things of God is *not* the imposition of some numerology mumbo-jumbo on Scripture. God Himself is triadic. This is elemental. This is foundational. As my colleague,

J. Michael Strawn, who with me developed the written underpinning of our teaching in the College of Biblical Representational Research at Trinity Southwest University, has stated, "The triadic structure of God Himself is like a stone in a pond—all the ripples of understanding that proceed out from that, come because of the nature of the stone."

To understand the things of God, we must look to the Lord: a triadic Being. And thus, logically, we can expect to see triadic, or trinitarian, structure in reality.

The Nature of Reality: A Triadic Structure

First of all, if we are going to accept the Bible as agent (the active element) and our minds as patient (or receptor), we would have to dispense with the notion that reality is something that exists outside of, or independently of, God. There is no such thing as time that pre-existed Him. There are no "invisible laws" like gravity or relativity that govern Him; if anything, He has established those determined relationships and when He happens to work within them, it is just because it pleases Him to do so. What we perceive as reality is a construct that He Himself created, and like Him, it is tripartite or trinitarian in nature.

But how to think correctly about reality?[48] One problem that has plagued Christian thinkers is the erroneous impression that there are two realities: a reality here on earth and a reality where God exists.[49] This erroneous thinking was identified in the book of James and personified by the double-minded man of James 1:5–8. Such a man does not seek the wisdom of God but operates on two separate tracks in his thinking, resulting in instability in all he does. By trying to reconcile two separate realities in his mind, he ends up being what the Greek in this text calls "two-souled." The result: he does not get what he asks for in prayer, he is plagued by doubts and tossed around like a wave of the sea in his thinking.

The truth is that there is only one reality. One reality, but it has, at least at first glance, at least two parts. There is the part you see and the part you do not see. We live here on this earth and are surrounded by the facts of our material existence, but there are other, invisible elements that are just as "real" as the ones we see. This can be compared to walking through your house at night during a power outage. With a flashlight, you can distinguish certain things, but even the things you cannot see at the moment must be counted as real as the things you can see—or you will surely stumble over that coffee table which is hidden in the shadows. There are not two houses: one that is dark and one that is partially illuminated. There is only one house, with parts you can see and parts you cannot; but all equally real.

Christians are urged throughout the Bible to operate on the basis that the unseen side of reality is just as relevant as the seen side. Consider the case of 2 Kings 6:8–20. Here we have the story of the prophet Elisha and his frightened servant in a besieged city. Elisha, who is accustomed to operating on the reality that is unseen, is not perturbed that the king of the Arameans has brought an army to surround the city and that from the visible aspect, things look grim. Elisha prays, "Lord, open the eyes of my servant so that he can see," and immediately the servant is able to see what others cannot: an angelic host greater than the physical, visible Aramean army. Here is an important truth in this story: the angelic army did not just spring into being for the benefit of Elisha's servant. They were there all along. They were as real as the Aramean army; in fact, they neutralized it. The only thing that changed was the servant's ability to see the angelic army.[50]

Ephesians chapter 6, the great "armor of God" chapter, emphasizes this truth. Our battle, Paul tells us, is against invisible beings that are just as real as the visible elements here on earth. That which is invisible is not part of another reality, but part of a single reality.

All biblical role models of faith have this in common: they give more weight to the unseen realities revealed to them by God than they do to what they can see. They reject what would be termed "common sense" and give the wisdom of God precedence. For example: each person listed as a hero of faith in Hebrews chapter 11 operates on information not immediately available here on earth. It was revealed information, given to them by God, a manifestation of His priorities and superior knowledge of the completeness of reality—which only He can reveal to us accurately. In fact, the ability to see the unseen actually gives one the ability to endure trial, as the example of Moses in Hebrews 11:27 shows us.

(Now, it is important to differentiate here between what we could call a plenary or complete view of reality, and the way that Christian Scientists and others deal with reality. For them, sickness, trouble, even death are only illusory and do not exist; therefore they just ignore them. The Bible never calls on us to deny the substance of the reality we see; it does, however, command us to operate first and foremost on the unseen but revealed realities from God about such things.)

The concept of "reality" is an active one in today's society. Modern and post-modern theologians do not believe that the events portrayed in the Bible really happened. In other words, they deny that the Bible accurately portrayed ancient reality especially in its depiction of supernatural events. (One of my recent books, co-written with Dr. Steven Collins, is gaining the respect of even agnostic archaeologists with its excavation-based assertion that one supernatural event of the Old Testament—the destruction of Sodom—can indeed be shown to have a basis in fact as demonstrated by the dig at Tall el-Hammam in Jordan.)[51]

Many Christians today would argue that the events and even the miraculous elements of the Bible really did happen, that the Bible did accurately portray reality at that time. However, in practice, it seems that few believe that the Bible accurately portrays the reality of *our day.* We believe we know "how things work," and ideas such as the intrusion or intervention of the supernatural into daily life don't "fit" with our experience. It takes mental discipline to internalize the concept that the Bible portrays, through the depiction of God's working in the past, the way that He can and does work today in health issues, geopolitics, meteorology, and countless other "secular" arenas where He has always worked so overtly before.

It was not just for first-century believers that Paul turns attention away from our human experience and affirms the truth of 2 Corinthians 2:18: "So we fix our eyes not on what is seen, but on what is unseen, since what is seen is temporary, but what is unseen is eternal." A little later in chapter 5, he sums this up: "For we live by faith, not by sight."

An objection will arise in the mind of many who would ask: "Do not all religions exist to show us how to access the unseen? We have our senses and our brains to assess the seen side of reality." And most religions—even pagan ones—tell us of an unseen side to reality. One of the biggest lures of Mormonism is its claim of its exclusive ability to provide information otherwise unavailable to humans.

But the question is: how does one without such futile devices as a seer stone or LDS priesthood hope to gain access to the side of reality we can't see? We need a link or *index*[52] (in actuality, a "dynamic system of indexing" as my mentor and colleague Dr. John W. Oller Jr.,[53] notes) between the seen and the unseen. There is no inherent link in the human thinking process between the seen and the unseen, the eternal and the temporal.

Paul in 1 Corinthians 1:16 asks the question, "Who has known the mind of the Lord, so as to instruct him?"

The question is rhetorical; for no one knows the mind of God unless God should choose to reveal it. In the vernacular, "You can't get there from here." The invisible has to come to you, you cannot go to it.

Thus the indexing or connecting action of the mind of God to ours is an active, kinetic one. But that action is asymmetrical, what my colleague Dr. J. Michael Strawn calls "non-commutative." A commuter, we know, is someone or something that travels back and forth between two sites. We say that the indexing action that connects the seen side to the unseen side of reality is *non-commutative*, for it originates not in the seen side with the mind of man, but in the unseen side, with the mind of God; nor does it commute back and forth with us informing God in the way that He informs us. In fact, the movement of power and instruction from the two sides of reality is always non-commutative; and it always originates from the unseen side.

(Strawn has actually developed a physical device he calls "The 3-D Model of Reality," a gable-like structure that demonstrates the two aspects of reality and the ways that God links them. It is versatile and thought-provoking: I have used it with kindergartners, middle school students, and adults just released from prison.)

Language: A God-Created Ability

Thus God's triune nature is something that is reflected in reality, which He creates and maintains. In fact, He operates on the unseen side as the Father, and came here to the unseen side as the Son, and we are able to know all about both of them through the Spirit, who has always functioned as a conveyer of information and comfort and advocacy for human beings. So, a triadic Deity created a triadic reality. Should we be surprised that His main medium of communication with us, language, is also trinitarian or triadic?[54]

Let us dispense immediately with any notion that language somehow "evolved," as sociologists would tell us, from primitive signs and grunts to a sophisticated method of interchange. We can dispense with that because it was with very specific language that God told Adam, "You are free to eat from any tree in the garden; but you must not eat from the tree of the knowledge of good and evil, for when you eat from it you will certainly die" (Gen 2:16–17). Now, if the first humans were incapable of developed language, they could pantomime "do not eat this," but could never cannot pantomime "you are free," nor the word "knowledge," nor "good" nor "evil." And in a world that did not know evil, that did not know death, no nonverbal precursor to words could convey such concepts. Only words could do it. Language did not evolve; God gave it to Adam.

Language is God's creation, and—no surprise—it is also triadic. There is not time here to give an extended linguistics lesson, but it is easy to see that a noun like "God" is only linked to a direct object like the world by a verb. God loved the world.

The invisible is thus linked by His love to the visible. "God loves" tells us about God, truth that we have to know and trust, but it only becomes complete when the noun is linked by the verb to something. "God loves" is information. "God loves me" is triadic, complete, satisfying.

The Nature of Symbols

By definition, representational research is about the study of symbols. Now, when most Christians hear the word "symbol," they rightly make association with many of our most treasured concepts. The Bible is full of symbols: a lamb, a staff, anointing oil, manna, living water.[55] We know that these objects are signs, and are meant to carry significance beyond themselves.[56]

We know, for instance, that two wooden beams that intersect carry more weight, symbolically speaking, than just any structure; a cross, Paul tells us in the first chapter of 1 Corinthians, can represent the power of God to those who are being saved.

But the very same cross, Paul tells us, is "foolishness to those who are perishing." Same cross, different meaning. It is remarkable that the LDS Church has historically been so adamantly opposed to any depictions of the cross on their buildings, and I didn't wear cross jewelry until I left the LDS Church.

In 2 Corinthians chapter 2, Paul said that the message which he called "the aroma of Christ" would be to some a sweet fragrance of life; yet to others the same thing would be a smell of death. Same message, same cross, different effect.

That is because a fact—a person, an object, an event, a circumstance—can be represented[57] in many ways.[58] Here is where representational research gets its name. And here is the core of all of representational thought. *We can either choose the biblical representations of God about reality, about the world, about every detail of our lives; or we can make our own representations and operate on them. It is that simple.*

The goal of representational research is to help people look at the way they represent the facts of their lives.[59] In order to do that, let us examine the way we form representations.

Thinking

Because the process of thought and its most precise manifestation, language, are so closely linked, it should come as no surprise that much of the terminology used in language studies is helpful in understanding the thinking processes that underlie language. Semiotics, or the study of signs, is particularly helpful. For our theological usage, representational thinkers have kidnapped some of the terminology of traditional semiotics and redeployed it for our specific use. Its precision in certain areas makes it ideal; while its unsuitability in others is overcome by carefully defining terms both from within semiotics and from without.

It is essential that we think about thinking.[60] Man alone of all the animals has this capacity of self-reflection and articulation about his own thinking processes; for while a monkey or dolphin can be taught to communicate in a rudimentary way that some term language, no other creature has the ability we call *recursive*—the ability to think about thinking and to analyze it. Much like the concept of a worldview which is "caught rather than taught," we assume that the way each of us thinks is natural and normal. Actually, our patterns of thought reflect both God's preprogramming of thought patterns in us which reflect His thinking processes as well as less-desirable forms and patterns from our sinful environment and nature.

To begin to ferret out how our thinking processes work, consider the triadic structure of thought. We are surrounded in our environment by those elements we could refer to as facts. Suspend for purposes of this discussion the element of "truthfulness" which we customarily assign to the word "fact." "Fact," as we will use the word here, refers to things, objects, persons, states of affair, events, etc. A thing like a table is a fact, an object like a house is a fact, the president of the United States (both as a person and as an office) is a fact, terrorism is a fact. All exist in our environment, all can be accessed through our senses in some way.[61]

Contrasted to the concept of "fact" is the concept of "representation."[62] A representation is a way of symbolizing or conveying the idea of a fact. For instance, the object upon which a computer customarily rests is a fact. The spelling out of d-e-s-k conveys an image of that object into the brain of a reader who does not have to actually see the solidity of the wood, feel its texture, or experience it with the senses at all.

Representations are the only access we have to the physical world that surrounds us—we access it through symbols.[63] When we see an object, for instance, and then turn away from it, the image that is in our brain is what informs us of the nature of the "fact" our senses access. We do not take a desk into our brains; we take a representation of that desk into our brains. We carry around not the fact of the desk but rather a representation of it in our brains: an image conveyed from our eyeballs through the nerves to the brain.

Here is where the idea of prescinding,[64] or cutting, is seen. A fact is not its representation. A representation is not a fact. In order to sort out which is which, one must mentally separate them in some way.

Representations have three different types: iconic, indexical, and linguistic/symbolic.[65]

Iconic Representations

Iconic representations have to do with sensory functions of our bodies and brains, and include information accessed through the five senses (seeing, hearing, touching, tasting, smelling). We have already observed how this works with sight. Consider how it works with touch, a sensation that Thomas in the New Testament thought was just as important as sight in verifying the reality of the risen Christ.[66] We might think that we are truly accessing a fact when we touch a hot stove, but really we are not accessing the stove itself but the sensations that our nerve endings carry to our brains. We do not have a hot stove in our brains but the icon or sensory image of the heat on our fingertips.[67]

We can readily see why iconic representations are so important and yet so unreliable. We put a lot of significance into such icons as hunger, pain, and blindness. And we can see throughout human history in the Bible how such things caused people to fall into sin. Consider hunger (Esau's selling of his birthright for food), pain (Saul's request for assisted suicide because of the pain of his battle wounds), the incapacity of blindness in the healing of the man born blind. *Yet the Bible shows us that, although God programmed iconic or sensory representations into our thinking, He nonetheless forbids us to operate on those things alone.*[68]

Another major drawback of iconic representations is that they are inherently only partial. For instance, while you might take an object like a pencil into your hand and turn it over and over, you can never see all the sides of it at once. Even if you used a complex of mirrors that might allow you to see all around, you still could not see its insides at the same time. Hidden from your view, for instance, might be the absence of lead in the top half of the pencil—something that would become quite significant when the lead broke in the middle of a timed exam!

The Index or Link

Another way of conveying information about a fact of our existence is through the second type of representations: the index or linking agent.[69]

Whereas iconic representations are sensory-based conveyers of information, the index (or gesture) connects two things. For instance, when you use the index of a book, the page numbers listed there point you to and connect the listing item to its actual location in the book. All indices connect something to something else. We say that indices are kinesthetic because they often involve some sort of action or movement. One good way of illustrating this is the action of pointing the finger: you are indexing or connecting the attention of an observer to what you want him or her to see. Though the icon of sight is involved, the main way that something is being conveyed is through the indexing action that connects the eyes to the object so indicated.[70]

Just as iconic representations are by nature partial, so indices as well are somewhat faulty because they are usually imprecise. If you have ever stood over someone's shoulder and tried to direct their line of sight to an object they cannot distinguish in the distance, you know that any number of things along the imaginary line you are pointing out could be indicated by your finger.

However, Scripture abounds in these "attention-getting" devices. The whole world, Romans 1:20 tells us, points toward the nature and power of a Creator. And other types of nonlinguistic communication[71] shout out from the Creation, as deep calls to deep, the morning stars sing together, the heavens declare the glory of God, and even rocks can cry out.

Many of the things we think of as "symbols" in the Bible are primarily indices. For instance, the elements of the Passover feast, the rocks piled on the shores of the Jordan River (Josh. 4), baptism and many other "signs" point to invisible realities. Relationships, too, critically involve links and function as indices: slave-master, child-parent, wife-husband, and church-Lord. All reflect a substructure of the universe: the submission of Jesus to His Father.

Aside from Jesus, the historical figure from the Bible who ideally portrays the essence of an index is Abel. We know about his exemplary actions, but the Bible *doesn't record a single word he spoke.* His actions connected the purposes of the unseen God onto the material world in the way that he chose and offered sacrifice. Even after his death, his blood conveyed information without speech: God told his murderous brother Cain that "your brother's blood cries out to me from the ground" (Gen. 4:10). Later in Hebrews 11:4, we read of the non-linguistic way in which he continues to serve as a symbol: "By faith Abel brought God a better offering than Cain did. By faith he was commended as righteous, when God spoke well of his offerings. *And by faith Abel still speaks, even though he is dead*" (emphasis added).

Linguistic Representations[72]

The third type of representations, linguistic or symbolic, are the most precise. Even though we have heard all our lives that a picture (iconic) is worth a thousand words, we need an explanation of almost everything we see. (A principal interviewing prospective teachers, for instance, would much prefer three letters of reference to even the finest photograph.)

Linguistic representations include written words, spoken language, and verbalized thoughts.[73]

The Three Kinds of Representations

Here is an example that will help to differentiate the three types. If someone wanted to introduce another person without his or her physical presence, one might show a photograph of that person, creating a visual icon in the mind (really, more precisely, an icon of the photograph, but let's not quibble). Or he or she might stand next to that person in a crowd and indicate (or index) that person by directing the line of sight to that person by pointing at him or her. Or our introducer might speak the unknown person's name and describe his or her attributes, personality, family history, and some anecdotes that illustrate the essence of that person, thus linguistically representing him or her.

Again, one important step in analyzing the process of thought involves prescinding the representations from the facts, recognizing that they are not one and the same. We have already shown that the icon of a mountain in one's head is not the mountain itself. That icon will go with you wherever you choose to take it; and it is substantially less heavy and cumbersome than it would be to carry the mountain itself around.

But the process of prescinding—or cutting—representations away from facts and seeing them as different entities is difficult. During an early stage of development between about the fourth and the sixth month, a normal child will cry inconsolably when his mother leaves the room because it seems she has ceased to exist suddenly. But we as adults have a similar problem; if we cannot see something, we may act as if it does not exist (the coming judgment of God, for instance). We may act as if hunger pains or physical difficulties are telling us the truth about a situation, when God asks us to depend on what He might say about the situation, not what our bodies or experiences are telling us. This shows up in Mormonism when Joseph Smith asked people to accept his version of what he said he iconically—through the senses— experienced in the "Sacred Grove" where he said he saw a God the Father who had flesh and bones, despite the Bible's insistence on the noncorporeal nature of God.

It will be easily observed that there is an increasing role of human will (and voluntary control) in the progression of the signs or symbols: iconic to indexical. For instance, one does not usually choose to "represent" scalding water as anything but painful. We react immediately and strongly to iconic representations especially when they are unpleasant. We can avoid such pain by being careful not to connect with scalding water; that is, in choosing what we will index or link to our own bodies through our actions.

But the greatest amount of voluntary control is involved in our use of linguistic or symbolic representations, and it through language that false religions such as Mormonism can be unmasked. Because we have such a wealth of written documentation of the LDS Church's history and personalities, we can see how this religion (and the willful way that many of its proponents such as Joseph Smith used language) hangs by the threads of words.

With words, we can represent the facts of our lives and any other aspect of reality truthfully. Or we can choose to fabricate fantasies, commit errors, or even invent lies if we choose.

It should come as no surprise that linguistic representations, not iconic (sensory) nor indexical (sensory-motor linking) ones, are the very kinds of representations that God chooses to use to deal with us.[74] We should be happy that He did not choose to "zap" information into us by electric voltage, for instance. (Some of us might behave better if He had!) Of course, there were times in the past where He did strike people dead for their sins (Ananias and Sapphira, for instance) but we would have to agree that they did not learn much from the iconic experience (being dead at that moment). But we who have access to the linguistic representations we read in the Bible can learn the lessons in a much less painful and ultimately more effective way. God also did not choose to let us know about Himself[75] by neon signs calling our attention to objects that might teach us about Himself (although Romans 1:20 does teach that just the created order ought to teach us about His nature and power).

Rather, God chose the most precise and multifaceted form of representation to convey His mind to us. Remember, He gave us language—which we can now agree, is the most accurate and potentially complete form of representing any fact. And the Bible is just that: a representation of His mind. He desires that we should rely on it, even above our senses, even above what we see, hear, and observe in other ways. Although our senses and their capabilities are given to us by God, He has specifically forbidden us to rely on them exclusively. While the icon of sight is useful, Strawn observes, in helping us to know which wall to walk toward in order to get through a door and not through the family portrait hanging on the other wall, its use is limited and always subject to examination of its worth.

Eve found this out in the Garden of Eden. She was faced with the choice of either going with what her senses told her about the fruit (it looked good) or what God told her (eating it would kill her). Furthermore, she knew about death the way all of us know about it: not from personal experience, but from being told about it. She balanced the iconic representation of the appearance of the fruit against the linguistic representation of God about the true, but unseen, nature of the fruit and its future effects.

In the same way, we are given the iconic urges of sexuality. As any teenager with active hormones will verify, sometimes there is not a great deal of will involved in deciding whether to be tempted or not. But even though God gave us those urges just as He gave us other iconic abilities, He has clearly limited their use. Just because God gave us the ability to do certain things does not mean He approves their wholesale implementation.

What does this imply about our thinking processes? Just because God gave us the ability to think and reason does not mean we can use that ability to come to conclusions He has specifically forbidden.

Let's return to the concept of prescinding, or cutting, a representation from a fact. We have already seen that the mountain in your head is not the same as the mountain out there. We have seen that a memory of Mommy in the next room is not the same as Mommy herself. Facts and representations are not only individual concepts, different in essential nature and substance; they are actually distinct and separate concepts.

We speak of a "gulf of incommensurability"[76] (the so-called "Einstein's gulf," because of that thinker's description of the difficulty of linking objects with abstracts)[77] between the two. Incommensurable are things that cannot be reconciled, that have no inherent connection, are not measured in the same way, are qualitatively different, "apples and oranges."

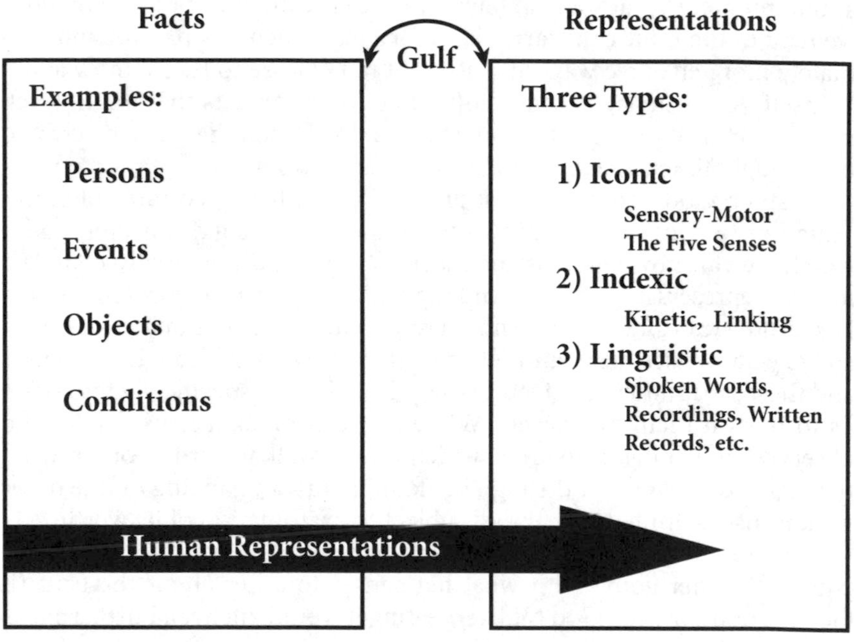

John W. Oller Jr.'s Pragmatic Map[78]

Let's take an example from the world of language. If someone wanted to tell about the small furry domesticated creature that meows, one might say the word "cat." An English-speaker would immediately access that linguistic representation and know that the reference was to a domestic feline. But a Norwegian could hear "cat" all day long and no useful information would be conveyed. That is because there is nothing inherent in the sounds of the word "cat" that will convey the image of a cat. In Norway another word would be required. But unless we find some way to link the sounds of the word "cat" to the Norwegian's concept of such an animal, no information will be conveyed about the animal in question.

Acts of linking representations and facts are performed routinely. A child in Spain soon learns to call that furry thing a "gato" and links the sequence of sounds of that word to that particular animal. All this occurs as a matter of course and with cultural consensus. Again, the concept of the involvement of human will and voluntary control, though, is seen in the progression of representations: We have little control over how we symbolize a cut finger, a little more over which things we point out or link with words; but a great deal of control over how we use words.

Consider once again the notion that we cannot directly access our surroundings. We have seen that we cannot directly put even the fact of pain in our bodies into our brains. If we hit our knee against an opened dresser drawer, we do not have the dresser in our heads. We do not even have the part of the dresser that struck us in our heads. We do not really have the pain in our knee there, either—just the iconic representation that informs our brain of what just happen and helps us step aside.

Whenever representational thinkers explain how we do not have direct access to the past, or even to the present except through representations, people have had a lot of trouble understanding that. But a movie recently came out that is very explanatory. Especially when talking to college students and other young people about representations, all that is necessary is the question, Have you seen the movie *Memento*? With anyone who has seen the movie, there is an immediate spark of understanding.

In this movie, the main character in this movie has had a traumatic experience, and as a result he has only short-term memory. Every time he falls asleep, he cannot remember anything of his past—not even his own name. He copes with that problem in a unique way: he takes photographs of people he will need to deal with the next day (he creates iconic representations) and creates linguistic representations by writing himself notes on paper and even tattooing crucial information onto his body. With no long-term memory, he has no access to the past except through representations.

At one point in the movie, a woman confines him in her home and insults him. She has cleaned out her house of all writing implements—there are no pens or pencils for him to record what happened. She knows that if she can just keep him there until he falls asleep, he will not remember a thing. He has no access to the past except through representations, and when he begins to change the written records he is keeping to reflect his own fears and desire for revenge, his past changes. All he has to go on are his representations.

Now, I do not advocate that everyone watch this movie—it is a disturbing film. But it concretizes a truth: *none* of us has access to our past except through representations.[79] We do not have the facts anymore—the events, for instance—we just have the representations of them. And we, like the man in the film, choose how we represent our circumstances.

Now that we understand that, we can see how all the facts of the present are converted into representations of one type or another—and that is what they will ever remain from that point on. Anything that we can access from the past, we access through representations. We can never recreate the past. For instance, a reader can go back to the beginning of this document and read it again, but will not be reproducing his or her actions. For one thing, he or she will have the memories of the first time it was read accompanying the second and subsequent readings.[80]

Where do people have the greatest problem with representations? It is with their own personal experiences. If there is something within their past, an event or a circumstance or even a feeling, they depend upon the force of personal experience because they believe they "know how things work," at least for them. Especially with past traumatic events, it takes a deliberate, willful choice to accept God's representations of His care even in those painful past events instead of what a person would remember and how it made him or her feel and continue to feel.[81]

It has been happening since the Garden of Eden. Look again at how Adam and Eve based their decisions to eat of the forbidden fruit. They had their own experience, which was that of perfection and eternal life. God gave them a linguistic representation: choose eternal life (which they had in their experience) or choose death (which they only knew about linguistically from the Lord). When it came time to decide to eat the apple, Eve lined things up this way: Her own experience did not include any kind of death. But she could represent the fruit iconically: it was good to look at and she thought it would be nourishing. God's instructions were a complete, reliable linguistic representation of that fruit, and the consequences of eating it.

Which did she choose?

What do we choose when faced with similar choices, when God gives us a linguistic representation of something that is either out of our personal experience or that is actually contrary to something we have experienced or felt?

Certainly this is a factor in what many Mormons would call their own personal faith or "testimony." Even when faced with Bible scriptures that contradict LDS scriptures, or when shown information that calls into question many of their cherished stories about Mormon heroes such as Joseph Smith, many Mormons lean most heavily on somatic or body-based evidence such as a "burning in the bosom" or some other sensation that they take as verification of LDS teachings.

The Bible speaks in Ephesians 1:18 of "the eyes of your heart." Paul prays there for the Ephesians that the eyes of their hearts may be enlightened. He is contrasting eyes of the heart with our physical eyes. Our physical eyes, indeed all our senses and our unaided powers of reasoning, will give us only a certain kind of information. They only create earthly representations. The Bible calls this natural state "the sinful nature," or "the fleshly nature." All that the best human mind and the best human body can conclude cannot co-exist alongside God's thinking: according to Paul in Romans 8:5–8, the sinful mind is actually "hostile" to God.

Just as one cannot serve God and money, we cannot let our minds try to operate on their own representational autonomy and still be pleasing to God.[82] It is a fundamental moral choice. For most Mormons, the thought of abandoning representational autonomy—the right to make spiritual decisions on physical sensations and what they might supernaturally "see"—feels unnatural and engenders suspicion. All their lives they have been told to depend on bosom-burning and the possibility of individual revelation wherein you might see a dead person while in the temple, for instance. For many, to give this up is a matter of great personal loss and confusion.

Where the Rubber Meets the Road: Implications for Our Lives

One thing that must be acknowledged in any dialogue between a Mormon and a Christian who is not aware of the intricacies of Mormon theology is that two such parties can think they are agreeing (using the same linguistic representations) when the facts they are trying to depict can be very different. One way that Mormon missionaries are trained to traffic in facts and representations is by their use of traditional Christian terminology to create a false sense of agreement between themselves and non-Mormons. "Do you believe in God?" a prospect might ask. "Why certainly," a missionary would answer, but the fact in the mind of the Christian's question (a timeless and eternal and noncorporeal Deity) has little common ground with the created, former-man, flesh-and-bone person Mormons call "Heavenly Father." Even though both parties are using the same representation, the same linguistic symbol "God," they are referring to quite different entities in the mind of each.

The second way in which the concept of the relationship of facts to representations has implications for Mormons is in dealing with what are popularly called "past issues." I think this is most useful when an ex-Mormon must deal with his or her past religious experiences and the guilt and other negative feelings they cause.

We are taught by therapists, both secular ones as well as most who wear the label "Christian," that the way to deal with past issues is to try to get back into the past where painful events or circumstances supposedly set up a chain reaction that makes us feel bad today. Sometimes this is done through hypnosis, sometimes through journaling or meditation, but mostly through talking about those past circumstances. It is important to realize that we cannot "get back into" the past of five minutes ago—the facts—much less into the circumstances that supposedly set up a chain reaction that makes us feel bad today. We cannot deal with past facts any more directly than we can deal with physical facts that surround us right now, *except through representations.*

We cannot change the facts of the past but we can change our representations of them, since they exists only representationally. The only way to "change" the past of a Christian is to accurately represent it within the context of the supervision of a loving God who was with us through it all.

That is the truth of Romans 8:28: that God causes all things to work together for the good of those who love Him and are called according to His purpose. This means that while both pleasant and unpleasant events and circumstances befall a believer, God has promised to make the events of both kinds "energize together" (a loose transliteration of the Greek) in such a way that the potential bad effects are not only nullified, they are transformed into good effects for the believer.

Here is another way to see it. Since the past exists only representationally, and the future exists only in the mind of God who wants the best for us because He loves us, then the arena of action is today, and the task of action is that of representing things as He would have us do, not as our senses or fears or inclinations would do.

When we say that we have perfect freedom to choose our representations, that does not mean we have unlimited latitude but only within the parameters God sets.[83] We tend to believe that certain "plain-as-the-nose-on-your-face" issues demand only one representation, but this is not the case. Take the example of the scouting party of twelve spies who went into the land of Canaan to survey it.[84] All twelve men saw the same giants, the same crops, the same high walls. In other words, they all had the same visual icons in their heads—and even brought back some giant grape clusters as visual icons for the rest of the people.

But how differently they represented the facts they saw! Ten of the men shrank to the size of grasshoppers in their own eyes when they compared themselves with the inhabitants of the land.[85] They spoke of dangers and fears. They advised caution. But Joshua and Caleb deliberately subjugated the images of power they saw in the land to the surpassing greatness of the God they served. They represented the land as conquered—a coming fact in the mind of God that He had verbally represented to them when He said "I give you this land."

And how did God deal with those who chose their own iconic representations over His linguistic ones? For forty years, there was never a day when the sound of mourning for the dead did not fill the camps of Israel, as all those faithless men died without ever again seeing the land.

When we say that we have perfect freedom to choose our representations of the past, this does not mean that one person's interpretation of a past catastrophe is as good as the next guy's, or that we can just choose to think about only pleasant things.

It does mean that if you believe God and adopt His representations of reality as seen in Romans 8:28, then He is at this moment filtering out, transforming and redeeming, even completely annihilating the bad effects of our circumstances so that they will ultimately be for our learning, growth, and good.[86]

The Chicken-Egg Question: Which Came First, the Fact or the Representation?

In one sense, it seems to us that facts precede—and almost force—certain representations. For most people looking at a just-unveiled new model of an automobile, for instance, the fact of its appearance will somewhat "automatically cause" a visual representation of it in the heads of the viewers. In that sense, the fact of the car preceded and to some degree formed the representation of it in our minds.

In another sense, however, the car existed representationally before it was constructed with metal, plastic, and glass. The designer's plans for it were a representation, one that preceded and (along with the indexing action of the manufacturing process, which linked the plan to the raw materials) then "caused" the car to come into being, to become a "fact," to move from the abstract representational form it had in the designer's mind to cold, hard, glistening reality.

The Bible's Unique Ability

The unique power that the Bible claims for itself, the ability to represent each fact in our lives, means that instead of the past forming what we are in the present, *we are rather always in the process of reforming the past (in the only way it now exists, as representations) right now in the present.*[87]

Paul the apostle understood this principle. When he looked at his past, he made this observation:

> I thank Christ Jesus our Lord, who has given me strength, that he considered me trustworthy, appointing me to his service. Even though I was once a blasphemer and a persecutor and a violent man, I was shown mercy because I acted in ignorance and unbelief. The grace of our Lord was poured out on me abundantly, along with the faith and love that are in Christ Jesus. Here is a trustworthy saying that deserves full acceptance: Christ Jesus came into the world to save sinners—of whom I am the worst. But for that very reason I was shown mercy so that in me, the worst of sinners, Christ Jesus might display his immense patience as an example for those who would believe in him and receive eternal life. (1 Tim. 1:12–16)

In other words, he chose to represent the bad things of his past as forgiven and even more as a source of encouragement for those who sinned much less grievously.[88]

However, he also chose the representations of the good things of his past in a way that God taught him:

> If anyone else thinks he may have confidence in the flesh, I more so: circumcised the eighth day, of the stock of Israel, of the tribe of Benjamin, a Hebrew of the Hebrews; concerning the law, a Pharisee; concerning zeal, persecuting the church; concerning the righteousness which is in the law, blameless. But what things were gain to me, these I have counted loss for Christ. Yet indeed

> I also count all things loss for the excellence of the knowledge of Christ Jesus my Lord, for whom I have suffered the loss of all things, and count them as rubbish, that I may gain Christ and be found in Him, not having my own righteousness, which is from the law, but that which is through faith in Christ, the righteousness which is from God by faith. (Phil. 3:4–9, NKJV)

(A parenthetical note here: Whenever you see the words "count" or "reckon" used this way in Scripture, you could substitute the word "represent" and be completely accurate.)

There is another specific way in which we can see, over and over in Scripture, how representations precede and form facts. It is often said that a majority, page-wise, of the Bible is prophetic in nature. (If you only count the prophetic books of the Old Testament, you have a substantial portion of the Bible, to say the least.) Without question, the Bible is filled with linguistic representations that precede—that is, come before—the facts they depict. And not only do they come before the events: the words of God have the ability to make reality conform to those words. *The representations of God precede and form facts.*

Let us look at how that happens. You may recall that we drew a distinction between facts and representations, showing that the first is illustrated in the physical world that surrounds us, and the second in the ways that we symbolize and access those physical realities. When we looked earlier at the nature of reality, we saw that there is a part of it which is seen, and a part which is not seen. We could call the seen side the world of facts, and the unseen part the world or realm of representations.

Now, while it is true that representations (language, for instance) take place here on the seen side of reality, we also can acknowledge that all that is seen begins as a representation. Our God is the originator of all representations, for all that has been created existed first representationally in His mind, which He linked to the material world in Creation through the Son,[89] and in communication through the agency of the Holy Spirit.[90]

Thus, we can identify that aspect of God that we refer to and personify as the Father; and we can see Him as the generator of perfect representations, the Great Representor. He can be identified with the unseen side of reality, the side of representations, where His will is done completely.[91]

On the other hand, there is a part of the Godhead which we have been able to see—of whom John said, "That which was from the beginning, which we have heard, which we have seen with our eyes, which we have looked at, and our hands have touched" (1 John 1:1). The Son, who lived among us, was literally representation made fact: Word made flesh. He embodies for us in our understanding of the Godhead the visible or seen aspect of God.

So we have the manifestation of representations, and the manifestation of fact; and of course we have the manifestation as we have already seen of the linking Agent, the Holy Spirit. The structure of language and the architecture of reality, let us emphasize, certainly do not "create" God: rather, their triadic structures merely (and must) reflect His own.

The Father, of course, is given supremacy by Jesus in every way. This was a conscious decision by Jesus who "being in very nature God, did not consider equality with God something to be used to his own advantage; rather, he made himself nothing by taking the very nature of a servant, being made in human likeness" (Phil. 2:6–7; other versions read that He "emptied Himself").

Perhaps one reason Jesus saw fit to do this was that the Father was to be seen as the Originator, the Representor; and He, Jesus, as the Fact.

The Trinity is itself as an entity "a model of how God runs the universe": the eternal linked to the temporal by means of a connecting agent, the Spirit.[92] These three form a unity and require, by their nature, that they be seen as such.

The "naturalness" of this is reflected in the unity, for instance, of language: under most circumstances one does not prescind or cut apart the unity of a mountain into its three parts in one's perception (the mountain itself, the icon in the head, and the connection one makes between the two.)

Let us return to our previous discussion of how representations precede and form facts.[93] We see this in any manufactured item: no car, for instance, "springs into being," becomes a fact, without having been represented first in the mind of the inventor and then in written or visual form of a blueprint or something similar.

Similarly, all of creation existed representationally in the mind of God before taking shape. He even used a type of representation—words—to speak light and all other elements of creation into existence.

Later, in the book of Leviticus chapter 26 (and many other places as well), we see that all of nature conforms to the representations of God. The people of Israel were told explicitly that their physical well-being, the abundance of their crops, the fecundity of their herds, their political stability—all of these depended on just a word from Him. He wanted the people to understand that they were not dealing just with the facts of their existence, but with the way they represented those facts.

He taught them clearly that all sin as a fact begins as a representation in the heart. One good illustration of this process is found in Micah 2:1 where a sinner is depicted as devising iniquity in his bed and then rising up in the morning to put that representation into practice as a fact.

This idea of a representation preceding a fact[94] is also illustrated in a scriptural device that is identified as type and antitype. In Romans 5:14, we see that Adam was a "type" of Christ: a representation of a coming reality of fact.[95]

Perhaps the most significant manifestation of this idea of things existing as representations before they have any status as facts is the deliberate inspired choice of terminology of the apostle John who begins his gospel outside of time, in eternity, saying that before He was flesh, Jesus was Word (representation) who then became fact. (This is not to say He was not "real" and "factual" before His Incarnation, of course.)

Test Case: Prophecy and False Prophecy

We have said before that the movement of ideas and power is always from the unseen side to the temporal or seen side. Certainly this is abundantly illustrated in the life of Jesus who looked to the Father for everything (John 12:49 and many other places). But prophecy, which permeates all of Scripture, also illustrates this movement in a linguistic way; for what is prophecy but verbal representations of things yet to be, or coming facts?

Because of God's foreknowledge, He represents all things truthfully, not only about events but about people as well. Jeremiah discovered that God had a specific mission in mind for him, one that had been in place in God's mind representationally before he ever even existed in the womb of his mother. Similarly, we have the privilege of participating in the great purposes of God: God has represented good works for us to do and gives us the joy of making those things facts (Eph. 2:10).

And what a protection we have built into the nature of prophecy when seen from a representational point of view! This has been so helpful to me, as an ex-Mormon and as a teacher and writer on cults, but also in assessing the prominent problem of false prophecy in Christian churches.

True prophecy, that which comes from God, is a verbal representation that will precede and form facts. True prophecy from God always eventually becomes fact on the "seen" side. But the converse is also true. If someone prophesies something (an event they say that God said is going to do: let's say, that He is going to heal someone or an event is going to happen at a certain time), then when the person dies or the deadline passes, you know that that was not a representation from God.[96]

Now, LDS history is replete with false prophecies. In fact, many significant instances in which groups of people left Mormonism during its early history can be traced back to disillusionment when some of the extravagant prophecies of Joseph Smith (verbal representations) did not take form—did not become facts—in the real world. A good example of this is found in Doctrine and Covenants section 111 where the "gold and silver" of Salem, Massachusetts, was prophesied to become the property of debt-ridden Mormons (which never happened).

(Of course, we must take into account the passage in Jeremiah 18:5–10 in which God demonstrates that He will relent from prophecies of destruction and reconsider prophecies of blessing, dependent upon the behavior of the recipients. However, this does not let the Mormon god "off the hook" for many other of Joseph Smith and Brigham Young's more extravagant prophecies, especially those concerning the end of the world.)[97]

Deuteronomy 18:22 says, "If what a prophet proclaims in the name of the Lord does not take place or come true, that is a message the Lord has not spoken. That prophet has spoken presumptuously." In representational language, that was not a representation from God, but from the mind of the individual. God's representations precede, and form, facts.

But do you know what people hold on to when someone they know has prophesied something that did not come true? They say, "Well, I know that person and his or her heart and I know they are sincere and good-hearted, so that could not possibly apply to them." I felt the same way when leaving Mormonism: What about all those wonderful people who said they had experienced visions telling them the Mormon Church was true? How could they all be wrong?

Here is the test, the same one Eve faced: Will I accept my own representations of the person, formed out of my experience, or will I accept the Bible's representation of a prophet whose words do not come true? How mighty is the hold that our own representations, formed out of our own experience, have on us.[98]

Perhaps as much as anything, the power of personal experience and personal assessment by oneself and one's peers holds great sway in Mormonism. "I've known the bishop all my life and if he says it, it must be true," is often the thinking, basing faith on the character of others. Barraged with conflicting information about the historical and other claims of Mormonism, its members who don't choose to engage issues directly are relying on the statements of Mormon apologists: if a Mormon scholar says it, it must be true." A current example of this is a short video produced by the LDS Church entitled *Alone*, in which a doubting young man is not given any data, sources, or other "hard" information to help him deal with his concerns about the connection of Egyptian papyri to the Book of Abraham; he is only assured that LDS scholars have the answers.[99]

A Representational View of History

When we looked at the apostle Paul's two representational views of his past—as an exemplary Jew on the one hand, and as "the worst of sinners" on the other—notice that Paul did not ignore the good or the bad things in his past. They happened, and ignoring them was not his choice. What he *could* choose is how he represented them, and he chose to do so according to the representations that God had for him.

Such choices are not made on worldly standards of what is accurate or complete.[100] One can have a very complete set of linguistic representations of an event (the closing documents on the sale of a house) but those representations might not tell you what is really important to know about that event (hidden damage in the ductwork, for instance).

The world regards historical accounts, especially those based on first-person witness accounts, as being the most reliable. However, human history is incomplete and faulty because it is written by humans with incomplete and faulty representational abilities. (In Strawn's words, "Human history is a function of personality."[101])

It is possible, according to researcher Craig Criddle, to ascertain the authorship of a book such as the Book of Mormon by identifying the persons—personalities—who contributed to it. He participated in a 2008 peer-reviewed text analysis of the Book of Mormon, published in the *Journal of Literary and Linguistic Computing,* that indicated "a prevalence of Rigdon and Spalding 'signals' in patterns consistent with Rigdon's modification of a base narrative text authored by Solomon Spalding."[102] In Criddle's words:

> The Book of Mormon is the Rube Goldberg literary product of a small group of financially desperate men. Each man attempted to imitate the writing style of the King James Bible and borrowed liberally from favorite books and sermons, including the Bible, View of the Hebrews, and The Late War.
>
> The forerunner to the Book of Mormon was "Manuscript Found," a book written by Solomon Spalding, a Dartmouth College graduate and veteran of the American Revolutionary War. Spalding submitted his manuscript to a Pittsburgh print shop for publication. Witnesses described the book as a Biblical-style fiction that traced the origin of Native Americans to migrations from the Middle East. Impoverished and unable to pay the printing costs, Spalding died with his manuscript unpublished. Sidney Rigdon, a tanner who supplied leather bookbindings to the shop, acquired the manuscript and modified it to reflect his religious views. Though Rigdon had suffered a childhood brain trauma that plagued him throughout his life, he was shrewd and intelligent and became a well-known Reformed Baptist Preacher, referred to by his peers as a "walking Bible." Driven by the voices in his head and by envy of his famous mentor (Alexander Campbell), Rigdon modified the Spalding document to reflect his religious views.
>
> He then teamed with Joseph Smith Jr., a man who Rigdon believed could bring the Book of Mormon to light and secure the funds needed for its publication. Smith was a convicted con artist who carried out his seer stone treasure-hunting cons in upstate New York and Eastern Pennsylvania. To bring the Book of Mormon to the attention of the public and to increase sales, Smith created a miraculous story of the book's origins and leaked word that he possessed golden plates of great value. To raise funds for printing, he targeted a gullible farmer named Martin Harris as his mark, and flattered Harris into serving as his scribe. Separated from Smith by a curtain, Harris recorded Smith's dictation. Once convinced that the manuscript would sell, Harris mortgaged his farm to pay for its printing. In the course of the con, however, Harris' wife Lucy stole the first 116 pages to test Smith's powers as a seer. Her act precipitated a hurried replacement and reorganization of the text. Rigdon worked in Ohio with Parley Pratt, his crafty and disingenuous protégé, to fabricate replacement text and to deliver it to Smith in New York. Pratt, a tin peddler, knew the route between New York and Ohio well. Smith dictated text received from Rigdon to his distant cousin Oliver Cowdery—a pious pamphlet peddler—who, like Pratt, also worked the route between New York and Ohio. Both Smith and Cowdery added inserts to the text, and The Book of Mormon version 2.0 was born. Just three months after its publication, Smith and Rigdon continued

> their collaboration—this time on the King James Bible, restoring to it "plain and precious things", including elements of Royal Arch freemasonry. The Inspired Version of the Bible and The Book of Mormon laid the foundation for a restoration of primitive Christianity and gathering of the faithful to a New Jerusalem in America. Within a year of publication of the Book of Mormon, hundreds of impoverished converts had gathered in Ohio, drawn by promises of "a land of milk and honey" and an "endowment from on high"—modern revelation penned by Sidney Rigdon and delivered by Joseph Smith.[103]

What Criddle was saying is that the Book of Mormon belies its authors. When one reads the historical account of an event, one is really reading the psychology of the writer—what he thought was important. Even if one reads the compilation of multiple experts on an event, he or she is still dealing with a collectivity of faulty and incomplete abilities to represent; and the finished product reflects this.

A very timely example of the way that "history" reflects the psychology of the writer of the history is illustrated by the recent tendency to "revise" history books for the public schools. The sensitivities of our generation are written back into the events of the past—which hardly adds more accuracy; it simply adds, at best, another point of view and, at worst, just more acceptability to the current reader.

But even the people who witness events cannot be relied upon to be complete and accurate from an eternal point of view, for each works from within the framework of his own proclivities and interests. Even an eyewitness to a battle, for instance, can only see part of the action and cannot correctly assess the importance of actions whose fruition may not appear for a generation or two.[104]

Thus we can begin to appreciate the immense value of the Bible: a complete and accurate accounting of the mind of God and its interworkings with the minds of men. Because the Bible is inspired by God Himself, it is the only reliable source of information about how to live life on this planet.

Though individual writers such as the physician Luke or the former tax collector Matthew may occasionally show us some glimpse of their personal interests, nonetheless the operation of the Holy Spirit with their minds[105] was such as to ensure that everything they wrote was not only accurate in conveying what happened; but more important, accurate in what was important about the events of which they wrote.[106] Thus the Bible reflects a mind's psychology as well: the psychology, if you will, of the Holy Spirit of God.[107]

TRUE NARRATIVE REPRESENTATIONS

It should be obvious from reading my description of representational research and its implications that this area of study has had a profound effect on my life. When I selected a topic for my dissertation, I surprised many people by not choosing a subject directly associated with Mormonism. However, I believe the principles of Representational Research are so practical and so applicable to so many areas of human thought that it seemed profligate of my time and efforts to focus on Mormonism. How much better to define and enable an excavating tool that could be used in so many places than to continue digging through the same (albeit constantly changing) theological site.

With this foundation of representational research's basic ideas, we can look at another very useful concept. My mentor and colleague—Dr. John W. Oller Jr., Doris B. Hawthorne/LEQSF Professor in Communicative Disorders III at the University of Louisiana at Lafayette (and also a member of my dissertation committee)—has outlined the relationship between "discursive representations and the facts of the material world"[108] using what Oller terms the "superior" brand of logic developed by logician Charles S. Peirce, the founder of American pragmatism.

Oller shows that any form of discourse must be seen as triadic. Thus it is that whether something be spoken or written, it must contain three parts: the icon, the index, and the symbol (iconic, indexic, and linguistic representations, as shown in the diagram given earlier.)

Oller used these three elements in many published studies examining the data of discourse to test grammatical theories. By using a Peircean approach, Oller could prove that only something known as a "true narrative representation" (TNR) could "provide a satisfactory basis for the determination of any meaning whatever."

Another colleague of mine at Trinity Southwest University (and the head of my dissertation committee) is Dr. Peter Briggs, who used the concept of a TNR—with a meticulous criterial screen and acknowledgment of TNRs as possessing determinancy, connectedness, generalizability, and necessary correspondence—to demonstrate the factuality of the conquest of the city of Ai as described in the biblical book of Joshua.[109] Yet another of my Trinity colleagues, Dr. Steven Collins, used the same principles to determine necessary features of the city of Sodom as he excavated, as I described in the book I cowrote with him, *Discovering the City of Sodom: The Fascinating, True Account of the Old Testament's Most Infamous City.*[110] Understanding and applying TNR theory can lead to versatile and quantifiable ways to understand contested narratives. Most significantly for Bible believers, TNRs can demonstrate the veracity of certain aspects of the Bible's historical record.

The three elements of a TNR can be illustrated with an exemplar true statement (I will use Oller's examples as illustrations in this present discussion). In Oller's explanation of a TNR, he said of himself, "I attended the Baltimore meeting of the American Association of Applied Linguistics in the spring of 1994." There would be checkable, verifiable evidences of that trip, what we would call facts. His statement that he did this would be his linguistic (verbal) representation of what happened. The linking or pointing out of the connection between the fact and the representation is an index.

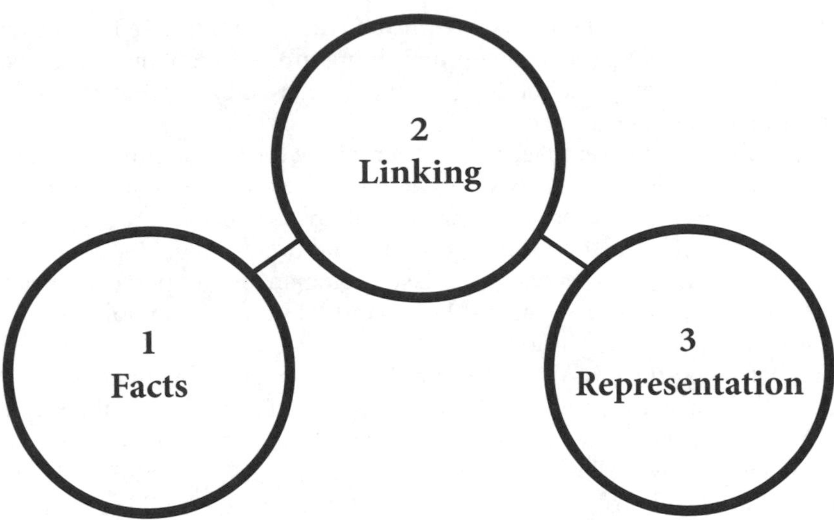

Figure 1: The underlying logical structure of every true narrative case

FICTIONS, ERRORS, AND LIES

In any such TNR, says Oller, the relationship (links) between facts, indices, and representations qualifies a statement as true, whereas if there is what he calls "degeneracy" in the elements or their relationships, they are no longer true narrative representations.

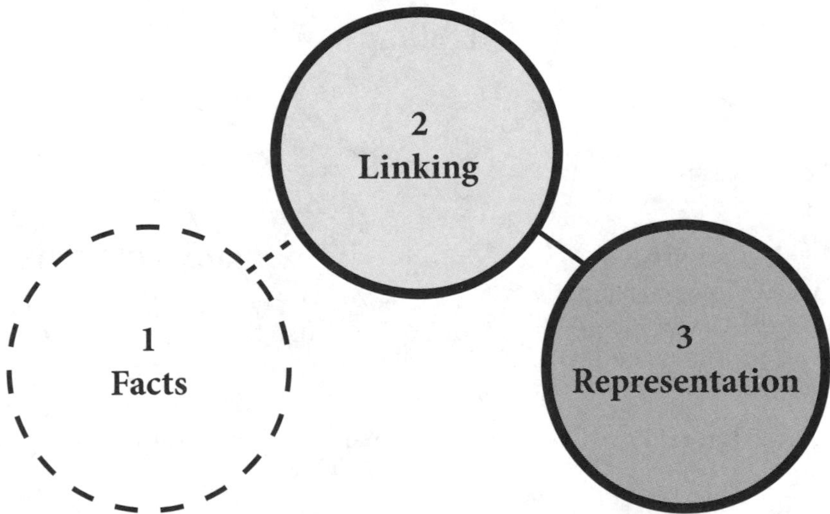

Figure 2: Fictions as a first degree of degeneracy from the true narrative case

A first degree of degeneracy from the true narrative case is a fiction. Oller's example is that of a person imagining himself grabbing the axle of an eighteen-wheeler and holding it over his head. In Figure 2 above,, such a narrative would be a fiction.

While the man's verbal account is actual (he formed a representation), the essence of his experience is not factual. Whereas Oller could produce airline tickets, an event program, or other items to substantiate the facts of his trip to Baltimore, the dreaming man could not do that.

"In fictions," says Oller, "the missing element is the perceptual part (the iconic aspect of the material facts) and its spatio-temporal connectedness to the material world."

That degeneracy of the triad of a TNR—the lack of iconic facts in a story—is how many intellectual Mormons would characterize their view of such things as Book of Mormon history. That book's events in its fictional geography, to hearken back to the comments of William Dever and Rabbi David Wolpe assessing the "truthfulness" of the Bible's Exodus events, have their value in the truth of the lessons they teach, not in the geography or any other solid factual basis.

Oller includes within errors—a second degree of degeneracy from the true narrative case—not only mistakes but also illusions, hallucinations, and the like. The degeneracy occurs when the fact of a situation and its representation have "gone wrong" and are not correctly matched to one another.

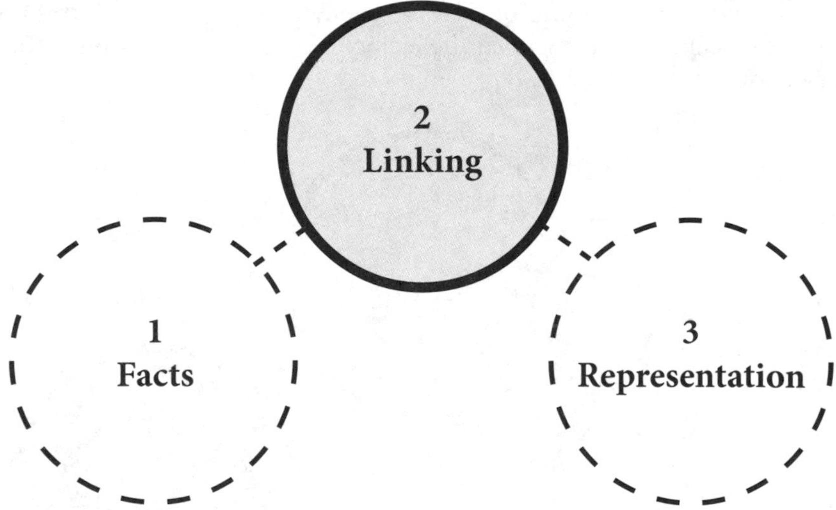

Figure 3: Errors as a second degree of degeneracy from the true narrative case

"As a result, the facts that ought to be represented are not, and the representations given (or taken) are also not as they should be," says Oller, offering the example of a driver who tells someone he sees a ground squirrel alongside the road, but it turns out to be a piece of cardboard that has accidentally turned sideways in such a way as to look like a squirrel. The facts aren't what the man originally said, and when he recognizes that, the representation would have to be corrected, too.

Probably most ex-Mormons would say that what they experienced in believing Mormonism was an error.

The third degree of degeneracy is deliberate, with the planned intention of using the representation to deceive someone. It is degenerate in all three parts, but it can be apprehended by someone as a true narrative representation; indeed, that is the intended aim of a lie. "The facts (as might be perceived or imagined iconically) are not as the representation at hand purports to make them out to be," says Oller. "The representation (as a symbolic description) does not truly correspond to the facts that do obtain. Further, the linking (the indexical part of the act of representing) has been deliberately corrupted by the producer."[111]

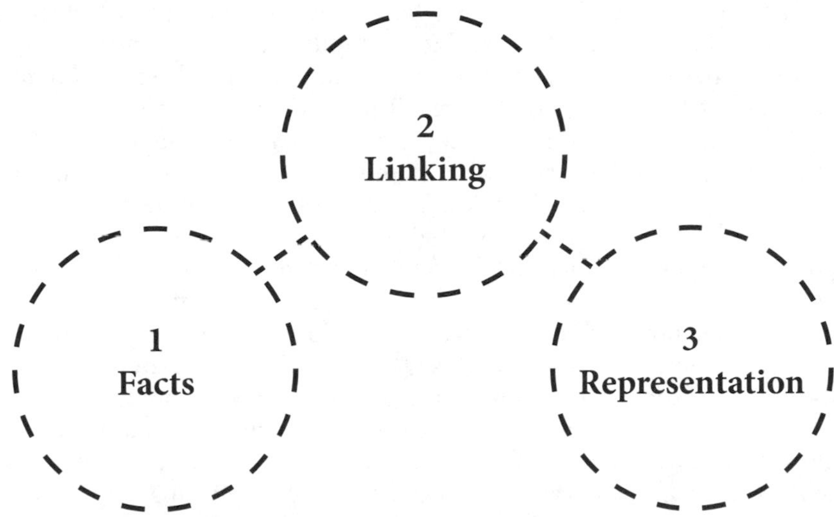

Figure 4: Lies as a third degree of degeneracy from the true narrative case

Oller wrote to urge language teachers to use only TNRs (or "well-instantiated fictions" such as drama or role-playing) in their instruction. (I strongly suggest that any reader access Oller's article; his pragmatic map that shows how representations merge with facts in the present is absolutely brilliant and is fertile ground for all sorts of exploration.)

Thus, anyone who is attempting to navigate in, around, or out of Mormonism can see the usefulness of the true narrative case and its degenerate forms.

We would have to say, for instance, that most Mormons who stand up in fast and testimony meetings and express their feelings are probably expressing an error. Their representation is heartfelt, and they are linking their words appropriately to concepts like "Joseph Smith was a prophet," or "The church is true," or "There is a living prophet today." Those of us who once said those very words—and meant them from the bottoms of our hearts—have now re-evaluated the "facts" of Mormonism (that wasn't really a squirrel by the road) and found them not to be what we once thought (they turned out to be an accidental thing for those born into it, and cardboard for all.)

Some of us have decided to change our former representations, our "testimonies," about Mormonism (hence, this book).

But even for many of those who don't speak up, who still attend church with family because they don't want to break hearts or bank accounts or reputations, they are nonetheless representing with inner dialogue that Mormonism is more than an error. It is the greatest mistake, or at least the greatest misfortune, many of them have in their lives.

The problem arises, of course, when someone points to one of them and says, "that person is kind and good (and/or educated and/or clever and/or a pursuer of truth)," and this confirms what the observer thought about staying in the Mormon Church. Thus, the error is perpetuated.

Many, many well-educated and lifelong Mormons, though, stay Mormons not because they are fooling themselves that maybe Mormonism might be true or because they desire to fool others. They recognize that from Joseph Smith onwards, this religion was about the creation of myths, and those myths have formed a lovely culture (sometimes a cultural heritage) they choose. For them it is a fiction, a beloved fiction.

There are thousands of us who have left Mormonism utterly. However, there are people within it who freely—and publicly—acknowledge the false nature of some of its claims, yet choose to emphasize other aspects of it. For instance, Grant Palmer, a high-profile Mormon who has been disfellowshipped from the LDS Church for his research on the problems with the LDS Church's claims about its own history, now puts his emphasis on the person and character of Jesus Christ, and not the Mormon trappings added to the biblical account of Him.[112]

There's a saying Mormons use to describe vocal ex-Mormons: "They left Mormonism, but they can't leave it alone." But Palmer and others who deeply love Mormon culture can't leave it, and can't leave it alone either.

I did give Mormonism a second chance of sorts about seven years ago. I had taken a trip to Texas to do some writing, and decided on a whim not to attend a church of my own denomination on Sunday. I selected a Mormon ward and attended there. I arrived late so as to not have to introduce myself (I do have a distinctive name I hoped not to have recognized). From the first moment I entered the building I re-entered a culture I dearly loved, from the ground-in Cheerios in the chapel carpet to the anxious but earnest speakers, to songs I remembered from decades ago. To be honest, it seemed as ordinary and un-cultic as anything I could imagine, nothing to demonize from what I saw and heard.

I managed to leave without much interaction and went back to my travel trailer and spent the next few days alone with no communication with anyone other than my husband over the phone. With me was a copy of my beloved *Mormon Doctrine* by Bruce R. McConkie, the nearest thing to a catechism and Talmud that existed when I was a Mormon.

I immersed myself in it, reading it from cover to cover, remembering what I had believed and why, *not just my present representations of what I had believed*. I found myself slipping into the logic of Mormonism. (I have often described Mormonism as one of the most logical systems of thought I've ever known; if you can accept as a premise that a man could go into a grove and ask God which church to join and God answered that he should to join none in existence, then everything about Mormonism flows out from that in an entirely coherent manner.)[113]

But I put the book away with both nostalgic regret and remorse. I know too much now to go back to a fictional god (no matter how winsome) who has stolen the identity of the God of the universe.

I have written about how beloved Mormonism was to me, and recounted in *The Mormon Mirage* how reluctantly I gave up some of its cardboard "facts":

> I felt a sense of personal loss, for instance, when I learned recently that the famous "miracle" of the seagulls in Utah was apparently not a miracle at all, at least not in the opinion of the people who witnessed it. According to Mormon lore, in 1848 the Utah pioneers had abundant, hard-earned crops, but a horde of crickets began eating the crops—until a great flock of seagulls miraculously appeared and ate all the crickets. But an examination of the diaries of the people who witnessed the event firsthand shows that most didn't even mention any seagulls, and the official First Presidency report that year said the gulls were "helpers but certainly not rescuers" of the harvest. In the words of journalists Richard and Joan Ostling, the story just kept growing far past the facts, an example of what they call Mormon "ritualized history."[114] It was one of the first stories I ever heard about the Mormon pioneers, and I cherished it even until a few months ago and only relinquished it with sadness and great regret.
>
> Those birds, like many of the elements I so loved about Mormonism, simply were never what the Church said they were.[115]

However, TNR theory and its depiction of lies is damning of early LDS leaders, and LDS General Authorities of all eras at least. It leaves no room to hide, once you can ascertain that Joseph Smith deliberately tried to fool people with fake plates, unverifiable visions, and self-aggrandizing statements intended to manipulate and dominate everyone around him.

For so long I wanted to believe he had participated in an error, that the visions he had were hallucinations or had some other natural explanation that made him as much a victim of Mormonism as anyone else. I wrestled with what to do with the experience he had in the "sacred grove," wondering what I would do with such an experience.

But then it crashed in on me, truth of all truths: that incident never happened. Moroni never came because Moroni never existed. The Mormon god couldn't get mad at anyone, or bless anyone, because he's not just someone's mistaken impression of a god, he's not just Joseph Smith's fiction, he's not even a he.

It's a 187-year old corporate, collusional lie, a degenerate representation which has no power over any people they don't give to it.

NOTES

1. Benjamin Franklin, *The Autobiography of Benjamin Franklin* (Cambridge: Houghton, Mifflin and Company, 1888), 88.
2. The sections "Meeting Dan" and "Retrospective" are reprinted with permission by Zondervan from: Latayne C. Scott, *The Mormon Mirage: A Former Member Looks at the Mormon Church Today* (Grand Rapids: Zondervan, 2009), 19–27, 269–78. I have made a few clarifications within that text.
3. As quoted by Jerald Tanner and Sandra Tanner, The Changing World of Mormonism, page 138, online at http://www.utlm.org/other/changingworld.pdf
4. Nathaniel Hawthorne, *Mosses from an Old Manse and Other Stories,* "Young Goodman Brown," online at http://www.gutenberg.org/files/512/512-h/512-h.htm#goodman (emphasis mine).
5. Charles Spurgeon, *The Treasury of David*, Psalm 30, online at *The Spurgeon Archive:* http://www.spurgeon.org/treasury/ps030.php.
6. The only literary works I have read that approach the articulation of this sense of loss are C. S. Lewis's *A Grief Observed* and Paul L. Maier's *A Skeleton in God's Closet.*
7. Note to the FARMS boys and their cousins: No, the school is not accredited; and yes, I did years of research and teaching, and wrote a dissertation on a subject other than Mormonism, a dissertation I defended before a committee of nationally-recognized academics.
8. Mormons in Transition provides a mentoring service for people coming out of Mormonism. I cannot imagine how better my life would have been had such a service been available for me. http://www.irr.org/mit/mentor.html.
9. James W. Sire, *The Universe Next Door: A Basic Worldview Catalog* (Downers Grove, Ill.: InterVarsity Press, 2004).
10. A Mormon term for optimizing your service or responsibilities in the Church.
11. Francis J. Beckwith, Carl Mosser, and Paul Owen, *The New Mormon Challenge: Responding to the Latest Defenses of a Fast-Growing Movement* (Grand Rapids: Zondervan, 2002). Mosser levels the charge that "some evangelical apologists jealously guard the kind of Mormonism they don't believe in" (81).
12. Standard Works of the LDS Church are its four books of scripture.
13. Review by Eric Johnson, "*The New Mormon Challenge*: *Responding to the Latest Defenses of a Fast- Growing Movement.*" Online at *Mormonism Research Ministry*, http://www.mrm.org/new-mormon-challenge
14. A previous version, "Mormonism and the Question of Truth", appeared in *Christian Research Journal,* vol. 15, no. 1 (Summer 1992). Online at http://www.equip.org/PDF/DM415.pdf.

15. President Harold B. Lee, "The Place of the Living Prophet, Seer, and Revelator," address to Seminaries and Institutes of Religion faculty, Brigham Young University, 8 July 1964, 14; as quoted in Adult Correlation Committee of The Church of Jesus Christ of Latter-day Saints, *Teachings of the Living Prophets* (Provo: Brigham Young University Press, n.d.), 148.
16. Brigham Young, *Journal of Discourses*, 11:272.
17. Ibid., 2:143.
18. Joseph Fielding Smith, *Answers to Gospel Questions,* II, (Salt Lake City: Deseret Book, 1958 edition), 188.
19. For a discussion of the context of Hinckley's statement, see "Dodging and Dissembling Prophet?" http://mit.irr.org/dodging-and-dissembling-prophet.
20. D. Michael Quinn, *Early Mormonism and the Magic World View* (Salt Lake City: Signature Books, 1987), as quoted on the book's jacket. A more detailed treatment of this idea appears on page x.
21. J. Reuben Clark, Jr., *Church News*, July 31, 1954, 9; as quoted in LDS, *Teachings of the Living Prophets*, 149.
22. Ibid., xiii.
23. Joseph Smith, *Teachings of the Prophet Joseph Smith*, comp. Joseph Fielding Smith (Salt Lake City: Deseret Book Company, 1976), 194.
24. See, e.g., Jerald and Sandra Tanner, *3,913 Changes in the Book of Mormon* (Salt Lake City: Modern Microfilm Company, 1965).
25. 2 Nephi 30:6. In *Major Problems of Mormonism* (Salt Lake City: Utah Lighthouse Ministry, 1989) 49, Jerald and Sandra Tanner note that "the original handwritten manuscript of the Book of Mormon, the first printing (1830 edition) and the 1837 edition all agree that the wording should be 'white.' The change, therefore, appears to be a deliberate attempt to change the original teaching of the Book of Mormon."
26. Vern Anderson, "Mormon Publisher Willing to Shake the 'Sacred' Tree," *Albuquerque Journal*, July 27, 1991, E4.
27. *Journal of Discourses* (London: Latter-day Saint's Book Depot, 1854–56), vol. 4, 49–50, 53–54, 173, 219, 220, and elsewhere, records the teachings of Brigham Young and other leaders that some sins are so grievous as to be beyond the power of the atoning blood of Christ, and mid-nineteenth century diaries and other writings by Mormons (e.g., John D. Lee's *Mormonism Unveiled*) tell of groups of Mormon priesthood holders who designated themselves "Avenging Angels" or "Danites" and went about shedding the blood of adulterers and murderers so that these sinners could receive forgiveness.
28. See, e.g., David John Buerger, "The Adam-God Doctrine," in *Dialogue: A Journal of Mormon Thought* 15:1 (Spring 1982), 14.
29. "LDS Speaker Admits Spicing Up Stories," *Salt Lake Tribune*, February 16, 1991, B1.
30. As quoted by authors Brian Waterman and Brian Kagel in *The Lord's University*: *Freedom and Authority at BYU* (Salt Lake City: Signature Books, 1998), online at http://signaturebookslibrary.org/the-lords-university-06/.
31. See Jerald and Sandra Tanner, *Mormonism, Magic and Masonry*, 2d ed. (Salt Lake City: Utah Lighthouse Ministry, 1988), online at http://www.utlm.org/booklist/digitaltitles/samplepdfs/mormonismmagicmasonry_sample.pdf.
32. D. Michael Quinn, "LDS Church Authority and New Plural Marriages, 1890–1904," *Dialogue: A Journal of Mormon Thought,* vol. 18, no. 1 (Spring 1985): 9–105.
33. As assessed by Robert Lindsey in *A Gathering of Saints* (New York: Simon & Schuster, 1988), 236, 238–39. This was also the conclusion reached by Stephen Naifeh and Gregory White Smith in *The Mormon Murders* (New York: Onyx Books, 1989).

34. J. Numano, "Perseverance amid Paradox: The Struggle of the LDS Church in Japan Today." *Dialogue: A Journal of Mormon Thought*, vol. 39, no. 4 (2006): 138.

35. Anderson, "Mormon Publisher Willing to Shake the 'Sacred' Tree," E4.

36. Richard R. Robertson, "Mormon Leader Admits Exaggerating Stories," *The Arizona Republic*, February 16, 1991, B10.

37. Elbert Eugene Peck, "Casting Out the Spell," *Sunstone 83*, 12.

38. Richard Abanes, *One Nation Under Gods: A History of the Mormon Church* (New York: Basic Books, 2003), 429.

39. Steve and Mary Ann Benson, "It's Becoming Red Square on Temple Square," *Arizona Republic*, May 22, 1994, "Perspective" section, 1.

40. *Empires* (video series), "Kingdom of David: By the Waters of Babylon" (Oregon Public Broadcasting, 2003), online at http://www.amazon.com/Kingdom-David-By-Rivers-Babylon/dp/B004AZSKK8.

41. See also "Doubting the Story of Exodus," *Los Angeles Times*, April 13, 2001. Online at http://articles.latimes.com/2001/apr/13/news/mn-50481.

42. *Empires*, "Kingdom of David: By the Waters of Babylon."

43. "Translation and Historicity of the Book of Abraham," online at https://www.lds.org/topics/translation-and-historicity-of-the-book-of-abraham?lang=eng&query=abraham.

44. "Translation and Historicity of the Book of Abraham."

45. Much of this information is from my dissertation, *A Definitional Study of Biblical Representational Research and Its Current Applications (*Albuquerque: Trinity Southwest University, 2003).

46. Page 16.

47. We might also add that God is not defined only by His Father-ness nor His Jesus-ness nor His Spirit-ness; though we might see each of these individually in passages of Scripture.

48. True objectivity, says Michael Polanyi, author of *Personal Knowledge: Towards a Post-Critical Philosophy* (University of Chicago Press, 1958), is "established contact with a hidden Reality," as quoted in *The Act of Bible Reading*, Elmer Dyke, ed. (Downers Grove, Ill.: IVP Academic, 1996), 142.

49. Note the differences between representational view of reality and that of Plato's cave. Plato argued that physical objects we see, trees for instance, are only "shadows" or copies of an ideal, unchanging, eternal tree. Though Hebrews 9 does speak of earthly objects in the tabernacle as being copies of corresponding heavenly realities, the Bible nowhere ratifies Plato's ideas as applying to all of earthly reality.

50. Dr. Oller points out that acknowledging only the two sides of reality here is dualistic, noting, "What is the third element? Is it not the present link between the seen and unseen? Is it not the intellect and understanding spirit that lives between and connects the two realms?" (Private correspondence between Oller and Scott.)

51. Steven Collins, Steven and Latayne Scott, *Discovering the City of Sodom: The Fascinating, True Account of the Discovery of the Old Testament's Most Infamous City* (New York: Howard Books, 2013.)

52. Use of the Greek word we have transliterated as "index" appears throughout Scripture: in verb form in Rom. 2:15; 9:17, 22; Eph. 2:7; 1 Tim. 1:16; Titus 2:10; Heb. 6:10–11. In noun form, it appears in Rom. 3:25, 2 Cor. 8:24, and Phil. 1:28. Each of these last three shows the noun functioning as a nonverbal director of attention to something—the exact function of an index as defined by both Peirce and Oller.

53. Oller is the Doris B. Hawthorne/LEQSF Professor in Communicative Disorders III at the University of Louisiana at Lafayette and also a member of my dissertation committee. (Private correspondence with the author.)

54. Strawn would go even further, asserting that "language is a property of God, and that our ability to use it is an extension of that capacity, not of human origin."

55. A paper by Lisa Young applies Peircean semiotics to the Hebrew Bible's use of the word for "sign," and concludes, "The writers of the Hebrew Bible, like Peirce, seemed to have been interested in the functions of 'signs,' which we equate with the modern field of semiotics." Lisa Young, "Peirce's Semiotics Applied to the Bible's Use of *Ait*." Paper presented at Proceedings of the Regional Meeting of the Central States ASOR and SBL, held in Kansas City, Mo., n.d., 4.

56. According to Oller, signs are "objects, actions, or marks standing for things beside themselves," whose understandability and meaningfulness is determined by the extent to which the signs are "consistent with what they are about . . . or with the material world." John W. Oller Jr., *Collected Background Readings* (Albuquerque: Trinity Southwest University), 1.

57. According to Umberto Eco in *Theory of Semiotics* (Bloomington, Ind.: Indiana University Press, 1979), 7, a representation or sign "is everything which can be taken as significantly substituting for something else." George Aichele in *Sign, Text, Scripture: Semiotics and the Bible* (Sheffield, UK: Sheffield Academic Press, 1997), 9, defines a sign as "any phenomenological object that may be taken to signify something . . . anything that might have meaning, anything that is potentially meaningful." Briggs defines a representation as "that which brings clearly before the mind; serves as a sign, symbol, counterpart, model or image; describes as having a specified character or quality." Peter Briggs, *Knowing the Fear of the Lord: A Brief Introduction to Biblical Representations,* Institute of Church-Based Theological Education, Academic Monograph Series, No. CBTE-5 (Albuquerque: Daystar Publications, 2003), 2.

58. We shall deal with the various types of signs later, but for now it is noteworthy that Oller regards all signs as triadic, according to chapter 2 of *Collected Background Readings.*

59. It won't escape the attention of a thinking person that symbols tend to pile on top of symbol in a way; talking about a sensory experience, for instance, is representing a representation, and someone's recounting of that telling is another representation on top, and so on.

60. I am aware that this discussion completely bypasses the concepts of inductive and deductive reasoning. Peirce would have said that there is a third way of knowing, one he called abduction. However, Strawn would insist that a biblical thinker would have to reject that kind of reasoning as well; because it, like both induction and deduction, has its origin in the nonabsolute: human intelligence. (Private conversation with the author.)

61. It may seem a bit circular to say, but a fact is that which can be represented.

62. Again, the pragmatic mapping developed by John W. Oller Jr. and used extensively in his teaching.

63. Peirce saw this clearly: "Since all that we know...we know through representations, if our representations be consistent, they have all the truth that the case admits of" in *The Charles S. Peirce Papers.* Cambridge, Massachusetts: Harvard University Library, Photographic Service, 1966; copies housed in the Institute for Pragmaticism, Texas Tech University. (Reference numbers as per *Annotated Catalogue of the Papers of Charles S. Peirce* by R. S. Robin.) Amherst: University of Massachusetts Press, 1967, 1865a:257.

64. About levels of abstraction, Oller (*Collected Background Readings,* 20–21) shows that separating the object from its context is *discrimination,* separating the percepts of the object from its materiality (in upwardly-spiraling, widening levels) is *precission,* and finally the idea to apprehend an object without its materiality is *hypostasis.* Such operations are essential for a Christian, who must not see all signs or symbols as homogenous nor equal; just as we have noted Christians must know the difference between a fact and any representation of it.

65. These three broad categories often contain complex combinations of the three types. According to Oller, all indices, for instance, consist of at least three distinct icons; and all symbols consist of what he calls "a Trinity of Trinities of the three basic kinds of signs. Thus every symbol can be analyzed into a Trinity of symbols and each of its symbolic elements is a similar Trinity." See John W. Oller Jr. and Steven Collins, "The Logic of True Narrative Representations" online at *Biblical Research Bulletin:* http://biblicalresearchbulletin.com/Biblical_Studies.html for a more complete look at this concept.

66. The word *icon* is the transliteration of a Greek word we find in Colossians 1:15 where Jesus is pictured as being a physical representation of the invisible God.

67. Strawn taught representational subjects to a small congregation in Whitharral, Texas, for many years. Among the members of the congregation was a six-year-old child, Sarah Board, who listened to Strawn's discussion of the difference between an icon in one's head and the physical object in the real world. Later Sarah was attending another church's Sunday school class in which the teacher held up a drawing of multi-colored, curved parallel lines and asked, "What's this?" The other children shouted, "A rainbow!" while Sarah calmly corrected them: "No, that's the *icon* of a rainbow." Proof, indeed, that even a young person can identify the difference between a fact and a representation of that fact.

68. In 1 John chapter 1, the apostle tells the readers of his epistle to appropriate his sensory experiences (what he saw, heard, and touched) as if they were our own. However, this is not a template for all Christians to follow: John shows repeatedly that what he'd experienced was no idiosyncratic event—it was an index to the reality of a living, resurrected Savior with whom he'd had firsthand experience and had divine authority to represent to others.

69. In Scripture, some unexpected things show up as links. For instance, in Philippians 1:28 the quality of courage is called an index (transliteration of the Greek word) because it connects the intentions of God to people, some of whom will be destroyed and others saved.

70. Of course, some words are indexical, like the words "this" or "that," as Eco points out. "Primary indexicality occurs when we attract someone's attention, not necessarily to speak to him, but just to show him something that will have to become a sign or an example, and we tug his jacket, we turn-his-head-toward." Umberto Eco, *Kant and the Platypus: Essays on Language and Cognition,* trans. Alastair McEwen (New York: Harcourt Brace & Company, 1977), 14.

71. "Speech is not limited to the field of spoken language: the heavens, day, night, all tell stories although their voice is not heard (Ps 19:2–5). Events, acts and behaviors are all said to be 'speech' (with a Greek word, *rhema,* used for that specific purpose) when they are spoken of, when they incite people to speak, or when they embody or incarnate speech (e.g., Gen. 15:1; 22:16; Deut. 4:32; 1 Kgs. 11:41; Luke 2:15, 17, 19)," according to Jean Delorme in Daniel Patte, ed., *Thinking in Signs: Semiotics and Biblical Studies, Thirty Years After* (The Society of Biblical Literature, 1998), 51.

72. Oller shows the versatility of linguistic signs, which may represent icons, indices, or other word-type symbols: "A linguistic sign may be used to represent any sensory sign, any motive sign, or any other linguistic sign. There is a generality of applicability of linguistic signs that is missing from the other two agentive sign systems." Oller, Jr., *Collected Background Readings,* chapter 2, 6.

73. For a fascinating discussion of facts and representations, Oliver Sack's *Seeing Voices: A Journey into the World of the Deaf* (New York: Harper Collins, 1990) recounts the way this famous neuroscientist demonstrates that formalized sign language functions as this kind of representation, and furthermore proves that without the ability to use language in some form, even the most intelligent human being is unable to even conceptualize abstracts. This book may be the very best illustration I discovered in "popular literature" of the use of "facts/representations" terminology and applications.

74. Oller points out that the sciences, including mathematics, cannot use signs in a "strictly consistent way," but the Bible shows a source of complete consistency in One who cannot lie (Num. 23:19), is always the same (Heb. 13:8), and the source of all perfections (Jame 1:17). *Collected Background Readings* chapter 1, page 2.

75. A compelling example of the power of linguistic symbols is seen in the emphasis God continually puts on His own name. Calling on that Name evokes a mental image of His attributes (who He is) and sets up a triad: the fact of His attributes, linked by the Holy Spirit's revelation of Him through Scripture, to the linguistic representation of His Name which carries power beyond the letters or phonemes that constitute its surface form.

76. We have previously seen in diagrammatic form a visual chart developed by Dr. John Oller Jr. known as a *pragmatic map* which demonstrates the gulf between facts and representations. Its

triadic structure has influenced the field of Representational Studies perhaps more than any other visual element. Oller equates it with Peirce's concept of "abduction" and quotes the philosopher's description of "a picture of all meaningful acts of representation" that "holds true regardless of whether we are thinking of the production, comprehension, or acquisition of sign systems." Oller also believed that the pragmatic map was a method that "clarifies a particular version of the correspondence theory of truth," according to the *Collected Background Readings* section, "Methods That Work," page 380. (Scott and Strawn later expanded on the correspondence and connected theories of truth—see "A Study of Angels: An Application of the Connective and Correspondence Theories of Truth" by Scott and "The Refuge" by Strawn.) As to the developmental forms of the pragmatic map, Oller himself recounts that in 1983 his friend Steve Kimble introduced him to a kind of diagram that Oller later developed into his pragmatic map. Since then, of course, Strawn has produced countless variations on the theme: God as ultimate Fact, the gulf unbridgeable except by Divine initiative, which comes to bear on this present world where we form and deal with representations.

77. As illustrated in Oller's "Einstein's Gulf: Can Evolution Cross It?", *Impact* #327, September 2000, http://www.icr.org/i/pdf/imp/imp-327.pdf.

78. One of Oller's greatest contributions is his pragmatic map, which shows visually the concept of the great "gulf" that exists between the realm of facts and the realm of representations, only bridgeable by an index or connecting element.

79. Oller shows that "the association of truth only with representations and not with concrete objects or states of affair is absolute" because "common sense is unaware that it knows facts only through representations." *Collected Background Readings* section, "Methods that Work," 381.

80. Eco uses the example of burning his hand on his coffee percolator one morning and then getting up the next morning and absentmindedly burning it again in precisely the same way. "The moment I feel the sensation of pain, a point in my nervous apparatus is activated that is the same one activated the day before and that point, in activating itself, in the same way makes me feel, along with the sensation of heat, a feeling of 'again.'" Eco, *Kant and the Platypus,* 103–104.

81. Collins and Oller demonstrate that "if the Bible is true, it can no more be tested against our experience (or against archaeology) than we can test the dictum that [an individual] was human and therefore destined to die against [that individual's death]. Nor could anyone test the statement that he or she must die by up and dying. Rather, if the Biblical narrative is true, archaeological claims must be tested against what it says. . . . the Bible is the basis against which our experience (archaeology included) must be tested. Only if the Bible is false can it reasonably be tested against experience." "Is the Bible a True Narrative Representation?" *Global Journal of Classical Theology,* vol. 2, no. 2, 8–2000; online at http://www.trinitysem.edu/journal/collins_ollerpap.html

82. Peter Briggs points out, "The essence of sin is to embrace the representations of material facts in preference to God's representations of those facts." Private correspondence, Briggs to Scott.

83. Linguists speak of "discourse constraints" which Strawn would identify as physics and physiology—in other words, the world would say we can only "sensibly" speak of those things that are conceivable as physically "possible." However, the Bible is replete with examples of God acting against discourse constraints and enabling His people to do so as well.

84. Deuteronomy 1:10–36.

85. Numbers 13:33.

86. Unfortunately, many Christians have a "dyadic" view of reality, in which things happen like dominoes —one event impacting and affecting the next. However, a Christian would have to see all events as triadic—in which there is an active, linking agent in a believer's life between such events (see Scott/Strawn: "The Domino Effect: The Myth of Dyadicity.")

87. Oller would qualify this statement: "The past is seen in the present. Therefore, if we have a true view in the present, the past is also truly understood. Both are transformed so completely as to be new creations. However, it is not true that the past is any less representational, nor any less real than the present. All is present from God's perspective; and His representations are the ones

that determine how things really are. Ours need to be subordinated to God's because His are true." Private correspondence, Oller to Scott.

88. When Paul chose this new representation of his past—acting on the premise that his sinful past didn't preclude his subsequent redemption—he concluded that what he knew could help others. In other words, his new representations could be the basis on which others would also build representations about their own pasts: they would *generalize* from his experience to their own.

89. Colossians 1:15–16.

90. 2 Peter 1:21.

91. Matthew 6:10.

92. Strawn. A recurrent phrase in his writings and speaking.

93. This is a bit sticky, for as Oller points out, the very idea of precedence involves material form in space and time. However, as Oller observes, God and His representations are both timeless and spaceless and boundless, yet they provide the "ground" for the creation of all other objects.

94. Again, from Oller's observation, this would be a timeless kind of precedence, seen as one thing preceding another in time only when viewed from the human (temporal) regard.

95. Jean Delorme, in *Thinking in Signs,* draws a distinction between the way that semiotic study of the Bible would see the type-antitype relationship, and the way that traditional exegesis would see it, saying, "Semiotics talks of 'figures' differently than exegesis that deals with the 'realities' of the Old Testament as 'figures' or 'types' of 'realities' of the New Testament" (47). Though both would involve what Delorme calls "a signifying process," he says that exegesis would see type-antitype as veiled-manifested; whereas semiotics would see the same figures as "a chain of signifiers that call each other."

96. Second Thessalonians 2:9 speaks of lying signs, which doesn't mean that the outward form of the sign isn't real, but rather that its intended purpose is not to promote truth. Deuteronomy 13:1–3 also speaks of "lying prophets" who can apparently produce "true" signs.

97. In 1835 Joseph Smith speaks of "the coming of the Lord, which was nigh—even fifty-six years should wind up the scene." (*History of the Church*, vol. 2, page 182).

98. Just because something is a representation does not make it true, as Oller points out in his helpful discussion of fictions, errors, and lies, in *Collected Background Readings* chapter 2, pages 9–10.

99. Online at https://www.youtube.com/watch?v=nR3uxbxRUz8

100. Representational language crops up in secular literature in surprising ways. A recent newspaper review (no author listed) of the book, *The Violet Quill Reader: The Emergence of Gay Writing After Stonewall,* quotes the editor as saying, "The very act of representing gay life altered that life, by indicating that it was worthy of depiction, of creative energy"—an acknowledgment that representations can indeed influence facts.

101. J. Michael Strawn in conversation regarding Psalm 145.

102. Online at http://sidneyrigdon.com/criddle/rigdon1.htm.

103. Personal correspondence, Criddle to Scott, 2015. Not all non-Mormon scholars would agree with former-Mormon Criddle's explanation of the origins of the Book of Mormon.

104. Strawn speaks of "the persistent absence of the apparency of correspondence between both human experience and the Word of God, and the sensorium and the Word of God," noting that experience routinely corresponds to the sensorium, leading most people to think these are both accurate because of that consensus. (Unpublished writings.)

105. 2 Peter 1:21.

106. Scott/Strawn's short article, "The Myth of Historical Distance," demonstrates that since we access all facts only through representations, then we are all equidistant to all representations. Thus it is nonsense to think of Bible events as being "way back there" in time, while thinking of our own experiences as more immediate and thus closer to us.

107. It is significant that God apparently chooses to limit what He thinks about. The book of Jeremiah depicts God as repeatedly saying that child sacrifice, for instance, was so heinous to Him that He declares that He never commanded or sanctioned such a thing "nor did it enter my mind." (Jer. 7:31; 19:5; 32:35)

108. "Adding Abstract to Formal and Content Schemata: Results of Recent Work in Peircean Semiotics" in *Collected Background Readings in Biblical Representational Research*, n.p. All the quotations from Oller in this section are from this article, which unfortunately as printed does not contain page numbers. It is also online at http://www.iupui.edu/~arisbe/menu/library/aboutcsp/oller/SCHEMATA.HTM.

109. Peter Briggs. "Testing the Factuality of the Conquest of Ai Narrative in the Book of Joshua" online at http://www.phc.edu/journalfiles/factuality.pdf.

110. Howard/Simon & Schuster, 2013.

111. Oller, Jr., *Collected Background Readings*.

112. See Palmer's website: http://mormonthink.com/gptimeline.htm.

113. Everything, that is, except for the one conundrum I've never been able to track logically in Mormonism: How, without a body, did the Holy Ghost get to be a god?

114. Richard and Joan Ostling cite witnesses who depict the historical accounts of the seagull incident as not at all the unique, supernatural event of Mormon lore. Richard N. Ostling and Joan K. Ostling, *Mormon America* (New York: HarperCollins, 2007), 241–42.

115. Scott, *The Mormon Mirage*, 293–94.

4

SOCIAL CONSEQUENCES OF MORMON TEACHINGS: FINDING POST-MORMON MENTAL HEALTH

Lynn K. Wilder

TESTIMONY

What's a BYU scholar to do? I was captivated by erudition. Hence, I conquered an undergraduate degree and persisted to a master's before our children were born. In 1977, I was earning a master's at Ball State University in Muncie, Indiana. Why Ball State? For my professional field of special education, focus in emotional/behavioral disorders, the program was ranked third in the nation. My grad student husband of three years, Michael, and I wanted to join a faith family and attend a Christian church. He had been raised Baptist and my family attended Presbyterian and Methodist churches. We both believed in Jesus and thought Christianity would give us a moral compass, but neither of us seriously read nor studied the Bible. We were nominal Christians with no real comprehension of who Jesus is or what He did for us, the very basics of biblical faith.

One day two Mormon missionaries knocked on the door of our little home just off campus on Rex Street. Michael was home alone working on his master's thesis. I was away teaching school to students who lived in abject rural poverty. The missionaries subsequently told us they were experts in "latter-days" (the Church of Jesus Christ of Latter-day Saints) or what biblical Christians call "last days" issues. This topic was of interest to me. I had just read in the Old Testament about Israel returning to her homeland which I knew happened in 1948 (Isa. 66:7–8; Ezek. 37:10–14; Deut. 30:3–5). After ten weeks of meeting with the missionaries two nights a week and being love-bombed and dined by local LDS ward (congregation) members, Mike took their challenge to ask God whether the Book of Mormon was true (Book of Mormon, Moroni 10:4–5).

I did not pray about it. If it was true, they said, Joseph Smith, church founder, *had* to be a prophet of God and the LDS Church the one true church. We assumed it was a Christian option and one that required full commitment. Michael had a dream soon after that prayer in which he was defending the Mormon people against their attackers. That was enough to convince him the Book of Mormon must be true and the Mormon people God's people.

Today we see our work as defending the dear LDS people against that which is *not* true. But I'm getting ahead of my story. After our study with the missionaries, we were baptized into the Church of Jesus Christ of Latter-day Saints Saturday evening October 28, 1977. Although I was skeptical at first, I told Michael I would try the faith alongside him. Immediately, we were given church callings to keep us busy and involved. Almost immediately, we connected with our new friends and their strange culture (that included such things as no beer at their parties), feeling we had a place among them. Within six months, I was weeping at the church pulpit, bearing testimony that the Mormon Church was the one and only church on the earth, with which the Lord was well pleased.

In Mormonism, we were taught that the obligatory role for women who wanted to obey Heavenly Father and the LDS prophets was to stay home and have a gaggle of children, and not pursue an academic career. To be a procreator with God was considered the highest honor for women. After five years of marriage, two years after joining Mormonism, our first precious baby came along. I was smitten and intended to obey the prophet, stay home and have a Wilder throng. I had labored joyfully in my chosen professional field until the children came. And then by the time I was thirty-three, we were blessed with three adored and active sons.

Independent, educated, and impassioned about my professional field, I loved my boys and desired to help the family financially by adding to motherhood part-time work in my field of training. Michael had been carrying the financial burden alone for some years now. Work took him away from us nearly twelve hours a day with a forty-five minute drive to and from his work and our now larger home in the country. Church leadership callings took him away another night or two a week and several hours on Sundays. When our third son was born, we looked for a way for Michael to be home with his sons more. Our solution was to move the family closer to the LDS ward building where we all spent so much time now. Mike moved his accounting business into our new home in Yorktown, Indiana, on seven acres along White River, and his parents moved into the home's mother-in-law apartment. I went to work a day and a half a week. We saw this as working together as an extended family and a solution preferable to one of us working long hours and the other raising kids with little support. Grandma and Grandpa Wilder were thrilled to be more intimately involved in their grandsons' lives.

For years I was able to teach GED (General Educational Diploma) in public school adult education, a juvenile center, a jail, a mental health facility, or the unemployment office. For a time, I worked as a coordinator of education programs at five homeless shelters. Later, I had a position with a federal Head Start grant and taught at a university. Social service work seemed a Christian thing in which to engage. Part-time work for me was the perfect answer to the problem of kids having a near-absent father. It renewed me. I loved it. My husband loved it. Life was good.

Our family read, heard, believed, taught, and defended Mormon doctrine from the words of the Mormon prophets and from LDS scripture. I truly believed it and strove to live as I was taught, as did Michael and the children. Besides teaching LDS seminary and serving as a Relief Society President, Young Women's President, and Stake Primary President over the years, I worked with Michael as an ordinance worker in the Chicago temple for ten years. We lived as faithful and active members of the Church of Jesus Christ of Latter-day Saints. My in-laws were delighted to watch the children just once a week and to be occupied with their own various activities. As Baptists, they were quite confused about something their pastor had told them: that we, as Mormons, believed we could have sex in heaven. Michael spent the one evening a week that I worked with our kids; he was home every night except when church callings required. Our boys—Josh, Matt, and Micah—were safe and happy, climbing trees, chasing frogs, and running, running, running in the woods. As they got older, they were allowed to fish at the river. In 1988, our last child and only daughter, Katie, was born.

As these precious children grew older, I ached to further my education, missing the rigor of absorbing new information. The world was so full of knowledge, and emerging technology made it more and more accessible. Loving the healing fields, I considered medical school, but that would be too difficult to manage with family and church responsibilities, and expensive as well. Loving logical sequential inquiry, I considered law school; my husband suggested my tongue needed no more honing. He was probably right about that. So, I acquiesced to the Mormon Heavenly Father and gave up on exercising my brain too energetically in ways that would lead to more time outside the home. My reading and studying were largely confined to teaching LDS seminary, conducting genealogical research, and other church-related classes. Occasionally, I read historical fiction. Ironically, I might have engaged the powers of reasoning more often in matters of faith. But life in Mormonism was good. I had no reason to doubt the Heavenly Father who blessed my righteous efforts with the good life. I chose to be content with family and LDS Church responsibilities, and I gave up any notions of researching anything besides genealogy—a staunch requisite from LDS scripture was to save my dead ancestors through LDS temple ordinances so I could save myself. I searched my family history for at least twenty years. In the words of LDS scripture: "And now, my dearly beloved brethren and sisters, let me assure you that these are principles in relation to the dead and the living that cannot be lightly passed over, as pertaining to our salvation. For their salvation is necessary and essential to our salvation, as Paul says concerning the fathers—that they without us cannot be made perfect—neither can we without our dead be made perfect."[1]

Spiritual Experience

Then in October of 1990, I experienced something that had never happened to me before. Something so strange and spiritual in nature, I hesitate to mention it, but it is central to my story. One night, at 2:00 a.m., I sat bolt upright out of a deep sleep. Did someone call my name? I could not go back to sleep the rest of the night. Typically if sleep did not come, I read my LDS scriptures to try to bore myself back to sleep and then I prayed. The next night, again about 2:00 a.m., I think I heard, "Lynn?"

Bolt upright. LDS scriptures and fervent prayer all night long. No sleep again. If I had known the story of Samuel and Eli in the Old Testament (1 Sam. 3), I might have suspected God was calling. But I didn't make the connection. Third night, same thing. I was getting bone-tired. I had four children, church callings, a part-time job, and now elderly and ailing in-laws to care for. I had completely conceded the idea of obtaining further secular knowledge some years ago. I was just too engaged in the role of the typical Mormon mom. Fourth night, "Lynn?"

What?! Bolt upright. This occurred fourteen nights in a row. And then it happened. I think God spoke to me. Being thoroughly exhausted and quite agitated, I called out to Heavenly Father in the early morning of the fourteenth night in a way a Mormon was not supposed to talk to him, disrespectfully. Instead, I was supposed to be courteous, deferential using King James English with "thee" and "thou." But I was depleted.

"If You want me to do something," I said, (because in Mormonism, it was always about me doing something to please Heavenly Father to make any glitches in life right), "just tell me because I *can't* stay up another night!"

That's when I heard—or did I sense—a voice say two things. One was, "I need for you to go back to school." *Did I really hear that? How odd. Why would Heavenly Father want me to go back to school?* The LDS prophet, Ezra Taft Benson, had spoken at a special "fireside" or informal meeting for women three years earlier to ask women to "come home from their typewriters."[2] As Relief Society president, I was the object of scorn from several women who did not want to support me as their leader precisely because I worked a day and a half a week.

Why then would God Himself ask me to go back to school? Wasn't that instruction in direct contrast to what the Mormon prophet, the mouthpiece for Heavenly Father on the earth, just said to women? Wouldn't a doctorate lead to full-time work in academia? Maybe God did speak to me and maybe He didn't, but this occurrence and the subsequent decision my husband and I made would play out for a purpose antithetical to Mormonism in years to come.

I took one doctoral course in educational leadership and hated it. So I didn't take a second. I ignored the middle-of-the-night communication partly because I was not sure it actually came from God. Then in December of 1994 and February of 1995, two months apart to the day, I was in two fairly bad automobile accidents. For the next eighteen months, I went to physical therapy twice a week, where a therapist worked on me ninety minutes at a time as I lay on a table with soft music playing. I was finally still enough from my harrowing LDS life to just think. My experience from 1990 was hard to believe but it seemed real. I remembered the instruction and thought about it often, lying still on that table, and finally decided I should return to school in earnest. So I took a job teaching at the university to pay my tuition and set on a course to complete the degree.

For four years, I taught at the university during the day, was home for my kids' activities after school and to make dinner, went to night class twice a week, studied often until 1:00 a.m. after class, and then got up to teach early morning LDS seminary for Mormon high school students in our home by 5:30 or 6:00 a.m. Michael helped out a lot on the days I just could not get out of bed that early, although some terms I had 8:00 a.m. classes to teach at the university anyway. We enrolled our two youngest, Katie and Micah, at Burris, the university lab school, so they were only blocks from me. I got to know their friends as we carpooled to and from school.

In the summer of 1999, I graduated with the Dean's Citation for Academic Excellence, doctorate in education, focus in emotional/behavioral disorders. The immediate and extended families came. Our oldest son, Josh, was headed to Indiana University in the fall. Matt completed his freshman year in high school; Micah, the eighth grade; and Katie, the fourth grade. I was now an "expert" for anyone who struggled to achieve academic and social success in school. I didn't feel like much of an expert, but as LDS, I felt pressure to appear like I was. The burden to be seen as something I knew inside I was not troubled me over the years. We good LDS members were to rise above the crowd in our jobs, the military, the CIA, the FBI, other government positions; and in academia, we should hail from the best universities, so others would admire us and want to join the LDS Church.

Now what? Well, we would love to move to Zion, the Mormon version of the Vatican, the center of the religious universe. Although Christ would return to Missouri to the Mormon priesthood first, we were taught that living in Zion meant we would be aware of the latest and most critical news for his people in these latter-days. Procuring an academic job at the LDS "school of the prophets"—Brigham Young University in Provo, Utah—would be a prodigious achievement and would move our family to the heart of Heavenly Father's kingdom in Utah. There was an opening in the Department of Counseling Psychology and Special Education at BYU; and with effusive gratitude, I received an invitation for an interview.

Brigham Young University

In order to become full-time professorial faculty at Brigham Young University, I had to be interviewed and receive the approval of an LDS general authority who could determine my spiritual "worthiness." My interview took place in May of 1999. As I sat in the exquisitely carved wood environment in the old church office building in downtown Salt Lake, dressed in a women's suit and nervously rubbing my conservative heels together, I was closely watched by starched security men who followed me even to the restroom and stood outside to await my return. I was mildly amused. During the interview, the general authority, Elder Dennis Neuenschwander, said something curious. He said, "I've been interviewing faculty for BYU for many years and I've never come upon someone like you."

"How's that?" I asked.

He replied, "You've never lived in Utah, you've never attended BYU, and you're a pure convert."

"Wow," I thought. "Among my professional colleagues, there will be few if any converts to the LDS Church, few who came from outside of Utah, and few scholars schooled somewhere other than BYU?" I deduced that since I was different, the Heavenly Father of Mormonism must have unique work for me to do there. In 1999, I thought it was about me and my works. The LDS instruction that the glory of God is intelligence (D&C 93:36) can cultivate some vast egos; it did mine. Mormons quote from 1 Nephi 19:23, in the Book of Mormon, that advises people to "liken all scripture unto us." The implication was that it's all about me—my journey to exaltation as a queen or priestess to my husband; my performance, my appearance, my callings, my works, my intelligence; my worthiness to enter the temple. At times, this was a great encumbrance. That was my Mormon mindset: focus on yourself; good works get you to the celestial kingdom.

Elder Neuenschwander determined I had sufficient testimony of Joseph's "restored gospel" and was worthy to teach at BYU, serving as a role model for women. In fact, he said Heavenly Father had called me to mentor female students. We moved the family to a quaint little mountain community, Alpine, Utah, and I drove the forty-five minutes to Provo for the next eight years. Mike established his own business. The three younger kids adjusted to life in Utah. My very life as a tenured professor at BYU exemplified and honored LDS doctrine and the men who preached it. I loved to go to work, taking scriptures to faculty meetings. I loved my colleagues. I loved that I could pray with my students, and I loved the Mormon Church and its leaders. When the prophet visited the Marriott Center to speak to the students and faculty, faculty were allowed to transit through the Marriot Center via the underground tunnels. Oh, how I hoped to come upon a general authority or the prophet himself as I sauntered slowly, dillydallying there. I knew that's where the revered men would transit from car to stage. I couldn't wait too long, though, or the good seats up front would already be taken.

In 2001, Matt graduated from high school and came to BYU on a scholarship. Josh had transferred from Indiana University to the University of Utah. Matt came to see me on Tuesdays so we could attend the weekly campus devotional and eat at a buffet, Chuck-a-Rama, afterward. (Eating is important to Matt.) In 2003, Micah also came to BYU on a scholarship. We always sat up front at devotionals in the Marriott Center with pens ready to take notes.

BYU was good for my professional career, providing what any professor would envy. The university paid research assistants to help with research, provided funds for me to travel to national and international conferences about four times a year, and encouraged me to join writing groups to publish. Colleagues were kind and collaborative. We worked together well. We had what we needed in terms of materials and supplies and clerical assistance. Life was good. As a hard-working individual, I was able to advance in rank to associate professor a year early and attain tenure the following year, in 2004. I began to write prolifically.

My students at BYU were intelligent, diligent, sincere, and religious, although sometimes lacking a bit in social and dating skills, something of which the university was cognizant and working to improve. LDS youth were expected to marry and have children as soon as possible. I loved them and they accepted me, working conscientiously in their academics. However, in due course, I began to wonder if something wasn't quite right at BYU and maybe in the theocratic system of Mormonism itself. One of my bosses used to say, "BYU, like the LDS Church, is a theocracy, not a democracy," as former LDS professor Michael Quinn describes.[3] As a BYU professor, I went into the heart of the Mormon Church to learn the heart of the Mormon Church and in some ways, it began to surprise me. Oh, at first I was extremely emotional about being on campus at the "Lord's university," feeling blessed beyond what I deserved to be in such an honored position. But, over time things happened that caused me to furrow my brow and wonder.

According to Mormonism, Dark Skin is a Curse

In the fall of 2000, I was assigned to teach multiculturalism/diversity. Given my experience with marginalized students (homeless, juvenile delinquents, special education students, English language learners, dropouts, ethnically diverse students, etc.), I was excited to teach this. In that first multicultural course, BYU students taught me about the inanity called "the curse of Cain" with its racist implications. They said it came from the Bible. Being LDS, I did not trust the Bible. The LDS Eighth Article of Faith says, "We believe the Bible to be the word of God as far as it's translated correctly…." Believing the Bible was often mistranslated, I didn't even go to the passage about Cain and Abel and investigate whether it said Cain was cursed with dark skin for killing his brother. I simply assumed that the unreliable, flawed Bible must teach something crazy and inaccurate like the dark-skin curse of Cain. Although I had taught the Bible (and the other LDS scriptures) as a Mormon seminary teacher, I did not remember that teaching. For my BYU students who were convinced that this dark-skin-is-a-curse notion had scriptural support, an open-minded class discussion about race was pointless.

At the time, I considered teaching this course as a challenge to change hearts, and I did see BYU students occasionally burst into tears as they realized the full import of their negative beliefs and actions on real people. I made it a service learning course requirement for students to go into a cultural environment different than their own for sufficient time for them to get attached to individuals from another culture and to rethink personal biases. Nevertheless, when students knew that racist ideas were defensible by LDS scripture combined with the statements of past prophets, making headway with them seemed nearly impossible. In fairness, I will say that current LDS general authorities have spoken against racism. For instance, from former prophet Gordon B. Hinckley in 2006: "Today, the Church disavows the theories advanced in the past that black skin is a sign of divine disfavor or curse, or that it reflects unrighteous actions in a premortal life; that mixed-race marriages are a sin; or that blacks or people of any other race or ethnicity are inferior in any way to anyone else. Church leaders today unequivocally condemn all racism, past and present, in any form."[4]

In fairness, many BYU students did not express racist ideas, and some of my current students, who are not LDS, do. Nevertheless, numerous racist scriptures still exist in official LDS sources that I was oblivious to at the time, the most indefensible being the Standard Works of LDS scripture.

Thus, seemingly on cue, our college was placed on probation by our accrediting agency for not meeting standards for diversity. The college diversity committee of which I was a member created occasions for both faculty and students to have crucial conversations about, and to implement, culturally responsive behavior. Colleagues and I wrote a grant, subsequently funded by the federal government, to provide scholarships for tuition and books that brought ethnically diverse, bilingual, and/or individuals with disabilities into a dual certification program to become teachers. As co-director of that program (the other director was off campus) and mentor for diverse students, I was wholly engaged in and loved the work of helping diverse students acclimate to BYU and the sometimes greater challenge of BYU acclimating to them. Students had my cell number and it rang all day and evening long, just as it had done when I was Relief Society president. As I immersed myself in multicultural issues and professional literature, I became increasingly disturbed about the history of racism in the Mormon Church. Blacks were restricted from holding the Mormon priesthood until 1978. Why would a loving God not allow one particular people group to live with Him in the next life? Doubts about Mormon teachings were surfacing. But they were not enough yet to rock my solid LDS testimony.

Typically, several times a year in my role as faculty, I present research at professional national/international conferences. If it hadn't been for a

Native American gentleman who stood up at such a convention and heckled me while I, representing BYU, was presenting research on a multicultural topic, I would not have known that blacks had not been allowed to attend BYU in the 1960s. This man stood and announced it to the crowd. Later when I returned to BYU and inquired about it, I was handed John Lund's book *The Church and the Negro*.[5] It contained some shocking truths about the racist words and policies of past prophets, apostles, and general authorities in the Mormon Church in fairly contemporary history regarding blacks. It was true. Blacks could not attend BYU in the sixties and interracial dating was forbidden. This provoked some *serious* reflection, but not yet ideas of apostasy.

Although I had known from the time we joined the church or soon after that blacks were only given the right to hold the Mormon priesthood in 1978, I never really thought about how that had kept them from the privilege of eternal life, defined in the LDS missionary *Preach My Gospel* manual, as living "forever as families in God's presence."[6] The priesthood restriction for blacks was so detestable a thought, I didn't like to think about it. That was behind us with the 1978 revelation to the prophet Spencer W. Kimball. Thank God. I was unaware, however, of the LDS black-skin-is-a-curse scriptures or that the Book of Mormon said the dark skin of some Lamanites (Native Americans and others) turned white when they became righteous. Instead of leading me away from the church, I wanted to be a part of the solution and teach this generation of BYU students that racism has no place in Heavenly Father's church. Maybe God woke me up fourteen nights in a row and eventually sent me to BYU to stem the tide of racism among Mormon youth, I surmised.

Eventually, in 2007, I discovered these racist teachings did not come from the Bible but from decidedly Mormon scriptures, the Pearl of Great Price and the Book of Mormon (see LDS scriptures: Abraham Chapter 1 and Moses Chapter 7 in the Pearl of Great Price; and references to "cursing" and "a skin of blackness" in 1, 2, and 3 Nephi, Jacob, Alma, and Mormon in the Book of Mormon).[7]

For me the existence of racist ideas in LDS scripture was a conundrum of mammoth proportions, but by the time I discovered the scriptures, I had already decided Mormonism was not true. Recent essays from the LDS Church on lds.org point to Brigham Young as the initiator of racism, but, truly, it was the church founder, Joseph Smith, who purportedly dispensed these scriptures from Jesus Himself. This topic of racist LDS scripture has been addressed in a chapter of my book *Unveiling Grace: The Story of How We Found Our Way Out of the Mormon Church*.[8] But for thirty years in the LDS Church, I never knew those scriptures were in our own Standard Works.

Modern-Day Polygamy

While supervising BYU student teachers in local Utah schools and visiting public places like restaurants, I encountered families who were obviously living polygamy. I thought polygamy was behind us as church members. Given the Doctrine and Covenants Section 132 scripture supporting polygamy that still exists in LDS scripture, and thus is doctrine, it was clear then as now that men could be sealed to more than one woman for time and all eternity in any LDS temple still today. However, a man was limited to one wife here on earth—the other wives would be for the eternities.

Doctrine and Covenants 132 taught and still teaches that polygamy is an eternal principle. We knew this because Mike and I had been temple workers for ten years. In addition, I heard a story from a reliable neighbor, Lauretta Larsen, about an LDS ancestor of hers who was a judge in Salt Lake and was called to live polygamy by the prophet himself years after the 1890 Manifesto (supposedly from God) was purported to have put a stop to the practice.

Michael and I were shocked to hear this. We could not fathom that the prophet would lie to the outside world while continuing to engage in a practice he had sworn had stopped in the LDS Church because of a revelation from Jesus Himself. Did the prophet lie? Why would he lie?

I did know that Joseph Smith had practiced polygamy before he told his wife, Emma, who was understandably not happy with this "revelation." The polygamy-is-an-eternal-principle revelation to Joseph Smith, Doctrine and Covenants 132, was the last revelation received before he was murdered. Joseph practiced polygamy (or perhaps in the beginning, adultery) since at least 1831 until his death in 1844, but he denied he was practicing it and the church did not make it scripture until 1876. He lied. I had read a biography of Joseph's long-suffering wife, *Mormon Enigma: Emma Hale Smith*, in the 1980s. Joseph Smith's own words in the month before his death were these: "What a thing it is for a man to be accused of committing adultery, and having seven wives, when I can only find one."[9] I didn't like that Smith had lied, but assumed he must have had reasons that involved protecting Jesus's church from the ravenous wolves.

As Relief Society president in our ward, I was charged to teach a lesson on polygamy each year. Like Emma, the women of the ward did not like the idea of polygamy as an eternal principle, either. While in Denmark in 2004 to pick Matt up from his LDS mission, we were embarrassed to watch the Danish news do a story on polygamy in Utah. The state of Utah had turned a blind eye to it (for one hundred years according to a magazine article) except for some feeble attempts to prosecute one woman during the time of the Olympics and the charge was not polygamy. From that article in *USA Today*: "The woman, Suzie Stubbs Holm, 36, is part of a polygamous household in rural Utah. But she is not directly charged with polygamy. Instead, she is accused of getting her sixteen-year-old sister to marry into the household."[10]

One early Mormon polygamist, apostle Orson Pratt (1835–1881), stated: "If the doctrine of polygamy, as revealed to the Latter-day Saints, is not true, I would not give a fig for all your other revelations that came through Joseph Smith the Prophet; I would renounce the whole of them . . . ."[11] Orson Pratt had ten wives. At the age of fifty-seven, he married a sixteen-year-old girl, younger than his daughter. I abhorred hearing about polygamy and so did Michael. He agreed never to take a second wife, even for the next life, so I tried to ignore polygamy unless it appeared in my scripture readings for the day. I learned from the Book of Mormon, Jacob 1:15 that some people began to "indulge "themselves somewhat in wicked practices, such as like David of old desiring many wives and concubines, and also Solomon, his son." And from Jacob 2:24, "Behold, David and Solomon truly had many wives and concubines, which thing was abominable before me, saith the Lord." These scriptures acknowledged for me that the Book of Mormon, the most correct book on the earth, taught that the actions of David and Solomon having many wives and concubines was an abomination before the Lord.

But later LDS doctrine says Jesus amended that teaching when he gave Joseph Smith Doctrine and Covenants 132:1, "Wherein I, the Lord, justified my servants . . . David and Solomon, my servants, as touching the principle and doctrine of their having many wives and concubines." This verse is in context and says the exact opposite as the Book of Mormon. In fact, the entire Section 132 supports the principle of polygamy, calling it the "new and everlasting covenant" and threatening Emma Smith, Joseph's first wife, with destruction if she does not abide this commandment (D&C 132:54). So Doctrine and Covenants 132:1 states that David and Solomon were justified in having many wives and concubines, but Jacob 2:24 in the Book of Mormon states the opposite: that David and Solomon's practice of having many wives was abominable before the Lord. As LDS, I was taught a modern prophet's voice trumped past words of prophets including words of scripture, so I assumed Heavenly Father changed his mind.

Mormons sometimes say that even the Book of Mormon does have one exception clause that actually supports polygamy for one purpose—raising up seed. We referred to Jacob 2:30 in the Book of Mormon, but it is not applicable when taken in context. "For if I will, saith the Lord of Hosts, raise up seed unto me, I will command my people; otherwise they shall hearken unto these things." The statement "raise up seed unto me" does not refer to the practice of polygamy. At the beginning of the Book of Mormon, Lehi's sons take wives that they might raise up seed unto the Lord (1 Nephi 7:1) and also says that "I, Nephi, took one of the daughters of Ishmael to wife" (1 Nephi 16:7). These instructions to Lehi's sons for raising up seed directed one man to marry one wife. The phrase "raising up seed" cannot be interpreted in Jacob 2:30 to mean one man must take several wives to do this. The context of this chapter of scripture wherein "raising up seed" is contained (Jacob 2:7–35) condemns the wickedness of the husbands for their abominations related to the practice of polygamy. Even if both the Doctrine and Covenants and the Book of Mormon could be wrenched to justify polygamy (which the Book of Mormon does not teach), modern Mormonism today distances itself publicly from the practice of polygamy. However, a worthy male priesthood holder can still be sealed to more than one woman in the temple to practice polygamy in the hereafter. Confusing? That's what the voice of a living prophet is for. (See the book *7 Reasons We Left Mormonism* for further information on polygamy.)[12]

Polygamy and racism were troublesome for me. These and other church-related issues in Utah surfaced as strange in Mormondom, but I did not research them too earnestly. I know that seems incredible to those outside of Mormonism, but I completely trusted the prophet, Gordon B. Hinckley, and the LDS Church. The polygamy I tried to ignore. That was for some in the next life and my own priesthood man said he wanted no part of it, so I figured I was safe. Although the LDS Church today vehemently denies that both polygamy and black-skin-is-a-curse teachings exist in the church, both doctrines *persist in LDS scripture.*

Truth Challenge

In 2001–2003 our first son, Josh, served an LDS mission to Russia. From 2002–2004, our second son, Matt, served his mission to Denmark. In 2004, our third son, Micah—zealous for the Mormon gospel—was assigned to serve in Mexico City. Those of us at home read our LDS scriptures, prayed for their success at spreading the Mormon doctrine, and went to church. While Micah was in the Missionary Training Center (MTC) in Provo, Utah, his lung collapsed and he was sent by the LDS prophet to Orlando, Florida, instead of to Mexico.

Within months we began to get emails from him that were full of Bible scripture. Micah was challenged by a Baptist pastor to read the Bible as a child would read it, and promised him his eyes would be opened and his life would never be the same if he did. Indeed, Micah read the New Testament perhaps a dozen times over during his mission, but not because he thought he had something to learn. Mormonism was certainly true, but he felt he had to find fuel to refute the biblical Christians he was stumbling upon and trying to teach on doorsteps in Florida, in the Bible Belt. Micah was a zone leader over about sixteen missionaries. As he read day after day, he came to trust Jesus's own words in the Bible and recognize that Jesus Himself opposed what Mormonism taught. Now, he didn't actually tell us this in his weekly missionary emails. He just sent us a lot of Bible verses to read and asked us to *please* read the New Testament.

I was really busy in my happy-valley Mormon life and didn't get around to picking up the Bible. Neither did Michael. Our prophet had challenged us to read the Book of Mormon every night as a family while Micah was gone. Once we finished, he asked us to read it again, this time in three months. I was an obedient servant of the LDS Church leaders and that was plenty of scripture reading for me. Scripture reading was perfunctory, an honest attempt to please the Mormon Christ, but not very interesting.

Three weeks before the end of Micah's mission, he was invited to stand before about sixty fellow missionaries in Florida to bear testimony of what he had learned on his mission. This opportunity was intended for a veteran missionary to remind the newbies and struggling ones that the Mormon Church is the one true church and Joseph Smith was undoubtedly a prophet of Heavenly Father. Once *extremely* zealous for the Mormon faith, Micah confessed at that pulpit what he knew for sure was that Jesus was enough. He had read in the Bible he didn't need a man (Joseph Smith) between him and God. Jesus was the only mediator between man and God. He wept as he shared that he knew Jesus had atoned for his sins on the cross. Mormonism has taught that the atonement happened in the Garden of Gethsemane. Micah asked the missionaries if they knew that Jesus loved them with a love they could not imagine. He knew he was loved like this. He asked them if each of them knew that Jesus saw their face as he looked down at them from the cross when he was paying the penalty for their sins (Isa. 53:10). Jesus took what we deserved, the penalty for our sins, and now it was finished. There was nothing Micah could do add to what Jesus had done for him. He was to believe in, to know Jesus Christ personally. He shed tears because Jesus loved him enough to do this for him and to give him an assurance of salvation. (This, too, refuted LDS doctrine since no Mormon has this assurance unless the prophet anoints his feet in the second anointing ceremony in the temple, an extremely rare occurrence saved for the most righteous leaders. LDS friends posted on Facebook that it happened to Mitt Romney right before the 2012 election.)

Two days later, Micah was called in by his mission president, quizzed for several hours, called an anti-Christ, told he had the spirit of the devil in him, made to relinquish his temple recommend, and threatened with excommunication from the LDS Church. Micah was unconquerable enough to tell the mission president he did not think he needed the Mormon Church to be saved. He knew Jesus had saved him. His leader deemed him unworthy to be a missionary of the LDS Church. As soon as Micah exited this meeting, he broke the missionary rules, and called me on his cell phone at home in Utah to say, "It's over," followed by a few brief details of the events of the meeting with his mission president. We did not know about his courageous testimony in front of the others at the time.

Soon we received a phone call from his mission president and our stake president, our regional leader in Utah. Both repeated much of what Micah had told us and said they would be contacting "the brethren" or "general authority" leaders in Salt Lake for a final decision about what to do with him. The next day they put him on a plane and sent him home. As soon as he landed, we were directed to take him directly to our stake president. This man was livid with Micah and cruel, declaring he had the spirit of the devil in him and referring to an anti-Christ named Nehor in Alma 1 in the Book of Mormon.

We were asked to bring Micah before the stake high council the next morning. If he professed biblical Christianity, we knew he would be "exxed." Mike and I looked at each other and shook our heads privately. We would not be taking him in. Within forty-eight hours, Micah left Utah for a job in Florida. We were glad to have him safely out of Utah and the arms of excommunication until we figured out what just happened to our most zealous son for the Mormon gospel. Before he boarded the plane for Florida, he begged, "Mom and Dad, *please* just read the New Testament like a child, with no preconceived ideas. Jesus is enough."

For Micah's sake and to figure out what he knew that was so powerfully impacting his young life (his twenty-first birthday was later that week), we said we would finally do so. Jesus (or Christ as I called him then) was the one, the only one, I thought I could trust in the middle of all this craziness. Truthfully, I did not trust the Bible, so I decided to go to the most correct book on the face of the earth first, the Book of Mormon, before the Bible to read the direct red-letter words of Jesus. Mormons don't have red-letters in their scriptures, but I remembered my old Protestant Revised Standard Version from my youth did have them. As a researcher, I considered Jesus a primary source of truth and the apostles and disciples who were with him secondary sources. Historical accounts like those of Josephus would be additional sources that triangulate the evidence.

I was surprised to discover that I couldn't actually find Jesus's words in the Book of Mormon, just in a small section of 3 Nephi—and at that, merely a copy of the Beatitudes from Matthew 5.

"Wow," I thought, "I guess I have to read the New Testament to hear what Jesus has to say."

Cautious of the Bible, I began in the book of John. I hadn't read far before I was learning things I hadn't known before about Jesus and his teachings; and little by little, I became insatiably hungry to learn. Again and again, I saw this gospel that Jesus and His apostles taught was *not* the gospel of Mormonism. What was I to do with that?! We had been taught the Bible had some of the truth and Mormonism built on that truth. But these truth claims were not at all compatible. They were contrary.

First, John the apostle taught in John 1:1 that Jesus was God from the beginning (eternity past). He didn't earn his way there. The Word, Jesus, came down and dwelt among men. I had to read that verse many times over for the full import of it to settle. John wrote one has the right to *become* a child of God through adoption at the point of believing in Jesus (John 1:12–13). No one is born a child of God, yet Mormonism teaches everyone is born a child of God. I learned when Jesus talked about the temple in John 2:19 he was referring to his body, not a physical temple. Later in Acts, I read that God does not live in temples made by human hands (Acts 17:24). A temple is not able to contain him.

In John chapter 3, I read that the born-again experience required for salvation does not necessarily include physical water baptism as the LDS

Church claims, but must include a baptism of the spirit. Jesus did not water baptize. His apostles did. This baptism of the Spirit mentioned does not require laying on of hands from a priesthood. I read in John 3:13 that no one has ever gone to heaven except the one who came from heaven, Jesus. What about the pre-existence? Didn't we live with Heavenly Father and Mother in heaven before we came to earth?

John 4:24 reports God the Father is spirit. He does not have a body of flesh and bone. John 5:24 delineates how to be saved. Hear my Word (the Word I'm reading and reading about), believe in God who sent the Word, and cross over right now. That's it. One can be assured of eternal life with God in the next life. "These are the very Scriptures that testify about me, yet you refuse to come to me to have life" (John 5:39–40). Ouch! It has to do with knowing Jesus, to surrendering to him to have life in him. Nowhere did I read that an organization represents him on the earth, although we as believers *are* the body of Christ, the church.

"How can you believe since you accept glory from one another but do not seek the glory that comes from the only God?" (John 5:44). The *only* God, not millions. All of those rules and measuring sticks in Mormonism are worthless? Micah had to report numbers of contact hours, numbers of people baptized, etc., on his mission. At BYU, I was feverishly counting publications and presentations and student evaluation numbers. I even had to report all of my church callings at BYU. Only God's praise counts?

In John 6, I read that the work God requires is to believe in Jesus. Period. It does not say genealogy or temple work, church callings or attendance, tithing or refraining from certain foods. It hit me hard that no one comes to Jesus unless the Father draws him. I knew I was being drawn. At that point, I promised not to read anything but the Bible for a whole year unless forced to do so for work. John 6:47 says, "He who believes *has* eternal life" (emphasis mine). Wow, no waiting to see if your works have mounted up to be enough for God's grace to kick in? Verse 63 says that these words are full of the Spirit. They are life. These words of life were having a powerful effect on me. I could not stop reading and pondering. John 8:47: "Whoever belongs to God hears what God says." I was beginning to hear. All these conflicts with Mormon teachings and scripture in just the first few chapters of the book of John. I've only mentioned a handful of the many I have marked in that first NIV student Bible. Two years ago, a friend took that old paperback, shabby and in-pieces student Bible and rebound it for me in leather. No better gift.

This Bible reading opened a whole new world to both Michael and me, as we labored in the Word, determined to find truth. And read we did, seriously, with our scientific-method, need-evidence-of-truth hats on (not our heads *in* our hats). In 2015, the LDS Church released a picture of the seer stone Joseph Smith used to "translate" the Book of Mormon: a seer stone placed in his hat, a known occult method of communication. One thing clear to me from my reading so far was that the words of Jesus Himself and the Bible teachings contradicted Mormon scripture and teachings—over and over and over again. Unfortunately, I could not recall a biblical Christian, in thirty years, ever telling me that Mormon Church teachings might need to be examined or that the Jesus of the Bible did not teach the same gospel as the Mormons. Or even that He loves me and saves me by his grace, that there is nothing I *can do* to add to what He did for me in love. I need simply to believe, to surrender my life, and to allow Him to work through me. Can't work my own way to be exalted. His works and plan for my life from now on. None of my own.

Micah had been challenging us to read the Word for months and months. When I finally did, I *loved* that the Bible invited me to investigate, to reason it out, to test all things. I could not put the Bible down. Its draw was stirring. I *did* believe in Jesus. But which one? The Mormon Jesus and the Bible Jesus taught different ways to be saved. They had different natures. Could I put aside the idea of "blind faith" in a living prophet and chase my doubts to their conclusion? There was no stopping me now.

My husband Michael was a high priest whom I revered for his dedication to his LDS faith. He had served in bishoprics and as a high councilor, a gospel doctrine teacher, seminary teacher, and temple worker. He, too, believed and trusted in the Mormon Church and the prophet—thirty years of dedication to this organization established by Joseph Smith. But he, too, loved his son dearly and took his challenge to read the Bible as a child. Months passed. We learned, thought, and talked. Mormonism had seemed like a great life, but was it all a ruse?

A Major Decision

Although racism and polygamy had bothered me for some time and the Bible was opening a whole new world, we kept attending church and praying with our children, not sure where all of this would lead. In the eighties and nineties, I had dabbled where I was warned by the LDS Church not to go by reading books like *Mormon Enigma: Emma Hale Smith* and Orson Scott Card's *Saints.* These books taught me the reality and horror of polygamy and Mormonism. I read *The Mormon Murders* about Mark Hofmann, and learned that this LDS counterfeiter and murderer was able to defraud church prophets, seers, and revelators by selling them forged historical documents. Did Mormon priesthood indeed have the ability to discern good from bad? I even read Hugh Nibley's daughter Martha Beck's books, *Expecting Adam* and *Leaving the Saints.* She claimed her famous BYU professor and church apologist father had ritually sexually abused her. I had no reason not to believe her. Why would someone concoct a story like that? Professor Nibley's funeral took place on campus in 2005 while I was teaching at BYU. I didn't attend, because I had read her first book.

In the summer of 2006, I was invited to travel with BYU colleagues to China for eleven days at the invitation of the Chinese Ministry of Education. I felt uncomfortable, as if someone might see the growing distrust of

Mormonism and hunger for Jesus on my face. I would characterize BYU professors as sacred cows. Our oldest Josh and youngest Katie went along on this trip. In the LDS Church, my husband and I and even our children held leadership callings and served diligently. Our kids knew we were questioning. However, that summer I was still trying to explain away the conflicts I was learning about with the whine, "But the Church is still true." It's a common refrain for those who put so many unresolved issues up on a proverbial shelf and ignore them. I was grateful to have family members traveling this road together, but we were not yet speaking up and out. We were still investigating the sense of something not quite right by using our analytical minds to think about it and trying to look at Mormonism from outside the box with an objective eye. The Bible helped me do this. Soon after we returned from China, I stopped "fulfilling my calling" at church. The reading continued and intensified.

One chilly October night in 2006, what I had been frantically reading for ten months came to a head. I *knew* Mormonism was not true: Joseph Smith's First Vision, the Book of Mormon and other LDS scriptures, the church organization, the temple ordinances, the priesthood authorities, none of it. I had endured some unexpected brutal blows to my sure testimony in that time, but once I started down the opening-my-mind-to-the-truth path, there was no turning back. The evidence was too persuasive and, the Jesus of the Bible at the end of the path much, much too compelling. I had a desperate desire to surrender my life to the Jesus of the Bible, to cross over once and for all from death to life. To rest in the work that He had done. That night after Michael and Katie went to bed, I lay facedown on the carpet, desperate to end the in-between and to decide. I stretched my arms out in the shape of a cross, and gave the rest of my life to the biblical Jesus. In fact, I did what I saw Martin Luther do and said the words I heard him say in the movie *Luther* that was the final straw culminating in a decision for Christ. "I'm yours. Save me." I didn't even know until 2014 that those words are in the Bible (Psalm 119:94). Everything changed.

What is unusual about my journey out of Mormonism and the journeys of family members is this. We did not learn Mormonism was false because we investigated LDS history like thousands have done. The Mormon Church currently is losing members at a distressing rate, according to Marlin K. Jensen, former church historian and general authority.[13] It wasn't the racism and polygamy that were the straws that broke my LDS camel's back. My knowledge of these things was quite surface, minimal. I was most comfortable ignoring them. *After* we decided Mormonism was false, we further investigated LDS history and discovered the skeletons in the closet and the LDS scriptures that were worse than we could have imagined. We were increasingly surprised to find Mormonism was not just a little off. The teachings and scriptures (such as man can become a god, dark skin is a curse, Native Americans are descended from Israelites, and polygamy is an eternal principle) were dangerous, poisonous, and an entanglement of outright lies. Now, the Mormon people were not perpetrating a false gospel on others knowingly. Mostly, they were innocent and unaware of what Jesus Himself taught in the Bible. They, as we had for thirty years, honestly believed what their leaders told them.

No, it was not LDS history that shattered my faith in the Mormon Church, but the living Word of God in the person of Jesus Christ. I came to know Mormonism was false because what the Mormon Church taught as God's truth did not line up with what Jesus Himself and his disciples taught as God's truth in the New Testament. The two cannot be reconciled. They are opposites. It came down to this. Either what Jesus taught in the Bible was true or what Jesus taught in Mormon scriptures was true. They could not both be true because they contradicted each other over and over and over again.

Or . . . perhaps there was no God at all. I considered this option briefly, but once I surrendered, God showed up in my life in very real and shocking ways that could have been nothing and no one else but God. Some of these experiences are illustrated in detail in the book *Unveiling Grace*. They go on and on as this enduring relationship develops. Here are a few brief examples.

First, with an extraordinary phone call I was offered a one-year visiting professorial job at a university in Florida *for which I never even applied*, at just the time I was desperate to leave BYU, the summer of 2007. Weeks later (nine months after giving my life to the God of grace), we packed up and left Utah. I was stunned; it seemed only God could have provided in this uncanny way. By the spring of 2008, I had officially resigned from BYU and my husband and I felt free to now resign from the LDS Church. Michael and I decided to write the resignations on March 16, 2008 in appreciation for the profound changes taking place and in honor of the reality of John 3:16. We now believed and had eternal life. Since this was a temporary one-year job in Florida, we still did not know what was next. I knew I could not go back to BYU, but would we go back to Utah? Michael's business was still mostly there and we seasoned hikers missed the mountains. We wondered if we should return to the home we still owned in Alpine, Utah. Could we live in the midst of LDS culture as Bible-believing Christians? Would anyone else be interested in what we had learned? We had great renters, so we didn't need to act immediately. We prayed God would let us know what to do.

In the course of traveling back and forth for business, Michael boarded a plane to Salt Lake to hand-carry our resignations directly to the church office building in downtown Salt Lake. Although he entered the building on a cloudy day, he emerged from the task into what seemed like God-ordained glorious sunshine. He called me feeling free and burdenless. Then he got a phone call. A couple from California had driven by our home in Alpine and wanted to see inside. How strange, we thought: that house was a block from national forest land—no one *ever* just drove through that secluded neighborhood. Before we had left for the job in Florida, we had two weeks' notice to put a for-sale-by-owner sign in our front yard and to put the house on craigslist. We did. But soon enough we needed renters to help cover the mortgage. That winter, the renters stayed and the for-sale sign was covered with snow. Now, in March, the sign, a mile high on the mountain, was barely visible again. On March 17, the day after we wrote the resignations, the couple drove by and called Michael's cell number on the sign. He called the current renters who let them in and a few days later, this couple offered a decent amount of cash for the house. Cash—in 2008 in the middle of a recession. We had heard that God opens doors that no one can shut (Rev. 3:8). Here was a prime personal example. We sold the house and took the offer as an answer to prayer. No going back to Utah, at least for now. By the end of spring term 2008, I was offered a permanent position at Florida Gulf Coast University among thirty-seven applicants and have been there ever since.

This personal and loving attention connected me to the God of the Bible in ways that I get frustrated trying to adequately describe. But with calm, confidence, and a sense of peace, I know what I know what I know. This testimony and this Savior departs radically from my former Mormon "testimony" and LDS "Savior" when I once said, "I know the church is true. I know Joseph Smith is a prophet . . . ."

It is simply this: God is truth. He lives. He's real. There is only One. He is personal. He loves me beyond what I could ever have imagined. He took the punishment on the cross I deserved so that I could have eternal life if I simply believe. He speaks to me and I get to know Him through his Word. He has a plan for my life that is unfolding even at my age. I have a desire to live and to see what is next like never before. Surrendering to Him changed me powerfully and permanently by transforming my thinking and then my behavior forever.

Mike and I joined Bible studies, tried various churches, and bombarded dear pastors and other Christians with our never-ending questions. One Monday evening at a Bible study someone else taught in our home, we were asked to pray this prayer from John 5:17, "In his defense Jesus said to them, 'My Father is always at his work to this very day, and I too am working.'" We prayed, "God show me who you are already working with around me, who you are drawing to yourself." The next day I went to work at the university and walked down a hall of offices; a woman I had worked with for four years but did not know personally was in her office. As I walked by, she said, "You! I dreamed about you last night." I went in and sat down where she waved her hand. "This is my dream. We went to a conference together in Washington, D.C. You were speaking. This voice kept saying to me, 'Where she goes, you need to go, and what she says, you need to hear.' I could not keep up with you, panicked, and hailed a cab. I said to the driver, 'Where she goes, I need to go, and what she says, I need to hear.' The cab caught up with you but the door would not open. I screamed, 'Where she goes, I need to go, and what she says, I need to hear!' Then she turned to me and asked, "What do you think of this dream?" I was thinking, *there's no way this has anything to do with what I prayed last night,* so I answered, "I have no idea," and walked out. Three days later, this woman came to my office and closed my door. Sitting down and leaning forward, she said, "I don't think you understand. I have been praying for a personal relationship with Jesus and I think He is sending me to you." Hit me over the head with a two-by-four! This *was* an answer to that prayer. Extraordinarily, she had joined Mormonism in Europe years earlier. How would I ever have known that?! Well, God did. Michael and I began attending Sunday school, church, and Bible study with her and with her husband and she was eventually baptized in a Nazarene church. Now, that's an amazing, personal God, a loving God of grace.

SOCIAL CONSEQUENCES OF MORMONISM: FINDING POST-MORMON MENTAL HEALTH

As the years wear on and I better understand by studying both Mormonism and biblical faith and communicating with so many leaving Mormonism, I am alarmed to recognize just how detrimental some LDS teachings are in the lives of some individuals. And then, to the contrary, I have watched the power of the biblical God of grace move through the lives of those willing to investigate, healing their past and giving them hope and a confident peace. Please do not misunderstand. I love the LDS people and wish them great contentment. It is the teachings of Mormonism that I will address as a social scientist, presenting academic, scriptural, and personal sources informing my theist worldview.

There are a number of teachings in Mormonism that would be considered by the professions of the social sciences—anthropology, sociology, psychology, cultural studies, marriage and family, and education—to be antiquated and even dangerous to the human psyche and the social conscience. I've thought a lot about the "fruit" of Mormon teachings. These include: (1) dark skin is a curse (racism); (2) polygamy is an eternal principle; (3) salvation requires obedience to LDS laws and ordinances and exaltation requires copious works; and (4) Mormons are Jews and the only true church.

Later in this chapter, I address the LDS teaching that the Bible is corrupt and the traditional Christian church is from Satan; and I examine the LDS practice of seeking the appearance of and communication with familiar spirits—the dead. The Word of God says one can tell believers by their fruit. LDS frequently say, "You can tell we are Christian because of our fruit." Let's examine some of this fruit of Mormonism.

Racism

The first fruit—racism in LDS scriptures—rocked my world when I taught diversity at BYU. My experience in this field at BYU and beyond led me to discover that blacks could not attend BYU in the 1960s. This shocked me and sent me searching further. A colleague at BYU whom I served with on the college diversity committee, Darron Smith, wrote an honest book about blacks in Mormonism and lost his job.[14] This was terribly upsetting. After years of teaching diversity and assuming the racist curse of Cain idea stemmed from the Bible—a book corrupted and not to be trusted—because one of my students had told me that it did, I discovered the racist scriptures were *not* in the Bible but in the Book of Mormon and the Pearl of Great Price.

Here's an example: "The skins of the Lamanites were dark, according to the mark which was set upon their fathers, which was a curse upon them because of their transgressions and their rebellion" (Book of Mormon, Alma 3:6). Plus, throughout history Mormon prophets made horrific racist statements that were written down and taught. The American Psychological Association (2015) describes the consequences of racism on their website:

> Racism in all its horrific forms is transmitted across generations and is manifested in individual behaviors, institutional norms and practices, and cultural values and patterns. Racism serves simultaneously both to rationalize the hierarchical domination of one racial or ethnic group over other group(s), and maintain psychological, social and material advantages for the dominant group. Both active racism and passive acceptance of race-based privilege disrupt the mental health and psychological functioning of both victims and perpetrators of racial injustice.[15]

LDS Scriptures "Utterly Reliable" and "Pure Truth"

In a recently released statement on the official LDS Church website lds.org on the subject of "Race and the Priesthood,"[16] the modern Mormon Church disavows its previous doctrines and public teachings by now denying "that blacks or people of any other race or ethnicity are inferior in any way to anyone else. . . ." This unequivocal truth is something that Spain (1542), Quakers (1600s), Pennsylvania (1790), England (1807), Abraham Lincoln (1865), and Christians of any era who believe the Bible, know. According to the Bible, God shows no favoritism—never by skin color—and commands his people to do the same.

Lincoln, who often quoted the biblical God, was displeased with the Utah Territory for its stance as a slave territory (and for its polygamy). Finally in 1978, 113 years after Lincoln and twenty-four years after *Brown v. Board of Education,* the Mormon Church gave black members of African ancestry (why not restrict Native Americans—they were the unrighteous dark-skinned Lamanites of the Book of Mormon?) equal access to the priesthood, and thus access to its celestial kingdom, eternal life, and the potential for godhood.

As a professor teaching multiculturalism, among other things, at Brigham Young University (1999–2008), I had some generational LDS students who proposed that those with black skin were blighted with something they called "the curse of Cain." Though the practices of *official* racial discrimination are not now active in the LDS Church, the LDS scriptures still exist, are read and revered. The lingering conundrum for the Mormon Church is this: How to explain the twenty-six verses of LDS scripture that can be considered racist? This new attempt to state a non-biased position on race, which falls short of an apology, ignores the challenge of present-day scriptures.

As well-intended as the latest words on the official church website are, they can effect no real change in policy or teachings because these scriptures remain. Why call these scriptures racist? The definition of "racist" is the belief that some races of people are better than others because of their race. This is precisely what the LDS scriptures *still* teach. Here are few examples just from the Book of Mormon: 3 Nephi 2:15, "And their curse was taken from them, and their skin became white like unto the Nephites"; and 3 Nephi 19:30, "And when Jesus had spoken these words he came again unto his disciples; and behold they did pray steadfastly, without ceasing, unto him; and he did smile upon them again; and behold they were white, even as Jesus." I doubt that Jesus had lily-white skin. As these passages explain, the Lamanites (forerunners of the dark-skinned Native Americans descended from the Jews according to the Book of Mormon) were given a mark of dark skin as a curse for their transgression, not toward God, by the way, but toward their brethren, the "righteous" Nephites. Later when some Lamanites became righteous, the curse was removed and their skin became white.

This repulsion for the LDS racist scriptures I had discovered softened my heart toward the biblical God. When I read the Bible, its teachings were unmistakably clear because they were repeated over and over. One of these undeniable themes is that God shows no favoritism, no *bias*. What, then, to do with the racist scriptures of Mormonism? If the LDS Church moves to remove them, then that calls into question all other things Joseph Smith wrote as scripture and said came from God. Can apologists say the scriptures are an allegory that means something other than what they say literally?

What do LDS Church leaders have to say about the reliability and accuracy of their own scriptures? According to LDS leaders, Mormon scriptures are "utterly reliable" and "pure truth." The current prophet, President Monson, declared on the official church website, lds.org: "The words of truth and inspiration found in our four standard works are prized possessions to me. . . . These holy words of truth and love give guidance to my life and point the way to eternal perfection."[17] In 2011, apostle Richard G. Scott taught, "Because scriptures are generated from inspired communication through the Holy Ghost, they are pure truth. We need not be concerned about the validity of concepts contained in the standard works since the Holy Ghost has been the instrument which has motivated and inspired those individuals who have recorded the scriptures."[18] And D. Todd Christofferson in 2012 said, "The scriptures are the touchstone for measuring correctness and truth....Where scriptural truths are ignored or abandoned, the essential moral core of society disintegrates and decay is close behind."[19] Additionally, this from apostle Robert D. Hales in 2006: "So essential are these truths that Heavenly Father gave both Lehi and Nephi visions vividly representing the word of God as a rod of iron. Both father and son learned that holding to this strong, unbending, utterly reliable guide is the *only* way to stay on that strait [*sic*] and narrow path that leads to our Savior."[20]

These men, considered "prophets, seers, and revelators," all describe Mormon scripture as words of truth and inspiration, strong, unbending, an utterly reliable guide, pure truth, and the touchstone for measuring correctness. If LDS scripture is reliable as pure truth from God yet the racist scriptures still exist, the only logical analysis is that the God of Mormonism was at the time the Book of Mormon was birthed and still is racist.

When I was LDS, I needed to trust Mormon scriptures as "strong, unbending, utterly reliable," but I could not wrap my head around the ones that suggest God cursed a people in the Book of Mormon with a mark of dark skin for their transgression. Exchanging my students' scripture-driven, dark-skin prejudices into impartial attitudes became my passion. I thought perhaps I could help fix the racism problem in the next generation of LDS students. But how could I when the scriptures taught that black skin was a curse?

In opposition, the God of the Bible made His stance crystal clear. He created humans in beautiful variability and is in relationship with people from every nation, tongue, and skin color—all members of the same human race. Skin color is never, ever, a determiner of value. He teaches not to judge by appearances (John 7:24). He does not show favoritism (Acts 10:34–35). The biblical God instructs individuals to show no partiality, meaning not to pay special attention to or honor someone because of skin color, wealth, social standing, position, authority, popularity, looks, or influence. If we do, it is so serious it is considered sin (James 2:9). Believers are charged to love other people as God loves them and treat them how we want to be treated.

Although the Book of Mormon states, "All are alike unto God" (2 Nephi 26:33), as long as racist scriptures still exist, are read, taught, believed, and made part of the culture, one may question the consistency of the "Race and the Priesthood" statement with the racist Mormon scriptures. The LDS Church is in a difficult position that is irrational, inconsistent, and illogical since the "Race and the Priesthood" statement and its own "utterly reliable" and "pure truth" scriptures collide.

Joseph Smith Founder of LDS Racist Scriptures and Teachings

In January of 1964, LDS apostle Delbert L. Stapley wrote to LDS Michigan Governor George Romney urging him *not* to support the Civil Rights Act; it would bring the integration of blacks. Of course, the apostle pointed out that he did not speak for the church. Stapley wrote that three U.S. Presidents and a friend who had disagreed with the Lord's voice on this matter met an untimely demise. He justified his counsel to Romney with the words of Joseph Smith from two sources.[21] Here's a sampling: "Had I anything to do with the negro, I would confine them by strict law to their own species, and put them on a national equalization"[22] And, "The curse is not yet taken off from the sons of Canaan, neither will it be until it is affected by as great a power as caused it to come . . . ."[23] According to these passages, Smith supported equalization but not integration. He wrote that the sons of Canaan (descendants of Cain) were cursed. It would take an act of God to remove that curse. The implication is it was an act of God that placed the curse in the first place.

In February of 1964, Congress passed the Civil Rights Act prohibiting discrimination according to race, religion, or sex. Four years later, Dr. Martin Luther King—pastor and Nobel Peace prize winner—was martyred for his role as a leader in the movement. After his death, black preachers continued to call for full integration of blacks into white restrooms, buses, schools, jobs, and neighborhoods. A full ten years passed after King's death until the Mormon priesthood, eternal marriage, and temple endowments were offered to the few black church members. Prior to 1978, blacks could only hope to be servants to the more righteous in the hereafter.

Roots from Joseph Smith

To imply, as the LDS "Race and Priesthood" statement on lds.org does, that racial bias began in the Mormon Church with second prophet Brigham Young is inaccurate.[24] Although the priesthood ban for blacks was not in force during the founding prophet's lifetime, the seeds of its justification were planted by Joseph Smith. The book of Mormon (1830) teaches that dark skin is the result of a curse for sin. The Book of Moses (1832–33) teaches that blacks descended from Cain. In the 1835 Book of Commandments, Joseph Smith added a statement (now Doctrine and Covenants 134:12) that the saints pledged not to "interfere with bond-servants...such interference we believe to be unlawful and unjust . . . ."[25]

Later in the Book of Abraham (1842), Joseph introduced the idea of "the right of Priesthood." Some could have it; some were restricted. Pharaoh was said to come from the cursed Canaanite lineage that could not have the priesthood. Abraham 1:21 states that the "king of Egypt [Pharaoh] was a descendant from the loins of Ham, and was a partaker of the blood of the Canaanites by birth." And Abraham 1:27 tells us: "Pharaoh [was] that lineage by which he could not have the right of Priesthood . . . ." It was Joseph Smith who taught that dark skin was a curse from God for iniquity. He was the one whose literary creation, the book of Abraham, taught that certain bloodlines were denied the priesthood power of God. It was Smith who supported segregation and did not want men to interfere with slavery. The 1842 Book of Abraham and the southern converts to the church were the final nails in the coffin for any abolitionist teachings from Joseph Smith.

LDS author Stephen Taggart writes that it was Joseph Smith who put all of the elements in place for the church to accept a priesthood restriction for blacks.[26] After Smith's death, the church's semi-official paper, *Times and Seasons*, printed in 1846 that the blood of Israel had exclusive rights to the priesthood, implying that other bloodlines such as the blood of Canaanites, did not. Patriarchal blessings identified Mormons with the non-cursed tribe of Ephraim from the 1830s.

Although at least two black men, Elijah Abel ordained by Zebedee Coltrin and Walter Lewis ordained by William Smith, received the priesthood during Joseph Smith's lifetime, Smith did not ordain them. Ordained in 1836, Elijah Abel could merely enter the Kirtland temple for foot washings and later baptisms for the dead. He was excluded from the Nauvoo endowment ritual. After Joseph Smith died, hundreds of endowments occurred in the temple before the exodus, but Elijah Abel was not among them. Irrefutably according to Mormon doctrine, he needed to receive his temple endowments to enter the highest degree of the celestial kingdom in a role greater than that of a servant. The same was true of Jane Manning James, once Smith's housekeeper. She pleaded with church leaders for decades to give her permission to take out her temple endowments. Smith did not offer the privilege to her, nor did Brigham Young after him, but in 1894 she was allowed to be sealed to Joseph Smith's family as a *servant*.

Taggart and Fawn Brodie[27] as well as some non-LDS historians suggest that the Mormon Church's anti-abolitionist, proslavery attitude began in Missouri in the 1830s. Missouri was a slave state and suspicious that the incoming "saints" might allow free blacks to come to Missouri. The LDS Church took a stand, non-LDS historians say, for survival. In the *Messenger and Advocate*, Smith declared that slavery was ordained by God and consistent with the gospel of Christ:

> We unhesitatingly say . . . the project of emancipation is destructive to our government, and the notion of amalgamation is devilish!-And insensible to feeling must be the heart, and low indeed must be the mind, that would consent for a moment, to see his fair daughter, his sister, or perhaps, his bosom companion, in the embrace of a NEGRO!

> We entreat our brethren of the Eastern, the free States, the Canadas, and all, wherever they may be found, not to be surprised or astonished at this step, which we have thus publicly taken: were they acquainted with the present condition of the slave, they would see that they could not be freed, and we enjoy our present, civil and social societies. And further, that this matter cannot be discussed without exciting the feelings of the black population, and cause them to rise, sooner or later, and lay waste and desolate many parts of the Southern country.

> This cannot be done without consigning to the dust thousands of human beings. And the bare reflection of being instrumental in causing unprovoked blood to flow, must shock the heart of every saint. [28]

Whether or not a few black men received the priesthood, as LDS apologists are quick to point out, those blacks were nonetheless denied the blessings of the temple endowments and sealings. Whether or not the racist posture coalesced in Missouri, it *originated* in the scriptures and the teachings that Joseph Smith himself brought forth. These are the very scriptures that the LDS Church teaches came from God Himself and are "utterly reliable" and "pure truth."

If the Foundation is Rotten, All that Joseph Smith Built Tumbles

The Bible invites people to "reason together" (Isa. 1:18, NKJV) to "test the spirits" (1 John 4:1) against the Word of God (Acts 17:11). What is rotten at the foundation, at the root, and does not "produce good fruit" will be hewn down. While I was still LDS, I read the following in the Bible and knew there was a problem with the foundation of Mormonism: "The ax is already at the root of the trees, and every tree that does not produce good fruit will be cut down and thrown into the fire" (Luke 3:9; Matt. 3:10).

For biblical Christians, the Bible is the standard for measuring truth. For Mormons, truth comes from four standard works of scripture and the words of prophets. The LDS prophets will never lead one astray, never mislead the saints, I was taught when I was LDS. "I say to Israel, the Lord will never permit me or any other man who stands as President of this Church to lead you astray."[29] From an official church gospel reference book, "You can always trust the living prophets."[30] There are many such quotes.

But what if a Mormon prophet did lead the church astray? Well, one could say he was speaking as a man and simply made a mistake, like Dieter Uchtdorf proposed in his conference talk October 2013. "And, to be perfectly frank, there have been times when members or leaders in the Church have simply made mistakes. There may have been things said or done that were not in harmony with our values, principles, or doctrine."[31] Okay, Mormon prophets are human and they make mistakes. It's difficult for any reasonable Mormon to know when a Mormon prophet, seer, and revelator is making such a mistake, to know when the prophets speak for God and when they err. Sometimes mistakes are made by eleven church presidents in a row: Brigham Young all the way to Spencer W. Kimball as the recent statement on "Race and the Priesthood" on lds.org concedes. I get it.

In recent years since Michael and I are in ministry and communicate every day with LDS folks and post-Mormons with questions and hear their stories, I have pondered the social and emotional consequences of some of these racist scriptures. What is the cost in human lives? Well, certainly today the LDS Church welcomes dark-skinned individuals not just to join but to be the representative face of their church. At General Conference (October

2015), some waited with bated breath to see if a dark-skinned person would finally be called to one of the three open positions in the LDS twelve apostles; but no, the new men called were all white. The LDS Church's PR videos make it appear that the church's diversity looks like the outside world but it does not. Today I communicated with an African American member of the Mormon Church who said in the past nine months, he has spoken eight times in sacrament meeting, once in stake conference, and was taken to Salt Lake City for General Conference. He said he receives dozens of emails and calls if he misses a meeting. He also admitted he knows if he ever renounces Mormonism all the people and their attention will go away. I have spoken to other dark-skinned individuals who have left the LDS Church because of the way they were treated by members who saw their dark skin as a curse because of what the LDS scriptures say.

However, what was once a great disadvantage may today be an advantage, if one can ignore the racist scriptures. In my experience teaching diversity at BYU, many generational Mormons still believe dark skin is a curse, and why not? It is still canonized scripture. So, does this flawed teaching come from Brigham Young or Joseph Smith? Does it matter if these were the mistakes of the *founding* prophet Smith?

What if a "mistake"—a false teaching—appeared over and over again from the establishment of the church in 1830 to 1978, for 148 years, in not just one but in several "official" places? What if it appeared in both the words of prophets and the words of other general authorities, say, when they spoke in conference? What if that "mistake" was still taught in two of the four standard works of Mormon scripture and *is still there today*? Now, what if that false teaching (e.g., racism) came from the *founding* prophet? Now *that* would be a problem, according to the Bible.

The LDS Church stands or falls on the foundation of Joseph Smith: his First Vision of the Father and Son with "glorified" bodies of flesh and bone, modern-day revelation, the principle of polygamy, and "translated" scriptures with racial bias. This foundation rests on "the arm of flesh" (2 Chron. 32:8), a man who described himself as a "rough stone rolling downhill."[32] One cannot be baptized into the LDS Church, receive the Mormon Holy Ghost, or work one's way to eternal life with the Father and the Son without professing that Joseph Smith was a prophet of God who restored Christ's original church in these latter days. In Mormonism, Jesus alone is not enough. Mormons must confess belief in Joseph Smith, even before baptism into the LDS Church. Without this acknowledgment, they cannot be exalted to the highest heaven. Joseph is the foundational key to Mormonism. One cannot be saved without accepting his prophet, seer, and revelator status and that of his contemporary substitutes.

Jesus Is Enough

Simply, the Bible is clear. Jesus *is* enough. He alone is the foundational cornerstone (Psalm 118:22; Matt. 21:42). He alone is the Mediator between man and God (1 Tim. 2:5). A prophet is no longer needed. God spoke through the prophets until John the Baptist (Luke 16:16). Then Jesus came and he as God spoke for Himself (Heb. 1:1–2) and He made it clear He again, does not show favoritism and is not a racist. The Bible establishes that if a foundation is rotten, the entire structure/organization/person/religion must go. Remember the house built on the sand of Matthew 7:26? And "no one can lay a foundation other than the one already laid, which is Jesus Christ" (1 Cor. 3:11). The house on the sand washed away.

Recently, I listened to a discussion taught by the LDS sister missionaries. They said the foundation of their building was Joseph Smith and the other prophets and apostles. Other members of the LDS Church form a pyramid structure with Jesus as the crowning stone on top. I wanted to comment about this issue of the foundation but did not. I had already rocked their world when I gently asked, "Hmm, how could the church have descended into a Great Apostasy when Jesus Himself said . . . well, why don't you read his words for yourselves and tell us what you think?" I turned to Matthew 16:18 and she read Jesus's own words out loud, "On this rock I will build my church, and the gates of Hades will not overcome it." Looking near tears, she kept reading, perhaps hoping some new words would mask the first ones. I kindly asked, "If Jesus Himself said the gates of hell would not stop his church, how could there have been a Great Apostasy after the original apostles died?" Pensive and uncomfortable, she offered, "We don't know everything yet. But the authority needed for Christ's church was lost when the apostles died." I delicately nudged on, "And there was no opportunity to pass on this authority you speak about? But couldn't John the apostle, who lived another sixty some years after Jesus's death [LDS teach John still walks the earth as do the three Nephites from the Book of Mormon], have had the opportunity to pass on any needed authority to someone in the rising church?"

Such compassion I have for the sincere devotion these sisters and so many others have, such as I once had, for a faith where the dots don't connect with teachings of the biblical God or even with commonsense reason and morality. Of course, the sister missionaries who gave that analogy of Jesus's church must not be aware that God's Word says Jesus Himself is the foundational cornerstone, the foundation without which there would be no building—no church—at all.

The LDS scriptures that teach dark skin is a curse may cause some church members to believe that, well, dark skin is a curse. This racist teaching, that dark skin is a curse, has proven psychological effects. This particular study demonstrated that white teachers perceive the behavior of ethnically diverse students differently according to their race/culture.[33] Many ethnically diverse report needing to work harder and longer and smarter to prove themselves in the work environment.[34] Racist beliefs may play out in behavior; for example, never dating or marrying a dark-skinned individual, never hiring someone with dark skin, not allowing their children to play with a dark-skinned child—the list is endless. The fruit of this teaching is abject racism—the belief that one skin color is better than another—and a very low rate of diverse faces in the Mormon religion. According to a study by the Pew Institute in 2009, only about 3 percent of Latter-day Saints in the United States are black.[35]

The next troublesome teaching for me from LDS scriptures is polygamy.

Polygamy

Did God give the commandment to practice polygamy in the Old Testament? Mormonism teaches he did. For biblical believers, how this question is answered will either verify or destroy the teaching of Joseph Smith on polygamy. The Bible is written in two modes. The first is *descriptive* which tells a story, describes something, and is not doctrine. The second is *prescriptive* which is doctrinal. Just because the Old Testament includes instances of polygamy with Abraham, Jacob, David, and Solomon participating, its narrative does not indicate that the God of the Bible commands or justifies these men's actions. Careful examination of biblical scripture will show that this practice in the Old Testament was *descriptive* and not a commandment from God, simply a description of what these men chose to do, not what God asked them to do. That would make it a doctrine of men, not of God.

Mormonism teaches the doctrine of polygamy came from a revelation directly from Jesus Christ to Joseph Smith recorded July 12, 1843, but was known by Joseph as early as 1831. This revelation exists today as Doctrine and Covenants Section 132 and contains sixty-six verses. Yes, polygamy like racism, is still in the "pure truth" and "utterly reliable" Mormon scriptures.

Brief History of Polygamy

Some early Mormons practiced polygamy from the 1830s until the U.S. government's anti-bigamy laws forced them underground or they fled to establish polygamy colonies in Mexico and Canada in the 1880s. The Mormon Manifesto officially stopped the practice in 1890, but there is evidence the prophets continued for some time to marry men to multiple wives in the temple. Joseph Smith had at least thirty-three documented wives (maybe more the official church essay on polygamy says), and Brigham Young, second prophet, had fifty-four. Seven successive prophets in all practiced polygamy. These facts are abundantly documented and easily found.[36]

The first edition of the Doctrine and Covenants printed in 1835 contained a Section CI on Marriage that on page 251 stated, "Inasmuch as this church of Christ has been reproached with the crime of fornication, and polygamy: we declare that we believe, that one man should have one wife; and one woman but one husband, except in case of death, when either is at liberty to marry again."[37]

At the same time this scripture was doctrine, polygamy was practiced by the prophet Joseph Smith, apostle Brigham Young, and other Mormon leaders. This doctrine of Section CI Marriage was not removed from Doctrine and Covenants until 1876 when it was replaced with Doctrine and Covenants 132, which remains until this day. Why did something so important from God to the Mormon Church as Doctrine and Covenants 132—with its new and everlasting covenant, D&C 132:4—take more than forty-one years to appear in the Doctrine and Covenants? Why was the doctrine of plural marriage officially announced in Utah by Brigham Young in 1852, but the Doctrine and Covenants Section CI Marriage was not removed from the Doctrine and Covenants until 1876?[38] Let's test Joseph Smith's polygamy revelation, Doctrine and Covenants 132, by comparing scripture to scripture.

Comparing Mormon Scripture to Mormon Scripture

Michael and I worked together to compare Mormon scripture to Mormon scripture and later Mormon scripture to the Bible (KJV). The following are Mormon scriptures related to polygamy. The interesting thing about looking at Mormon scripture is it sometimes conflicts from one standard work to another, like in the case of polygamy. These inconsistencies occur between the Book of Mormon and the Doctrine and Covenants. From the Book of Mormon, Jacob 1:15, we read that some people began to "indulge themselves somewhat in wicked practices, such as like David of old desiring many wives and concubines, and also Solomon, his son." And from Jacob 2:24: "'Behold, David and Solomon truly had many wives and concubines, which thing was abominable before me,' saith the Lord." These scriptures verify that the Book of Mormon teaches that the act of David and Solomon having many wives and concubines was an abomination before the Lord. I liked this scripture. It comforted my anxiety about having to maybe practice polygamy someday (or at least my husband would be doing most of the practicing).

In direct opposition to those scriptures from the Book of Mormon, the Doctrine and Covenants 132:1 states, "Wherein I, the Lord, justified my servants . . . David and Solomon, my servants, as touching the principle and doctrine of their having many wives and concubines." This verse is in context; the entire Section 132 supports the principle of polygamy, calling it the new and everlasting covenant and threatening Emma Smith, Joseph's first wife, with destruction if she does not abide this commandment (D&C 132:54). So Doctrine and Covenants 132:1 states that David and Solomon were justified in having many wives and concubines, but Jacob 2:24 states the opposite, that David and Solomon's practice of having many wives was abominable before the Lord.

How can both be true? According to the rules of logic, which God recommends in Isaiah 1:18, one scripture has to be right and the other wrong or both are wrong. Both can't be true if they contradict each other. It is thought-provoking to notice that the Mormon Church has one scripture to refute their belief in polygamy and one to support it. Polygamy is not the only topic with contradictions between LDS scriptures.. Can a faith that contradicts its own teachings with conflicting scriptures hold up to a standard of truth? Interestingly, there are scriptures on both sides of several issues for LDS to utilize depending on what the world outside Mormonism is most comfortable hearing. One such example happened when Prophet Gordon B. Hinckley was asked in a 1997 interview for *Time Magazine* if Mormons teach they can become gods. Then, when asked whether the LDS Church "holds that God the Father was once a man, he sounded uncertain, 'I don't know that we teach it. I don't know that we emphasize it . . . I understand the philosophical background behind it, but I don't know a lot about it, and I don't think others know a lot about it.'"[39]

That interview was in August. Soon after, my husband was in a priesthood meeting where the prophet said to his leaders by satellite that he knew his doctrine. Michael took this to mean that he applied the "milk before meat" principle in not admitting to the outside world that Mormons teach they can become gods since that seems incredible to Gentiles (those outside of the LDS Church). Don't tell them anything they are not ready to accept or would treat as unholy. Robert Millet, former Head of the Religion Department at BYU, tells his students in a video how to avoid a direct answer. Instead "answer the question they should have asked."[40]

The Mormon scriptures in Doctrine and Covenants 132 teaching that polygamy is an eternal principle to be lived in the millennium and the next life by those working their way to godhood would be another of the LDS teachings I knew the outside world would not accept and, where, like the racist scriptures, the milk before meat principle applied.

If the fullness of the everlasting gospel was contained in the Book of Mormon, as delivered by the Savior (*Joseph Smith History* 1:34), why does the Book of Mormon not justify the practice of polygamy for any of its historical people groups from 600 B.C. through A.D. 421, including the Jaredites? No one was given the authorization by God to practice polygamy in the Book of Mormon. Plurality of wives is condemned throughout the Book of Mormon (Jacob 1, 2, & 3; Mosiah 11:2; and Ether 10:5). No wonder that fifty years ago when asked which one is correct regarding polygamy, the Book of Mormon or Doctrine and Covenants 132, Mormon apostle LeGrand Richards couldn't "reconcile" the two statements.

What Does the God of the Bible Say about Polygamy?

Now to the Bible. Did God give the commandment to practice polygamy in the Old Testament? Doctrine and Covenants 132 says He did. In the Bible, the first indication of marriage is found in Genesis 2:23–24 (KJV) where a man "shall cleave unto his wife: and they shall be one flesh." Note the verse did not state "wives." The Genesis verse is also confirmed by the words of Christ in Matthew 19:4–6 (KJV) "and they twain shall be one flesh." The word "twain" means only "two," no more. Also note in the New

Testament that church leaders, as stated in 1 Timothy 3:2, 12 and Titus 1:6, should be the husband of one wife.

The first to practice polygamy in the Bible was Lamech, who was a descendant of Cain. He acted on his own and took two wives, but was not commanded by God to do so (Gen. 4:19). Man started the practice of polygamy, not God. Polygamy flourished in the times before Noah: "and they took them *wives* [italics added] of all which they chose" (Gen. 6:1–2). "And God saw that the wickedness of man was great in the earth (Gen. 6:5). This happened before the flood. In Genesis 7:13, it states the only people on the ark saved during the flood were Noah and his wife, Shem and his wife, Ham and his wife, and Japheth and his wife. If polygamy was to be the law of God, would this not have been a logical time to start with Noah and his three sons? But the Bible is very clear that Noah and the three sons only had one wife each.

Now look at Abraham. Abram was promised seed in Genesis 15:5. It was Abram's faith in the Lord that was counted to him for righteousness (Gen. 15:6). Abram was given a second wife by his first wife Sarai (see Gen. 16: 1–4), because Sarai had borne no children for Abram. She became impatient and took matters into her own hands to fulfill God's Word (Gen. 16:2). God never told Sarai to give Hagar, Sarai's bondwoman, to be Abram's wife. Abram also erred when he hearkened to the voice of Sarai (Gen. 16:3). In Genesis 16:4 Hagar conceived and in 16:5 Sarai realized that what she did was wrong and she complained to Abram. Abram in Genesis 16:6 stated, "Thy maid is in thy hand; do to her as it pleaseth thee." Sarai dealt harshly with Hagar. This procedure was not the order of God. Abram's marriage to Hagar was not ordained by God. Due to pressure from Sarai, Hagar did flee into the wilderness, but an angel told Hagar to "Return to thy mistress, and submit thyself under her hands" (Gen. 16:6–9, KJV). Notice that the angel said to submit unto Sarai not Abram, for Hagar was not under the authority of Abram. God did not recognize Hagar as Abram's wife, but only as a bondwoman to Sarai.

Abram and Sarai were impatient to bring forth seed; therefore they followed the law of man and did not wait on the Lord. But in Genesis 17 God covenanted with Abram and changed his name to Abraham. God called Sarah, Abraham's wife, (17:15–16) to bear a son. The name of the son should be Isaac (17:19). Abraham's son by the slave woman was born according to the flesh, but his son by Sarah was born as the result of a divine promise" (Gal. 4:21–23). The above scriptures clearly demonstrate a contradiction with Doctrine and Covenants 132:34 and 65 where the LDS god commanded Abraham to take Hagar to wife, and Sarah gave Hagar to Abraham.

In Doctrine and Covenants 132:37 it states, "Abraham received concubines and they bore him children; and it was accounted unto him for righteousness, because they were given unto him." This statement is in error because (1) God counted Abraham righteous because of his faith not because he received concubines and wives (Gen. 15:6). This happened when Abraham had one wife, Sarah. (2) God did not give Abraham concubines, but only one wife, Sarah, who bore a son named Isaac. The Bible states in Genesis 22:2 that God said, "Take now thy son, thine only son Isaac, whom thou lovest." God even repeats in Genesis 22:12, "thine only son." This was stated by God after Hagar had given birth to Ishmael. God only recognized one son, Isaac.

In Doctrine and Covenants 132:65 it states, "I commanded Abraham to take Hagar to wife." If this is true, where is the second witness in the Bible? There is none. Nowhere in the Bible does God tell any man to take another wife while he is currently married. If Doctrine and Covenants 132:65 is true then why was the covenant (Gen. 17:19) and promise (Gal. 4:22–23) not given to Ishmael instead of Isaac? In Genesis 21:10, Sarah stated, "Cast out this bondwoman [Hagar] and her son: for the son of this bondwoman shall not be heir with my son, even with Isaac." God stated to Abraham in Genesis 21:12, "in all that Sarah hath said unto thee, hearken unto her voice." God never referred to Hagar as the wife of Abraham but only a "bondwoman." Why would God command Abraham to marry Hagar and have a son, only to later cast them out and never acknowledge the son, Ishmael? Abraham only remarried after the death of Sarah (23:2), which is when he married Keturah (25:1). Abraham only had one wife at a time after he received the covenant from God in Genesis 17.

Polygamy was never justified in the Old Testament by Abraham, Isaac, or Jacob as per Mormon doctrine; nor was it justified in the New Testament. Here are a few Bible verses to research: Genesis 2:22–24; Deuteronomy 17:17; Matthew 19:4–6; 1 Timothy 3:2, 12; Titus 1:6; 1 Corinthians 7:2; Ephesians 5:28–33.

LDS Church's Current Position

To clarify the Mormon Church's current position on polygamy, the church still teaches the eternal principle of plural marriage to members in their various church programs and classes. It appears in their scriptures (D&C 132) and church lesson manuals. They teach it will be practiced in the hereafter. The Mormon Church does not practice physical plural marriage/polygamy today, but does seal men to more than one woman in the temple to be a family in the next life. The 1890 Mormon Manifesto was given to stop the earthly practice of polygamy, but not the belief in polygamy. Even as the Mormon Church in 2008 was supporting a constitutional amendment defining marriage as only between one man and one woman, temple sealers were marrying men to a second wife for time and eternity after the first wives died. The Mormon Church teaches that any man sealed (married) for eternity with two or more wives will have his multiples wives with him in the celestial kingdom. This is the practice of spiritual polygamy, and this doctrine exists today.

M. Russell Ballard, current Mormon apostle, warned members in 2009 not to waste time trying to justify the practice of polygamy during Old Testament times. Elder Ballard: "We follow Jesus Christ by adhering to God's law of marriage, which is marriage between one man and one woman. This commandment has been in place from the very beginning. God said, "Therefore shall a man leave his father and his mother, and shall cleave unto his wife: and they shall be one flesh" (Genesis 2:24). God instructed Adam and Eve to "be fruitful, and multiply, and replenish the earth, and subdue it" (Genesis 1:28).

If God's law of marriage is between one man and one woman, what about the principle of plural marriage in Doctrine and Covenants 132? What about Joseph Smith's own polygamy? Will the LDS Church remove the section and denounce the practice? How do we explain Joseph Smith being married for eternity to at least thirty-three women (with one as young as fourteen and eleven married to other men) when he was alive, and then being sealed to hundreds of women after his death? What do we do with Brigham Young being married (sealed) to fifty-four wives and with five additional latter-day prophets who practiced polygamy? What do we now do with Doctrine and Covenants 132? What about the other current apostles who are sealed to two wives each, although the first one has passed on? Are they breaking the "one man and one woman" commandment that apostle Ballard says has been in place from the beginning? Which doctrine is true—the doctrine of polygamy in Doctrine and Covenants 132 or marriage of one man to one wife?

It's interesting that Doctrine and Covenants 132 was the last revelation received by Joseph Smith before he was murdered. Joseph Smith had practiced polygamy for many years before his death in 1844, but he denied he was practicing it. He lied. His own words in the month before his death: "What a thing it is for a man to be accused of committing adultery, and having seven wives, when I can only find one."

If the LDS Church teaches that polygamy is an eternal principle and that revelation came from the Mormon Jesus (D&C 132), then the church has received an answer from a different Jesus than the One in the Bible, because those two Jesuses disagree. The biblical Jesus does not command polygamy; the Mormon Jesus did. For Michael and me, this was another conflict of doctrine that led us out of Mormonism. One day in 2007 after I had already decided to follow Jesus, all alone in the celestial room of the Mount Timpanogos Temple, Mike, desperate for an answer, asked God if polygamy was from Him. He got his answer. Mike said it was like someone reached down and whispered in his ear, "No, it's not from Me. It's from man." That was a stunning answer right there in a Mormon temple and the first time anything like that had happened to him. What the Bible taught about this principle helped Michael leave Mormonism and accept the biblical Jesus.

Human Cost of Scriptures Supporting Polygamy

There is a human cost for the teaching of polygamy that Joseph Smith introduced to North America in the 1830s. Fundamentalist LDS polygamy colonies and other aberrations of Smith's teachings still exist in the U.S., Canada, and Mexico. The Canadian and Mexican colonies appeared when

U.S. President Grant put undue pressure on the Mormons to stop practicing polygamy in the United States in the 1880s, so many fled the country.[41] The tens of thousands who continue to practice polygamy in the U.S. today stem largely from Smith's Doctrine and Covenant 132 teachings, except for perhaps a small percentage of Muslims and Africans currently living polygamy here. Practicing polygamy may encourage male priesthood to exercise unholy domination over women and children, sometimes resulting in sexual abuse of young girls and early teenage motherhood as starkly discovered in Warren Jeffs' and other fundamentalist groups.[42] Typically, in polygamy, the man legally marries only his first wife in order to stay within the current U.S. law (which may be rapidly changing in favor of polygamous unions). Some women and children survive in wretched poverty and some may collect government assistance since technically they are "single mothers" able to receive benefits.

I have wondered: if the *practice* of polygamy can result in the abuse of young girls, what are the results of the current *teachings* of polygamy as an eternal principle in the minds of some LDS men? One former LDS priesthood holder, Andy Poland, tells the story of how the teachings led him to imagine a second wife and have an affair. Andy left Mormonism and embraced biblical Christianity. His marriage was restored.[43] We worked with an LDS family whose father was having an affair when he was called in by church leaders for instruction to prepare to become a bishop. He confessed his affair and was excommunicated from the LDS Church. His wife left him. Both became biblical Christians and remarried each other to the joy of hundreds of Bible believers in attendance at their wedding, a great blessing to watch. Their marriage is strong today.

Now, I have no data to prove a correlation between the teaching of polygamy as an eternal principle and men's thoughts about additional partners; I only know that these thoughts have influenced the thinking of some LDS men who we have encountered in ministry. We have met former LDS women relating stories of sexual abuse by priesthood-holding brothers, fathers, and neighbors. Some have been the victims of occult ritual abuse by church members. The book *Paper Dolls*[44] gives a horrific account of sexual abuse in an LDS neighborhood in Utah. Stats show the rate of reported rape in Utah is consistently higher than the national average.[45] One third of Utah inmates are sex offenders, about three times the national average (12.4%).[46] In a study published by the *Journal of Economic Perspectives* in 2009, Utah ranked number one among U.S states in Internet porn subscription.[47]

The Centers for Disease Control study the effects of sexual abuse on the abusers' prey and divide them into four categories: physical, psychological, social, and health. Physical symptoms could include migraines, gastrointestinal disorders, chronic pain, gynecological complications, and/or genital injuries. Psychological effects of sexual abuse are devastating: depression, anxiety, fear, withdrawal, anorexia and bulimia, guilt, shame, distrust of others, anxiety, PTSD, flashbacks, and suicide. Social consequences include strained relationships with family, friends, and intimate partners; less emotional support from friends and family; less frequent contact with friends and relatives; lower likelihood of marriage; and isolation or ostracism from family or community. Health consequences may include engaging in high-risk sexual behavior, using harmful substances, unhealthy diet-related behaviors, juvenile delinquent and criminal behavior, and failure to engage in healthy behavior.[48]

Tragically, there is evidence that, occasionally, priesthood members of the LDS Church have sexually abused children. Even more tragically, too often alleged abusers and their abuse went unreported by church authorities aware of it in their ecclesiastical positions to government agencies, as required by law in many states. In some cases, abuse was reported to congregational leaders, both male and female, at a ward council meeting or other leadership meeting and no one reported it to government authorities. For a comprehensive compilation of LDS alleged abuse cases, see Diener (2017).[49]

In ministry, we met a woman who left Mormonism, who told us she was forced to be a victim of occult ritual abuse by adult family members of the LDS Church. We have also ministered to a woman whose priesthood father used his temple recommend on the nightstand as justification to seduce his daughter into sex for many years. "You are my special daughter. I'm not doing anything that Heavenly Father has not done with his special daughter, Mary." In no way can we say these practices are common; however, the teaching of polygamy made both Michael and me ill, and the more we read the Bible, caused us to deduce that something was terribly morally amiss.

Another teaching with serious social and mental health consequences is the LDS teaching that one must become perfect as Jesus is perfect.

Salvation Requires Obedience to LDS Laws and Ordinances

It is well known that Mormonism requires works to gain eternal life. Mormons do many good works and when I was LDS, I saw these "Christ-like works" as evidence to others that I belonged to the one true church. The LDS scripture from the Pearl of Great Price, the Third Article of Faith, states that salvation comes by "obedience to the laws and ordinances of the [Mormon] gospel." I address this issue because the need to continually perform in an effort to become perfect—an impossible standard for any man or woman (without the righteousness imputed to us by the biblical Jesus)—has many consequences in terms of human effect. Unfortunately, statistics and studies over the years have shown that suicide is more prevalent in Utah than the national average. According to the Centers for Disease Control statistics from 2012, Utah ranked fifth in the U.S. for suicide.[50] Is the pressure to live impossible standards related to behaviors such as lying, depression, cutting, judging, shunning, pornography, prescription drug addiction, divorce, white collar fraud, bankruptcy, and loss of jobs, friends, and family? There is a great need for hard data on these issues.

As I read the Word, I was faced with another biblical teaching conflicting with Mormon doctrine—this time Ephesians 2:8–9. This verse impacted me like an iron mallet. This teaching was opposite Mormon doctrine—the exact opposite. "For it is by grace you have been saved, through faith—and this is not from yourselves, it is the gift of God—not by works, so that no one can boast." The Bible clearly teaches we are saved, or receive eternal life, by grace alone through faith in Jesus. No works of ours can save us or earn for us eternal life. But Mormonism requires that one continues in good works until the end of life in order to gain eternal life (in LDS theology called "exaltation"). I will show some contrasts between biblical eternal life and Mormon eternal life (exaltation).

Let's examine the requirements for gaining eternal life in Mormon theology. In the Book of Mormon we read, "For we labor diligently to write, to persuade our children, and also our brethren, to believe in Christ, and to be reconciled to God; for we know that it is by grace that we are saved, after all we can do" (2 Nephi 25:23). In LDS theology, grace is not given as a free gift as it is in the Bible, but eternal life is earned from God through merit, *if* one has done all he or she can do first. In Mormonism, individuals can never know personally if they have done enough: Heavenly Father decides in the end. If someone would have asked me when I was LDS if I was saved, I would have answered, "I hope so." I hoped that by the end of my life I would have done enough. For Mormons, eternal life is earned only by members of the LDS Church in good standing after working their way, through a process of obeying LDS laws and ordinances, to the top heaven in Mormonism, the celestial kingdom. Only in this top of three heavens can they have access to all members of the godhead so biblical eternal life and Mormon eternal life are similar in that sense.

This coveted LDS top heaven, the celestial kingdom, is divided into three levels. Only by being sealed to a worthy LDS spouse in a temple marriage can a woman earn the uppermost of the three levels in this top kingdom. The husband, not Jesus, will resurrect his spouse. In the *Preach My Gospel* manual used by Mormon missionaries, on page 70 we find an LDS definition of eternal life: "Eternal Life: To live forever as families in God's presence." Technically, this means a Mormon must reach the uppermost part of the celestial kingdom to have eternal life. Mormons strive to earn this right to live as a forever family in the next life through remaining temple-worthy to the end. Both spouses and the children must stay worthy and do good works until the end to have the hope of eternal life with family and with deity.

Of course, biblical eternal life is not earned but given freely by God's grace by believing in Jesus. The Bible teaches one *has* eternal life here and now at the point of belief. The Bible's definition of grace is: unmerited favor freely given. In contrast, the LDS Bible Dictionary states this about grace in Mormonism: "The main idea of the word is divine means of help or strength . . . . This grace is an enabling power that allows men and women to lay hold on eternal life and exaltation after they have expended their own best efforts.

Divine grace is needed by every soul in consequence of the Fall of Adam and also because of man's weaknesses and shortcomings. However, grace cannot suffice without total effort on the part of the recipient. Hence the explanation, 'It is by grace that we are saved, after all we can do' (2 Ne. 25:23)."[51]

On December 9, 1982, Ezra Taft Benson, then a member of the twelve apostles and later a prophet, gave a talk entitled, "After All We Can Do," in which he said the following: "What is meant by, after all we can do?' 'After all we can do' includes extending our best effort. 'After all we can do' includes living His commandments. 'After all we can do' includes loving our fellowmen and praying for those who regard us as their adversary. 'After all we can do' means clothing the naked, feeding the hungry, visiting the sick and giving 'succor [to] those who stand in need of [our] succor' (Mosiah 4:15)—remembering that what we do unto one of the least of God's children, we do unto Him (see Matthew 25:34–40; D&C 42:38). 'After all we can do' means leading chaste, clean, pure lives, being scrupulously honest in all our dealings and treating others the way we would want to be treated."[52]

In addition to a professing faith in the Mormon Jesus, the Mormon gospel, and the Mormon prophets—and the above requirements—"all you can do" also includes obedience to the laws and ordinances of Mormonism. The Third Article of Faith states, "We believe that through the atonement of Christ, all mankind may be saved, by obedience to the laws and ordinances of the Gospel." One may be saved by obedience to the laws and ordinances of the Mormon gospel. What are these saving ordinances?

In the current LDS manual *Duties and Blessings of the Priesthood: Basic Manual for Priesthood Holders, Part B*, it reads, "In the Church the word *ordinances* usually refers to rites and ceremonies that the Lord has given us for our salvation, guidance, and comfort." This priesthood manual also teaches: "Ordinances that are necessary for us to return to Heavenly Father include baptism, confirmation, the sacrament, conferral of the Melchizedek Priesthood (for brethren), the temple endowment, and temple marriage."[53]

Let's look at each of the ordinances necessary for Mormon eternal life/exaltation.

Baptism by Immersion

The first saving ordinance is baptism by immersion performed only on individuals age eight or older. Water baptism is required for eternal life and is only valid if performed by a Mormon male with priesthood authority and accompanied by priesthood witnesses who make sure no hair has gone unsubmerged. Mormons teach baptism accomplishes remission of sins. Baptism is the gate to becoming a member of LDS Church. Acts 10:43 is a biblical passage to consider: "All the prophets testify about him that everyone who believes in him receives forgiveness of sins through his name." In this passage, remission of sins is received through faith in his name, not water baptism. (Of course water baptism as a saving ordinance is argued for and against among Christians as well.)

Confirmation as a Member of the Church of Jesus Christ of Latter-day Saints

Immediately after baptism by immersion (within twenty-four hours in my experience), the individual must receive the Holy Ghost. This is also required for eternal life and must be given through the laying on of hands by those in authority, which means the Mormon priesthood. This gift of the Holy Ghost and confirmation of membership in the LDS Church are bestowed together.

A biblical passage I read that refuted this idea is Acts 10:44–45: "While Peter was still speaking these words, the Holy Spirit came on all who heard the message. The circumcised believers who had come with Peter were astonished that the gift of the Holy Spirit had been poured out even on Gentiles." The Holy Spirit fell on them without the laying on of hands. In the next passage, the Spirit fell on the audience without the laying on of hands as well. "As I began to speak, the Holy Spirit came on them as he had come on us at the beginning. Then I remembered what the Lord had said: 'John baptized with water, but you will be baptized with the Holy Spirit.' So if God gave them the same gift he gave us who believed in the Lord Jesus Christ, who was I to think that I could stand in God's way?" (Acts 11:15–17). In Galatians 3:2 and Ephesians 1:13 the Holy Spirit is received by hearing with faith, "I would like to learn just one thing from you: Did you receive the Spirit by the works of the law, or by believing what you heard?" (Gal. 3:2). Again, laying on of hands is not part of the gifting. "In him you also, when you heard the word of truth, the gospel of your salvation, and believed in him, were sealed with the promised Holy Spirit" (Eph. 1:13). Note that baptism by immersion and LDS Church membership are also bestowed on the living in proxy for the dead in the temple as part of the laws and ordinances necessary to salvation after this life, something the Bible never mentions at all.

Sacrament (Communion)

The next ordinance required for Mormon exaltation is the weekly taking of the sacrament during the Sunday seventy-minute sacrament (church) service. The sacrament must be taken on a weekly basis so that one will remain "worthy" and be cleansed of sins committed during the previous week, like a spiritual recharge. Mormons use water instead of fruit of the vine (wine or grape juice), and leavened bread. Some biblical passages that I read are: Luke 22:17–18 where Jesus gave the fruit of the vine to His apostles to drink. "And he took a cup, and when he had given thanks he said, 'Take this, and divide it among yourselves. For I tell you that from now on I will not drink of the fruit of the vine until the kingdom of God comes.'" And, in John 2:6–11, Jesus turns water into wine. This "fruit of the vine" is significant in Christianity partly because of the biblical metaphor that Jesus is the vine, we the branches, and we bear fruit in Him.

Conferral of Melchizedek Priesthood (for Men)

The Melchizedek priesthood is necessary for a male member of the LDS Church to receive in order to achieve eternal life with God and Christ in the celestial kingdom. There are several biblical passages that shook Michael and me about this priesthood that we had so esteemed for thirty years. Michael was a high priest in the LDS Church, which office is required to hold certain leadership callings. The following passage of the Bible would be great to consider with your Mormon friends; the rich words in Hebrews chapters 7–13 are powerful. This passage states that Jesus's position of high priest is for One only. It is nontransferable. This passage explains how the temple ordinances were a shadow of Christ's sacrifice and how the temple rites are no longer needed. It is accomplished. Mormonism tries to resurrect Old Testament law, but it is a skewed and inaccurate interpretation of such.

First Peter explains that true believers are living stones built up as a royal priesthood, the body of Christ (see 1 Peter 2:4–9). This body is not exclusively male. The one and only high priest is Jesus Christ Himself (Heb. 10:10–21). He meets our need for a holy, blameless, and pure high priest who offered Himself once for all. The Hebrews section makes it clear that there is one high priest forever and that is Jesus Christ Himself. There is no other. Ephesians 4:11–13 describes apostles, prophets, evangelists, pastors, and teachers as critical to the body of Christ, the New Testament church. High priests are not mentioned.

Temple Endowment

The LDS temple endowment is an additional requirement for eternal life. The temple endowment is performed by those with Mormon priesthood authority in secret behind the walls of the Mormon temples. The endowment ceremony is Masonic in nature and involves taking oaths of secrecy. The first time one goes through the endowment, it is received personally. Thereafter, it is performed in proxy on behalf of someone who is dead; the temple patron or attendee is given the name of the dead person for whom he or she is standing in proxy. While living near the temple in Utah, I went frequently. Our son, Micah, tried to go every morning, about 5:00 a.m., his last year of high school. Husband Michael, son Micah, and I all worked in the temple.

The most impactful passage of biblical scripture I read that related to the Mormon temple was Acts 17:24: "The God who made the world and everything in it is the Lord of heaven and earth and does not live in temples built by human hands." I had never seen that verse before (or at least I never noticed). God doesn't dwell in temples made by men. When LDS, I believed that one could get closer to God in the celestial room of the temple than anywhere else on earth. I also found scriptures warning against making oaths (Matt. 5:34; James 5:12) like we did in the temple. It seems that once I surrendered my life to Christ's keeping, my eyes were opened as I read the Word and everything became clear over a period of time. It took a while to shed the untruths and replace them with biblical truth—for me, nearly five years.

I also read the scriptures that clarify that Jesus did nothing in secret (Matt. 10:26–27; Mark 4:21–22; John 18:20). I began to understand what it meant that the temple veil was torn in two when Jesus died. We now have direct access to the Savior. No believer should be ashamed of the gospel. We should shout it from the rooftops. There is no biblical reason for secrecy. Even the Book of Mormon warns against "secret combinations" in more than twenty scriptures.

Temple Marriage (Sealing)

According to the Priesthood manual and Doctrine and Covenants 132, it is necessary to be sealed to a worthy spouse in a Mormon temple in order to reach the highest rung of the highest heaven to live with Heavenly Father after this life. The temple sealing binds the couple in marriage for this life and the next. Mormons believe in marriage beyond death, although the Bible teaches the opposite (Luke 20:34–35; Matt. 22:30; Mark 12:25). Only those Mormons who are "worthy" enough to hold a temple recommend can attend a temple wedding/sealing ceremony. A non-Mormon can never enter a temple. Having family members and friends left out of the wedding ceremony is a huge flash point of emotions for many families and may encourage the newly married couple to look to other temple sealed members as family before their own. These are the ordinances of the Mormon gospel, now the laws. The laws are additional (see below). Before one can receive many of these saving ordinances exclusively offered in Mormonism, it is necessary to first prove oneself worthy by obeying the laws of Mormonism.

The Laws of Mormonism

The Word of Wisdom

The first such law is the Word of Wisdom. This is a code of conduct regarding what Mormon people can and cannot consume, a health code of sorts. It includes abstaining from alcohol, tobacco, coffee, tea, and harmful drugs. It includes dietary suggestions, such as eating meat sparingly, grains (wheat is for man, the other grains for animals), herbs, and fruit. The Word of Wisdom is specified in Doctrine and Covenants Section 89. It includes blessings if one obeys, such as health, protection, knowledge, wisdom, and strength. "And I, the Lord, give unto them a promise, that the destroying angel shall pass by them, as the children of Israel, and not slay them. Amen" (D&C 89:21). Obeying the Word of Wisdom is one of the many requirements that must be kept in order to be worthy to receive a temple recommend so one can enter the temple to earn eternal life. It is not an option for one who intends to go to the celestial kingdom to live with the Mormon Jesus and the Mormon god in the hereafter. One must go to the temple and do the ordinances. In their own words from the LDS website: "While the Word of Wisdom requires strict obedience, in return it promises health, great treasures of knowledge, and that redemption bought for us by the Lamb of God, who was slain that we might be redeemed"[54] The prophet Joseph Fielding Smith asked: "Are you letting a cup of tea or a little tobacco stand in the road and bar you from the celestial kingdom of God, where you might otherwise have received a fulness [*sic*] of glory?"[55]

There are several noteworthy Bible passages that refute the need for the Word of Wisdom. A good passage is Matthew 15:10–20. Here Christ explains that it is not what goes into a body that defiles it. What goes in just comes out the other end. It is what comes out of a man's mouth that comes from his heart that defiles him. Out of his heart comes evil. Romans 14 teaches us not to pass judgment in matters of food and drink. Another powerful place to read is Colossians 2:16–23 and then 1 Timothy 4:2–5. Paul rails against human commands, teachings, and regulations that have an appearance of wisdom but have no value.

The Tithe

For members of the LDS Church, paying tithes (10 percent) or "tithing," as Mormons say, to the Mormon Church is obligatory and must be documented in a yearly personal meeting with the bishop or a representative. It is a requirement for those who wish to attend the temple for the hope of gaining eternal life. Only temple-goers can reach the celestial kingdom where they earn eternal life and live with Jesus and Heavenly Father (and Heavenly Mother) in the next life. So in a sense, paying money to the Mormon Church gets one to the best heaven. Only temple-going males can become gods, so for faithful Mormons who wish to reach the celestial kingdom, tithing is compulsory. Without it one cannot receive a temple recommend. Without the recommend, one cannot go to the temple. Without the temple endowment, one cannot go to the celestial kingdom. The biblical Old Testament tithe was largely agricultural and received by the Levites. In many ways, Mormonism appears to live the old law but it is a distortion of the actual Old Testament law.

According to Christ himself, he has fulfilled the law. The law was a schoolmaster to bring us to Christ. "For all who rely on the works of the law are under a curse, as it is written: 'Cursed is everyone who does not continue to do everything written in the Book of the Law'" (Gal. 3:10). Anyone who tries to live one part of the law is obligated to all parts and to live them perfectly in order to be saved. This is impossible for man. One who tries to live the old law but stumbles on any part of it, transgresses the entire law (Gal. 3:10; James 2:10). "For whoever keeps the whole law and yet stumbles on just one point is guilty of breaking all of it" (James 2:10). Instead, as followers of Christ, we now recognize that all that we have, surely our material things but even our breath and life, belongs to him and depends on Him.

The Law of Chastity

Mormons are taught there is to be no sexual activity of any kind before marriage, and complete faithfulness during marriage. Living this law is a requirement for "worthiness" to receive a temple recommend and attend the temple.

Keeping the Sabbath Day Holy

Mormons are not supposed to shop, watch television, work, etc., on Sunday; they must attend church and all other meetings. The church block of time is typically three hours and includes three meetings. Most people will have callings to fulfill on Sundays. Lay members provide leadership, nursery workers, Sunday school, youth and adult teachers, etc. Church attendance is a necessary requirement for temple ordinance worthiness; attending your meetings is temple recommend requirement number eight. These rules about the Sabbath reveal a lack of knowledge concerning the biblical Sabbath and fulfillment of the law (Rom. 14:5; Col. 2:16–17). Again, Mormonism attempts to live a brand of Old Testament law that is not in sync with the Bible. If Mormons were consistent with the other Old Testament laws, they would have animal sacrifices in LDS temples and members would abstain from pork.

The Law of the Fast

Mormons have a mandatory corporate fast day once a month on Sunday. The fast sacrament service is different from a normal Sunday. Fast Sunday is an "open microphone" testimony meeting which can be quite emotional. This specific law is not necessarily a requirement for temple ordinance "worthiness," but is noteworthy because it reveals unfamiliarity with what the Word of God teaches in Matthew: "But when you fast, put oil on your head and wash your face, so that it will not be obvious to others that you are fasting, but only to your Father, who is unseen; and your Father, who sees what is done in secret, will reward you" (Matt. 6:17–18).

Other laws Mormons follow are: obey the prophet, keep the Ten Commandments, obey and honor the law of the land, fulfill your callings, do service to others, and on and on. Are you exhausted yet simply reading this? My family had a never-ending trail of things to do and were decidedly busy. As a reminder, largely the Mormon people truly believe they are following the right Gods and most are very sincere in their efforts to please them. If you have Mormons in your life, it is important to understand that it can be a very harrowing trying to measure up to the many high standards set all the while not knowing if they have done enough to be exalted. There is data that suggests religion is helpful in preventing poor mental health;[56] however, I believe there are consequences for Mormons persistently striving to be perfect. Given 2013 data, Mental Health America ranked Utah sixth from the bottom of the U.S. states for overall positive mental health.[57]

Thus far, I have addressed the social consequences of the teaching that dark skin is a curse, that polygamy is an eternal principle, and that works-based salvation can bring undue pressure on many to be perfect. Each of these has a cost in terms of social consequences. This next topic, too, has social consequences related to LDS beliefs.

The Only True Church

In 2007, I attended a multicultural conference in Baltimore. Between sessions, I was in the hallway browsing items on a table for sale, when a man read my nametag: Dr. Lynn Wilder, Brigham Young University. He approached me and introduced himself as a Palestinian Muslim. "I have one question for you," he said rather loudly. He assumed I was LDS, although by now I was mostly out of the church in my head if not yet officially on paper. "I used to live in the Phoenix area and I met some Mormons and I want to know why you people think you are Jews?!" I frowned, pondering, and said something like, "Well, we *are* told in our patriarchal blessings what tribe of Israel's blood flows through our veins or whether we have been adopted into a particular tribe." Whoa, that question stuck in my gut and ate away at me for days. Do Mormons think they are Jews? Yes, we believed we were a gathering of the lost ten tribes, it says on lds.org. But, were the descendants of Ephraim (my husband and most LDS priesthood leadership) and Manasseh (my purported tribal affiliation) really lost? In addition, we were taught that the Nephites and Lamanites, Book of Mormon peoples, were both descendants of Jews from Jerusalem and ancestors of Native American tribes in the Americas, so Jewish connections abound in Mormonism. (As an aside, Jews are aware that when Levi is recognized as a tribe, Ephraim and Manasseh, the sons of Joseph, are considered one tribe—Joseph—to keep the integrity of exactly twelve tribes.[58] When Levi is not mentioned in the Torah as one of the twelve tribes, then Joseph's sons Ephraim and Manasseh are each given a tribe. Many Mormons' patriarchal blessings give them lineage from Ephraim and Manasseh, so we can assume the Mormons do not recognize Levi as a tribe, which is interesting since Mormon men hold the priesthood and ordain high priests, but these male LDS leaders do not come from the tribe of Levi. Most come from Ephraim.)

Lost Ten Tribes

Only years later (2011/2012) when traveling to Israel did I learn from archeologist Joel Kramer that the ten tribes are not actually lost! In the eighth century B.C., after the reign of King Solomon, Israel was divided into two kingdoms, the nation of Israel in the north with ten tribes and Judah in the south with the remaining two tribes, Judah and Benjamin. Assyrian kings Shalmaneser and then Sargon attacked the northern kingdom of Israel in a twenty-year ongoing war. Just like refugees running from ISIS, the Islamic State, are doing today, inhabitants of Israel gathered to Israel's larger cities, which were better defended, especially the capital city of Israel,

Samaria. Fearful that even Samaria would fall, the king of Israel sent representatives from all ten tribes from Samaria to shelter in Jerusalem, where he believed they would be safer. Jerusalem welcomed the refugees and extended its boundaries to accommodate people from the ten northern tribes by building the broad wall. (On our visit, Michael and I saw remnants of the broad wall in Jerusalem.) A later Assyrian, King Sennacherib, did camp outside Jerusalem with the intent to capture the southern kingdom of Judah; however, a remarkable event happened to Sennacherib's army. One morning the king awoke to find 144,000 of his men dying of a disease. They packed up and went home.

Several years into my investigation into biblical faith, I discovered these Bible scriptures: "I know your afflictions and your poverty—yet you are rich! I know about the slander of those who say they are Jews and are not, but are a synagogue of Satan" (Rev. 2:9). And, "I will make those who are of the synagogue of Satan, who claim to be Jews though they are not, but are liars—I will make them come and fall down at your feet and acknowledge that I have loved you" (Rev. 3:9). Of course this applied to the believers in Jesus of John's day who thought all believers in Jesus, including non-Jews, should keep all of the Jewish laws; however, I wondered if that scripture didn't have a more modern application. Readers may come to their own conclusions. Regardless, the LDS organization does teach that it is the sole authority for the "fullness of truth," and that members of the LDS Church are the only true Christians and members of the lost ten tribes of Israel. Again, from the Book of Mormon: "And he said unto me: Behold there are save two churches only; the one is the church of the Lamb of God, and the other is the church of the devil; wherefore, whoso belongeth not to the church of the Lamb of God belongeth to that great church, which is the mother of abominations; and she is the whore of all the earth" (1 Nephi 14:10). The Mormon Church in this scripture teaches that it is the church of the Lamb of God. By default, that makes all who are not Mormon in the church of the devil. Mormons believe they are the Lord's chosen people, leaders from the tribe of Ephraim. Others outside the Mormon faith are Gentiles. There is LDS scriptural support for Mormonism being the one true church.

What follows here are some LDS scriptures that appeared on the official church website lds.org under the heading of *Mission of Latter-day Saints* in 2012. (Three years later, this section was not found on the website, however.) These LDS scriptures indicate who Mormons believe they are as followers of the LDS Church and what their roles and responsibilities are: "light unto the Gentiles, Doctrine and Covenants 86:11; saints . . . armed with righteousness, 1 Ne. 14:14; bring forth and establish the cause of Zion, Doctrine and Covenants 6:6; called to bring to pass the gathering of mine elect, Doctrine and Covenants 29:7; New Jerusalem should be built up upon this land, Ether 13:6; this church have I [Jesus] established, Doctrine and Covenants 33:5; sent forth to preach the everlasting gospel,

Doctrine and Covenants 36:5; not sent forth to be taught, but to teach, Doctrine and Covenants 43:15; Missouri . . . consecrated for the gathering of the saints, Doctrine and Covenants 57:1; New Jerusalem shall be built by the gathering of the saints, Doctrine and Covenants 84:4; they are accounted as the salt of the earth, Doctrine and Covenants 101:39; put on the authority of the priesthood, Doctrine and Covenants 113:8; gather ye out from among the nations, Doctrine and Covenants 133:7; by the hands of the . . . children of Ephraim, Doctrine and Covenants 133:32; gospel shall be preached unto every nation, Doctrine and Covenants 133:37; prepare the weak for those things which are coming, Doctrine and Covenants 133:58; faithful elders . . . continue their labors in the preaching, Doctrine and Covenants 138:57; Zion (the New Jerusalem) will be built upon the American continent, Articles of Faith 1:10."

Therefore, Mormons belong to Jesus's one true church, their leaders are from the tribe of Ephraim, it is their role to gather the lost ten tribes to Mormonism, it is their role to preach the Mormon gospel to all nations, and it is their responsibility to build the New Jerusalem in Missouri.

This certainly gives them a perceived position of elitism from their Heavenly Father among the faiths, a belief that is indeed not unique to LDS. It is reported that Joseph Smith prophesied that one day the Constitution would hang by a thread and a Mormon elder would ride in on a white horse and save it.[59] In a faith where God is more like a man, does this man-god need assistance from a Mormon elder to set the world stage for LDS dominance in order for Jesus to return to rule and reign? I once entertained this idea. Secular leadership presence in the CIA, FBI, military, academia, government, and other secular institutions once seemed necessary to me for the return of the LDS Christ, although these teachings are not substantiated in LDS scripture, but simply in cultural ideas.

Authority and a Great Apostasy

However, Mormon teachings do claim Mormons are more than just Christians; they are the only true church. That's why biblical Christians, most of the converts to the LDS Church, must join the Mormon Church to earn eternal life. There are several reasons Mormons claim this. Their scriptures say, "And also those to whom these commandments were given, might have power to lay the foundation of this church, and to bring it forth out of obscurity and out of darkness, the only true and living church upon the face of the whole earth, with which I, the Lord, am well pleased, speaking unto the church collectively and not individually" (D&C 1:30). Here allegedly Jesus Himself gives Joseph Smith and the other early church leaders power to lay the foundation of the only church with which he is well pleased, that foundation of prophets and apostles previously described. The Mormon Church was in its first year of existence when this revelation was received. So, there is and has been scriptural support from the beginning for its exclusivity. Joseph Smith stated in the scriptural account of his First Vision that all other churches of his time (Presbyterian, Methodist, etc.) were an abomination before God and that God asked him to join none of them. Deity then promised Joseph that he would restore the Lord's true church to the earth. Because Mormonism believes it is the one true church, Mormon missionaries try to convert traditional Christians to the fullness of the Mormon gospel. More than 80 percent of converts to the LDS Church come from biblical Christianity.[60]

According to LDS teachings, the foundation of the Mormon Church had to be laid so the Lord could restore his true and living church. The true church had to be restored because it had been lost from the earth after the original apostles died. This is called the Great Apostasy. This quote from the official Mormon Church website explains the Great Apostasy: "When individuals or groups of people turn away from the principles of the gospel, they are in a state of apostasy. One example is the Great Apostasy, which occurred after the Savior established His Church. After the deaths of the Savior and His apostles, men corrupted the principles of the gospel and made unauthorized changes in Church organization and priesthood ordinances. Because of this widespread apostasy, the Lord withdrew the authority of the priesthood from the earth. This apostasy lasted until Heavenly Father and His Beloved Son appeared to Joseph Smith in 1820 and initiated the restoration of the fulness of the gospel. Latter-day Saints believe that, through the priesthood conferred to Joseph Smith by the ministering of angels, the authority to act in God's name was brought back to the earth. This is 'restored' not 'reformed' Christianity."[61]

This original passage, too, has been changed from the official website since 2012, but I have presented the current passage here. To reiterate, Mormons believe the "true gospel" (Mormonism) was lost from the earth until Joseph Smith restored it for these reasons: (1) The Bible had been changed and was corrupt, and the "true gospel" was removed from it. (2) The priesthood authority was lost when the apostles died. (3) The loss of priesthood authority resulted in no man being able to receiving the Gift of the Holy Ghost from the time the apostles died until Joseph Smith restored the "true church" and the priesthood. Therefore no *true* Christians or *true* church existed from that time until Smith restored the true gospel.

Mormons suggest that biblical Christians reject the Book of Mormon because Christians are a product of the Great Apostasy and erroneously believe that they already have the fullness of truth in the Bible. Mormons believe they need more direction from extra-biblical latter-day scriptures like the Book of Mormon, Pearl of Great Price, Doctrine and Covenants, and the words of their prophets, seers, and revelators. 2 Nephi 29 verses 6 and 10 from the Book of Mormon state: "Thou fool, that shall say: A Bible, we have got a Bible, and we need no more Bible. . . . because that ye have a Bible ye need not suppose that it contains all my words; neither need ye suppose that I have not caused more to be written."

The Book of Mormon also says plain and precious teachings are lost from the Bible. It does not contain all of God's words, hence the need for the latter-day extra-biblical scriptures. What if the Bible actually records accurately the word of Jesus? I would want to read it.

Great Mormon Church Exodus

This LDS Church or church of the Lamb of God (1 Nephi 14:10) is accepting of its exclusivity and its secular accomplishments. The church claims more than fifteen million members worldwide (in reality the activity rate may be a fraction of that number), has more than 85,000 full time missionaries worldwide, 177 temples around the world, four church-owned undergraduate schools, and an estimated worth of thirty billion dollars.[62] A 1997 article in *Time Magazine* and a 1999 book by the same author as the article, Richard Ostling, called it one of the world's wealthiest churches per capita and goes into detail.[63] The LDS Church owns numerous for-profit corporations, businesses, land, mines, etc. Recently it was reported in the *Orlando Sentinel* that the LDS Church owns more land in Florida than any other private entity, amounting to 2 percent of Florida.[64] Although the Mormon Church teaches one is blessed in temporal things for keeping the commandments (see Mosiah 2:41) and itself exemplifies what is impressive in worldy terms--wealth, land holdings, for-profit corporations, and powerful and influential members in important institutions, Christians consider prosperity teachings an aberrant theology (1 Timothy 6:5)

Mormonism has a closet full of historical and doctrinal skeletons waiting to be opened by anyone who takes the time to investigate. The advent of the Internet has made a wealth of information available to the general public, including lesser-known church history and doctrines that would normally not be taught to a new member of the LDS Church until after a person is baptized (see the missionaries' manual, *Preach My Gospel*).[65] This has resulted in a decreasing number of converts per year and difficulty with convert retention.[66] In 1999, each LDS missionary baptized an average of 5.23 people. In 2008, it was 3. In 2015, it was about 3.5 converts per missionary, according to LDS records.[67]

Discontent with Mormon teachings burgeons as more and more members of the LDS Church and anyone willing to research on the Internet discover various sordid details of events in Mormon history, such as the Mountain Meadows Massacre, the banking practices of Joseph Smith, his polygamy, as well as others previously unknown to them.

A month before the book *Unveiling Grace: The Story of How We Found Our Way Out of the Church* came out, an article appeared in the *New York Times* that chronicled the journey of Mormon Church European Area Authority Hans Mattsson (who served from 2000–2005) and approximately 600 Swedish LDS saints as they grappled with questions from church history that Mattsson's superiors were inept at answering.

LDS apostle L. Tom Perry met with Mattsson, a stake president, and a few members in 2005 but had no real answers for them. Swedish dissatisfaction spread and in 2010 the LDS Church sent Marlin K. Jensen, church historian, and others to meet with about twenty-five members. The leaders took questions from the audience. There were approximately fifteen major questions the members posed to Jensen and to Turley, Kopischke, and Olsson, who accompanied him. Jensen explained that every day we deal with the spirit of Christ and the spirit of the devil and in the midst of this battle, every day we choose whether to believe or to doubt. He went on to tell them that many who decide to believe are aware of all these issues and more. But they still believe.

By 2011 the crisis was growing. Marlin K. Jensen, now retired general authority and historian of the LDS Church, was asked if the LDS leaders knew that Mormons, not just in Sweden, were leaving the faith in droves, typically after discovering troubling aspects of church history online. He responded:

> The fifteen men [First Presidency and Quorum of Twelve] really do know, and they really care. And they realize that maybe since Kirtland [1830s], we never have had a period of, I'll call it apostasy, like we're having right now; largely over these [historical] issues.[68]

Never had a period of apostasy like we're having right now. Perhaps the "Great Apostasy" they believe in will be their own. Evidently in response to the increasing number of Mormons disturbed by researching sensitive topics on the Internet, on September 9, 2014, the LDS Church issued a letter to all church leaders starting with general authorities and ending with bishops and branch presidents inviting them to direct members with doubts to the accurate information from this reliable church source instead of from those who may be posting inaccurate information about church history and doctrine. The church also invited programs in each ward (congregation) to submit the names to their priesthood superiors of two people each week who may be questioning their LDS faith or in some kind of need. We talked with a family last summer who had left the LDS Church when this directive came down. They could no longer be members of a church that kept such close watch on their members.

Regardless of these in-place measures to present "authentic" church history and maybe because of them, Latter-day Saints continue to doubt their faith by the tens of thousands.[69] The LDS Church attempted first the Swedish saints' rescue and during summer of 2015, the Boise, Idaho saints' rescue. Neither has proved largely successful. Absent convincing answers to very real questions, the discontent surges. In October of 2013 at the LDS Church's General Conference, Dieter F. Uchtdorf, member of the LDS First Presidency, acknowledged that leaders have made mistakes doing things that could cause people to question. His advice if this happens, however, is to doubt your doubts before you doubt your faith.[70]

Social Consequences of Mormonism

Racism

In summary, to a social scientist, it is the social consequences of Mormon teachings that cause the greatest trepidation. Even a nonbeliever with no faith anchor likely agrees that the teaching that any skin color is a curse is outrageously destructive within the stratified power structures of social societies and institutions. Most social scientists would concur that teachings of the superiority of any race do not promote civility and equality nor harmonious living among racial groups of humans. Most would condemn the genocide of entire groups as unethical and immoral. Now, Mormonism does not suggest negative behavior toward those with dark skin; however, the essence of morality belies the credo that dark skin is a curse, a teaching remaining in twenty-six verses of supposed "pure truth" LDS scripture. How any Mormon interprets that "truth" in behavior is up to them. However, I cannot deny that this ideology can lay the foundation for racist practice and, for that reason, can be dangerous. I have published professional articles on what I call a "moral multiculturalism." In other words, rather than allow each group to socially construct their own reality and accept each group's stance as morally equitable, I implore rational multiculturalists to examine and consider the moral status of group positions when they are extreme, threatening, and violate the human rights (as in the case of the behavior of genocide, not in the case of beliefs not acted upon) of other groups.[71] It is the action—the behavior—not the beliefs that are inherently perilous, although immoral beliefs can lead to immoral behavior.

Polygamy

Since practitioners of various LGBTQ lifestyles can now participate in legalized unions in the United States, it may be that polygamy will be legally accepted soon as well. If this is the case, it is still incumbent upon a moral society to protect the rights of children from sexual and emotional abuse and male domination resulting in the violence present in some polygamous communities and to set legal boundaries for all families. Under no circumstance is the rape or other physical or emotional abuse of children acceptable. Utah has a dreadful record of not prosecuting those practicing polygamy or impregnating young teen girls. Some mainstream LDS parents have expressed concern that Mormon priesthood holders have queried their children about sexual activity such as masturbation without the parents' presence or even their knowledge in some cases. The LDS Church has an abysmal record of not reporting sexual abuse to government authorities,[72] as can be deduced by searching the Internet for instances of sexual abuse in Mormonism and reading various blogs of personal experiences. Michael and I, of course, hear such stories firsthand in our own ministry. A careful search will provide data on lawsuits or near lawsuits that have resulted from this grievous practice of not reporting, particularly regarding pedophiles never reported who abused repeatedly. Sometimes pedophiles use Mormonism, like other religions, to hide or to try to justify their abuse by using church teachings, like Brian David Mitchell did when he abducted and repeatedly raped 14-year-old Elizabeth Smart, claiming her as a second wife in polygamy.

The idea that Jesus resulted from sexual relations between Heavenly Father and Mary has been clearly taught in the LDS Church by leaders including Brigham Young, Orson Pratt, Heber C. Kimball, Joseph F. Smith, Joseph Fielding Smith, James E. Talmage, Melvin J. Ballard, J. Reuben Clark, Bruce R. McConkie, and Ezra Taft Benson.[73] Many Mormons believe that Jesus Christ was literally the son of Heavenly Father, the only begotten of the flesh. The teaching that he may have impregnated Mary "in the usual way" is a detrimental teaching that has resulted in at least one man sleeping with his young daughter. The viewing of Internet pornography is rampant in Utah, perhaps as an outlet for sexual tension experienced by singles before marriage. Or pornography is perhaps a factor for married men thinking of someday having another wife. As previously noted, rape rates are higher in Utah than the national average and the Utah prison population has more pedophiles than the national average. In ministry, we have even run into stories about occult ritual abuse of children by active members of the LDS Church in local/stake leadership.[74] In recent years, progressive LDS women formed the Ordain Women movement. "Based on the principle of thoughtful, faith-affirming strategic action, Ordain Women aspires to create a space for Mormon women to articulate issues of gender inequality they may be hesitant to raise alone."[75] I was always confused about why LDS women who cannot hold the Mormon priesthood would not simply accept the royal priesthood offered by Jesus in the Bible, available to all believers. Why try to change an institution immovable on this issue? Why not just investigate faith in something better? "Someone greater than the temple [or anything else] is here," Jesus said about himself (Matt. 12:6). His priesthood extends to all believers. The role of women in Mormonism and the issue of sexual abuse is a subject vast enough for an entire book.

There is great need for solid, up-to-date data on these matters to determine the scope of the problems and to test correlations.

Works

The third topic addressed, works-based religion, has a wider range of negative social consequences given the fact that individuals respond to pressure and stress differently according to their personalities, past experiences, and biology. Among them may be: anxiety, depression, PTSD, prescription drug abuse, lying, cutting, suicide, judging others, shunning, or divorce (especially when one spouse is not "temple-worthy" or decides to leave the LDS Church). White-collar fraud and bankruptcy rates have been high in Utah over the years, perhaps as a result of the pressure on LDS men to be exemplary wage earners and to support large families. Surely paying 10 percent of gross income to the LDS Church for a chance at eternal life is a burden for some. Latayne Scott's book *Mormon Mirage*[76] has two chapters describing the challenges facing Mormonism in this century, including the issues of gender, race, the Internet, politics, public former Mormons, polygamy, and others. More research on the Mormon challenges and their social consequences is required.

The Book of Mormon teaches that those who keep the commandments of God (the righteous) will be "blessed in all things, both temporal and spiritual" (Mosiah 2:41), but I knew those blessings would come from the work of my own hands. I was taught that God helps those who help themselves. Biblical Christians know this is not Jesus's teaching. The result of those choosing to leave the works-based faith can be loss of job, friends, and family, even spouse. We have talked with many in this predicament. It is possible there is no direct connection from LDS culture and teachings to some of these social consequences, but without correlational research, we cannot positively say one is related to the other. We can only ask questions and look at the data we do have in Utah—polygamy is openly practiced with no legal repercussions; there are high rates of depression, suicide, prescription drug addiction, bankruptcy, white-collar fraud, pornography viewing; and there are high rates of rape, with leaders in the LDS Church sometimes not reporting abusers.[77]

One True Church

The "only true church" teaching also has social consequence of defensiveness and isolationism. Because I believed it was the Lord's own church with the Lord's own prophets, seers, and revelators and because I worked at the Lord's own university, the School of the Prophets, I felt protective. I felt defensive. I was taught everyone was out to persecute the Mormon Church and Joseph Smith and so viewed the outside world from a shielded bubble. Once I saw the prophet lie on TV. At first I was shocked and disturbed, but then he told the brethren in a priesthood meeting that he knew his doctrine. In other words, he fudged on purpose to the outside world who would not understand the sacred things of our faith. "Lying for the Lord" was a term coined by Brigham Young to justify not telling the outside world the whole truth and stems from the LDS scripture in the Book of Abraham where God tells Abraham to lie to Pharaoh and say Sarah is his sister (Abraham 2:22–25). The Bible does not say that God told him to lie. The lie was Abraham's own idea to save his skin. Yes, humans are sinful from birth, not born as children of God as Mormons teach. I've heard returned missionaries wonder if they had perhaps deceived investigators to Mormonism by not telling them whole truth. I know I was reluctant to tell the truth about my questions and struggles and, of course, my sins to other church members who might tell my bishop. I tended to embellish the church's value and my own and definitely Joseph Smith's, who in the end, had many failed prophecies, and to feel justified in promoting this only true church.

Apostates were something to be feared and I was to stay away from this work of the devil. I believed I was a Jew, the real chosen people, gathered to do the work of the latter-days and that I must work continually so God would be pleased with me and, at the end of my life if it's been enough, offer his grace. While working in the temple and while doing the work for my own family's dead, I longed for spirits of my dead ancestors to appear to me. The Bible calls this necromancy, the stuff of séances, and one should run like hell. As a woman I would never become a god, but I could be eternally pregnant and a happy servant to my god-husband. Salvation came through my husband and he, not Jesus, would resurrect me from the dead. If I ever got divorced, I would be a second-class citizen unless I married a righteous priesthood holder—and these are becoming scarce, especially in Utah.[78]

When we were LDS, traditional Christians had nothing to offer us. I dismissed anything they tried to tell me, although I don't recall one ever trying to tell me that I should rethink Mormonism or that there was a God that was real, not impotent, and able to do amazing things in my personal life. Honestly, when I discovered the God of grace, I was a little peeved no Christian I knew had tried to tell me about who He is and what He can do. I was also taught as LDS that "if Mormonism is not true, nothing is." This, too, I found to be a lie, yet so many we talk to who leave the LDS Church still believe it and it leads them nowhere, paralyzed to test whether there might be a real God. One of the most insidious things I believed from Mormon scripture that impacted my point of view was that the Bible was mistranslated, corrupt, and not to be trusted. The Book of Mormon was the most correct book on the face of the earth. This teaching kept me from reading the Bible and from taking seriously the things I did read there.

Truth is, the archeological, physical, historical, botanical, and geographical evidence is so overwhelming for the Bible people, places, and events, it is as if this God actually wants people to know Him. That one thing—opening my heart and mind to the possibility there is a real God, a God of grace, and that His words are recorded accurately and I can trust them—has changed my life forever. Jesus truly is enough, and I know peace.

NOTES

1. Doctrine and Covenants (D&C) 128:15, https://www.lds.org/scriptures/dc-testament/dc/128.15?lang=eng#14.
2. Address given by LDS prophet Ezra Taft Benson February 22, 1987 entitled *To the Mothers in Zion,* 2015, http://emp.byui.edu/websterb/links/Mothers%20in%20Zion.htm.
3. D. Michael Quinn, *The Mormon Hierarchy: Origins of Power* (Salt Lake City: Signature Books, 1994),
4. Gordon B. Hinckley, "The Need for Greater Kindness," *Ensign* and *Liahona,* May 2006, 58–61.
5. John L. Lund, *The Church and the Negro* (Lund, 1967).
6. The Church of Jesus Christ of Latter-day Saints, *Preach My Gospel*, (Salt Lake City: Church of Jesus Christ of Latter-day Saints, 2004) 70.
7. Jerald and Sandra Tanner, *Curse of Cain? Racism in the Mormon Church* (Salt Lake City: Utah Lighthouse Ministry, 2004), http://www.utlm.org/onlinebooks/curseofcain_contents.htm.
8. Lynn K. Wilder, *Unveiling Grace: The Story of How We Found Our Way Out of the Mormon Church* (Grand Rapids: Zondervan, 2013).
9. Joseph Smith, *History of the Church*, 7 vols., comp. B. H. Roberts (Salt Lake City: Deseret Book Co., 1975), 6:411.
10. "Utah Woman Charged with Aiding and Abetting Polygamy," *USA Today*, 2005, http://usatoday30.usatoday.com/news/nation/2002-10-14-utah-woman-polygamy_x.htm.
11. *Journal of Discourses*, vol. 17, pp. 224–25.
12. Michael and Lynn K. Wilder, *7 Reasons We Left Mormonism* (Palm Springs, CA: ATRI, 2012).
13. Peter Henderson and Kristina Cooke, "Mormonism Besieged by the Modern Age," *Reuters*, January 31, 2012, http://www.reuters.com/article/2012/01/31/us-mormonchurch-idUSTRE80T1CM20120131.
14. Newell G. Bringhurst and Darron T. Smith, *Black and Mormon* (Chicago: University of Illinois Press, 2004).
15. American Psychological Association, "Racism," 2015, http://www.apa.org/pi/oema/programs/racism/un-conference-plenary.aspx.
16. LDS Church official website, "Race and the Priesthood," 2015, http://www.lds.org/topics/race-and-the-priesthood?lang=eng.
17. LDS Church official website, "Heritage, Study, and Blessings," 2015, http://www.lds.org/scriptures/heritage?lang=eng&country=car.
18. LDS Church official website, Richard G. Scott, "The Power of Scripture," 2015, https://www.lds.org/general-conference/2011/10/the-power-of-scripture?lang=eng.
19. LDS Church official website, D. Todd Christofferson, "The Blessing of Scripture," 2015, http://www.lds.org/general conference/2010/04/the-blessing-of-scripture?lang=eng
20. LDS Church official website, Robert D. Hales, "Holy Scriptures: The Power of God unto Our Salvation," 2015, https://www.lds.org/general-conference/2006/10/holy-scriptures-the-power-of-god-unto-our-salvation?lang=eng.
21. Delbert Stapley Letter, January 23, 1964, http://mormonmatters.org/wp-content/uploads/2008/01/delbert_stapley.pdf.
22. Joseph Smith, Jr., compiled by Joseph Fielding Smith, *Teachings of the Prophet Joseph Smith*, (Salt Lake City: Deseret Book Company, 1976), p. 270.
23. Joseph Smith, Jr. and B.H. Roberts, *History of the Church*, Vol. 2, p. 438.
24. LDS Church official website, "Race and the Priesthood," 2015, http://www.lds.org/topics/race-and-the-priesthood?lang=eng.

25. LDS scripture, D&C 134:12 http://www.lds.org/scriptures/dc-testament/dc/134.12?lang=eng.
26. Stephen G. Taggart, *Mormonism's Negro Policy: Social and Historical Origins* (Salt Lake City: University of Utah Press, 1970).
27. Fawn Brodie, *No Man Knows My History* (NY: Vintage Books, 1945).
28. *Latter-day Saints' Messenger and Advocate*, vol. 2, no. 7, Kirtland, Ohio, April, 1836. [Whole No. 19], http://www.centerplace.org/history/ma/v2n07.htm.
29. *Teachings of Presidents of the Church: Wilford Woodruff*, (Salt Lake City: Church of Jesus Christ of Latter-day Saints, 2004), 199, 201.
30. *True to the Faith: A Gospel Reference* (Salt Lake City: The Church of Jesus Christ of Latter-day Saints, 2004), 129.
31. LDS Church official website, Dieter F. Uchtdorf, "Come Join with Us," 2015, http://www.lds.org/general-conference/2013/10/come-join-with-us?lang=eng.
32. Richard Lyman Bushman, *Joseph Smith: Rough Stone Rolling: A Cultural Biography of Mormonism's Founder* (NY: Alfred A. Knopf, 2005).
33. Lynn K. Wilder, Terry L. Shepherd, Francie Murry, Eric Rogers, et al. (2007), "Teacher Ratings of Social Skills across Ethnic Groups for Learners with Mild Disabilities: Implications for Teacher Education," *Curriculum and Teaching* vol. 22 (1), 47–66.
34. Elia Vázquez-Montilla, Lynn K. Wilder, and Robert Triscari, "Ethnically Diverse Faculty in Higher Ed: Belonging, Respect, and Role as Cultural Broker," *Multicultural Learning and Teaching* vol. 7, no. 1 (April, 2012), http://www.degruyter.com/view/j/mlt.2012.7.issue-1/issue-files/mlt.2012.7.issue-1.xml.
35. Pew Research Center, "A Portrait of Mormons in the U.S.," http://www.pewforum.org/2009/07/24/a-portrait-of-mormons-in-the-us/.
36. B. Carmon Hardy, *Solemn Covenant: The Mormon Polygamous Passage*, (Chicago: University of Illinois Press, 1992).
37. LDS scripture, Doctrine and Covenants, Section CI Marriage, 1835, http://www.physics.byu.edu/faculty/rees/325/documents/ArticleMarriage.pdf.
38. Jerald and Sandra Tanner, *Mormonism: Shadow or Reality?* (Salt Lake, UT: UTLM, 2008), pp. 202, 228.
39. LDS apologists argue this quote was taken out of context http://www.fairmormon.org/perspectives/publications/does_president_hinckley_understand_lds_doctrine.
40. Robert Millet; see 1:30 into the video https://www.dailymotion.com/video/x1kt8h_robert-millet-short-version_news.
41. B. Carmon Hardy, *Solemn Covenant: The Mormon Polygamous Passage*, (Chicago: University of Illinois Press, 1992).
42. Susan Ray Schmidt, *His Favorite Wife: Trapped in Polygamy* (Susan Ray Schmidt, 2006).
43. *Andy Poland's Story*, https://www.youtube.com/watch?time_continue=75&v=OBda3vWOBsU.
44. April Daniels and Carol Scott, *Paper Dolls: A True Story of Childhood Sexual Abuse in Mormon Neighborhoods* (Scott's Valley, CA: Recovery Publications, 1993).
45. Utah Department of Health, Public Health Indicator Based Information System: Utah's Public Health Data Resource, *How Do We Compare With the U.S.?* https://ibis.health.utah.gov/indicator/complete_profile/Rape.html.
46. For Utah statistics from Pew Charitable Trusts on inmates who are sex offenders, see Marissa Lang, "Sex Offenders Driving up Utah's Prison Population," Salt Lake Tribune, September 15, 2014, http://archive.sltrib.com/story.php?ref=/sltrib/news/58406311-78/offenders-sex-prison-utah.html.csp. For federal statistics on inmates who are sex offenders, see U.S. Department of Justice Office of Justice Programs Bureau of Justice Statistics, Prisoners in 2015, p. 14, https://www.bjs.gov/content/pub/pdf/p15.pdf.

47. Benjamin Edelman, "Red Light States: Who Buys Online Adult Entertainment?" *Journal of Economic Perspectives*, 23 (1) (Winter 2009), http://people.hbs.edu/bedelman/papers/redlightstates.pdf.
48. Centers for Disease Control, "Sexual Violence: Consequences," 2015, http://www.cdc.gov/violenceprevention/sexualviolence/consequences.html.
49. Deborah J. Diener, Compiler, Instances of Child Sexual Abuse Allegedly Perpetrated by Members of The Church of Jesus Christ of Latter-day Saints, a History 1959-2017. Soon to be available on the Internet.
50. Sterling C. Hilton, Gilbert W. Fellingham, and Joseph L. Lyon, "Suicide Rates and Religious Commitment in Young Adult Males in Utah," *American Journal of Epidemiology*, Vol. 155 (5), 413–419. http://aje.oxfordjournals.org/content/155/5/413.full.
51. LDS Bible Dictionary (Salt Lake City: Church of Jesus Christ of Latter-day Saints, 1990), 697.
52. Ezra Taft Benson, "After All We Can Do," Christmas Devotional, Salt Lake City, Utah, December 9, 1982. Quoted in *The Teachings of Ezra Taft Benson*, 354.
53. *Duties and Blessings of the Priesthood: Basic Manual for Priesthood Holders, Part B*. http://www.lds.org/manual/duties-and-blessings-of-the-priesthood-basic-manual-for-priesthood-holders-part-b/priesthood-and-church-government/lesson-4-the-purpose-of-priesthood-ordinances?lang=eng. Bruce R. McConkie, *Mormon Doctrine*, 2nd ed, (Salt Lake City: Bookcraft, 1966), 548–49.
54. President Boyd K. Packer, How to Live the Word of Wisdom, https://www.lds.org/youth/article/how-to-live-the-word-of-wisdom?lang=eng
55. Joseph Fielding Smith, *Doctrines of Salvation*, 2:16, (Salt Lake City: Bookcraft, 1955).
56. Kenneth I. Pargament, Kenneth I. Maton, Robert E. Hess, eds., *Religion and Prevention in Mental Health: Research, Visions, and Action*, (NY: Haworth Press, 1992).
57. Mental Health America, "The Ranking America's Mental Health: An Analysis of Depression Across the States," http://www.mentalhealthamerica.net/issues/ranking-states#Overall Ranking.
58. Jewish Virtual Library, "Ancient Jewish History: The Twelve Tribes of Israel," http://www.jewishvirtuallibrary.org/jsource/Judaism/tribes.html.
59. Joseph Smith, "White Horse Prophecy," http://www.mrm.org/white-horse-prophecy.
60. Pew Research Center, "Portrait of Mormons in the U. S.: Religious Beliefs and Practices," http://www.pewforum.org/2009/07/24/a-portrait-of-mormons-in-the-us-religious-beliefs-and-practices/.
61. LDS Official website, Topic "Apostasy," https://www.lds.org/topics/apostasy?lang=eng.
62. Richard and Joan Ostling, *Mormon America: The Power and the Promise* (New York: HarperCollins, 1999), and Richard Ostling, "Kingdom Come," *Time Magazine*, August 4, 1997.
63. Ibid., 1999 and 1997.
64. Kevin Spear, "Mormon Church Completes Huge Buy of Land—Now Owns 2 Percent of Florida Land," *Orlando Sentinel*, March 6, 2014, http://articles.orlandosentinel.com/2014-03-06/news/os-mormon-florida-land-deal-sealed-20140306_1_mormon-church-north-florida-utah-based-church.
65. The Church of Jesus Christ of Latter-day Saints, *Preach My Gospel*, (Salt Lake City, UT: Church of Jesus Christ of Latter-day Saints, 2004). See pages 29 and 82.
66. ABC News, "Number of Faithful Mormons Rapidly Declining," 2015, http://www.abc4.com/content/news/top_stories/story/Number-of-faithful-Mormons-rapidly-declining/rvih3gOKx-Em5om9IYJYnRA.cspx.
67. 2014 Statistical Report for 2015 April General Conference, http://www.mormonnewsroom.org/article/2014-statistical-report-for-2015-april-general-conference.
68. Marlin K. Jensen, "Q&A," John A. Widtsoe Association for Mormon Studies, Utah State University (November 11, 2011), http://mormon-chronicles.blogspot.com/2012/01/rescue-plan-toaddress-difficulties-of.html.

69 Peter Henderson and Kristina Cooke, "Mormonism Besieged by the Modern Age," *Reuters*, January 31, 2012, http://www.reuters.com/article/2012/01/31/us-mormonchurch-idUSTRE80T1CM20120131.

70. Dieter F. Uchtdorf, Second Counselor in the First Presidency of the Church of Jesus Christ of Latter-day Saints, General Conference Talk, Come Join with Us (October, 2013), https://www.lds.org/general-conference/2013/10/come-join-with-us?lang=eng.

71. Lynn K. Wilder, "Reflections on a Moral Multiculturalism and Post-Modern Thought" in *White Voices in Multicultural Psychology, Education and Leadership: Inside the Walls of American's Higher Education*, ed. Jeffrey Bakken. (Boston: Elsevier Science, 2014).

72. Deborah J. Diener, Compiler, Instances of Child Sexual Abuse Allegedly Perpetrated by Members of The Church of Jesus Christ of Latter-day Saints, a History 1959-2017.

73. Mormon Think website, "Birth of Jesus Christ," 2015, http://www.mormonthink.com/QUOTES/birthofjesus.htm.

74. James Coates, "Mormon-affiliated Group Linked to Rituals of Devil Worship, Occult," *Chicago Tribune*, November 03, 1991, http://articles.chicagotribune.com/1991-11-03/news/9104080968_1_satanic-abuse-mormon-tabernacle-choir-8-million-member-church

75. Ordain Women, Mission Statement, http://ordainwomen.org/mission/.

76. Grand Rapids: Zondervan, 2009.

77. Deborah J. Diener, Compiler, Instances of Child Sexual Abuse Allegedly Perpetrated by Members of The Church of Jesus Christ of Latter-day Saints, a History 1959-2017; Jana Riess, Mormon Statement on Child Abuse: Move Along, Folks; We Don't Have a Problem, Religion News, February 2, 2016, http://religionnews.com/2016/02/02/mormon-statement-on-child-abuse-move-along-folks-we-dont-have-a-problem/

78. Jana Riess, "More Mormon Men are Leaving the LDS Church, Say Researchers—But Especially in Utah," Religion News Service, September 16, 2015, http://janariess.religionnews.com/2015/09/16/more-mormon-men-are-leaving-the-lds-church-say-researchers-but-especially-in-utah/.

5
WRESTLING WITH NATURE AND GOD

James Vincent Eccles

TESTIMONY

Early Scientist

Jim and Nanette Eccles had just purchased a brand-new home in a neighborhood midway between the Wasatch Mountains and the Great Salt Lake in northern Utah. The small, three-bedroom house was a wood-frame dwelling common to the post-WWII years. Every house on our street was a home to a family with kids. Every yard was covered with a lawn lined with flower gardens. The neighborhood was the first encroachment into the farm pastures, fruit orchards, and wheat fields of Sunset, Utah.

The blue skies of Utah in the late 1950s were very clear during the day. Sometimes the clouds had fine-line details rarely seen through today's pollution haze. The extreme dark of the night revealed a wondrously starry sky. I remember lying in my father's military-issue down sleeping bag just outside the pup-tent door in our new backyard. Thousands of stars spread out in the sky above me with an occasional shooting star punctuating my wonder.[1] Each star seemed to be a brilliant pinprick in the black dome. I wondered how many stars I could actually see distinctly. I knew that there were still many more stars in the fuzzy splash of light called the Milky Way. My father explained that each star was a sun and some may have planets. The universe was very big and visually wonderful for this six-year-old boy.

My parents encouraged my curiosity in nature and science. Both my mother and father had graduated from college. My mother had studied journalism and my father had studied English and psychology and he eventually obtained a master's in government administration. History, science, and politics were among the topics of our dinner conversation. During one particular summer evening's dinner we talked about the size of the universe. That the universe had a size was a new idea for me.

"How can the universe have a size if it is everything? It doesn't go on forever? What does the edge look like? What's beyond the edge? What if

I flew a rocket to the edge, what would I see?" I was envisioning a fuzzy, glassy boundary.

I remember my parents' smiles and my father answering, "Well, it would take a very long time to get to the edge.[2] There may not be an edge exactly, but I don't understand the science. It takes a long time for light to travel from here to there and your rocket goes much slower than the speed of light. Your journey is going to take a very long time."

"But what do I see if I get to the edge? Can I turn my rocket and fly past the edge?" I repeated without even considering the fact that light traveled with a particular speed.

"I don't think that's possible. Albert Einstein was a very smart man. He thought about these things. You will have to ask someone who knows his theories about the universe."

Later that night I visualized my rocket ship hopping from earth to a bright star, then to a dimmer star. Someday I hoped my mental ship would get to the edge of the universe. What *is* the edge and what *is* beyond the edge?

Mormon Ancestry

The Eccles name is well known in Utah. If you visit the two oldest state college campuses, you will find a number of buildings with the Eccles name attached. Most Utah Eccles families descend from a single family from Glasgow, Scotland. William and Sarah Eccles and their five children lived a meager life. William was mostly blind but made wooden cooking utensils to earn a living. His children would sell them on the streets of Glasgow. William and Sarah Eccles converted to Mormonism and boarded a ship to the New World and eventually they arrived in Utah, in 1863.[3] Once the family got settled in their new home in Eden, Utah, the two oldest sons, David and William, established themselves as hard workers in Utah's lumber industry. The two brothers made their way to Oregon where they worked as lumberjacks, then purchased their own log wagons, then hired workers, and eventually established the very successful Oregon Lumber Corporation. The two Oregon tourist railways, Mt. Hood Railroad and Sumpter Valley Railroad, were originally built by the Eccles to carry logs from Oregon forests to the Eccles lumber mills. David returned to Utah and William remained in Oregon. The Eccles brothers were the first entrepreneur multimillionaires in the Intermountain West. David expanded his enterprises into construction, sugar, and banking while William stayed in lumber. I am the great-grandson of William Eccles.

My mother is from the Mormon working class of Utah. There were farmers, blacksmiths, coal miners, railroad employees, and a Utah sheriff. She has wonderful stories of these common folk. My heritage is definitely embedded in the tapestry of Mormon culture. There are threads of the wealthy and the worker; of polygamists and monogamists; of missionaries and scoundrels. There were a few wonderful non-Mormons added to add to the weave.

My parents attended the famed Mormon academy, Brigham Young University (BYU). My father was a BYU quarterback in the late 1940s long before BYU became known as Quarterback U for producing a succession of NFL quarterbacks in the 1980s. After college, Nanette and James married and quickly became pregnant with my lovely sister, Leslie. I was born three years later in Seattle during my father's graduate education. They named me James Vincent Eccles. James, after my father, and Vincent, after Vincent van Gogh. The popular book *Lust for Life* by Irving Stone had reinvigorated public interest in the extraordinary painter. I don't know why my parents named me after a tormented soul like van Gogh, but I consider it an honor. I resonate with his fuzzy and vivid vision of the world and I have experienced to a lesser degree his struggle with depression. In the book *Lust for Life* I also discovered that we Vincents were captured by a faith in the God of Christianity. My struggles with depression have roots in heredity and in the uncertainty generated by my parent's stormy marriage. They were not particularly good spouses for one another. They divorced . . . twice, but they were exceptional parents. My three siblings are wonderful human beings and each sibling has made the trek from Mormonism into a Traditional Christian[4] faith in Jesus Christ as Savior and Lord. I was first to leave Mormonism and the first to become a Christian during the evangelical, "born-again" movement of the 1970s.[5] But first, I visit my Mormon Spiritual roots.

Young Theologian

During my preteen years our family was involved in church activities of the local Mormon ward. We attended the meetings. My mother played the organ and piano for the choir and for the congregational singing. I remember having religious sensibilities that predated my interest in science. Every good Mormon family has a Family Home Evening (FHE) event once a week.[6] The nuclear family gets together to read scripture, hear a religious lesson, and play games. One early FHE is particularly memorable to me. I was about five years old. At the end of our FHE, we knelt in a circle in the middle of the living room. Father was holding my left hand and Mother my right. Leslie knelt across from me, head bowed. My father and mother took turns praying with thees and thous as they talked to the Heavenly Father, the most frequent title given to God, in a manner that reflected respect and demonstrated an expectation that God was present and listening. My undisciplined mind wandered away from the content of the prayer as I envisioned a light of God's presence hovering back behind my sister. I knew that I was imagining rather than experiencing something real, but it seemed that the real presence of this unseen God was listening. I had intuited or absorbed the idea that God's presence was like light—a real but invisible light. Absolute dark frightened me, and the thought of God's presence kindled a quiet peace like a little light in a dark night. I remember thinking about God listening to all the prayers in the other homes of our neighborhood. God was everywhere. I don't remember ever having in my mind that God had a body.[7] I did accept some anthropomorphism, but it didn't even dawn on me that God could be a human-like being. God was . . . something else. I remember envisioning people praying their evening bedtime prayers at all the different hours of the day as the earth turned under the sun. It was a wave of evening prayers following along with the sunset in each country. God was always present and listening to each prayer of this collective wave across the planet.

I was confused about how Jesus and God were related. I learned in my Sunday school lessons that Jesus was a special and kind man. The teachers used felt-covered storyboards to display Jesus sitting on a rock with children and lambs gathered around him. Jesus was called Son of God, but that seemed to be an honorary title rather than a reality. Jesus was a man and God was something else. Both Jesus and I had real human fathers. I wasn't too specific in my theological imaginations, but I was clearly not understanding what my Mormon teachers were intending to teach me.

Both my spiritual sensibility and my scientific inquisitiveness were undisciplined. I was mostly inattentive in our Mormon ward meetings. One of my most frequent activities during church services was to sit quietly in the pew and visualize gravity being turned off. The congregation would float to the ceiling (gravity was always turned off slowly). I would then visualize my climb from the high ceiling of the meeting hall to the doors at the back of the room. I examined every hand and foothold in my reverse climb. My mental adventure was to get to the bathroom or to the drinking fountain. Occasionally I would wonder what would happen if I exited the church and floated up to the clouds or moon. Despite my mental distractions in church, I was spiritually inclined. I talked to God freely. Conversing with God was just a natural extension of my acceptance of His invisible and real presence through all time and space. It was a decade later that I thrilled as I read in *Confessions* by Augustine of Hippo (A.D. 354–430) descriptions of the God I had always envisioned:

> So also did I endeavor to conceive of Thee, Life of my life, as vast, through infinite spaces on every side penetrating the whole mass of the universe, and beyond it, every way, through immeasurable boundless spaces; so that the earth should have Thee, the heaven have Thee, all things have Thee, and they be bounded in Thee, and Thou bounded nowhere.[8]

At eight years old I was baptized into Mormon Church membership. The baptism event remains a bit fuzzy in my memory, though I knew that the ritual act "did the thing." The baptism was the magical act that made me a member of the Mormon Church. There was no emotional or intellectual connection for me with the ritual event. However, the next day I officially received the Spirit through the biblical practice of laying on of hands.[9] The ward bishop, the first councilor, and my father gathered around me as I sat in a cold metal chair in the middle of a Sunday school room with their collective hands weighing on my head. I don't remember a word of the bishop's prayer. My father had spent the previous night writing his prayer for me. He did not like spontaneous prayer or predetermined prayer formulae for special events. I remember the prayer being close to this paraphrase:

> Our good Heavenly Father, I thank Thee for the gift of thy Spirit. I pray for my son, James Vincent Eccles, to receive this heavenly gift of the Holy Spirit into his life for guidance and consolation. I pray that he will always seek Thee and desire to please Thee. As Jesus said in Matthew 5, "Blessed are the peacemakers, for they shall be called sons of God." This is my prayer for my son. Make him a peacemaker that he will always seek to bring your peace to his relationships and community. And as a peacemaker he shall be called a son of God. Amen.

This was beautiful to me. I resonated with beautiful ideas rather than physical ritual. I fully desired and desire to live the answer to my father's prayer. This remains my most vital and spiritual connection to my deceased father. More than being another quarterback or being a worldly success, I wanted to be a peacemaker and be a son of God. There were two conclusions I came to that day. First, I was not automatically a child of God. Second, I desired peace between people. Certainly, the arguments between my parents had already placed this into my personality. An argumentative countenance is incredibly disturbing to me. I cannot converse with someone who yells with polemic attacks. Abusive anger is used not to convince but to overwhelm another human. I often receded in terror as a child, but now I move to stand between the abuser and abused.

In my teens I read and re-read the gospel according to Matthew to learn more about Jesus. This gospel contained the source text for my father's prayer. Jesus and the Sermon on the Mount were my touchstones for beautiful ideas about God and a good human life.[10]

Young Intellectual

Mormonism permits a broad variance of belief. The community judges more strictly against variance of practice than of thinking. If a Mormon is baptized, attends meetings, pays tithing, and avoids alcohol, then she will be judged as a Mormon in good standing. It is not a big problem if a Mormon does not embrace every jot and tittle of the theological statements of the Mormon prophets as long as theological divergence is not too vocal, too public, or too critical. My parents considered themselves Mormons and attempted to live good lives within the context of their Mormon culture. I was pursuing the same as a youth.

During my parents' education in the 1940s, Mormon intellectuals at the University of Utah and Brigham Young University were working to integrate Mormon theology into the larger tradition of Western Christianity and philosophy. After my father's death I spent some time organizing his books and files. I read through his university notes and assignments from religion and philosophy classes. The BYU professors had assigned diverse writings from Plato, Hobbes, Thoreau, and Schweitzer. The high point of this Mormon intellectual and liberal theological trend occurred during David O. McKay's presidency. This intellectual effort was interrupted in the late 1960s by President McKay's death. There was a deliberate return to a more fundamentalist interpretation of the Mormon prophets and Joseph Smith.[11] This conservative theological return was embodied by the now out-of-print book *Mormon Doctrine* by LDS apostle Bruce R. McConkie. Many of the theological presentations in the book are not official LDS doctrines, but his book does represent the literal teachings embraced by many Mormons. My parents had a more liberal and perhaps a less clear understanding of Mormon theology. They used traditional Christian language when talking about God and they never taught their kids the McConkie-ite theological particulars of the Mormon faith.

My father nurtured respect for knowledge. Honest treatment of historical and scientific evidence was the basis for human understanding. Questioning was permitted because truth can defend itself. My father was a ferocious reader and had little patience for shoddy presentations of history or unscientific thinking. Cleansed presentations of Mormon history seemed to be the strategy of the Mormon Church in the late '60s and '70s to deal with the messiness of early Mormon events. My father pursued an honest investigation into Mormon history, yet he remained a Mormon, but a questioning Mormon, into his last years. Near his last days my sister, Leslie, spoke loving words of grace to our more child-like aging father. He freely asked for forgiveness from the merciful God, who offers peace to those who will receive.

Traditional Jewish and Islamic stories about Abraham, the father of monotheism, suggest that Abraham's father was a polytheist and had household idols. These oral traditions generally tell us that Abraham chastised his father and destroyed the idols. The truth about Abraham's break from his inherited religious culture could have been closer to my story. I imagine that Abraham's shepherd father had negative opinions of the Mesopotamian warrior gods and god stories. The criticism gave Abraham permission to take the next step to move away from the Mesopotamian culture and follow another god. Abraham heard the call from a different god and he followed without looking back. This is what my father did for me. He did not intend to leave Mormonism, but his questioning of Mormon dogmatists gave me permission to seek elsewhere for reasonable answers to life. I also eventually took the step away from Mormonism.[12]

Young Naturalist

My mother, Nanette, is one of the best of human beings. She was born in southern Utah and learned to see the beauty of desert landscapes. Horny toads, snakes, and bareback horse rides through the sagebrush were a part of her youth. Through all her days she loved to wander the byways of Utah's mountains and canyons. She became a part of the natural lore of Utah as fly fishermen would ask for snippets of her brilliant red hair to tie their fishing flies. She was photographed holding a fishing fly near her red hair in a naturalist magazine in the 1950s.

Mother practiced her small town sensibility in the gardens around our house and yard. I hated to weed for her, but her flower and vegetable gardens were bursting with color and eatables. A vast array of bugs visited her gardens especially in the evening. Huge, colorful ranchman and white-lined sphinx moths would flutter around the row of four o'clock blossoms. My mother would expound on the art of natural defenses for gardens as we planted the phalanx of marigolds around the vegetable garden or moved found ladybugs to combat an aphid colony. I remember her walking boldly through a swarm of wasps that had made its home in the backyard potato cellar. Her calf length skirt swayed from side to side with a dozen orbiting wasps. She didn't bat an eye. This was another Eve walking through her little Eden.

My mother's smiling eyes seemed to see beauty in all humans. It did not matter what shape and color of the person, there were wonderful stories to discover within the expanse of each human soul—humans are all bigger on the inside. In 1954, my father pursued a master's degree at the University of Washington and my mother was pregnant with me. My father, mother, sister, and pre-born me lived at the top of the hill on Yesler Way above Seattle's Puget Sound ferry terminal. In the apartment next to ours lived a young African American couple. They were also with child. My mother freely embraced her new friend and companion in pregnancy. When my mother was invited to her friend's home for tea, the woman said that my mother was the first white person to come into her home for a visit. My father had a liberal mindset and hated racism as an intellectual. My mother's was not an intellectual stand; it was just her natural way of seeing the world. She continues to collect people to fill her rainbow of friends and acquaintances.

I was born and my parents suffered a divorce soon after. My mother moved to Utah to work and live as a single mother with two children in her brother's basement, which sported one bedroom, a bathroom, and a kitchenette. I remember sitting on my mother's lap in the dark kitchenette taking my One-a-Day vitamin before being dropped off at the sitter's home. I would watch her drive off to work. After a couple of years, my father returned to Utah and re-proposed marriage. The options are always limited for a single mother, but in the 1950s it was a path with no options. She accepted. Nanette worked in various jobs throughout their marriage. She had decided to have her own career because she feared that my father would divorce her again. A divorce would leave her in poverty in her retirement years unless she provided for her own financial stability and retirement. My father did divorce my mother after thirty-three years of marriage and she survived. For most of these years my mother worked in Utah Family Services as a social worker. She helped families obtain services for physically and mentally disabled kids. She developed long-term friendships with these oft-neglected humans and occasionally introduced her children to her favorite friends, such as Kim Peek, the real Rain Man of the 1988 movie of that name. My mother was a living lesson of loving acceptance.

Young Rebel

My first irritations with Mormon culture are not specific to the Mormon culture. Ugly behavior occurs in all faith communities, but what cracks they cause!

It was not apparent to me as a young child, but I learned during my college years that my mother had suffered under the overt disrespect of the women of the Relief Society, the Mormon organization for women. My mother worked. To them she had chosen a career over her children and husband. In the 1960s this was cultural heresy in most religious communities. Additionally, her position as a civil servant in Utah Family Services was a doubly evil career choice. The godly choice would have been for her to volunteer at Mormon Church Social Services. When I learned of the spurning my mother suffered, I was already experiencing disillusionment with religious culture in general. My mother's case became a buttressing argument for my growing Mormon disillusionment.

Overt racism in our religious community was frequent in the late 1960s. In 1968 our family moved a few miles south to a larger home. My parents showed our for-sale home to an African American pastor who was moving his family to Utah to lead a small church that served African American military families at Hill Air Force Base. A Mormon neighbor (or neighbors) lit a burning cross in the grass of our front lawn that night. My father was furious. His anger and athleticism could cower anyone within sound or sight of his volcanic eruptions. No one ever admitted to the threatening sign, but my father discounted the price of the house to encourage the pastor's purchase. The pastor did not buy the house, but moved to a neighborhood closer to Hill Air Force Base.

There were other overt expressions of racism made in my Sunday religious classes. There were extreme statements spoken about Martin Luther King Jr. and civil rights supporters with suggestions of "blasts of my shotgun, if they ever set foot near the Salt Lake Temple." The teacher pronounced this explicit threat in my priesthood meeting class.

In high school I started indicating to my peers that I was planning to be an astrophysicist. This was my new goal in life. I no longer intended to go on a mission for the Mormon Church. Attending BYU was dropped entirely. Instead, I started to admire my science and math teachers in high school, who were indeed admirable people. The algebra teacher was a retired captain of a Navy battleship. His gruff dry humor made algebra an entertaining subject. I enjoyed talking with my chemistry/physics teacher who loved to surprise his classes with explosions or fascinating displays of physics. In one conversation he mentioned he was an atheist, the first I knowingly had ever spoken with. He was a severe diabetic and knew his health would decline rapidly within a decade. His conclusion from the pain of all his insulin injections and the vision of his future was that the universe was not managed by a loving God. I did not necessarily agree with his conclusion, but I understood and understand the discouragement of his situation.

The math and science teachers were easy to talk to and the grading was straightforward. I found myself struggling to generate acceptable essays for teachers of less objective subjects of English and history. So I gravitated towards math and science. Math was simply a set of enjoyable puzzles to solve and science was a wonderful exploration of how the world works.

At the same time as my intentional move towards science studies, the bishop of our Mormon ward started circulating short propaganda filmstrips on communism and evolution for interested families. They were used during Family Home Evenings. My parents would never show these propaganda presentations, but I was invited to my best friend's Family Home Evening a couple of times. I sat through filmstrips that decried the evils of evolution and communism. I felt tension as I was at that time convinced that science held better answers on creation of the universe than the literal six-day creation interpretation of Genesis in the Bible. I was reading a number of lay-level books on the Big Bang theory and stellar evolution. In spite of rejecting the Genesis creation myth, a Creator God and the evolving universe never seemed to be a contradiction to me. The cartoon filmstrip related the stellar evolution proposal of Immanuel Kant to communist teachings. The propaganda logic drew a line from Kant to Hegel to Marx and (somehow) to Darwin as a demonstration of the inherited evil in both evolution and communism. The second cartoon filmstrip showed young minds chained by the communists as they spread atheist, socialist, and evolutionist lies in America. I was upset at the emotional anti-science propaganda and my soul was further loosed from Mormonism.

These three examples of social judgment, anti-scientific rhetoric, and racism cited above were repeated many times in various degrees in my Mormon community. Let me warn the reader to not color Mormons as having a unique hold on these opinions. There seems to be an extreme vein within all religious groups that generates ugly and unfortunate characteristics. When I became a born-again Christian in 1975, I sadly discovered religious social judgment, bigotry, and anti-scientific rhetoric embraced by some within my newly adopted Christian culture. Eventually the discouraging extreme views led me into a second crisis of faith. These attitudes were so opposite of how I viewed Jesus in his own community of religious hypocrites.[13]

Good students from committed Mormon families mostly defined my circle of friends. We enjoyed the typical high school social life as science and math geeks. In the midst of my typical Utah experience, my intellectual skepticism towards Mormonism itself was awakened rather abruptly by a blunt presentation by my Mormon priesthood teacher. I went to my usual Sunday morning priesthood class and we had a special larger group teaching from an excited teacher in the ward. The teacher was a prototypical geek engineer with short-sleeved white shirt, black tie, and pen-filled pocket protector. Hi appearances had no bearing on my dismissal of his presentation of Mormon doctrines. I was headed toward similar geek regalia. He gave an energetic and clear description of conservative Mormon theology to the thirty boys in the class.

The teacher's description was literalistic and devoid of nuanced meaning. He explained the following: Humans were birthed spirit children in the pre-existence. We are all children of the Heavenly Father, which is not a metaphor for the Creator God, but He is our literal father. The Heavenly Father had a body of flesh and bone. He lives on a planet orbiting the star called Kolob at the center of the universe. The Heavenly Father could only be in one place physically because the physical laws of the universe binds His physicality. However, he had progressed in the knowledge of divine truths and was now the all-knowing and powerful God over us. Jesus was his eldest son, had earned his divine standing, and was a part of the godhead, which was composed of the three individual gods—the Heavenly Father, the Son, and the Holy Ghost. Humans had been birthed into this physical world to receive physical bodies to go with our spiritual bodies and we were born to live lives of obedience to the teachings of the Mormon Church. We too could progress to a glorified state and some of us with our spouses might reach an exalted state to oversee a world of our own spiritual children. This was a stark portrayal of the populist and literalist Mormon theology preferred by many conservative religious Mormons. I note that these theological teachings are currently receiving nuanced and metaphorical interpretations through Mormon scriptures by a new generation of moderate Mormon theologians.

I was completely stunned by this one Sunday morning lesson. My mental jaw dropped and my own theological understanding sat in contrast. God with a physical body bound by physical laws with a home on a planet somewhere was unbelievable in my mind. I rejected it out of hand. From my earliest memories I had intuited that God was spirit and everywhere. God was creator of the universe and not a creature in it. God was not a human and humans could not become gods. No apologetic could move me to accept this peculiar Sunday revelation. Why were there three gods in the godhead? I was a monotheist. From that single hour priesthood lesson, Mormonism no longer made sense to me. I don't even remember talking to my parents about this Sunday revelation. Their marriage was troubled and I preferred to keep my distance from their difficulties, so I started my journey of skepticism alone.

Utah Mormon teenagers have access to religious studies during high school in a Mormon seminary building adjacent to high school campuses. Most of the teaching in seminary was on the life of Joseph Smith and the Mormon pilgrimage to Utah rather than any focus on religious metaphysics or comparative religions. Mormon history has its admirable stories and there are several wonderful stories from my own Mormon ancestors. However, I started asking unfortunate questions on theology and on Mormon history of my seminary teacher, ward bishop, and stake president. I read *No Man Knows My History* by Fawn Brodie, which catalogues a number of human failings in the life of the first Mormon prophet, Joseph Smith.

During this time I re-read the gospel of Matthew instead of reading my seminary texts. The person and teachings of Jesus were captivating. Some teachings seemed impossible, but Jesus was concerned for the poor, the sick, the lost, and the sinner. Even better, he was angry with the legalistic religious leaders of his day. This New Testament gospel watered a different seed of faith in the Jesus mentioned by my father as he had prayed over me nine years earlier.

I continued to prefer my earliest intuitive conclusions. I remember asking my stake president, "Why does Jesus say that Peter did not receive his knowledge of Jesus being the Messiah from flesh and blood?[14] Maybe his knowledge came from God, who is spirit."

"Well, first of all," came the response from my stake president, "we cannot trust the Bible as a perfectly true scripture. It has probably not been translated correctly and has been under the influence of evil men. Second, it says flesh and blood not flesh and bone. The Heavenly Father has a body of flesh and bone."[15] The stake president was a good man and I even had a teenage crush on his daughter, but the answer left me desiring a bit more rigor.

By the time of my high school graduation, I did not consider myself a Mormon. This did not matter greatly to any of my friends or family. I was still on the rolls of membership and my intellectual disagreements did not change that fact. I tossed Mormonism and Christianity out of my purview and my conversations with the God-who-listened stopped. In the depths of my soul remained a shrinking but beautiful memory of Jesus in the gospel of Matthew.

The embarrassment of a dogmatic and literal religion seemed obvious to me. It seemed to produce self-righteous people who despised my wonderful working mother. It seemed to require interpretations of Scripture that were difficult for a scientific thinker to accept. I began to make arguments to dismiss traditional religious beliefs in general. Science was an evidence-based study. Humans might have wrong ideas in science, but this was only a temporary situation. The evidence will eventually overcome bad ideas in the orderly scientific process. I went off to college to study physics and mathematics. My new self-identity was as an enlightened human whose education would be based on trust in science and on skepticism of religious dogmas. Perhaps like Douglas Adams says in his absurd novel, *Hitchhiker's Guide to the Galaxy*, "Isn't it enough to see that a garden is beautiful without having to believe that there are fairies at the bottom of it, too?"

Young Mountain Climber

I worked at Jenny Lake Lodge in Grand Teton National Park during the summers of 1972 and 1973. There was an extraordinary group of people working as busboys, waitresses, maids, bellhops, dishwashers, and horse wranglers. They were diverse, talented, and accepting of one another. I had many conversations about Transcendental Meditation, Broadway plays, various sexual preferences, Mormonism, Christianity, horse wrangling, secular skepticism, and many more fascinating topics for an eighteen-year-old young man. There were several Christians who helped me become aware that traditional Christianity is more than superficially distinct from Mormonism. There were also several colorful pagans who loved to discuss the meaning or meaninglessness of life. Most of the conversations were often in deeper waters than I could swim.

Rex, a Christian, used very strong language as he argued against Mormonism with statements punctuated by short thrusts with his very large Bible. Rex was a Christian seminary student and a severe Reformed theologian. His witness was unappealing. A couple of Mormon missionaries visited the employee cabins to present the Mormon gospel to anyone willing to listen. Rex expertly used his Bible foil with lunges and parries in his arguments against the young missionaries. It was obvious to me that Rex knew the Bible well and the missionaries had been trained with a script that used only a few Bible verses. I jumped into the fray to defend Mormonism: "Rex, calm down. Both sides are based on unprovable mythologies and questionable histories." I am certain the missionaries were not appreciative of my particular line of defense.

Another Christian, Eddie, affected me more. Eddie was a Chinese American from Idaho Falls, Idaho, a descendant from one of the working families brought from China to build the American railways during the 1860s when my own ancestors arrived from Scotland. Eddie had applied to enter a Franciscan lay order to live his love for Jesus in a celibate religious community.[16] He was working at Jenny Lake Lodge while he waited for their response. Eddie was the embodiment of kindness. He never sat me down to convince me with Christian apologetics. He never argued with pagans or Mormons or anyone. Instead, the joy of life overflowed from him, with frequent acclamations like "Praise the Lord, that was wonderful!" A plastic Jesus was glued to the dashboard of his mammoth 1968 Pontiac Bonneville. Many would make fun of Eddie's simple happiness, but his guileless joy was a beauty that delighted me all summer. It still does.

One of the lodge's cooks, Michael, a bellman, Steve, and I were frequent hiking buddies. We were becoming known for our late night returns from excursions on Teton trails and peaks. We would stumble back from our treks in the dark until we arrived at the Lodge in time to get a couple hours of sleep before our shifts began. We occasionally brushed past a moose and once startled a bear on our returns to the Lodge. One late return put us at the Taggart Lake Trailhead at 3:00 in the morning. We walked to the nearby Climber's Ranch to call the Jenny Lake Lodge front desk and ask the night watchman to wake a friend to come and get us. The only person who would come pick us up at that time was Eddie. About twenty minutes later, Eddie drove up in his big Bonneville and he jumped out of the car to welcome us back from our trek. His infectious big smile was a brilliant light to my tired soul. The little plastic Jesus stood on the dashboard with arms held wide, blessing the conversation during the ride back to the lodge. Eddie's joyful and ever-present "praise the Lord" meant more to me than any rigorous doctrinal apologetic. He had awaked something in my heart that was beyond reason.

One late June weekend I decided to do a solo hike up a rarely visited peak called Mount Saint John. I planned to think about a number of my summer conversations with pagans, Christians, and Buddhists. I vaguely knew that Saint John was the New Testament gospel writer and I also realized that Eddie had arrested my cynicism towards religion. The hike to the top of Mount Saint John is not technical, but is a very steep hike. I left Jenny Lake Lodge on foot with a very light pack. It carried a couple of water bottles, a sandwich, and my down sleeping bag. The trail starts at String Lake and winds around the north end of Jenny Lake; then one must turn up the very steep Hanging Canyon trail. Upon reaching Ramshead Lake I unstuffed my sleeping bag and sat down to enjoy the last bit of sunlight hitting Symmetry Spire peak overhead. In the morning I ate the egg salad sandwich and started the steep hike up the southern slope of Mount Saint John. The day revealed an incredibly blue, cloudless sky and the alpine flowers were covering the mountainside. I knew that there would be a spectacular view of the Grand Teton from the top of Mount Saint John so I doggedly kept my face to St. John's slope as I hiked to the ridge. I intended to not look at the Grand until I had signed the season's registry of ascents in a little metal canister at the top. My memory is full of superlatives—the flowers, the sky, and then finally the Grand Teton soaring two thousand feet above me to the south. I was overwhelmed at my first gaze towards the Gran—God's creation magnificently displayed. Eddie had challenged my conclusions about religion and this view finished blowing out the cobwebs of my skepticism. With every edit of this paragraph I tear up at the memory of the experience. Creation's loud praise of God was in perfect harmony with Eddie's joyful "praise the Lord."

I prayed a two-sentence prayer: "God, Creator of the universe, I don't know you. I want to know you." This quiet prayer was the only intrusion that I could put forward in Nature's visual chorus, but it was not a discordant note.

Mount Saint John is an uninteresting Teton climb in terms of its technical challenge, so I was the only one to visit the top that June day in 1972. I started down the peak with a lingering sense of my visitation with something divine during my literal mountain-top experience. It still is my most memorable view of the Grand Teton and the most emotional religious experience of my life. I have since felt more frequently the absence of God, sometimes to the point of despair. My memory of this silent witness on the perfect day revives my unsteady faith even now. I felt "looked for" upon Mount Saint Johns. I felt found.

I remember hiking down later that afternoon on the steep Hanging Canyon trail with a lingering joy. My egg salad sandwich had introduced a bit of food poisoning into this blissful day, so I was occasionally barfing off the side of the trail. Closer to the valley floor I encountered a young couple hiking up to spend the night at Lake of the Crags.

"Hello," I smiled, and then dry heaved off the trail.

"Are you OK?" the man asked with real concern.

"I'm fine. Just a bit of . . . (dry heaving) . . . food poisoning. The hike is absolutely gorgeous. You will love it . . . (dry heaving)." I was guessing that God was listening again . . . and laughing . . . in a good way.

My Heresies Become Orthodoxy

Even with this stunning day and Eddy's joyful countenance, I wasn't immediately swept into Christianity, but I had initiated a more earnest pursuit of the Creator. I explored Transcendental Meditation with one of the housemen at Jenny Lake Lodge. I occasionally talked with other hiking partners about the basics of traditional Christianity. I struggled to integrate my scientific understanding with conservative interpretations of the Genesis creation story. I also struggled (and continue to struggle) with the co-existence of beauty and ugliness, joy and sadness in the world. How could God create such a beautiful yet ugly world? How can humanity be in the image of God and be so incredibly evil at times?

At least I had initiated a new search. As a youth, I had imagined turning a rocket ship continually towards the edge of the universe. As a physicist in training, I knew that this thought experiment was more of a metaphor of a new flight past the edge of physics towards the Creator above and beyond the universe. Science has clear methods for the pursuit of physical understanding. It is still the most honest and capable human methodology for expanding our understanding of the world. How could I organize a proper search into religions? This realm hovered above physics—beyond physics. Science seemed incapable of accessing concepts like meaning, love, or beauty. An objective reality of goodness and of a Creator might be beyond science, but these truths should at least seem reasonable if explored honestly. "Being reasonable" does not mean that there cannot be mystery or paradox, but the found truths cannot be silly or ugly. God is not a rock or an alien from another planet. I could only come up with a few criteria to assess religious metaphysical teachings. I brought my earliest understandings of God to the investigation and added a few more:

1. There is one God.
2. God is Creator of everything, and nothing in creation is God.
3. God is ultimately good and beautiful.

4. The world and I both have goodness and evil, beauty and ugliness. Something is wrong. God must hold the solution to this broken situation.

5. The essentials of the truth about God and humanity had to be accessible on some level to a child but also had to be deep and even inaccessible to the smartest human. However, truths cannot be stupid; that is, they must be reasonable.

These seemed reasonable criteria and I will revisit these later in this chapter. The first and second criteria seemed to discount Mormonism in my basic understanding of Mormon doctrine. The last one was important for a five-year-old child and a twenty-year-old physics student to both experience an awe of a God who listens to a billion humans in a moment and a Creator who could overwhelm a lonely soul on a mountain peak. I also acknowledged that there was a possibility that there is no god, because axiom 3 need not be true and axiom 4 may have no solution. However, I yearned for a positive meaning for life and a god of goodness over all. I desired something like the creation myth of *The Silmarillion* to be real.[17] J. J. R. Tolkien imaginatively writes of the One Creator who initiates a beautiful world by replacing the empty void with a beautiful musical symphony of creation. Created angels begin to participate in the creation symphony as they begin to understand the vision of the One Creator. Soon one powerful creature rebels against the Creator and works to destroy the beautiful symphony by adding harsh discordant sound. The Sovereign continually adds counterpoint to each line of evil cacophony to resolve the flaw into even more beautiful symphony. I yearn for this resolved chord even now.

My trust of the Bible had disappeared with my rejection of Mormon scripture and theology. I was open to anything but Christianity. However, during my junior year as a physics student at Utah State University, a Campus Crusade for Christ student minister named Stu offered to talk with me about traditional Christianity and religion in general. I relished the argumentative possibilities. In one of the early conversations Stu shared Jesus's claim in John 10:30, "I and my Father are one." I mentioned that I couldn't trust the Bible and I even used the Mormon phraseology, "We can only trust it as far as it is translated correctly" (which implies that we should not trust it). Stu pulled out his Greek New Testament and turned to the appropriate page and started to read the verse in Greek. Being a studying mathematician, I knew the Greek alphabet and their sounds. It was apparent that he was reading the Greek. I could even recognize the Greek word for father—*pathr* or *patér* from "paternal." Not only was he translating the Greek right there, I was stunned that he held a book of the Greek text in his hands! As a Mormon, the translation of manuscripts into the King James Bible was something that happened many years ago. It was supposed to be a lost art.

This misunderstanding makes no sense to me now, but this stunning revelation of Stu translating New Testament Greek in front of me helped free me to reconsider the Bible with greater intellectual honesty. Stu started handing me books about biblical archeology by William Albright and manuscript studies by F. F. Bruce to address my skepticism of the Bible and its history. Stu also gave me a couple of books of apologetics that seemed to aggrandize every conceivable evidential support of Christianity regardless of reliability, robustness, or reasonableness. This was not a help to me. I have always been of the opinion that God is God and He should be able to defend Himself. Why make bad arguments in defense of God?

Many of the traditional Christian concepts like grace and propitiation were completely new to me, though I had an intuitive sense of God's forgiveness even from my earliest recollection. It took me some time to get an intellectual foothold to properly consider what the apostle Paul was saying in his letters to city churches. This is probably true for every Mormon embedded in the Mormon hegemony. The understanding and language gap between traditional Christians and Mormons can only be overcome with long and kind discussions.

Jesus and the Gospels had always drawn me toward a faith in God, but it was the book of Exodus in the Old Testament that suddenly grabbed my religious imagination while my rational mind struggled with New Testament Epistles. Exodus 3 tells us that when Moses turns aside to see the burning bush that was not consumed, he meets the angel of the LORD within the bush. Moses asks for God's name. Moses wants to relate this divine appearance to one of the many god stories that Moses knows. There are many god stories from Egypt and the area around Palestine at this time. Moses was hoping for a name to identify the god and the story. God instead gives the Ineffable Name, YHWH, with the implied meaning of "I AM WHO I AM" OR "I SHALL BE WHO I SHALL BE." In other words, "Never you mind, Moses. You cannot put me in a god story. You cannot know who, what, or how I AM." I was stunned. I could not believe that a 3000-year-old story could be so silly and so deep simultaneously. A burning bush? I had heard this story before, but this time the depth of the Ineffable Name immediately brought me to the edge of a very deep ocean of religious thought. The God of my youthful faith had now become wondrously deep. I heard in my wonder, "Vince, 'I SHALL BE WHO I SHALL BE.' You will never come to the end of wonder if you pursue Me." (The fifth criterion.)

After a number of discussions and readings with my mentor, Stu, I was beginning to understand that Jesus was God made flesh—incarnate. God coming in human form was just as surprising as appearing in a burning bush. However, all of the sudden the one Creator God above all creation and Jesus who taught the Sermon on the Mount came together into a single point of religious focus through the lens of traditional Christianity. Humanity is called to live lives of goodness. Unfortunately we have failed in big and small ways. Humans (me) are carrying heavy burdens of failure and ugliness. We cannot escape the weight of our terrible behaviors before a beautiful and perfect God. Jesus is perfect divinity and perfect humanity, but He took on the weight of our failures, sins, and illness in our place on the cross. My fourth criterion was addressed. God offers two things to humanity—forgiveness and a way forward. First, Jesus has taken the burdens of my sin onto his shoulders, so forgiveness is now offered. Second, God offers a new life through His Spirit working directly in our lives to help us live in kindness, joy, and beauty.

On December 17, 1975, I embraced a faith in Jesus, the Son of God as the one who saves my life. The Creator, whom I desired to know from a mountaintop, the Son, whom I had loved at my Mormon baptism, and the Spirit, whom I envisioned as a young child in our family circle, all came together within the Triune mystery of Christianity. In a parallel fashion to G. K. Chesterton, I discovered that my heresy within Mormonism was orthodoxy in traditional Christianity.[18] I trust and hope for a God-breathed transformation into the likeness of Jesus . . . to be more like Eddie. Praise the Lord. I am not yet transformed into Eddie's lightness of soul. Maybe I should get a plastic Jesus for my car's dashboard.

Saints of the Faith

The following several summers I worked at a recreational camp for individuals with disabilities in Minnesota. Camp Courage was an amazing blessing to my young faith. The job as cabin counselor demanded a focused commitment to act selflessly towards the campers who would come to the camp for a couple of weeks to enjoy sports, arts, boating, and entertainment. During the first week on the job, I was reprimanded firmly by the camp director. I was sitting next to another counselor as the entertainment progressed. I had figured that the campers were being entertained, so I could befriend another counselor. The camp director tapped me on the shoulder and said, "If you look to your left and right and don't see campers, then you're in the wrong place." The job taught me to pursue unselfish friendship towards humans whom I had avoided previously. This was one of the great blessings of my life—not because I was *forced* to befriend individuals with disabilities, but because I discovered what exceptional human beings they are. The challenges were various: cerebral palsy, muscular dystrophy, brain injury, spina bifida, lost limbs, etc. These exterior disabilities and anomalies of the body are what most people see and use to define the disabled individual. In reality, people are so much larger on the inside than our small exteriors suggest. And frequently, humans with disabilities are larger of soul than people without physical disabilities. It surprised me how many campers had upbeat personalities and a strong faith in God. I had a grumpy intellectual faith in comparison.

The camp was organized into two-week sessions, each for a particular age range. The first session was the 20- to 35-year olds. They are the robust adults who had been to camp many times and could withstand the missteps of an untrained camp counselor. They acted as generous one-on-one trainers on how to move someone from wheelchair to toilet or from bed to wheelchair or how to patiently feed someone while you also ate your own lunch. It was entertaining to receive a jovial running commentary by a mature camper on the proper placement of a silver bullet, the suppository laxative for a late bowel movement. Every experience at Camp Courage was a tremendous life lesson.

I was helping out on Sunday morning services for interested campers by playing my guitar and leading singing, so I got to know many who were joyfully and patiently "waiting on the Lord" for their physical restoration in this world or the next. I once read a wonderful short story (I thought by Mark Twain, but I cannot find the story) about a young boy who lived next door to an invalid girl of the same age. The boy would see her in a wheelchair on the porch of her family's home. Because he was from a Christian family, they often visited and even brought gifts of food to this neighboring family, which was close to poverty due to the requirements of care for their disabled daughter. The boy excelled in his school, which she did not attend. He went off to Bible College to study Greek, Hebrew, and theology, while her aging parents cared for her needs. His talents as an orator eventually brought him fame as a traveling preacher. He drew huge crowds to his gospel tent-meetings. Many people were drawn into a commitment to following Jesus Christ. The boy grew into an old man and eventually met death with a firm faith in God. He walked through the pearly gates of the-world-to-come to be greeted by a large crowd of angels, family, friends, and converts. He is ecstatic when he hears the voice of his Lord coming from the heavenly clouds, "Well done, good and faithful servant." Thus, he is joyfully received into his eternal home. After about a half an hour, the skies brighten markedly. A million angels fill the skies, millions of people wait near the pearly gates, and Jesus descends on his great throne. The preacher turns to see whose great arrival is portended. At the gates the parents of the invalid girl are waiting. An old invalid woman in a wheelchair passes through the gates and she leaps up with youth and vigor into Jesus's arms as the multitude of angels burst into song. The preacher is taken up with the emotion of this reunion, but then questions come to his mind. He asks a nearby angel, "Isn't this the girl of the family that we helped with food when I was young? I am just wondering why my arrival was so modest in comparison." The angel said, "Ahh! She was bound tightly within her weak body, but her enormous inner life was expressed in every breath. Her continuous prayers rose to heaven for the needs of others. She prayed for you and others to find God, for your success at college and for your ministry. She prayed for the people at your meetings to have soft hearts. God knew her well from her continuous conversation with Him. Please be happy, you did marvelous things in your life, but she befriended God in her every breath."

At Camp Courage I met a similar woman, who is indeed created in the image of the Most High God. JoJo, a diminutive woman with a large soul, was in her 20s when I knew her. She had cerebral palsy, was nearly blind, and required a wheelchair for mobility. Her parents and caretakers helped her in dressing, bathing, and other personal needs. It is a national blessing that a slice of our Social Security system helps provide for her care through life. While JoJo's physical shortcomings limited her physical life, she always displayed the same loving-kindness that was overflowing from Eddie's soul. JoJo spoke very naturally about Jesus and she shone with joy in her conversations. She took an interest in me as a new follower of Jesus and asked how she could pray for me, telling me, "I cannot do anything else, so I pray for people."

I do not know what heaven looks like, but I look forward to the welcome JoJo will receive in the-world to come because it will be a glorious greeting. I also look forward to meeting Eddie again. These two probably still radiate a level of god-likeness that I will never attain. Genesis indicates that humans are created in the image of God. It is clear to me that this image is not reflected in the perfection of a physical body. Instead it shines in the expansive goodness of the soul. I cannot define God's *image* or *likeness* with precision, but I have *seen* it.

Growing in Knowledge

I have attended conservative evangelical congregations since my first days of becoming a follower of Jesus Christ. Many kind friends and thoughtful mentors have blessed me in the evangelical community. I met my lovely wife in the same church community that we then attended for thirty years. We have served in ministries for youth, small groups, Bible studies, and music. I have been quick to serve as Bible teacher, small group leader, or building custodian. Kathy and I had three wonderful kids. Our family benefited greatly from the friendships and fellowships of our small churches.

I have been very slow to take on the mantle of elder leadership. In Protestant Christian circles as in the New Testament, an elder is often a recognized wise leader in a local congregation.[19] In my thirties I was asked to preach during the summer when the pastor's family was on vacation. I declined. To me, a teaching elder from the pulpit should really be an elder, an older, wise Christian. Perhaps I am arriving now at the requisite age, but I refrain from taking on elder status within my congregation. I perhaps excel in knowledge but not in requisite wisdom.

As a traditional Christian I have loved to explore the Bible with the aid of a rich collection of writings on history, praxis, and theology. I read many contemporary works, but I more frequently explored the classic writings of Christianity, such as *Confessions* by Augustine of Hippo and *Imitation of Christ* by Thomas of Kempis. Christianity has a whole universe of ancient writings to explore. Through these writings I have gained an appreciation of other Christian traditions in the Great Church.[20] An important discovery for me in my move from Mormonism to traditional Christianity was that I was now participating in a much larger community of believers. Many wise saints have helped me refine my understanding of Christianity and of the Christian life. There are certainly anachronisms and ugly thoughts embedded in Christian writings. For example, Augustine's *City of God* is one the most influential Christian books ever written. There is beauty to be found there, but from his deep-seated Roman cultural background he writes that judges should torture accused criminals to determine their guilt.[21] Similarly, the *Imitation of Christ* was one of the most published books behind the Bible for 400 years after its initial printing in 1471, a mere fifteen years after the Gutenberg Bible's first printing,[22] but its monastic advice of self-mortification sounds strange to the modern Christian. It is necessary to see each author embedded in the culture of his or her time. As an honest explorer I must face both the beauty and the broken aspects of Christians through history, in my local community, and in me. Humanity is always flawed, even the most godly among us. I trust that God is continuously working out the salvation of his people towards greater and greater goodness. It is the task of each generation to speak against the ugly teachings in their community and their history.[23] We must read with a heart of humility. Christians over the 2000 years of the Church era are my brothers and sisters in Christ.

One of the high points of the Christian tradition has been the life and few writings of Francis of Assisi. He shines, like Eddie. I'm pretty cerebral and dull. This humble Catholic saint is my highest hero. Francis's humility and service for others encourages us to live in imitation of Christ. Even as a monk he did not exclude other life paths in God's service. He sought a place for women who desired to practice poverty and celibacy in service to God by establishing the Order of Saint Clare. Similarly he established the Third Order of Saint Francis for people of all walks of life including married couples. I am especially excited to praise the God of creation just as Francis did. He recognized that creation is filled with our co-created siblings of brother Sun, sister Moon, brothers Wind and Air, and sister Water, all under the One True God.[24]

Marginalized Moderate

It is unfortunate that being a scientist and evidence-based thinker often puts one at odds with some Christians. Science has a well-established method of assessing the best explanations of what is observed in the natural world. Interpretation of the Bible is not so definitive. There are a number of reasonable hermeneutical approaches. I always have had this one assumption as I approach the Bible: my particular interpretation of a passage must accommodate my understanding of the natural world. This is not a problem for me since the Bible says very little about science directly. The pastors of our churches have often but not always been kind towards my preference of theistic evolution on both cosmological and biological scales. They did not consider a particular interpretation of the opening chapters of Genesis as a necessary doctrine of Christian orthodoxy. I have rarely discussed my views of theistic evolution, but gossip is an important mode of communication in churches, so I received occasional ribbing from particular congregants about what they thought my views on Genesis were. In the churches my family and I have attended, many held to the six-day creation (young earth) and others held to a six-period creation (old-earth) interpretation of Genesis, but generally it was an avoided topic. Only a few would have agreed with theistic evolution as a viable biblical option. There was an occasional invitation to college Sunday school class to present my views on Genesis 1–3. I would explain my interpretative approach and present the evidences of standard scientific conclusions associated with big bang cosmology and evolution. Often I was asked to read and assess a book about young-earth creationist theories, but eventually I had to decline these requests, as my reviews were generally not appreciated. I have always been kind in the discussions and never took an absolute stand against someone's interpretive preference, but there was always a subtext of disapproval from a few church members. Some parents refused to let their teenagers come to the Sunday school classes I taught no matter what the topic. There were letters circulated about perceived heresies taught in the small group home studies that Kathy and I helped start. These eruptions from the more fundamentalist members of our church were rare, so Kathy and I were able to serve and be served in a number of wonderful ministries.

It is important to carefully define *conservative*, *moderate*, and *liberal* as terms within traditional Christianity as well as my usage of the frequently used term *fundamentalist*. I have always viewed myself as a moderate Christian with conservative leanings in theology. The conservative traditional Christian generally embraces the standard orthodoxy of the reality of God's incarnation as the Son of God. Jesus is the unique Son of God[25] who lived, died, and was resurrected within human history as presented by the New Testament[26] and interpreted by Christians through the ages.[27] I have embraced conservative orthodoxy in that I recognized my sins and failures as a selfish human who needs God's saving grace through the life, death, and resurrection of Jesus Christ. This conservative orthodoxy sees real actions of a real God in real human history and in my human life. To the conservative Protestant Christian the Bible is the defining document of orthodoxy and orthopraxy, which I have accepted.

Liberal theology arises primarily from the seminal theologians Friedrich Schleiermacher (1768–1834) and Adolf von Harnack (1851–1930). Their theology and histo-theological analysis, respectively, separated heaven and earth into categories of universal transcendental idealism and historical realism. Pastor Friedrich Schleiermacher was concerned about the shallow criticism of Christianity made by the Enlightenment thinkers of his day. The Protestant movement had lost trust in the authority of Catholic Church hierarchy and the Enlightenment had caused many to doubt the miraculous events within and historicity of the Bible. These two foundations of faith for the traditional Christian message were growing weak particularly among the educated Protestants of Europe. Schleiermacher suffered under the same doubt in the conservative orthodoxy as well, but he desired to continue in his Christian faith. He wrote an influential book entitled *On Religion:*

Speeches to its Cultured Despisers that puts the Christian faith into the philosophical language for the educated elite of Europe. He proposed that faith in the Christian message of forgiveness of sins and a new life through God's Spirit was based on the soul's intuitive feeling of dependence on the infinite God. This religious feeling was a deep psychological and creaturely connection to universal transcendental truths of God. This religious feeling as a basis of faith becomes important during the decades of Joseph Smith's youth. Perhaps the *burning bosom* feeling of the modern Mormon testimony arises from the same Romantic Era notion as Schleiermacher's religious feeling of dependence. As Schleiermacher expressed the doctrines of Christian orthodoxy he used the language of Romantic Idealism and this language remains embedded within liberal congregations today. Jesus becomes the idealized heavenly savior of humanity in which the believer's inner experience of faith accesses forgiveness. Jesus's resurrection into a heavenly Christ need not be an actual event in history, but God uses the story to point to the powerful ideal of heavenly forgiveness and new life in God. The Enlightenment had brought the authority of the Bible into question, but Schleiermacher worked to recover the Bible as trusted scripture, Schleiermacher taught a new hermeneutical approach to biblical interpretation. The Bible was not directly interpreted as God's words speaking directly to the reader. He proposed that one had to strive to think of what the writer of the text intended to say to an ancient audience. This introduced a layer of contextualization for the reader to use as a filter prior to doctrinal interpretation and application in the modern church community. Our modern studies even in conservative churches depend on his hermeneutical approach of contextualization.

About a century later, Adolf von Harnack fully embraced the historical requirements of contextualization for Scripture. He worked to discover the historical human Jesus in the New Testament writings which were to be separated from the European misconceptions and legends of the Christ. We have benefited from Harnack's project of the deconvolving of European cultural views of the Bible from the ancient Hebrew and Greek cultures of the Old and New Testaments. The liberal academics of Europe have given us a rich milieu of ancient cultural understanding to aid in better Bible interpretations. However, the move of doctrines into philosophical idealism and the filtering of Bible texts to exclude the supernatural have moved liberal Christianity towards an idealized heavenly Christ and an earthly Jesus. Jesus Christ was torn in two.[28] Through philosophical idealism, liberal Christianity becomes a religion of ideas of God, forgiveness, salvation, love. The religious feeling about religious concepts make them experientially true to the believer.

I define myself as a moderate Christian, one who remains theologically conservative believing that Jesus is the Son of God who lived, was crucified, was buried, and was resurrected. Jesus is the Christ who saves us from our sin and offers us a new life in God's Spirit. These conservative orthodox doctrines are embedded in both heaven and earth. However, the moderate Christian also benefits from Schleiermacher's Bible hermeneutic of striving to understand the intentions of the authors towards their ancient audience and from Harnack's historical contextualization to help the reader separate the timeless message from the culturally and historically bound content in the Bible. Additionally, the moderate Christian embraces conservative orthodoxy but with a recognition of scientific knowledge. It is the recognition of culture, history, and science as important facets of understanding the Bible that makes one a moderate. As one explores medieval and early documents of Christianity, the moderate theologian becomes accustomed to seeing the continuous thread of a consistent theology but with variations associated with the culture and science of that time. As a result, the conservative theologies of Eastern Orthodox and Roman Catholic Christians are more easily accommodated because of the core beliefs. The moderate can look past a ritual or metaphysical disagreement and see the core. The use of non-Protestant traditions does put the moderate Protestant at odds with conservative Protestants, but there are excellent inquiries to be found in other traditions that can aid in resolving the conflicts within into the difficulties of discussing an objective divine authority with the plethora of Protestant denominations.[29] God has been speaking continuously to the Church, and it becomes important to incorporate Christian voices from Eastern Orthodox and Roman Catholic traditions into a deeper understanding of Christian orthodoxy and orthopraxy.

A common set of labels for these theological categories within Protestant Christianity is *orthodox* (conservative), *neo-orthodox* (moderate), and *liberal*. It is important to recognize that both the conservative and the moderate Christian stand under the care of a real God, who acts in history to save His people. The differing hermeneutics of the conservative and moderate will sometimes lead them to different conclusions on specific topics, ethics, and politics, but courtesy and humility should abound within the Christian body between conservative and moderate believers. I will let God decide where liberal Christians stand as believers, but there are serious questions about the positional stand of a human trusting in God compared with that of a human trusting in the idea of God.

Fundamentalism is generally associated with conservative theology. Originally "fundamentalist" was the name of a Christian movement that desired to take a stand against growing strength of liberal theology and the liberal hermeneutics within Christian academic institutions, particularly in Europe. A group of seminary professors met in 1910 to write ninety essays in support of conservative theology based on a literal hermeneutical approach to Scripture. The resulting document is called *The Fundamentals*. The document limited conservative orthodoxy to a conservative Protestant Reformed Theology that stood against socialism, atheism, and evolution. The unfortunate extent of the document on many cultural as well as theological issues make it a document of legalistic exclusion. The more recent usage of the term *fundamentalism* has been generalized to apply to any religious group with large systems of orthodoxy and orthopraxy which are required for all true believers. Any deviation from the system places one outside the circle of true believers. I use "fundamentalist" in this more general usage. Fundamentalism exists in every religious movement. The ultra-orthodox Jews, Fundamentalist Latter-day Saints, and fundamentalist American Christians are extreme conservatives in their religious orthodoxy, but it is their exclusionary certainty of their large doctrinal and cultural stands that become the hallmarks of fundamentalism. With this last phrase one can envision a usage of *fundamentalism* with radical atheists like Richard Dawkins, who condemns any theist as evil. Indeed, there is a bit of fundamentalism in each of us as we defend our own thinking and declare dissenters our enemies.

As a moderate lay theologian, I live in a fuzzy neo-orthodoxy required by the recognition of my doubts about human access to absolute knowledge. Humility of a precise interpretation of Scripture is often the hallmark of the moderate. Admittedly it is a difficult place to live as one strives to submit to the teachings in Scripture when using an interpretive approach that recognizes human culture embedded in Scripture. To the moderate and conservative Christian, Paul of Tarsus advises unity and acceptance of those who believe (trust and rely upon) Jesus as their Lord and Savior.[30] Paul even spends some time on identifying disputable issues in Romans 14 and 1 Corinthians 8–10. I agree with the oft quoted proverb, "In essentials unity, in non-essentials liberty, in all things charity."[31]

In 2007, our pastor of twenty-plus years announced his retirement. The congregation voted me onto the five-member pastor search committee. Many church members respected my long service in the church community and my moderate views on many church issues. The search committee members reflected the diverse congregation of our university town. The committee had two conservative members inclined towards Southern Baptist fundamentalism, two charismatic members inclined toward Pentecostal gifts of the Spirit, and me, the moderate theologian/scientist. The members voted me as committee leader perhaps because I represented a middle ground. My intentions for the pastor search team were to help the congregation find a theologically conservative pastor who could accommodate the diversity of our university community church. The two conservative committee members began to communicate their fundamentalist preferences for the pastor selection. They identified some of my questions to various candidates as inappropriate and they grew suspicious of my intentions. These two conservative committee members put one candidate particular forward. All agreed that he was a good candidate to lead a church, but the three other members voted against this candidate as being too narrow in his very conservative fundamentalist views for our congregation. The two fundamentalist members insisted that the three members bring the candidate before the church for a vote of acceptance. During one discussion, I was accused of being a liberal unbeliever who should never have been permitted on the committee. Eventually, the three nays submitted to the two yeas and we presented this fundamentalist pastor to the church for consideration. Indeed he was a very good and very conservative pastor, but probably less likely to accommodate moderate or Pentecostal views. The church voted to offer him the position. I was happy to be finished with the pastor search task. The committee sat down with the presumed new pastor and he refused the offer. His reason? I was an unacceptable liberal Christian in the church's leadership. He left the meeting to return home, and the fundamentalist committee members blamed me for his refusal. In the next few weeks a polemic letter written by a prominent member in the congregation was circulated. It attacked the liberal theological heresies in the leadership of the church. Now I just wanted the committee to end. We quickly invited a second fundamentalist pastor candidate and he accepted the invitation. I resigned all my positions to be a member with no responsibilities.

After several months the new pastor asked Kathy and me to breakfast. Kathy and I sat in the local IHOP across from the new pastor. I encouraged our new young pastor to enjoy the maturity and diversity of our congregation associated with the college milieu. About halfway through the breakfast, the pastor moved to his main purpose. He stated that I could not teach any Bible studies or small groups associated with the church and declared, "You must not speak your theological views on church property." I laughed at the declaration. The pastor did not.

Religious fundamentalists within Christianity and Mormonism are often very good human beings striving to please God, but they view any deviation from a literalistic orthodoxy as a threat to true faith. I was viewed as a cancer to true believers. My pastor imposed silence on me as a heretic and it slowly worked into my soul over the course of months. I wondered whether I had a place within conservative traditional Christianity.

I desired to investigate other churches in our city beginning with a couple that I thought were more moderate in their theology. Kathy is definitely a conservative Christian and she did not want to leave the conservative milieu or leave our friends of our church community. We stayed, but I moved to the rarely used last pew in the church's balcony. The back wall of the balcony is the eastern wall of the church. The east wall is favored in European synagogues—the wall closest to Jerusalem. So I sat at the edge of fellowship near the favored wall and wrestled with the parameters of my newest exile.

Scientists as Heretics?

I have always been aware of a subtext of disapproval of my theistic evolution views in the three conservative evangelical churches I have served and attended, and in the Mormon Church of my youth. I am a scientist, and the evidences of Big Bang cosmology, of planetary and stellar evolution, and of biological evolution are substantial. I must merge science with my biblical understanding. This is not going to change. Most people accommodated my views but not many agreed with them, and a minority expressed strong disagreement. The fundamentalist minority stood at a distance and talked with the pastors about my heresies.

The Christian Church has reprimanded several scientists without trusting the ability of science to determine the validity of the scientific claims. Most famously, Galileo championed the sun-centric theory of Copernicus. Galileo turned his telescope towards the heavens and saw the moons of Jupiter changing their positions around Jupiter. He presumed their motion to be orbits around the distant planet. Galileo proposed in his "Starry Messenger" publication[32] that the motion of these moons around the planet Jupiter were similar to the motion of the planets around the sun as the theory of Copernicus proposed. This theory of a sun-centric solar system was disputed by other scientists who had reasonable criticisms based on the lack of observed parallax motion in the stars if the earth orbited the sun.[33] The stars would have to be incredibly distant to remain motionless in the sky. Eventually, the huge distance to stars was demonstrated.[34] As the scientific discussion continued, Galileo received a letter from a friend and mathematician about the apparent disagreement of the sun-centric view with biblical texts like Psalm 104:5 ("He set the earth on its foundations; it can never be moved."). Galileo replied in his responding letter that the theory was not in conflict with the biblical texts because the Bible was not intended to be a textbook on science, but the Bible was an authority on faith and human praxis. Galileo's letter was circulated widely.[35] In 1615 the Roman Inquisition reviewed Galileo's writings and declared them dangerous because they contradicted many parts of the scriptures. Galileo traveled to Rome to defend Copernicus's theory, but he eventually was ordered to abandon the theory and was found guilty of heresy. He was sentenced to imprisonment (house arrest) and publication of his writings was forbidden.

What is the issue between science and religion? I have had conversations with professors and educated friends who condemned Christianity for the demise of scientific progress during the opening centuries of the Christian era (A.D. 100 to 900). I dispute the suggested causal link because there were trends in Greek philosophy that diminished the value of scientific study as well. For example, the pre-Socratics in the teacher-student line of Thales of Miletus were intensely interested in explaining the natural world using reason. Socrates also had an early passion for natural science, but he decided that all the explanations of *how* things happened never addressed his questions of *why* things happened.[36] Socrates and his student, Plato, moved away from natural science into questions of virtue, goodness, and government. To a large degree, Western Christianity followed this Platonist trend of disinterest in natural science. The occasional confrontations were not based on any necessary contradiction between science and Christianity. Even during Galileo's argument with the Church of Rome, there was a vibrant community of scientists at religious universities. In the modern scientific era, there have been many religious Christians involved in brilliant works of scientific discovery including Isaac Newton, James Clerk Maxwell, Leonhard Euler, George Lemaître, and more recently, Francis Collins.

The Christian theologian who set the stage for the modern scientific revolution was a portly Dominican priest named Thomas of Aquinas (A.D. 1225–1274). Plato's most famous student, Aristotle, influenced Thomas's scientific views. Thomas Aquinas managed to moderate the influence of Platonism on Christianity and integrate Aristotle's scientific empiricism into a Christian view of knowledge. Aristotle was an empiricist with an intense interest in biological science. His scientific method was purely observational with the goal of categorizing things by properties. Some of his scientific conclusions were incredibly misguided. However, Christian Europe's eleventh century interest in Aristotle increased investigations in the natural world. Thomas Aquinas produced one of the world's most complete philosophical-theological systems by integrating two sources for human knowledge—natural revelation and biblical revelation. One is a revelation by nature for humanity to explore directly. The other is a revelation by God of heavenly knowledge that is not available to humanity through natural science. Thomas also proposed a third category of human knowledge where one could explore theological truths based on reasoning from within creation as an effect of God. Most importantly for any scientist who is also Christian, Thomas Aquinas envisioned that investigations of truths from the Bible and from nature could not conflict in the final understanding. At essentially the same time, a Franciscan friar, Roger Bacon, developed the basics of the scientific method for a critical investigation of nature. From these Christian roots, modern science developed quickly in Europe and scientific discoveries began replacing the previous culturally bound mythic explanations of the natural world. It is important for Christians to take the view of Thomas Aquinas and embrace the integration of natural and biblical revelations. We are suspended between the mud of earth and the breath of heaven. We cannot ignore either.

So what is the core of the religion-science conflicts? Science and religious traditions only have difficulties when there is an enormous worldview shift required by scientific discovery. Several enormous paradigm shifts required by science have been resisted by scientists as well as theologians, but religious adherents have been slowest to adjust to these discoveries long after the evidences have thoroughly justified a new theory's value. The four largest paradigm shifts in science that have required changes to Christian worldviews have been Copernicus's sun-centric solar system, Kant's nebular evolution of the solar systems, Darwin's evolution of species, and Lemaître's big bang cosmology. All received aggressive resistance for a short time from scientists. The last three still are resisted by a significant percentage of Mormons and traditional Christians. Each theory has received refinements and corrections, but the seminal ideas initiated enormous leaps forward in human understanding of the natural world.

The difficulty of these paradigm shifts for religious fundamentalists is that they require an interpretative shift to metaphorical language rather than literal language when approaching some portions of scripture. The earth is not set firmly on foundations as indicated by a literal reading of

Psalm 104. However, the earth has an unmoving quality in the human existential experience. For example, the cattle are made after their kind in Genesis 1:25. This can no longer be viewed as a special creation of static species. Instead it is an expression of the stability of species over the timescales of human experience, but not over evolutionary timescales. The biblical interpretations of the physical world must become metaphorical to properly integrate the new scientific paradigms. This is particularly difficult for the religious fundamentalist.

The merging of science and Scripture has never been a problem for me. I continually ruminate on the beauty of Genesis 1–3. These chapters are foundational stories of meaning that apply to creation and to all humanity.[37] I also interpret the flaming sword at the end of Genesis 3 as a declaration against humans returning to Eden by measuring these stories with scientific or historical methods. Genesis 1–3 become stories of powerful truths that cannot be interpreted as events connected to humanity's historical timeline in some fashion. We are cut off from these chapters. While we cannot enter into Genesis 1–3 using human investigations, the religious meanings flow out as great truths about the existential experience of creation and humanity.

So in the end I really have no issues with traditional Christianity based on scientific understanding. There are serious approaches in theology that integrate science and history thoroughly. My difficulties within Mormonism and traditional Christianity have been with the insistent religious fundamentalists who find it difficult to integrate these scientific paradigm shifts into their worldview. I can accommodate their literalism as a courtesy, but they generally consider my views as heresy.

Faith in Crisis–Doubled Down

My exile from ministry occurred simultaneously with several other difficult life issues. My youngest son, Patrick, was seriously injured during a trip to Europe. He required two separate surgeries to save his life. Also, my father was rapidly decaying with debilitating dementia. My siblings and I had to move our father out of his home against his wishes. We shared responsibilities to care for him for a short while, but it became necessary to place him in a memory care facility. We chose one near our home in Logan, Utah. He lived well but he continually asked me when he could return to his home in Oregon. I would take him for frequent walks, car rides, meals, and family gatherings, but his typewriter often held a sentence or two about his bewildering son who imprisoned him away from his home. There is tremendous guilt to be found in the perceived failures of parenting and caring for a parent. At the same time as these family difficulties, science funding decreased as a national priority and it was becoming increasingly difficult to maintain a career as a research scientist. Thus, I had a perfect storm of crises in my fifties at the time of my exile. Perhaps it was unnoticed by friends, but I descended into a dark night of the soul where hope dies. I had retreated from my Christian community and God seemed hidden.

As an anathematized outsider to the religious fundamentalists of my local congregation I felt released to explore religious questions again. My own existential lost-ness is a common experience in the Bible.[38] Jacob wrestled with an apparent theophony in Genesis during a night of uncertainty, as he was about to re-enter the land of promise.[39] I wrestled with God's apparent absence in my own dark night.

Descending the Ladder[40]

A new exploration of faith had begun. I had an incredible weariness of dealing with people who knew all the answers based on a narrow vision of faith in things unseen. So I sat quietly in the balcony and read during the worship and sermons.

My reading moved through the eras of philosophy: classical, medieval, modern, and post-modern. It was a whole new exploration so it held my interest: Plato, Aristotle, Descartes, Locke, Hume, Hegel, Schopenhauer, Kierkegaard, Nietzsche . . . I respected many of the insights and hated some of the writing styles, but generally enjoyed new horizons. The beautiful pessimism of Arthur Schopenhauer was wonderful to read and I spent significant time with the pseudonymic Søren Kierkegaard. Kierkegaard became a companion outsider since he also was at odds with his own Christian community in Copenhagen. Writing as Climacus, Kierkegaard elevated the humility of Socrates by drawing a parallel between Socrates and Jesus. Socrates advances humility in the realm of reason by stating that one becomes wise when one admits not knowing wisdom. Jesus advances humility in the realm of righteousness by teaching that one becomes righteous when one confesses sin and cries out for mercy. To Kierkegaard paradox and distance are the existential parameters of the human relat,ionship to God. This did not confound my faith; instead it helped me relax with my doubts in the midst of mystery. I now believe that my questions will always be questions. Wrestling with the questions is the important thing to help one live towards a humble goodness.

As one must when reading philosophy, I was confronted by Friedrich Nietzsche. His atheist conclusions of radical existentialism are an intellectual bomb to any faith in the unseen worlds of religion. There were ancient philosophers with the same message of complete skepticism, but they do not carry the modern literary power of Nietzsche. I experienced what he intended to do in his denigration of philosophical systems and the Christian religion:

> I know my fate. There will come a day when my name will recall the memory of something frightful—a crisis the like of which has never been known on earth, the memory of the most profound clash of consciences and the passing of a sentence upon all that has before been believed in, demanded and sancti-

> fied. I am not a man, I am dynamite. And with it all there is nothing of the founder of a religion in me. Religions belong to the rabble; after coming into contact with religious people I always feel that I must wash my hands. I do not want "believers," I think that I am too full of malice to believe even in myself.[41]

Perhaps it was my inevitable dark night of the soul, but Nietzsche's writing gave voice to the thoroughness of my growing uncertainty. He left no ground for ethics, goodness, or God as real categories. He was indeed doing philosophy with a hammer.[42] Humans have always used mythic, rational, or doctrinal systems to define truths about life and death, good and evil. Nietzsche's first message is that religious and philosophical systems are generally unprovable; thus, he intentionally smashes systems in front of the foolish idol worshippers just as Moses smashes the golden idol into dust. For Nietzsche, religious doctrines were created for a priest-cast to control the humans beneath them. *Don't do that, do this, don't believe that, believe this, or you will be assigned to eternal hell.* The religious words of heaven, hell, soul, spirit, salvation, etc., are words with no concrete definition. What is soul? What is spirit? All religion is devoid of any measurable human reality, so Nietzsche declared God dead and instructed humans to believe their eyes rather than their dogmas. I agree to a degree. Christians sometimes think that their particular theological system is identical to the mind of God. Smash the idol—it is not God.

Nietzsche's positive philosophy advises that the human must step forward and choose to be his own hero—to be übermensch, superman. The übermensch must choose without regard to cultural obligations or ethics—he is above systems that define good and evil. The one requirement for this new human is to make a life choice as if each moment is to be lived 1000 times exactly the same way. This is the opposite of the movie *Groundhog Day,* where infinite repetition of opportunity is given to Bill Murray for the perfection of his character. He repeats the same day thousands of times in pursuit of his best self and then he experiences salvation as a better human. Nietzsche's infinite recurrence of single-moment decision is really the better advice for a life lived once. Salvation to Nietzsche is the freedom to be one's own hero in each moment of time.

Even as I agree broadly with Nietzsche as the destroyer of faux systems, I must also recognize the unleashing of a terrible beast. Nietzsche's philosophical musings became doctrinal propaganda for the Nazi's reign of terror. Watsuji Tetsuro (1889–1960), a Japanese philosopher, identifies the most unfortunate aspect of Nietzsche's great philosophical success in killing God for the modern world—Nietzsche fails to kill Satan as well. If we release ourselves completely from religious calls to live ethical lives, then we give permission to the insanity of extreme immoralists. Extremism is not a category reserved just for the religious. Instead Watsuji advises that people must listen to ancient doctrines, but must add their own voices towards a better understanding of a good life lived. This is not ethical relativity. It merely recognizes that no generation is in full possession of an absolute system of ethics. Systems must always be deconstructed and then reconstructed by every generation in a respectful and humble transfer of wisdom. The Nietzschean effect of no-ethics and no-God releases humanity to become self-indulgent narcissists at best and societal monsters at worst.

Nietzsche's declaration of the death of God caused me to think again of the fundamental questions: What is God? Where is God? I yearned for a good God, but I wandered to the edge of an abyss of no-faith, no-god, no-people[43] and peered in. Perhaps there is something new to be gained when one walks in the dark valley. John of the Cross recognizes this state of sickness as standing at the bottom of a ladder of ascension towards God.

> This sickness and swooning to all things, which is the beginning and the first step on the road to God, we clearly described above, when we were speaking of the annihilation wherein the soul finds itself when it begins to climb this ladder of contemplative purgation, when it can find no pleasure, support, consolation or abiding-place in anything soever. Wherefore from this step it begins at once to climb to the second. The second step causes the soul to seek God without ceasing. Wherefore, when the Bride says that she sought Him by night upon her bed (when she had swooned away according to the first step of love) and found Him not, she said: "I will arise and will seek Him Whom my soul loveth." This, as we say, the soul does without ceasing as David counsels it, saying: "seek ye ever the face of God, and seek ye Him in all things, tarrying not until ye find Him;" like the Bride, who, having enquired for Him of the watchmen, passed on at once and left them. Mary Magdalene did not even notice the angels at the sepulchre.[44]

Ascending the Ladder to Faith

The post-modern theologian Paul Tillich places faith in God at the very edge of the abyss of no-god. Faith in the God-who-saves is the *groundless ground* for believers in this existential world. Proof of God is never direct.[45] Tillich does theology under the constraints of Nietzsche. The absurd groundless ground became the initial descriptor of my wilderness faith experience. Indulge me. I will start from physics and strive to ascend one step at a time on the ladder of faith. Because of my lostness I had to determine what can be said without the aid of Scripture about the very ground of our existence or, in more traditional words, our Creator.

The foundational assumption for the scientist is that reality reveals itself through evidences. The problem the modern Christian must face is that science has explained so much of observable reality that God has receded from interpretations of every human experience of reality. The wonders of creation have become embedded within nature itself and God's participation has become subtle. The martyred German pastor, Dietrich Bonhoeffer, in his *In Letters and Papers from Prison,* struggled with similar conclusions from within his Nazi prison cell:

> The movement beginning about the thirteenth century (I am not going to get involved in any arguments about the exact date) towards the autonomy of man (under which head I place the discovery of the laws by which the world lives and manages in science, social-political affairs, art, ethics and religion) has in our time reached a certain completion. Man has learned to cope with all questions of importance without recourse to God as a working hypothesis. In questions concerning science, art, and even ethics, this has become an understood thing which one scarcely dares to tilt at any more. But for the last hundred years or so it has been increasingly true of religious questions also: it is becoming evident that everything gets along without "God," and just as well as before. As in the scientific field, so in human affairs generally, what we call 'God' is being more and more edged out of life, losing more and more ground.[46]

The world demonstrates an extraordinary degree of naturalism. From the distant galaxies to the center of the earth, from the point of creation to the end of the universe, from the touch of our fingers to the depths of our brain, science is revealing that it is "physics all the way down." Many scientists are even concluding that the human mind can be reduced to the interactions of physics and chemistry. We are merely wet machines. What happens to Christian adherents if spiritual experiences are demonstrated to be associated with certain measurable brain activity?[47] Is there to be an inevitable demise of spirit-based religion and a move to a religionless Christianity as Bonhoeffer proposed?[48] As he ruminates, it seems that Bonhoeffer envisioned that God would have to be met at the center of life being lived rather than in spiritualized worship. I do not believe he retreats from faith in God even though he does feel that God has retreated from human experience.

One conclusion of a fully natural universe is provided by the brilliant physicist, Stephen Hawking, who replaces the hubris of religious mythos with the hubris of scientific modernity:

> A well-known scientist (some say it was Bertrand Russell) once gave a public lecture on astronomy. He described how the earth orbits around the sun and how the sun, in turn, orbits around the center of a vast collection of stars called our galaxy. At the end of the lecture, a little old lady at the back of the room got up and said: "What you have told us is rubbish. The world is really a flat plate supported on the back of a giant tortoise." The scientist gave a superior smile before replying, "What is the tortoise standing on?" "You're very clever, young man, very clever," said the old lady. "But it's turtles all the way down!"[49]

Many scientists prefer to see reality as "physics all the way down." Ethics, goodness, and beauty become existential preferences of the individual or community in a thoroughly material existence.

As a scientist and a pursuer of God I need to address this modern conundrum of physics all the way down. Where is the interface of God and human? I need to think about the turtle under the last layer of physics, the turtle that is the ground of existence and the ground of order we call physics.

Divine Ground of Existence

Thomas Aquinas excels in exploring the edge between reason and faith. His Five Ways or Five Proofs of God's existence are wonderful to think about.[50] Many philosophers have dismissed these thought experiments with a wave of the hand, and some theists have embraced them as real proofs of God. Neither of these extremes should be taken. The Five Ways should be meditations on the hints about God based on questions about reality. The logic experiment of the First Way circumscribes a definition for the word "God" as the Unmoved Mover, the initial cause of all transient motion in our world. The second follows back the chain of cause and effect to the Uncaused First Cause. In these mental excursions to the origin of what we observe, God can be defined as the Divine Ground[51] of existence and the one turtle that supports all the layers of explorable physics. This Ground of reality is beyond exploration, but the observable effects arising from that Ground hint or point out beyond experiential reality. Thomas admits that God is a middle word that sits between the question of existence we raise and the underlying basis of existence. Princeton theologian Hugh T. Kerr explains in an introduction to one of Thomas Aquinas's writings that the cause is the proof of the effect, but the definition of the cause stands for the cause's actual existence. Thus, the word "God" stands in the place of the Cause of creation, which is the effect we observe.[52]

Thomas Aquinas fills out the word "God" circumscribed by the First Way and Second Way as *that which nothing greater can be conceived.*[53] By definition "God" is a word that represents the ultimate ground of all that exists. In this view the Divine Ground is just beyond physical reality that we can observe, thus, is immaterial because it is beyond physical reality. Potentially, the Divine Ground is the universe itself as proposed by Baruch Spinoza, a seventeenth century Jewish philosopher. This pantheist God would be Divine Existence rather than the Divine Ground of existence—in either case they are beyond measure because we cannot measure reality in its entirety or measure that which sits behind reality. Isaiah 6:3 says "Holy, holy, holy is the Lord," which is translated more literally as "Separate, separate, separate is the Lord." God is the complete Other from every created thing and all of creation.[54] God is not a thing that exists within creation—He is Other. I will return to this idea below.

Can science say anything about that Divine Ground? Perhaps. In recent history the CERN supercollider was smashing protons together in hopes of observing evidence of the Higgs boson, the particle that completes the standard model of physics. This boson explains why particles are observed to have inertial mass. Two competing physics theories gave different predictions of the mass of the Higgs boson. A particular observed mass would permit physicists to draw interesting conclusions about the underlying answers to "Why is there an ordered something rather than something else?" One interesting problem in modern physics is the longevity and complexity of the existing universe that we observe. The universe has an incredibly fine-tuned physics that permits a long-lived universe where galaxies, stars, planets, life, and intelligent life can evolve. The finely-tuned physics makes this universe extremely improbable. If fundamental constants of the physical forces in the universe were to differ in the slightest, then the universe would collapse or expand far too quickly for our situation of earth's billion self-aware beings. The "multiverse" theory solves this conundrum of the improbable universe by proposing a frothing chaos with an infinite number of universes popping into existence—each with a different physics. The chaotic froth births all possible universes and ours is just the rare accident. The multiverse theory predicts a heavy Higgs boson.

A second theory called "supersymmetry," or "SUSY," predicted a lighter Higgs boson, but SUSY depends on a finely-tuned physics for our observed reality. That is, no explanation of the finely-tuned physics comes from the theory. The SUSY could suggest that an intentional design is embedded within this one, very unlikely universe.

The scientific world waited with excitement for the results from the CERN supercollider search for the Higgs boson. On March 14, 2013, CERN scientists announced with great certainty (a term with definable rigor) that they had observed the Higgs boson. It turned out to have a mass in between the two theory predictions. There were congratulatory remarks between physicists even in my own university department as scientists felt privileged just to be a part of the human effort to understand nature. The measured mass of the Higgs boson brings many questions for physicists to work on, but an intentionally fine-tuned creation remains one of the explanations of observed reality.[55]

I have always used "God" as the word for the Divine Ground of existence regarding which nothing higher can be considered. This is reasonable and (by definition) compatible with science. "God" is a word representing the answer to "Why is there something?" and "Why is there order?" In this definition is a necessary monotheism. There can only be one ultimate Divine Ground of all existence. Additionally, this Divine Ground is that which is beyond the last layer of measurable physicality, the turtle that supports physics all the way down as it were. This view points to classic theism, that God is not physical, that is, God is immaterial.[56] Monotheism and classic theism are my preferred conclusions on theism—though Spinoza's pantheism is also a possible conclusion so far.

If eventual evidence supports the multiverse theory, then God is the chaotic sea from which this creation birthed, though one might still see intentionality towards the goal of a finely-tuned creation with conscious, self-conscious, and other-conscious beings. There are several early Jewish rabbis who propose that there were several creations prior to this particular one.[57] Certainly the finely-tuned universe provides a greater hint of intentionality by the Divine Ground. Intentionality is an unnecessary anthropomorphism, but I use it to set up a second question. Is there intended goodness as an objective reality? Is God good?

Divine Ground of Good

Our impossibly finely-tuned physical universe arises from the Divine Ground by my definition. Neither traditional theists nor atheists need be offended by this definition. For the theist, using existential as the proof of the Divine Ground of existence is begging the question par excellence for faith's sake. For the atheist the Divine Ground of existence is merely a set of words representing existence. Spinoza and Einstein used the word "God" in this way. Saying there are intentions in the Divine Ground apply a bit of anthropomorphism into the word "God". Intentions presume a direction to creation and one particular direction arises by asking, "Is the Divine Ground Good?" I will use Plato's term, the Good, to identify idea of transcendental good.[58] For Plato, the equivalency of the Good and the Ground for existence provides a transcendental footing for valuing as an activity within reality, that is, valuing qualities like kindness, beauty, justice, or meaning. Is valuing an existential evolutionary tool of human survival or a hint of transcendental goodness?

C. S. Lewis' moral theory in *Mere Christianity* identifies the universal human desire for fairness as an indicator that the idea of justice resides as an objective reality.[59] His nuanced presentation is convincing for the convinced. It is logically similar to Plato's discourses on the form of the Good.[60] Humans cannot give a precise definition of fairness, piety, goodness or courage, but they recognize these values when they occur. The Good is the form or divine concept from which all good forms arise and these valuing qualities are something real to be recognized. Nietzsche rails against Plato for beginning the lie of the objective reality for valuing qualities like good and evil.[61] C. S. Lewis would reply to Nietzsche, "Why do you rail? You judge Plato and Christianity to be evil? Apparently you feel a wrong otherwise you would not be so upset." I suggest that Nietzsche is correctly upset at arrogant system builders who impose their earthbound dogmas on others as if it were transcendent truth. However, Nietzsche overlooks the gentle humility of Socrates when approaching objective goodness in the Dialogues of Plato. Humans can never lay hold of transcendent things in their existential experience, but they recognize kindness, justice, and beauty as hints of goodness in reality that point to a transcendent Good. Socrates was as much of a system destroyer as was Nietzsche. The Athens community condemned Socrates to death for demonstrating the foolishness of commonly held dogmas. Instead of elevating the self into a superman, Socrates remained a humble pursuer of the Good—pursuing but never fully grasping hold.

I still ask, *Is there goodness as an objective reality?*

Anselm, the scholarly Bishop of Canterbury from eleventh century England, put the oft-discounted ontological proof of God forward. Anselm uses a chain of goodness to point to the ground of goodness similar to Aristotle's chain of causality pointing to the First Cause. Anselm's begins by observing that humans value the goodness of things and actions. Knowing goodness is itself very good.[62] Humans judge beings by the goodness of their actions and qualities. There must be one being of highest goodness, who is highest of all beings. Anselm takes one more step above the highest being in his chain of superlatives with an arrow that points beyond created things to the self-existent being through whom all good beings exist. This self-existent being is "that than which nothing greater can be conceived." Anselm's phrase is later used by Aquinas, but many any enlightenment philosophers criticize this last step. Bertrand Russell demonstrates that conceiving of something does not prove its existence. He imagines the existence of a flying teapot to demonstrate the absurdity of the ontological proof. However, this criticism is ignoring that Anselm begins from a reality (of good or intelligence or power) and defines God as the end of the infinite inference from reality. The critique is misguided. The Prime Mover argument of Aristotle can be used in this same manner. We perceive movement or action that has a causal action, which itself has a causal action. At the end of the causal chain of actions in the world sits by the definition the Prime Mover, which has no cause (self-existent) . . . the Divine Ground discussed above. At the beginning of the argument is the existential experience of actions from causes that one cannot deny is the hint that begs the question, "Why is there something happening at all?" The Prime Mover or Divine Ground merely becomes the representative words that answer the question. The ontological argument applied to the Good must be questioned at the beginning of the chain of arrows in the perceived goodness as a real thing experienced within the depth of the human soul. Maybe goodness is not a real thing. Anselm recapitulates his argument by acknowledging that without the objective standard of highest goodness then goodness does not exist in reality. Good and evil then become relative levels of pain and pleasure in our evolutionary physicality.

The twentieth-century philosopher Ludwig Wittgenstein proposed that all philosophical questions are based on word games[63] that can be reduced to existential valuing words of *ouch* and *ahh*. However, this philosophical reductionism merely uses belittling words to trivialize the human quest for transcendence. If nothing else, *ouch* and *ahh* do exist. The Good becomes the ultimate *ahh* and the Evil becomes the ultimate *ouch*. Heaven and hell, God and Satan, or existentially, Francis of Assisi and Hitler of Braunau am Inn. The dichotomy of *ouch* and *ahh* simplifies the bliss and suffering of the human experience, but it does not demand that humanity to merely mud.

The important sociologist Peter Berger wrote on the development of religion as a social construct for ancient humanity.[64] Many praised his work as a demonstration of the foolishness of religion and faith. In reply to this hasty conclusion he wrote a small book called *A Rumor of Angels*. Like C. S. Lewis he also sees hints of transcendence as well:

> We have come a long way from the gods and from angels. The breaches of this worldly reality, which these mighty figures embodied, have increasingly vanished from our consciousness as serious possibilities. They linger on as fairy tales, nostalgias, perhaps as vague symbols of some sort. A few years ago, a priest working in a slum section of a European city was asked why he was doing it, and replied, "So that the rumor of God may not disappear completely." The word aptly expresses what the signals of transcendence have become in our situation—rumors—and not very reputable rumors at that.[65]

Valuing is the activity that suggests that humans are at least transcending beings that exist between mud and sky. Most humans still lift their hands to the sky because they sense there is something there. This is only a hint, but it is a hopeful hint. C. S. Lewis describes the depth of humanity's involvement with valuing of beauty and goodness:

> We do not want merely to see beauty . . . . We want something else which can hardly be put into words—to be united with the beauty we see, to pass into it, to receive it into ourselves, to bathe in it, to become part of it.[66]

It is here I step towards faith in things unseen. I do not see a definitive argument for a transcendent good, but I recognize goodness as hinting towards a transcendent good. I yearn for goodness to be real and, like C. S. Lewis writes, I desire to participate in goodness and beauty. I also recoil at the thought that rape, child abuse, the twentieth century Holocaust are merely things that happen. A Divine Good and a Divine Ground as God is not a very specific God for one's faith, but it is as far as reasoning can take me. Thomas Aquinas also identifies revelation through Scripture traditions as a realm of knowledge not available to natural reason. I have explored the evidences of the Bible as a reliable religious history and Mormon scriptures less thoroughly. I know where I stand on the Bible's reliability, but the reliability of other various scriptures (Quran, Bible, Book of Mormon, etc.) is beyond my purpose here. Let me merely just examine the revealed truths about God in Mormonism and traditional Christianity in relation to my speculations above about God as the Good Divine Ground. What does the Bible reveal about God, the Good Divine Ground of all creation?

REASONS

God Is One; God Is Spirit; God Is Love

Traditional Christianity has interesting variations of doctrine and practice within the Oriental, Orthodox, and Western Churches.[67] I see more agreement in the essential beliefs of these broad sectors of traditional Christianity than many Mormons think (even more than many Protestants think). The Apostle's Creed and the commentaries of the early church fathers capture the core agreements of these broad denominational lines. Mormonism is substantially different from all these denominational lines. There are some agreements between particular Mormon doctrines and teachings of several heretics in the early centuries of Christianity.[68] Did early Christianity mislabel a heretic?

Mormonism and traditional Christianity maintain metaphysical positions that are impossible to prove unless one assumes a particular Scripture is the true revelation of God. Adherents can organize verses from their recognized scriptures to support or detract from their favorite metaphysical position. Arguments from scripture and logic cannot be considered objective proofs for a skeptical listener. The skill of the rhetorician is generally more important than the veracity of the metaphysical interpretation of a given Scripture. Certainly, the Jewish and Christian Testaments of the Bible have received an extraordinary amount of extra-biblical support for the religious history presented within, but this does not ensure that the religious teachings are necessarily true. While most mainstream historians and archaeologists do not accept the historicity of the Book of Mormon, this does not necessarily invalidate the metaphysical teachings of Mormons.[69]

My previously stated criteria for assessing the metaphysical doctrines of a faith community are still reasonable to me. My five criteria are here repeated:

1. There is one God.

2. God is Creator of everything, and nothing in creation is God.

3. God is ultimately good and beautiful.

4. The world and I both demonstrate goodness and evil, beauty and ugliness. Something is wrong. God must hold the solution to this broken situation.

5. The essentials of the truth about God and humanity had to be accessible on some level to a child but also had to be deep and even inaccessible to the smartest human. However, truths cannot be stupid, that is, they must be reasonable and/or embedded in mystery.

These are consistent with my musings on God as the Divine Ground and the Divine Good. From a biblical perspective I will approach these through the three positive creed-like statements from the Old and New Testaments: *God is One, God is Spirit*, and *God is Love*. These address criteria 1, 2, and 3. Wrestling with the depth held in these three simple statements satisfies 5 for me.

God could be the universe as for a pantheist, but good and evil have no real distinctive separation within pantheism. Reality just is. A separate God from created reality seems necessary for a transcendent and objective

Good. If a good God is not objectively real, then faith questions have no import. However, with one last push against the position of No-Good and No-God, a Jewish philosopher, Martin Buber, relates a tale of a young enlightenment scholar who was accustomed to arguing with Jewish scholars about the existence of God.[70] Torah[71] scholars had presented arguments for faith and serving God from the Torah, but the atheist countered every presentation with excellent rhetorical arguments. The atheist then visits a famous local rabbi to destroy his old-fashioned faith in God. The rabbi paid little attention to the arguments; after a time he raised his hand to dismiss the young man and said, "But what if it is true, my son?" The young man stopped speaking and thought deeply for a moment. He tried to steady himself against the simple WHAT IF. In time the young man sought to study the Torah to live in the light of WHAT IF.

Negative, Analogy, Reality

There are three broad approaches to discussing the relationship between God and humanity: negative, analogy, and reality theologies. Negative theology and the theology of analogy are recognized and well-established categories. I perhaps invent the category of *reality theology* to place Joseph Smith's teachings on God. The position of reality theology insists on the direct connection of our human life experience with the Heavenly Father. In reality theology the difference between God and man is only a matter of degree. The advantage of a reality theology is that God becomes accessible and understandable. The love of God is the most beautiful version of human love. This parallels the "univocity of being" approach championed by Duns Scotus, a scholar of the high middle ages, who disliked the *theology of analogy* detailed by Thomas Aquinas.

Negative theology, or "the way of negatives" (*via negativa* in Latin), proposes that positive knowledge about God is impossible for humanity. God can only be described through statements of negation. Biblical statements in the way of negatives can be found. For example, references to the ineffable God are in Old and New Testaments—"God is not human" (Num. 23:19), God is not a created thing (Col. 1:16), and The thoughts and ways of God are not the thoughts and ways of man (Isa. 55:8). These are completely true statements through the way of negatives. The negative theology has long been an intellectually deep rumination on God. The ruminations provide a path towards veneration of the Most High God. The votary contemplates the elevating negative truths of the Ineffable God and contemplates the infinite difference between the created worshipper and the Divine Creator. Negative theology is both ancient and new. An Christian theologian known as Pseudo-Dionysius the Areopagite, from the fifth century A.D., influenced subsequent generations of theologians with his books entitled *The Divine Names* and *Mystical Theology*. A number modern philosophers[72] and theologians[73] continue to explore the mystic tradition of the way of negatives. The beauty of negative theology is the elevation of Ineffable God. The dreariness of the approach is the sense of the infinite distance of the unknowable God from the finite human being. During the deepest depression I could only speak of and to God through the way of negatives. Prayers seemed earthbound, but the way of negatives still gave me a context of hoping for hope.

The thirteenth-century Dominican Friar Thomas Aquinas was influenced by the earlier negative theologians of Christianity (Pseudo-Dionysius), of Islam (Averroes), and of Judaism (Maimonides). The famous twelfth-century Rabbi Maimonides embraced negative theology in total. One could not say that God existed, only that God does not *not* exist. The famous rabbi suggested that positive statements about God were merely religious expressions created for the benefit of less-educated followers of the Ineffable God.[74] Thomas Aquinas appreciated the way of negatives, but he also acknowledged the positive truth statements about God within the Jewish and Christian scriptures. He recognized a human capacity to understand God but only through analogies based on our earthly experiences. This is the *theology of analogy*.

The most fundamental Old Testament positive statement might be summarized in *God is One* (Deut. 6:4b), which the book of Isaiah supports. Important New Testament positive statements are *God is Spirit* (John 4:24) and *God is Love* (1 John 4:8).

Without any depth to my youthful faith, I clearly approached God with a simple theology of analogy because God was unlike anything in my physical experience. God was a loving Heavenly Father like and unlike my loving but flawed father. I thought that the term "Father" was applied to God to aid in my relating to God as creator. I had only one father in reality and another analogous Father, who was Father over all Creatures in a more fundamental way. God was a present, but unseen, spirit in the midst of our little family prayer circle. As a teenager I was surprised at the Mormon presentation of the Heavenly Father in a reality theology. In recent years God has been more hidden from my experience and the way of negatives was strangely more accessible.[75]

The ruminations above foreshadow my conclusions below. Even now as I look at the simplicity and depth of these three positive statements about God (one, spirit, and love), I feel confident that the classic theism and monotheism of traditional Christianity satisfies my criteria 1, 2, 3, and 5 for a reasonable faith. My fourth criterion requires God's action in the world as a redeemer to set things right. This is indeed the literal crux of Christianity and to a degree of Mormonism.

God Is One

To most of the contemporary religious world there can only be one God. God has no peer. The most common interpretation of Mormon theology is that there are at least three individual and separate gods: the Heavenly Father, Jesus, and the Holy Ghost. Within traditional Christianity there may be many gods[76] with a small "g," but traditionally these are created beings (human princes, angels) that are given places of authority under the One God (capital "G"). My first criterion for faith is closer to the traditional Christian teaching of monotheism, but it is clearly just a personal intuition since polytheism was widely embraced in the past. I can articulate personal reasons for my intuition.

In ancient polytheism there was generally a recognized most high god over the many gods. That highest god had to earn the position through an act of conquest described in a god-story. The designated father of monotheism, Abraham in Genesis, likely grew up hearing the Mesopotamian creation myth called Enuma Elish. It is a story of a war among the gods and the subsequent creation of our ordered cosmos.

Enuma Elish begins with the first primordial god of the peaceful sweet waters, Apsu, and his wife, Tiamat, the goddess of chaotic seas. They come together to beget a plethora of children gods. Soon the primordial world is filled with the laughter and carousing of many children gods. The first father-god decides to kill off his noisy children so he can sleep. His eldest child, Ea, hears of the plan and decides that he must kill the father god to save all his siblings. The first-son god murders the first-father.

The mother goddess is overwhelmed with anger at the murder of her husband. She takes a new husband and enlists a number of children-gods to wage a war against Ea and his allies. Tiamat creates eleven terrifying sea monsters to strengthen her army. The children gods are frightened by their apparent doom. Eventually, a powerful grandchild-god is chosen to fight the mother goddess directly. If he can kill Tiamat, then the remaining children gods will join him to battle the sea monsters and Tiamat's army of loyal gods. The chosen warrior god, Marduk, brings his weapons of the whirlwind, the hurricane, and lightning bolts to fight Tiamat. He is able to kill the mother goddess and the rest of the children gods join in to defeat her armies. As a reward for his victory he is given the title of "god of gods." The body of the first father god becomes the earth and the first mother goddess's body is split in two by Marduk to make the firmament that separates the waters above from the waters beneath. Humans are made by dripping the blood of a dead god on the dirt of earth to make the red mud body of humans. The humans are created to serve the gods by bringing food to the tops of zuggarnauts, the stairways to the heavens. Marduk earned his place as highest god of gods as a warrior god.

Traditional extra-biblical stories say that Abraham breaks from his Mesopotamian culture and gods when he hears the voice of YHWH, which is the *God of the unpronounceable name* who later meets with Moses in the burning bush. To Abraham, YHWH is, first, the god-who-calls. Abraham obeys his new god and goes to a new land. YHWH is an invisible, relational god who speaks to Abraham rather than a warrior god of a primordial god-story. There is no god story for YHWH. I ponder whether Abraham even thinks of YHWH as the One God at this first call.

In Genesis 14 Abraham becomes the hero of the War of Nine Kings when he rescues his nephew, Lot, and the people of the five defeated cities of the Jordon River valley from captivity by the four invading kings from Mesopotamia. After Abraham's triumph, there is an amazing meeting of key biblical characters: the king of Sodom, Abraham, and the king of Salem (Jerusalem) come together in Salem. The king of Sodom rules over the violent and licentious culture of Sodom. Abraham is a wealthy shepherd wandering in the mountainous regions above the Jordon valley. The king of Salem is named Melchizedek, which means king of righteousness. Melchizedek blesses Abraham with a prayer to God Most High (*El 'Elyon*):

> Blessed be Avram by El'Elyon, maker of heaven and earth. And blessed be El 'Elyon, who handed your enemies over to you.[77]

Melchizedek's God Most High was not the-most-powerful-warrior god of a god story; instead God is maker (*qanah* in Hebrew.) In this meeting Melchizedek, the priest of God Most High, may have helped Abraham make a leap in his understanding of YHWH. Maybe it is at this time Abraham finally sees YHWH, the god-who-calls, as God Most High and Creator of all.

In one fascinating Jewish tradition, Melchizedek is Shem, one of the three sons of Noah. In the biblical counting of years Shem is still living at this time, which is incredible since Abraham is a ninth-generation descendent of Shem. Shem was given YHWH as his God of promise through the blessing of his father, Noah.[78] Thus, the important understanding of the One Creator (the Divine Ground of existence) is possibly passed on to Abraham through Shem. Even if Melchizedek is not Shem, knowledge of YHWH as Most High Creator God likely comes through the line of Shem to Abraham.

After Abraham's merging of the God-who-calls and the Creator God, he then converses with the inhospitable king of Sodom in an important juxtaposition of the shepherd of hospitality and the king of the proverbial inhospitable city.[79] Abraham proclaims YHWH is God Most High and *qanah* (maker) of heaven and earth.[80] All biblical metaphors of God seem to be tied up in this one word (*qanah*), which carries the main meaning of creator or maker, but secondary meanings of possessor, purchaser, and redeemer. Abraham's declaration is his creedal statement and it may be a seminal version of the *Shema Yisrael*.[81] This broadly interpretable Hebrew word for creator differs significantly from god stories within polytheism where a god must demonstrate and earn his elevation over other gods. This Hebrew word jumps past the warrior story and settles on creator and possessor of all. Abraham's understanding possibly leaps to his own version of the One Divine Ground of existence—monotheism.

The biblical creation story has similarities with Enuma Elish, but the differences are most significant. Genesis chapter 1 begins with a simple "In the beginning God." There is no peer. There is no god story. God just is. The Creator pauses before and above creation in verses 1 and 2, while creation waits in a chaotic angst. The God speaks with creative goodness and life to the cosmos throughout chapter 1. The cosmos and Creator are in relation as peers perhaps, but with the cosmos as a contingent peer. I interpret "Creator" to be the One Divine Ground of existence who has directed goodness towards creation. God exists before and above and apart from creation.

Greek philosophers started exploring the world as a reasonable world. They could see organization that was accessible to their reasoning minds. Some concluded that a single Divine Mind was behind the pervasive unity observed in the natural world. The ordered universe arises from divine rational concepts (*logos*) from a single cosmic mind (*nous*). With our human minds we perceive the order. As mentioned earlier, in the twelfth century, Thomas Aquinas presented five arguments for God's existence. His fifth argument of Governance articulates the same conclusions of the ancient Greek philosophers. It is a thoughtful argument for the modern scientist. In short, the Governance Argument states that the universe is filled with mindless objects, but they seem to follow orderly actions. There must be a governing cause or mind behind this orderliness. This goes deeper than just pointing to a set of physical laws. set of physical laws. God is the answer to the question, "Why is there order rather than chaos?" of where order arises.[82] As a physicist I can pose the One Divine Ground to this reality as the "meta" of my physics.[83] As far as humanity has probed out into the skies or down into the atom, there is a consistent physics underlying the observations. This requires a single Divine Ground for the unifying vision of the entire universe. A Creator—One God.

The universe of polytheism did explain the seemingly capricious events of nature to ancient humanity who only saw uncorrelated catastrophes. Different gods who vacillated between calm and rage controlled volcanoes, earthquakes, and violent storms. The Greek philosophers made a move toward rational investigations of nature and toward monotheism (platonist version of The Good) and some moved toward atheism.[84] As a scientist I agree with the Greeks, the world is orderly and wonderfully so. The unity of physics for the observable cosmos suggests One Mind (without definition) from which existence and order flows.

The seventeenth-century Jewish philosopher Baruch Spinoza saw the universe as being identical to the thought and expression of the Spirit of God, in other words, the universe is God. To Spinoza, all that happens and exists are deterministically occurring in a complete unity. He contested the concept of a God that transcends the universe with anthropomorphic responses to the events within creation. Instead, unity of physical reality was identical with the word "God." This is a suitable conclusion as well. I generally consider atheists to be theists in the line of Spinoza with an impersonal God, the Universe. Ultimately, there can be only one Highest God. This God must either be the universe itself or a single, separate (holy), Divine Ground for the universe. Traditional Judaism and Christianity see God as Other in relation to creation. One Creator, Father of all things, is creedal Christianity.

"We believe in one God, the Father Almighty, Maker of all things visible and invisible." (Nicene Creed of A.D. 325).

Mormon theology teaches that there are three gods in the godhead of the heavenly court—the Heavenly Father, the Son, and the Holy Ghost. These are three individual gods and free agents presiding in a bishopric over all.

> There are three separate persons in the Godhead: God, the Eternal Father; his Son, Jesus Christ; and the Holy Ghost. We believe in each of Them. From latter-day revelation we learn that the Father and the Son have tangible bodies of flesh and bone and that the Holy Ghost is a personage of spirit, without flesh and bone. These three persons are one in perfect unity and harmony of purpose and doctrine.[85]

This Mormon teaching in its reality theology form implies three separate beings of divine standing with a unified purpose to support a doctrine of the *Godhead is One*. Mormon doctrine for humans and gods emphasizes free agency. Traditional Christianity acknowledges that God is completely free but also completely good. All other beings have limited freedom of varying degrees; humans have some freedom in choosing their actions, animals have less freedom, plants have very little, and non-life have none. My criticism of three gods in a Godhead is that one of the three perfectly free Mormon gods may choose to wage a war of divine wills against the other two in some distant future. The Mormon culture of familial authority is the obvious solution to the possibility of war within the godhead. The Heavenly Father is perfect in righteousness and the other two are true spirit sons of the Father. They will ultimately agree with the one who is highest in perfection and the Father God over all.

This is the slight nod of Mormons for the Heavenly Father to be Highest God without peer. The other two gods of the Mormon Godhead, Jesus Christ and the Holy Ghost, become gods with a small "g." This preserves a Mormon monotheism and this was probably embraced by most Mormons I knew as I was growing up. There seemed to be only one Most High God in my home. Quotes of Mormon authorities demonstrate a breadth of the theological stands. Some authorities emphasize reverence towards the single Highest God in closer agreement with traditional Christianity. Even in Bruce McConkie's *Mormon Doctrine* there exists the traditional language of reverence towards the supreme God:

> "There is a God in heaven, who is infinite and eternal, from everlasting to everlasting the same unchangeable God, the framer of heaven and earth, and all things which are in them." (D&C 20:17.) He is not a progressive being in the sense that liberal religionists profess to believe; he was not created by man; and he was not a God of vengeance and war in Old Testament times and a God of love and mercy in a later New Testament era. He is the same yesterday, today, and forever.

> God is only known by revelation; he stands revealed or remains forever unknown. He cannot be discovered in the laboratory, or by viewing all immensity through giant telescopes, or by cataloging all the laws of nature that do or have existed. A knowledge of his powers and the laws of nature which he has ordained does not reveal his personality and attributes to men in the true gospel sense.[86]

In a generous view of Mormon doctrine, I can accept a Mormon monotheism with the Heavenly Father as the One God. However, in recent essays on the LDS.org website, the LDS Church has permitted the explicit presentation of a Heavenly Mother.[87] The Heavenly Father and the Heavenly Mother are our Divine Heavenly Parents in Mormonism's reality theology. This complicates the pursuit of a Mormon monotheism.

Traditional Christianity must deal with its own scandal of the Trinity against a more singular version of monotheism. The ecumenical councils of bishops of the early church worked very hard to remain connected to Jewish monotheism of the Creator God,[88] but the New Testament introduced a number of ambiguities with respect to the Spirit and the Son.[89] Some New Testament writings also seem to elevate Jesus into unity with the Father (e.g., John 1:1, 14; 10:30). The unity claimed by Jesus in John 10 suggests a unity in essence, which traditional Christianity defines as Divine essence or pure God nature. Also the oneness of the Creator, Jesus Christ, and the Spirit is suggested by the interchangeability of the phrases "Spirit of God" and "Spirit of Christ" in Romans 8:9.

I have a preference for monotheism and I have a difficult time accommodating three individual gods in the Godhead. There can only be one Divine Ground for our unified physical existence. If Mormons see the Heavenly Father in this way, then I can let them embrace a Mormon monotheism with the Holy Ghost and Jesus as individual gods (small "g") apart from the One Highest God.

God Is Spirit

The Doctrine and Covenants indicates that the highest Mormon God, the Heavenly Father, has a physical body of flesh and bone.[90] Classic theism of traditional Christianity holds that God is Creator of the material universe, and, thus, is an immaterial God. There is no positive knowledge in saying immaterial God. It says that God is not material, for example, not flesh and bone. It does not say what God's essence is. I emphasize again the importance of the theology of analogy when using the Greek and Hebrew words for *spirit.* "Spirit" more literally means breath or wind, but these are merely word pictures that humans must use to think about the biblical Creator God. When we, traditional Christians, read the conversation between Jesus and the Samaritan woman in John 4 where he states that "God is spirit," we think we understand something. We understand nothing. What is spirit? "God's spirit is like the wind," Jesus says redundantly in John 3. God's

Spirit is also light (I John 1:5). In this statement there is an implication again of God being immaterial, but also with goodness as an identity. My youthful thoughts of God's Spirit were of a light appearing (but not actually seen) behind my family as we prayed. This is still my most knowledgeable vision of God's presence. I have gotten no further in understanding the material goodness of God's essence.

God is immaterial or God is Spirit, I believe are essentially identical statements. However, there still remain views within traditional Christianity about a heavenly physicality. The Catholic theologian, Stephen H. Webb, writes about heavenly flesh in his recent book, *Jesus Christ, Eternal God: Heavenly Flesh and the Metaphysics of Matter*. If this remains a discussion of afterlife, of angels, of the risen Jesus, then this can be within traditional Christian views. However, if the physicality is used to describe the Creator God, then it is a minority opinion against the majority opinion of classic theism. God, YHWH, seems to appear in forms several times in the Old Testament; the broadly accepted position of classic theism is that these theophanies are only forms of appearance for the purpose of communication between the infinite and the finite. Evangelical Christian theologians have inferred that human form theophanies in the Old Testament are of the pre-incarnate Christ.[91] However, this is not a necessary conclusion since the New Testament rarely connects Jesus with Old Testament theophanies.[92] God appears as a burning bush to Moses, but God is not a burning bush. God appears on Sinai to the elders of Israel in an anthropomorphic form with feet and hands, but God is not a man.[93] However, a couple of chapters later in Exodus, Moses asks to see God and Moses is only permitted to see the "back of God's glory" as God passes by.[94] The non-seeing of God continues in the New Testament when John writes in his gospel, "No one has ever seen God."[95] There is no definitive interpretation of theophanies, but the broadly accepted classic theism of traditional Christianity contends that God is immaterial and theophany appearances are God 'stooping low' to communicate with humanity.

Catholic theologian, Stephen H. Webb, argues for a physicality of God and seems to support a view similar to Mormon theologians that there are divine bodies of heavenly flesh. To the best of my knowledge, the Mormon general authorities teach that the Heavenly Father has a heavenly physical body of flesh and bone in a literal Reality Theology. We are like God in reality not in analogy. After the early church councils of traditional Christianity, God's heavenly physicality is almost exclusively held within Mormon dogma and by Stephen Webb, who stands essentially alone among traditional Christian theologians on this issue.

Curiously, Joseph Smith seems to deny the possibility of immaterialism in his statement in *Doctrine and Covenants* Section 131:7–8:

> There is no such thing as immaterial matter. All spirit is matter, but it is more fine or pure, and can only be discerned by purer eyes; we cannot see it; but when our bodies are purified we shall see that it is all matter.

Though the first sentence is confusing (why is Joseph Smith criticizing immaterial matter?) the second sentence clarifies that spirit is still a material substance and thus spirit is not immaterial. Joseph Smith strives to ameliorate the physicality of the flesh and bone body of the Heavenly Father by pronouncing spirit is matter as well. This places the Mormon Heavenly Father within a larger material existence where his flesh-and-bone body must live. This God living within a physical realm never made sense to me. The Creator cannot be a being within creation. Even if the Heavenly Father exists as a bodily being within a higher physicality above this universe, then he becomes a being within that larger physicality. There still must be a Divine Ground of this larger spiritual/physical existence. My definition of Highest God is the very Ground of all existence for all things created "visible and invisible."[96] Even from my earliest intuitions about the One God, a Heavenly Father with a physical body cannot be the Ground of all that exists. To me the Mormon Heavenly Father becomes a god among gods and not the One God.

I prefer the monotheism and classic theism of the early church fathers. While the Triune God adds mystery to the Oneness of God, it still represents monotheism more directly than the Mormon Godhead of three individual gods. Tatian the Syrian (A.D. 110–180) states it well:

> Our God has no introduction in time. He alone is without beginning, and is Himself the beginning of all things. God is a spirit, not attending upon matter, but the maker of material spirits and of the appearances, which are in matter. He is invisible, being himself the Father of both sensible and invisible things.[97]

Notice this quote indicates that even traditional Christianity recognized created spirits as residing within physical creation as "material spirits." This agrees with Joseph Smith's statement of spirit being material. However, Joseph's extension of physicality to God is counter to the implications of *God is Spirit (Breath).*

God Is Love

My examinations of the doctrines of *God is One* and *God is Spirit* are dry ruminations on analogies about God. Monotheism and classic theism are my most natural conclusions. Meaningful expansion into a fuller description of how God interacts with creation and humanity depends on the third statement, *God is Love*. Without this third dogma, the first two become static doctrines. In theological ruminations I prefer the Jewish view. Theological correctness is not an important pursuit within Judaism. Instead the Jewish tradition after the first century permits a variety of opinions on theological topics that Christians might require agreement on. Dogmatic insistence on theological purity becomes counterproductive. For instance, if I dogmatically insisted on the immaterialism of God then I might be inclined to toss out Jesus's parable of the Prodigal Son who leaves his corporeal father, the God figure in the story. The Jewish Jesus used parables as stories of meaning, in which details were not as important as the meaning embedded within the story. For the modern Jew, the theological details become secondary to answering the question, "How do I treat my neighbor?" *God is Love* becomes the dogma of preeminence and stories of meaning become more important than systematic theologies because they help us understand *God is Love*. A range of theological opinions in Judaism is actually valued in their tradition. They will label a particular opinion the majority view while others are minority views. The minority views are regularly taught along with the majority view to aid the pursuit of deeper insights into a question.

The *Shema* might be the one dogmatic touchstone of Judaism: "Hear, O Israel, the Lord our God is One." It resembles a Christian creed with one difference—the *Shema* does not start "We believe." Instead it begins as a call, "Hear, O Israel, ..." or "Hear, the one-who-wrestles-with-God . . . ." The call is to wrestle with a teaching, not to believe a static dogma. This is even more true with *God is Love*.

The details of *God is One* and *God is Spirit* are metaphors to wrestle with, but there is an important caution: these dogmas are useless by themselves. One God? So what? Immaterial God? Big deal. I have explored the intellectual implications of these two dogmas above and I demonstrated that I think like a traditional Christian rather than a Mormon about God. Now what? These really do not affect my life in any meaningful way. It is tempting to build my theological system about Oneness and Spirit and think I understand God. In the hands of hubris ,the system becomes an idol of witless worship and a bludgeon to attack others. This is foolishness. If I listen to my heart, then it does not yearn for one god or for three gods in a godhead. My heart does not cry out that God be the immaterial Divine Ground of existence or a Heavenly Father of flesh and bone. Religious systems of dogma are houses built from thick wire and these wire walls do not warm those that live there.[98] I ache for *God is Love*—for sadness to be turned to joy, for injustice to be resolved to justice, for desolation to be made beautiful. Like Jacques Derrida, even if there is "no god" I would still cry out to the heavens with prayers and tears in hoping for hope that *God is Love*.[99]

Traditional Christian doctrines get their substantial meaning *only* through the third dogma—*God is Love*. Paul exhorts, "If I have the gift of prophecy and can fathom all mysteries and all knowledge, and if I have a faith that can move mountains, but do not have love, I am nothing" (1 Cor. 13:2). Once *God is Love* becomes the goal of interpretation, then traditional Christianity becomes a beautiful gospel of love to humanity. However, it also becomes apparent that the Mormon version of *God is Love* can provide wise guidance for good living on this earth.

Love is a squishy word. It can bring to mind romantic bliss, committed friendship, parental concern for a child, or kindness offered to a stranger.

The Greek philosophers and the New Testament writers used different words for different kinds of love. Most Christians know of the Greek word *agape*, which refers to a selfless love that expects no return benefit. *Charity* is the old English word of the King James for *agape*. Generally Christians will indicate that agape love by humans is impossible unless empowered by the Spirit of God. Certainly we have a difficult time untangling our selfish motives from any free-will action of charity.

From its opening chapters, the Bible calls humans to be like God and this is tied specifically to this third divine declaration of *God is Love*. Let me take a bit of time to define love in my understanding.[100] Love is expressed through internal intention and outward action simultaneously for the good of something. It has little to do with a fuzzy feeling. Both intention and action are necessary components. Jesus corrects the view of the Pharisees of his day that only external actions matter. He emphasized that the condition of the inner life of the human is as important as the external action because the soul is the fountain from which external actions flow.[101] His brother, James, corrects a Christian misinterpretation of Jesus by explaining that internal intentions without external actions are also useless.[102] I can see no better definition of love . . . intention and action for the good of something.

A bedrock biblical foundation of love is self-love. This is assumed as a starting place. Leviticus 19 is a litany of hateful actions that one can perform against a neighbor, an employee (slave), a stranger, or an animal. At the end of the list is the guiding summary of verses 17–18: do not hate your neighbor . . . love your neighbor as yourself. Love of self is assumed as a natural good, but God gives an ethical principal to avoid hateful actions against others Twentieth-century America seems to have embraced the lowest bar of ethical guidance. Ayn Rand defines a proper ethic as reasoned self-interest, which is essentially identical with the ethical low bar of Nietzsche's übermensche will-to-power. They have both chopped off the first half of the biblical guideline. They leave self-love in isolation. Rand and Nietzsche have no regard for one's neighbor.

The simplicity of the levitical ethics is based on the principle of reciprocity. One must consider an 'other' as another 'self.' The ancient Jewish sage, Hillel the Elder, summarizes the biblical ethical baseline using the negative version of the Golden Rule: "Do not do to others what you do not want to be done to yourself." Hillel the Elder has a long teaching ministry in Jerusalem just before Jesus was born. Hillel gives the negative statement of the Golden Rule to a Gentile who is interested in the Jewish Torah during this period of domination by Roman political influence. Hillel tells the interested Gentile that all of the teachings in the Books of Moses (Torah) are just an extended commentary on this negative statement of the Golden Rule. I believe that Hillel refrains from giving the Gentile the Leviticus law stating, "Love your neighbor as yourself" perhaps because Hillel does not consider this Gentile as a neighbor; instead the Gentile is a stranger (also discussed in the Torah). Thus, Hillel gives the negative version of the

Golden Rule to accomplish what Leviticus 19 intends, "Do not do this to your neighbor because it is hateful."

Jesus moves beyond ethics into kindness, or the biblical term, loving-kindness with his positive statement of the Golden Rule: "Do to others as you would have them do to you" (Luke 6:31). Indeed, when a Jewish Torah scholar asks Jesus about how one inherits the world to come, Jesus ties love of God, love of your neighbor, and love of self in his response.[103] Afterwards the Torah scholar asks, "Who is my neighbor." He perhaps wants Jesus to place the boundary of neighbor to be a Jewish neighbor. Hillel the Elder may have had this boundary, but he still honored the stranger as someone included in ethical reciprocity. Instead Jesus extends the definition of neighbor beyond the circle of one's own group and even into a group considered enemies! In the Sermon on the Mount, he explicitly calls us to love our enemies. Loving-kindness goes beyond ethics. Ethics can be seen as the avoidance of hateful actions against another based on reciprocity. Loving-kindness becomes a gift with purposeful intention and actions of good for an other. This is also based on reciprocity.[104]

Living a biblical life seems to be defined by these three concerns. First, it is assumed that we will live in health through our concern for the good of self. Second, we must strive to live as ethical humans through avoidance of hateful actions towards others. Third, we can live in the original intention of Genesis as images of God by living with loving-kindness with intention and action for the good of the other.

God instructs that humans are to be shadows of God[105] on earth by presiding over God's vision of goodness towards creation and creatures. We are like God when we express concern through intention and action towards the good of other humans and other creatures. Being like God in loving-kindness is the context of Jesus stating "Be perfect , therefore, as your heavenly Father is perfect."[106] God sends refreshing rain for the righteous and the wicked alike, so, be like God in intention and action towards the good of others. This provides a concrete definition of love without specifying emotional, romantic, or familial components. There is nothing exclusionary about this definition of love. It can be used to expand the different metaphysical understandings of traditional Christianity and Mormonism.

God Is Love within Mormon Christianity

God is Love has a direct unfolding out of the experiences of family life and parenting. The Mormon Heavenly Father and Heavenly Mother love their children fully. This Reality Theology provides a direct understanding of the call for both male and female humans to be loving parents and humans in life. The whole Mormon society is based on teaching families how to love children, love siblings, and honor parents. Additionally, Mormonism sees every human as a sibling and child of the Heavenly Father. This translates into a transparent interpretation of loving even your enemies because they are really no enemies—they are family. The divine family is a very good metaphysical story of meaning about *God is Love* in human relationships. Mormons build a differently shaped theological house than traditional Christians do, but they give their house warmth and protection using the teachings on a divine family. Communities with dominant Mormon populations are frequently safe and friendly communities. Their vision of *God is Love* is evident in many ways within their community.

The great limitation of the Mormon metaphysics of Divine Parents and humanity as the children of God is that it encodes love within the context of a particular familial structure. This makes it more difficult to extend love into categories not associated with the nuclear family. This is the key problem with reality theologies; they strictly codify a definitive human structure. The Mormon metaphysics of family cuts off other metaphoric interpretations for *God is Love*. For example, the earth is not included in a context of family and, thus, the earth and other creatures in nature become objects with no ethical standing. There are divine beings and children of divine beings, but the earth is just a stage where the story develops. Additionally, the emphasis of the traditional family leaves the unmarried adult and childless couples as appendages of incompleteness in the Mormon community. Single adults are merely humans-to-be-married-later and childless couples are left without evidence of heavenly blessing. The Mormon Reality Theology also leaves the alternative of human relationships without models of love.

Moderate versions of Mormon theology might produce a Mormon theology of analogy to accommodate other creatures, unmarried humans, childless couples, and gays struggling under the reality theology of a narrow family vision. Without humor I suggest the Divine Family needs to include an unmarried aunt or uncle.

God Is Love within Traditional Christianity

In negative theology, *God is Love* becomes a complete mystery. In the theology of analogy we begin to get some help in understand what love looks like through the best examples of human acts of love on earth and then we merely pronounce that for God it is more so. The Mormon reality theology of the Divine Family has a distinct advantage of clear application when it comes to the doctrine of *God is Love*. However, there are many analogies within the Bible for traditional Christianity to use. God loves the church as the groom loves his bride (Eph. 5); God loves creatures as a father loves his children (Rom. 8:14–16); God cares for creatures as a mother cares for her children (Deut. 32:18, Isa. 66:13); Christ rules with love for the church as the head (Christ) unites the body parts (Christians) in unity (Church) (1 Cor. 12). These metaphors can be used to explore the intention and action of goodness for the other.

Let us address the failings of Christian orthodoxy first. There are similar limitations to the triune heavenly Father, the only begotten Son, and Holy

Spirit since that concept codifies masculine familial preferences in theological language as does most of the Bible. This is a flaw of ancient Jewish and Christian culture and not of God. There is every opportunity given within the Bible for traditional Christianity to break free from historical and cultural prejudices. Biblically, the one divine Creator expresses maleness and femaleness since Genesis 1 includes male and female in the verses referring to the image of God.[107] I enjoy the Jewish insight that the first human, Adam, is androgynous prior to the separation of male and female from Adam. The Hebrew word *adam* is best interpreted *human* and not *man*. Maleness and femaleness become apparent only in the separation, but both are included in the concept of the image of God.

I have no problems with the feminine aspects of the Divine. I enjoy the writings of Julian of Norwich, an anchoress of a small church in England during the fourteenth century, who writes the first English book by a woman author. She extols the loving-kindness of God as motherly affection.[108] Her emphasis of God as Mother might be based on her negative experiences of earthly masculine failures, but it is not without biblical support (see Isa. 49:14–16). My reference point is the incredible example of my own mother, who walks through this fallen Eden with an amazing acceptance and love of humans and nature. My father loved his kids, but it is my mother's love for others, enemies, and all creatures that extends my understanding of *God is Love*. To evangelical Christians who prefer masculine pronouns for God, I say, "Get over it." It is a culturally codified preference of the past. The very expression of God's presence in the world is the feminine Hebrew word "shakinah" or "glory." God as creating Father is the One who works to order creation for goodness. God as consoling Mother is the glory of the caring Spirit in the lives of God's people.[109] Our allegorical views of God suffer within traditional Christianity only in the dryness of our vision of *God is Love*. This dogma should be expansive in its interpretation and application.

Indeed, traditional Christianity has had many contemplations on *God is Love* which cause the dogmas of *God is One* and *God is Spirit* to explode with meaning.

Within God's oneness there is a triune community where relational love is expressed timelessly and eternally as a perfection of God. Trinitarian theology becomes a necessary addendum to Christian monotheism if love is to be found in the transcendent Divine Ground. Love finds no foothold with *God is One* if oneness is identical with the number one. I have delayed my investigation of the Trinity in the face of the doctrine of *God is One* until I also address *God is Love*. Both Mormon Christianity and Christianity have a problem of threeness within the Godhead. Mormon threeness is explicit; Christian threeness is subtle and dangerous. Both are scandals to my intuitive definition of the One God. The Mormon doctrine of three individual gods in one Godhead seems an obvious error to me as Deity is atomized into individual gods. So I remain a traditional Christian, but the Trinity is still a dangerously subtle scandal for monotheism. Early

Christians boldly embraced the Jewish monotheism of a Creator God as they spread across the polytheistic Roman Empire. The church leaders following the apostles had to accommodate peculiar statements about God, Jesus, and the Spirit in the teachings and writings of the apostles. Within Jewish culture it was simple enough to think of the Spirit as God's unseen presence and action in the created world; thus, there was no discussion of a "bi-une" God of the Father and the Spirit. However, Jesus's relationship to the Creator God introduced a complexity that needed to be addressed in the decades after Jesus's crucifixion. Within the Gospels, Jesus experiences a full human life while praying to God in heaven as Father. This separateness seems apparent enough, but the Gospels and the New Testament Epistles speak of a unity or oneness of the Jesus and God the Father.[110] The precise formula for discussing the One God as three persons, the Father, the Son, and the Spirit, took several centuries to complete.

A reconciliation of *God is One* with *God is Triune* can be found in the ancient meaning of the word "person." "Person" has drifted to mean an atomized individual in modern thought. In traditional Christianity, there is One God with three Persons, but not three atomized individuals. The word "person" in Greek and Latin referred to a mask of an actor on a stage. One actor could be different persons in a stage play by changing masks to represent the different personages to the audience. Karl Barth, a twentieth-century Protestant theologian worked to re-educate modern Christians on the ancient definition of "person" as differentiated from "individual" in regards to the Trinity. Clearly "mask" can only be used in analogy when discussing the Persons of the Trinity. One must avoid the modalist heresy (Sabellianism) which suggests that God relates to creation and humans through the modes of the Father Creator, the Son, and the Spirit. To avoid modalism, the persons of the Trinity must be in true relation to one another as well. This is an important aspect of the Trinity, because even as there is one God there is also community within God to provide the transcendent ground for *God is Love*.

Augustine of Hippo expresses the triune God using a description of mutual love exchanged eternally between the Father and Son.[111] The Spirit is the divine person who proceeds from the Father and Son as mutual love exchanged between the Father and Son. Augustine's mutual love model of the Trinity becomes an excellent picture of the three dogmatic truths within the Triune God, which accomplishes *God is One*, *God is Spirit*, and *God is Love*.

I conclude again that I am a traditional Christian with monotheism, classic theism, and trinitarian theism in terms of my religious thinking and worldview, but this still leaves me a dry shell with *God is Love* objectively residing above the highest heavens. It has all been a theological discussion and there has been a deadly failure to bring love to earth. Somehow I do not think my gospel of the Divine Ground will bring new converts into traditional Christianity. The ruminations on theological speculations about God can be endless and loveless. All I have done is demonstrate that I have never thought about God in the way the leadership of the Mormon Church does. I will not return to the religion of my youth.

The Mormon gospel (good news) for humanity has some compelling features. We are all children of God. We were birthed as spirit children to our Heavenly Parents before our births on earth. At our proper time we are born to earthly parents, who are also children of God, and we pass through a veil of forgetfulness about the things of our pre-existence. On earth we gain our physical bodies and strive to learn the path that leads back to our Heavenly Father. The Mormon Church holds the fullest teachings of the return path. Our goal is to follow a godly path, have children, and help our earthly families follow godly paths to achieve our levels of glory in the worlds to come after death. The Mormon Church holds the keys to important church-related activities within the temples, of giving (tithing), and helping in welfare activities of the church. These activities are important for Mormons to participate in order to return to the highest heaven where the Heavenly Father and Heavenly Mother live. Other religions will teach paths of goodness and adherents will achieve certain levels of glory but not the highest levels. It is important to acknowledge that Jesus's death and resurrection makes the return to the future worlds-to-come (or heavens) possible and God's Spirit is a guide to help one along the path. I am certain Mormons can express the Mormon way with more eloquence. It is a well-defined path of necessary efforts to return to our primary home in the Heavenly Father's household.

Socrates presents a similar gospel. We are in the presence of heavenly beings (the stars) in our pre-existence. We come to earth and pass through a veil of forgetfulness. We have a vague remembrance of heavenly truths. Our task is to become the wise philosopher who strives to remember the form of The Good and live a life of goodness. Failed lives get recycled through reincarnations, but eventually we learn the path to return to a place among the heavenly stars. It is a story of striving towards goodness and a return to the home of God's presence.

Biblical Christianity tells a different story. It is the story of God's relationship of love towards creation and humans, one based on God's kindness towards those who are destitute and lost. The Bible walks through God's love in six primary actions of God's loving intentions that reach across the infinite ontological gap between the immaterial Divine Ground and the contingent beings of material creation.

First, *God is Love* is expressed through the goodness and beauty of the creative acts of Genesis 1–2. Intentions of beauty and diverse life were pronounced good after each work of God's breathed declaration.

Second, *God is Love* is expressed through the call of a purpose for humanity to be shadows of God through their own intentions and acts of goodness towards the creation that God loves. The story of God's love is interrupted by the horrors of human history. Humans have all gone astray

(Is. 53:6). We all sense the monster lingering within each of us and see the collective atrocities of our human family.

Third, God redeemed a people from slavery and made a covenant with them at Mount Sinai. They would be God's special people and they would agree to live as a separate (holy) people living between the dirt of earth (material life) and the light in the heavens (spirituality) in their ethical calling. This was a renewed call to live as "shadows of God" in the world for the world.

Fourth, the Separate, Separate, Separate God emptied himself to walk in our midst in the likeness of a human. Jesus is the unique Son of God. In John 14, Jesus proclaimed to his disciples, "I am the way and the truth and the life." One disciple, Philip, then asks, "Lord, show us the Father." Moses asked the same in Exodus 33, to see God's manifest glory (*kavod* in Hebrew.) God replied to Moses that he would instead see "all my Goodness" pass by and God would also pronounce the unpronounceable name, YHWH. Jesus's response to Philip carries all the same meaning. (In paraphrase) "Philip, don't you know that if you have seen me you have seen the Creator? I am living 'all His Goodness' in your midst. And now you can make requests to the Father in my name, which you know!" God is seen and his name is known because, now God is with us (Immanuel), Jesus Christ. He becomes *God is Love* in our sight as we read the Gospels in the Bible.

The story of *God is Love* is interrupted as God is lead by humanity to the cross of execution. This is not a human story of Sadducee temple priests or Roman soldiers. It is my story of choosing to live life AS IF God is dead. With every breath that does not give a thanksgiving for life, with every hidden intention of jealousy, with every open action of hate, I strike the nails that hanged God. In foolishness we declare with our lives, "God is dead! I will do as I please." The Son hanging on a Roman cross of torture looked down to fallen humanity and breathed a powerful whisper, "Father, forgive them" and then God died. Forgiveness offered, not earned.

Fifth, a new life of hope is proclaimed in the gospel of traditional Christianity through the forgiveness offered in the power of the Son's resurrection, and the empowered life offered through God's Breath (Spirit) given to us. This gospel is the good news. A new life given to us is a renewed call to live in the likeness of the Son of God. This is like the original call to live as shadows of God with intention and action of loving-kindness towards all of creation.

Sixth, and lastly, there is a promise for the final resolution for all creation and history in *God is Love*. We live in the midst of our tragic history still. I have no idea what this resolution will look like, but I live in hope for a merciful and just resolution in God's love.

These six actions of intentional love expresses that *God is with us* and *God is for us*. In this story of love, it always begins from above through God's kind grace and mercy. As contingent creatures we are utterly dependent on the God of love. We need only hear the whispered call to be forgiven and receive new life by calling on a name we know, Jesus. Incredible. This is my hope as one who has no human hope.

Most significantly to me, in traditional Christianity Jesus becomes the central focus of my worldview. Jesus, even from my youth, is the one who displays "all God's goodness." He displays what love looks like. In the New Testament Jesus sees, speaks, feels, heals, cries as God the Father does. He sees with compassion the suffering people in his community.[112] He speaks comfort and forgiveness with his voice to those who cry out for mercy.[113] He brings wholeness with his touch to those who are sick.[114] He dies for us and forgives his executioners from the cross.[115] We are called to live in the likeness of Jesus as true shadows of *God is Love*. Lastly, Jesus and Saint Francis remind us that we have siblings in creation. Brother wolf, sister sparrow, and even sister lily are under God's divine care. God's loving-kindness is not just for humanity, it is for all creation.

> For God was pleased to have all his fullness dwell in him and through him to reconcile to himself all things, whether things on earth or things in heaven, by making peace through his blood, shed on the cross.[116]

The basis of Christianity is captured in the story of the Prodigal Son in Luke 15. Here is love of God overcoming hopelessness. The wayward son returns from the worst of life, only hoping for hope that his father will receive him back as a servant in the household. The father rushes out to the grimy, dirty son to embrace him. In the depths of my struggles at the edge of the abyss of no-god, I continued to get up from my balcony seat in my small community church to take the Lord's Supper. In the evangelical churches, the Lord's Supper is a symbol of faith that Jesus had given his body and blood for our salvation. Strangely, when I could only hope for hope, I still shared in the Lord's Supper hoping that this was a real sacrament of the ancient Christian church. From the earliest fathers of faith, Christ's real presence was in the elements. The Eucharist dispensed real grace to the partaker as a place in space and time where heaven and earth were mysteriously connected. With the inability to muster up the work of a certain faith I would weakly lift the bread dipped in wine[117] to the heavens and cry out in hoping for hope that God would meet me at His table. Now, while the rest of my church partakes in the symbols of their faith, I join with them in celebrating the mystery of sacramental grace that God is with us. I believe that the Lord's Supper in part held the elements of my continuing life of faith.

FINAL THINGS

My recent faith crisis in my evangelical community allowed me to wander through many brilliant insights within secular, Christian, and Jewish literature. The Jewish community is perhaps 2000 years older in wisdom than Gentile Christianity (and it often shows).[118] I contemplated the value of becoming a Jewish proselyte. Jews often seem to embrace a thorough integration of religion and science more easily than my evangelical Christian community. They accept theological deviation with greater ease. They are also a religion about God's grace and mercy. However, the move would have been a great divide between Kathy and me and, in the end, I could not step away from the central person of Jesus as Messiah found in traditional Christianity. It was too large a hole. Jesus is my 'seen' measure of Divine Goodness. I can see *God is Love* in the Bible just as I have seen the likeness of Jesus in Eddy, in JoJo, indeed, in my mother, my siblings, my wife, my kids, and others. My hope is for God's help and mercy that *God is Love* can be seen in me.

Because of my wilderness wanderings, I must probably consider myself a post-evangelical Christian. My Christian intellectual understanding is traditional and creedal but with a few Jewish insights into Scripture. I employ Schleiermacher's hermeneutical approach to see through the eyes of the Jewish culture within the Bible. Obviously I have become a bit of a mongrel of religious thought, but I am a follower of Jesus the Messiah, God incarnate who, because of love, became the atoning sacrifice for my sins.

As a scientist, I will wait for the main body of evangelical Christianity to move beyond their insufficient integration of science and biblical revelation. There are a growing number of evangelicals with a better view of science, which is encouraging, but I wait with a bit of impatience for the rest.

I have always intuited the majority views of traditional Christianity identified as monotheism and classic theism. I learned to embrace the triune theism of traditional Christianity because it incorporated Jesus as the central figure of God's love towards me. These three intuitions about God remain as barriers to my return to Mormonism. However, the credo of *God is Love* exhorts me to evaluate the Mormon tradition with more kindness and humility. The reasons I originally left Mormonism were in reality tied to the failures of humanity that I find even in myself. The Mormon stories provide very different details in cosmology and eschatology than traditional Christianity. Mormons do seem to be a disconnected appendage of the Great Church of Christianity, but they have always intended to be. In recent decades many Mormons desire to be seen as a Christian religion. Are Mormons Christians? Strangely, the first Mormon Scripture, the Book of Mormon, contains a very clear trinitarian statements (2 Nephi 31:21), though the Mormon creedal Articles of Faith declare tritheism. The later Mormon scripture of the Doctrine and Covenants initiate many distinctive doctrines of Mormonism. It cannot be denied that the Mormon religion comes from the Christian tradition. But the cosmology and theology of Mormonism are not traditional Christianity. I believe it is best to acknowledge the differences under different labels. If Mormon's prefer to be labeled Mormon Christianity, I am not opposed, but they must remember that differences from traditional Christianity are substantial. It is the reality theology of Mormonism that makes it particularly difficult for me, as a scientist and rational thinker, to accept Mormonism. Maybe a retired Mormon scholar or theologian will sit down and write out a new analogy theology of Mormonism. Then in a couple of generations of general authorities, Mormonism might move towards traditional Christianity in substantial ways.

Are Mormons included within the saving grace offered by God through Jesus Christ, the Son of God? Giving an answer to that question is specifically not in my job description.[119] In faith I believe that God forgives those who cry out for mercy for their failures and broken lives. I presume that includes the failures regarding misconceptions about God. The cry of a contrite heart is the ground of our receiving God's mercy. However, I would still profess the Good News of a new life through Jesus's death and resurrection. God's merciful offer to create in me a new life of goodness in the Spirit is indeed a saving grace. In all discussions I will still try to see others in the best light while I share my hope in Christ.

I recently attended my cousin's memorial after cancer ended his life. Greg was a wayward Mormon. His youngest brother described Greg at the funeral as a rebellious and heroic blend of James Dean, Clint Eastwood, and Goofy. I could clearly see the blend. Even as Greg rebelled against his Mormon past and against other religious structures, he still declared his faith in God based on the miracle of creation and on the miracle of Christ's redeeming atonement of his own rebellious life. God was his Creator and Jesus was his Redeemer. I do not know how Greg wrapped his mind around those words. Greg had avoided any attempts at a detailed theological specificity. Until told otherwise, Greg is my saved brother in Christ Jesus. I hope in faith that *God is Love* so, like Karl Barth, I say, "I am not a Universalist, but I am hopeful."[120]

As a mongrel creedal Christian, I love the Maasai Creed representing the statement of traditional Christianity from within their East African culture.[121] I declare it in my hoping for hope and in my hope:

> *We believe in the one High God, who out of love created the beautiful world and everything good in it. He created Man and wanted Man to be happy in the world. God loves the world and every nation and tribe on the Earth. We have known this High God in darkness, and now we know Him in the light. God promised in the book of His word, the Bible, that He would save the world and all the nations and tribes.*
>
> *We believe that God made good His promise by sending His Son, Jesus Christ, a man in the flesh, a Jew by tribe, born poor in a little village, who left His home and was always on safari doing good, curing people by the power of God, teaching about God and man, showing the meaning of religion is love. He was rejected by his people, tortured and nailed hands and feet to a cross, and died. He lay buried in the grave, but the hyenas did not touch him, and on the third day, He rose from the grave. He ascended to the skies. He is the Lord.*

We believe that all our sins are forgiven through Him. All who have faith in Him must be sorry for their sins, be baptized in the Holy Spirit of God, live the rules of love and share the bread together in love, to announce the Good News to others until Jesus comes again.

We are waiting for Him. He is alive. He lives. This we believe. Amen.

NOTES

1. This was the same scientific and mythic wonder Huck Finn held for the moon and stars. "We had the sky up there, all speckled with stars, and we used to lay on our backs and look up at them, and discuss about whether they was made or only just happened. Jim he allowed they was made, but I allowed they happened; I judged it would have took too long to make so many. Jim said the moon could a laid them; well, that looked kind of reasonable, so I didn't say nothing against it." Mark Twain, *The Adventures of Huckleberry Finn*, chap. 19.
2. Cosmology is a fascinating subject with many questions still being discussed. The universe may be finite and have a size, but it also might be infinite. If it is infinite, then the observable part of the universe still has a size.
3. L. Arrington, *David Eccles: Pioneer Western Industrialist*, (Logan, UT: Utah State University Press, 1975).
4. I use 'traditional' to identify the core Christian faith that has been common to Christians for 2000 years. This core faith is the subject of C.S. Lewis's *Mere Christianity*. I will compare traditional Christianity to Mormonism below.
5. I am using the common evangelical usage of Christian as one who confesses their sinful inadequacy and receives God's forgiveness through the life and death of Jesus, Son of God. The Christian also commits to be a follower of Jesus Christ, who commands loving God and loving one another as the primary rule of life through the power of God's Spirit in his or her life.
6. Family Home Evening is a required Mormon practice that should be widely embraced by every family—secular or religious, traditional or alternative. The time solidifies relationships and also requires intentionality in teaching children directly in the many things parents wish to transfer to their progeny.
7. The Mormon Heavenly Father has a material body. (D&C 130:22)
8. Augustine of Hippo, *The Confessions of St. Augustine.*
9. Acts 8:14–19.
10. Leo Tolstoy in "*What I Believe*" also sees the Sermon on the Mount as a primary Christian text. He has doubts about Christianity because he sees the beauty and the impossibility of living the precepts presented by Jesus in the Sermon on the Mount. He states, "Of all the gospels, the Sermon on the Mount was the portion that impressed me most, and I studied it more often than any other part. Nowhere else does Christ speak with such solemnity; nowhere else does He give us so many clear and intelligible moral precepts, which commend themselves to everyone. If there are any clear and definite precepts of Christianity, they must have been expressed in this sermon; and, therefore, in those three chapters of St. Matthew's gospel I sought the solution of my doubts."
11. I am not referring to the polygamous sects of the Fundamentalist LDS living in isolated Utah communities. In this writing I use the term *fundamentalist* to refer to insistent and narrow interpreters of a religious tradition. The religious fundamentalist will generally hold all other interpretations of their religion as heresy. Note that there can be atheist fundamentalists in this usage.
12. "There are only two mistakes one can make along the road to truth—not going all the way, and not starting." The Buddha.

13. William Golding's revealing book *Lord of the Flies* resonated with me as I read the following sentence in chapter 12: "Ralph wept for the end of innocence, the darkness of man's heart, and the fall through the air of the true, wise friend called Piggy."

14. Matthew 16:17.

15. My stake president could have presented several Mormon answers without criticizing the New Testament. For example, the Holy Ghost is a person of the tri-godhead and has no physical body. Additionally, some interpret Luke 24:39 as indicating that resurrected bodies are flesh and bone rather than flesh and blood, blood being a component of this world's biologic life. Some even see the pre-fall of Adam and Eve as having these glorified bodies of flesh and bone (Gen. 2:23). However, Judges 9:2 (in many translations) uses "flesh and bones" for regular humans.

16. I suspect that Eddie was a young homosexual man who was struggling under the strong cultural judgment of the era before the tragedy of the AIDS epidemic. He was denied his entry into the Franciscan community at the end of that summer. I know he was crushed, but he continued to express kindness towards everyone. I have not seen Eddie since that summer, but he remains one of my favorite humans ever.

17. I didn't read *The Silmarillion* until after I was a Christian. The beauty of its creation story was what I hoped for as a mythic reality behind the last curtain of the material universe. Like J. J. R. Tolkien and C. S. Lewis, I now appreciate the value of myth as a story of meaningful truth. If one relates the scientific understanding of how the universe was created, then the factual presentation is devoid of meaning. This is true whether one relates the details of the current big bang theory or a literalist's six-day creation theory. These presentations are devoid of meaningful truth. The truth that resides "above" the how-it-happened details is the "mythos" of the story one tells.

18. G. K. Chesterton, *Orthodoxy*.

19. E.g., 1 Peter 5:1,5 and 1 Tim. 5:17–19 use the Greek word *presbyter*, meaning an older or senior member.

20. The Great Church or *Ecclesia Magna* in Latin broadly refers to the great traditions of Christianity aligned under the Nicene Creed: Orthodox and Roman Catholic churches. Both the Orthodox and Roman Sees generally view the Protestants as wayward children of God under the See of Rome. I generously include most Protestant denominations within this Great Church.

21. Augustine of Hippo, *City of God*, book 19, chapter 6.

22. W. P. Anderson and R. L. Diesslin, *A Journey Through Christian Theology* (Minneapolis: Augsburg Fortress, 2000), 96.

23. Two giants of Christianity, Martin Luther for the Protestants and John Chrysostom for the Orthodox, are revered Bible interpreters, but both wrote hateful polemic homilies toward the Jews and the synagogues. In *On the Jews and Their Lies*, Martin Luther essentially gives permission for atrocities against the Jews. In *Against the Jews*, Chrysostom attacks the Jews with slanderous accusations and labels them "fit for slaughter" (Ch. 1:6). The Russian and eastern European pogroms find their basis in the Christian writings of this saint.

24. Search out the full "Canticle of the Sun" by Francis of Assisi.

25. John 3:16.

26. First Corinthians 15:1–19 is Paul's description of the Christian message with the literal crux in 3 and 4.

27. I can read Justin Martyr from the second century and Karl Barth from the twentieth century and see the same interpretive thread on the life of Jesus Christ that Paul presented in his letters to the first-century churches.

28. Adolf von Harnack, *What is Christianity?*, 1901. This is still a classic of liberal theology. To Harnack, Jesus is the Son of God because of his self-conscious pursuit of knowing God and his obedience to the rule of love (p. 128 in the 1957 Harper Torchbooks edition).

29. *Suffering Divine Things: Theology as Church Practice* by Reinhard Hutter works to address the question of authority in the Protestant movement of traditional Christianity. The authority comes from the three-fold reality of Scripture of God, the Spirit of God, and the community of God.

30. Romans 15:7.

31. It is a paraphrase of a longer sentence from an essay by Rupertus Meldenius (aka Peter Meiderlin) called *A Reminder for Peace at the Church of the Augsburg Confession of Theologians,* written in 1626.

32. *Sidereus Nuncius or Sidereal Messenger,* by Galileo Galilei, 1610.

33. D. Danielson and C. M. Graney, "The Case against Copernicus," *Scientific American* 310 (2014): 72–77.

34. James Bradley (1693–1762) worked to measure the parallax motion of stars in the sky but observed an effect called the "aberration of light." His interpretation was that the seasonal changes in the aberration of light demonstrated the earth's motion around the sun, but the parallax motion of stars was too small to measure by his instruments directly. Indeed, stars are incredibly distant.

35. M. A. Finocchiaro, ed., *The Galileo Affair: A Documentary History,* (Berkley: University of California Press, 1989).

36. Plato, *Phaedo*, 95–100.

37. John Stott embraces the evidence of the evolution of earth and of life. The Genesis poetic verse describing mud-to-man takes billions of years of evolution guided by God's metaphorical hands. Stott suggests a good interpretation of Genesis 2 to be a description of God's forming of the human animal, homosapiens, as a suitably soulful vessel for the image of God. At some point God "breathes" into homosapiens to create a first *homo spiritus* couple, Adam and Eve. This is a reasonable and encouraging interpretation that blends natural and biblical revelations.

38. Consider Job, Elijah, or Jeremiah as they wrestle with issues of how life and faith collide. Each does not get their questions answered, but they move through their questioning into faithful submission—*in spite of* life. Their support communities generally heaped criticism on them rather than encouragement.

39. Just as Jacob became Israel in Genesis 32:28.

40. *The Ladder of Divine Ascent* by John Climacus in the seventh century is a classic monastic treatise in the Eastern Orthodox tradition for pursuing greater participation in the Divine life.

41. Friedrich Nietzsche, *Ecce Homo*, trans. Anthony M. Ludovici and Paul V. Cohn, Gutenberg Project.

42. *Twilight of the Idols or How to Philosophize with a Hammer,* by Friedrich Nietzsche, damns all systems built by rationalism or religion. "The will to a system is a lack of integrity." (p. 34) Systems merely unload one's own will to a philosophy or church doctrine. Nietzsche's "will to power" advises one to take full responsibility for life in this real world. There is no reward in another world to come. That would diminish the reality of the world you live in.

43. Deuteronomy 32:20–22.

44. Saint John of the Cross, *Dark Night of the Soul*, trans. E. Allison Peers, chapter 19, paragraph 2.

45. Kierkegaard spends a great deal of time discussing indirect and direct knowledge in *Practice in Christianity*. One never has direct access to knowledge about God. Even Jesus avoids direct declaration of his relation to the Father. Only the eyes of faith see that he is the divine Son of God.

46. Dietrich Bonhoeffer, *Letters and Papers from Prison*, 194.

47. Craig Aaen-Stockdale (2012), "Neuroscience for the Soul," *The Psychologist* 25 (7): 520–23.

48. Dietrich Bonhoeffer, *Letters and Papers from Prison*, letter of April 1944.

49. Steven Hawking, *A Brief History of Time*. Note that Steven Hawking misrepresents the source. John R. Ross suggests that the philosopher William James is the source. John R. Ross, *Constraints on Variables in Syntax* (PhD diss., Massachusetts Institute of Technology, 1967).

50. Thomas Aquinas, *Summa Theologica*, Part I.

51. I capitalize Divine Ground or Ground or the Divine because I am referring to the unique, absolute God.

52. Hugh T. Kerr, *Readings in Christian Thought*, 113.

53. Aquinas is using Anselm's ontological argument here to broaden the meaning of the word "God."

54. The second-century early church father, Irenaeus, seems to view the Creator God in terms of a total reality outside which nothing can exist, but he also understood the otherness of God in relation to creation. See *Return to Mystery* by Hans Boersma, 125.

55. The movie *Particle Fever* is a reasonably exciting documentary about this search for the Higgs boson.

56. Pantheism is an option where God is the totality of the physical universe. Traditionally, a Good God must stand separate from a fallen creation.

57. Genesis 2:4 in the RSV states, "These are the generations of the heavens and the earth when they were created." The Hebrew can suggest generations of creations. One interpreter suggests the first creation in chapter 1 was too perfect and humanity (*adam*) did not grow soulfully. The second creation in chapter 2 was created with imperfections to encourage growing to meet the difficulties. God's goodness could not be fit into our creation so goodness broke into sparks of light that lay hidden in the world for humans to find and reveal. The Jewish call to *repair the world* is this task of revealing God's hidden sparks of light.

58. The Good is the highest form in Plato's *Republic* (book 6, section 508e).

59. C. S. Lewis, *Mere Christianity* (1952; New York: HarperCollins: 2001), 38–39.

60. Plato, *The Republic*, 508e2–3.

61. Friedrich Nietzsche, *Beyond Good and Evil*, Introduction.

62. Anselm of Canterbury, *Monologion.*

63. Ludwig Wittgenstein, *Philosophical Investigations* (Blackwell: Oxford, 1997).

64. Peter L. Berger, *The Sacred Canopy: Elements of a Sociological Theory of Religion*, 1967.

65. Peter L. Berger, *A Rumor of Angels: Modern Society and the Rediscovery of the Supernatural,* 1967.

66. C. S. Lewis, *Transposition and Other Addresses*, 1949.

67. C. S. Lewis addresses the core similarities of several Western traditions in *Mere Christianity.*

68. Arianism of the third century A.D. held that the Heavenly Father created the Son of God. Thus Jesus Christ was not consubstantial with the Father as Trinitarian theology requires.

69. It is difficult to find unbiased publications on the historicity of the Book of Mormon. Mainstream historians and archaeologists of the Americas generally ignore the Book of Mormon as a source for organizing their investigations.

70. I read this story in Cardinal Ratzinger's *Introduction to Christianity*, p. 46.

71. Torah is the first five books of the Old Testament, often called the Books of Moses.

72. Ludwig Wittgenstein, twentieth-century philosopher, answered an interviewer's question about belief in God with, "What we cannot speak about we must pass over in silence." Jacques Derrida, the post-modern deconstructionist philosopher, insisted that he was an atheist but he often deconstructed the language of his Jewish religious experience. See John D. Caputo, *The Prayers and Tears of Jacques Derrida: Religion without Religion* (Bloomington: Indiana University Press: 1997).

73. Jean-Luc Marion, a Catholic theologian wrote *God Without Being* to explore negative theology with new post-modern philosophical approaches.

74. M. Maimonides, *The Guide of the Perplexed*, trans. D. Frank, 1995.

75. God's hiddenness became a central theme to my thinking in this recent decade. Even when Isaiah experiences God's presence in the temple in Isaiah 6, God was still hidden by the heavy

smoke of incense. The theophanies of the Old Testament preserve the hiddenness of God through language of analogy. For example, he appears in the likeness of a man to Ezekiel (Ezek. 1:26). Analogy remains as a cloud to ensure human humility as we strive to see into the incense cloud before the altar in the tabernacle of the Hebrews.

76. Psalm 82 and John 10:34–35.

77. Complete Jewish Bible, Genesis 14:18–20.

78. Genesis 9:26.

79. Genesis 18 and Genesis 19.

80. Genesis 14:22.

81. "Hear, O Israel, the Lord our God, the Lord is one" (Deut. 6:4).

82. Physicist John Polkinghorne reminds us that science cannot free itself from metaphysics in *Science and Theology*. Metaphysical assumptions remain even within the most radical view of scientific reductionism. For example, an electron is described as being a wave or a particle in various experiments. These are essentially metaphysical analogies used to describe what an electron is like, but what an electron is is still not defined.

83. *Metaphysics* is a short book written by Aristotle, which precedes his book entitled *Physics*. It means literally "*before physics*." *Metaphysics* discusses first principles of being, knowing, and cause before Aristotle begins discussing the empirical knowledge of nature more directly in the second book, *Physics*. God (whatever the word means) is a metaphysical basis for the physical universe.

84. Democritus and other atomists were atheists.

85. From the article on Godhead in "The Guide to the Scriptures" (https://www.lds.org/scriptures/gs/god-godhead, September 6, 2015).

86. McConkie, *Mormon Doctrine*, p. 317–18.

87. https://www.lds.org/topics/mother-in-heaven, 2015. Genesis 1:26–27 becomes a proof text for Heavenly Parents. The "us" in Genesis and the plurality of *Elohim* ("gods") can be interpreted that humans are like the Heavenly Father and Heavenly Mother—male and female. This provides immediate advantages of including the feminine in the story of the divine.

88. Justin Martyr provides one of the earliest post apostolic writers to indicate the Creator God as the primary identification of the Christian God. In "Plea for a Fair Hearing" (13), he writes, "What sound-minded man will not admit that we are not godless, since we worship the Fashioner of the universe, declaring him, as we have been taught, to have no need of blood and libations and incense, but praising him by the word of prayer and thanksgiving for all that he has given us?" This ties strongly with Jewish tradition of prayers of thanksgiving to the Creator (King of the Universe) who provides wine, bread, and everything else for our life and enjoyment.

89. In Matthew 3:16, the Father's voice is heard from heaven as Jesus is baptized and the Spirit descends like a dove upon Jesus when he comes up from the water. The threeness is obvious in the story.

90. Doctrine and Covenants 130:22.

91. Jonathan Edwards infers that Christ is in the furnace in the book of Daniel (*Works of Jonathan Edwards*, p. 534). Evangelicals generally interpret all human form theophanies as the pre-incarnate Christ (J. A. Borland, *Christ in the Old Testament: Old Testament Appearances of Christ in Human Form*, 2010). However, other traditions are less insistent on this interpretive connection.

92. Although Genesis 14 does not indicate that Melchizedek is a theophany, Psalm 110 suggests that Melchizedek is a messiah archetype, which Hebrews 5:5–6 alludes to.

93. Exodus 3; Exodus 24.

94. Exodus 33.

95. John 1:18.

96. Nicene Creed (A.D. 325).

97. Tatian the Syrian, *Address to the Greeks*, ~ A.D. 170, trans. J. E. Ryland. From *Ante-Nicene Fathers*, vol. 2, 1885.
98. Anatole France captures the beauty of an ancient medieval story in his writing, *Le Jongleur de Notre Dame*. It is found in the English translation *Our Lady's Juggler*. A simpleton juggler becomes the dearest worshipper in the midst of intellectually and artistically talented monks of an abbey.
99. Caputo, *The Prayers and Tears of Jacques Derrida*.
100. Much of this definition comes from Martin Buber's *I and Thou*. The book provides a philosophy of relational ethics based on reciprocity. It is very Jewish in approach to philosophy but helps Gentile Christians understand Jesus and Paul in their Jewish modes of thinking. It is a difficult book to read, but very fruitful for the diligent reader.
101. Matthew 5:21–22, 27–28.
102. James 2:14–17.
103. Luke 10.
104. The "gift" is explored by Pope John Paul II in *Theology of the Body*.
105. The Hebrew behind "image of God" can be literally translated as "shadow of God."
106. Matthew 5:43–48.
107. Genesis 1:27.
108. Julian of Norwich, *Revelations of Divine Love*, trans. Elizabeth Spearing, 1999.
109. Romans 8:11.
110. John 1:1, 14; John 8:58–50; John 20:28–29; Rom. 9:5; Col. 2:9–10, Titus 2:13; 2 Peter 1:1; Heb. 1:8–12.
111. Augustine of Hippo, *On the Trinity*.
112. Matt. 9:2, 22, 36.
113. Luke 23:34.
114. Matt. 8:3,15; 9:28–30; 20:34.
115. Luke 23:24.
116. Col. 1:19–20.
117. Grape juice in our conservative church.
118. John Howard Yoder observes in the opening pages of *The Politics of Jesus* that the teachings of Jesus were best displayed within the Jewish ghettos rather than the European Christian hegemony during the last 1500 years.
119. Matthew 7:1–2.
120. Timothy Gorringe, *Karl Barth: Against Hegemony* (Oxford: University Press, 1999).
121. Jaroslav Pelican, *Credo: Historical and Theological Guide to Creeds and Confessions of Faith in the Christian Tradition*, 2005.

6
WHY BELIEVE IN GOD? OBJECTIONS TO FAITH BY THE NEW ATHEISM

Corey Miller and Lynn K. Wilder

In this final chapter, we address some objections to faith in God presented by the New Atheism that many, swept in the current exodus from Mormonism (and other faith traditions), embrace. We acknowledge our ex-LDS (Post-Mormon) friends who question or renounce faith in God altogether, an understandable direction after the blistering experience of leaving Mormonism, which can be especially difficult on relationships. These post-Mormons, like us, are savvy to the historical, archeological, botanical, DNA, language, and doctrinal problems and the social consequences of false religion. Like us, they have thrown out the dirty bathwater of false religion. But unlike us, many of them have thrown out the baby (faith in God) along with it. Atheism is a natural jump after Mormonism for several reasons. Where post-Mormon atheists and the authors of this book differ is that we *do* believe God exists and we believe there are rational, evidential reasons for that faith. The very first person who read *Unveiling Grace* when it was released in August of 2013 and called was a gentleman in his early forties who had left Mormonism for atheism twenty years earlier. He was living and working in Washington, DC. He had just finished the book when he declared to me (Lynn), "I had no idea there was a God who can do the things you describe in this book! If there is, I would be willing to give him a try." C. S. Lewis, once atheist and later a believer in Jesus, said this: "Christianity claims to give an account of the facts—to tell you what the universe is really like. Its account of the universe may be true or may not, but once the question is before you, then your natural inquisitiveness must make you want to know the answer."[1] Unfortunately, many post-Mormons are too burned out with *religion* to investigate the existence of a real God.

In this chapter, we dismantle three arguments presented by the New Atheism against faith in the Christian God, countering with rational arguments that support faith in the Christian God. Although having room for only a brief discussion here (myriads of books have been written on these topics), we examine in detail the following three objections that New Atheists make in their writings to faith in the Christian God. They are: (1) the problem of evil, (2) the Bible, rationality, and modern science, and (3) the problem of the historical trustworthiness of the Bible. In this chapter, we also point out several logical fallacies—examples of faulty reasoning—taught in Mormonism. Reason is a critical part of faith, and thinking well is foundational to faith in God.

Some atheists tell us we drank that Kool-Aid, now we drink this Kool-Aid; it's all just Kool-Aid for ignorant folks. But many of these "ignorant folks" who believe in the Christian God of grace have terminal doctoral degrees, are trained in analytical thinking, and do apply reason in the area of faith. Faith to us does not mean setting the intellect aside and following something or someone blindly (arguably an LDS idea). Often atheists define faith as leaving your brain at the door, but this is *re-defining* Christian faith. Ignoring evidence is not the "faith" of a Christian. Atheist Richard Dawkins defines faith like this: "Faith is the great cop-out, the great excuse to evade the need to think and evaluate evidence. Faith is belief in spite of, even because of, the lack of evidence."[2]

On the contrary, faith to a biblical believer includes reason, logic, and scientific and other evidence. We profess faith *supported by* reason, not faith without reason. The God we believe in invites us in Isaiah 1:18 to reason these things out. Faith utilizes the mind (the intellect) as well as the will (freedom to choose) and the heart (feelings, emotions). Given this more comprehensive definition of faith, then faith and science are not opposites, as many atheists propose. The real contrast is not between faith and science anyway, but between the worldviews of theism (belief in an omnipotent being who grounds reality) and naturalism (belief that reality is limited to all things material).

Even the conscious mind can create a problem for naturalists. The mind, to some, consists of nothing but evolutionary goo whose fundamental purpose is survival and reproduction rather than, say, seeking truth. Some atheists even argue that rape is an explicable product of human evolution. (More later on the topic of evolutionary naturalism and morality.) One of Lynn's doctoral professors was an ardent atheist and a behaviorist. Students were advised to leave any talk of God and any acknowledgment of reasoning taking place in the mind at the classroom door. Humans, he taught, were simply reactionary, biological machines responding to external stimuli. Only what was observable and measurable was real. Incongruously, scientists themselves use the conscious mind to induce and deduce theories and natural laws from research. If the mind is not a reliable entity of reality, then neither are the theories and laws that come from it. The ideas of "truth" or "morality" have no meaning to strict naturalists. Survival is the game and death is the end. That is not to say that atheists cannot act in ways that are moral or develop personal standards for morality. (Morality is addressed under "The Problem of Evil" below.)

To theists, truth *is* important. The theistic universe is broader and not limited simply to the material, the natural world. It may include things like super intelligence, free will, reasoning, miracles, and maybe angels and spirits (although some theists argue the latter may consist of extremely fine material, placing them in the naturalistic realm). To us, the mind exists and is capable of thinking beyond what might be expected by environmental stimulus/response reactions and survivalist reactions. The notion that the mind can reason makes good sense. Solomon states in Proverbs 21:16, "Whoever strays from the path of prudence comes to rest in the company of the dead." Interestingly, atheists purport the end is death and nothing more. When Paul stood before Festus to plead his case, he said, "I am not insane, most excellent Festus, ...What I am saying is true and reasonable" (Acts 26:25). Truth, reasonableness, and morality are central to Christian faith. They matter to theists, and our thinking about them with our conscious minds should be sound.

CLEAR THINKING AND LOGICAL FALLACIES

In order to think clearly about arguments (two or more truth claims linked together toward an idea or conclusion), those arguments should prove to be sound. There are standards for determining sound arguments. Truth claims that lead to a conclusion must be unambiguous and accurately reflect facts. Each claim should not contradict the one before it. The logic must be valid; the conclusion makes sense and follows from the accurate truth claims. We think of science as being highly accurate in its conclusions, but even science cannot always *directly observe* what it is investigating, like the big bang, evolution, or the end of the dinosaurs. Conclusions/ideas/theories are deduced using logical reasoning with the evidence or apparent evidence available. These conclusions are theories, sometimes forming natural laws, that best describe the original events; but as more data is available, theories can change. Failure to meet standards of sound reasoning creates logical fallacies, faulty thinking.[3]

After leaving Mormonism, we realized that much of what we had been taught were faulty truth claims that, further, did not lead to logical conclusions. Now as Christians, we do not run from logic but utilize it. We are cautious of logical fallacies. Both of us are now in Christian ministry and talk with former LDS who once truly believed in the Mormon god, decided Mormonism is false, and are now sincerely perplexed about whether God exists, who the real God is, and whether they can ever trust again. In our work with LDS finding their way away from Mormonism and wondering what is true and what is not, whether or not there is a real God is a common post-Mormon dilemma created by a Mormon truth claim that sometimes leads them to a logical fallacy.

If the LDS Church Is Not True, Nothing Is

When LDS, we were all taught, "If the Mormon Church is not true, nothing (no other god or church) is true." It took awhile after leaving to realize there were many ideas, both religious and cultural, we had been taught in the LDS Church that were still stuck in our heads, even years later. But were they *true*? Each and every one of them required re-examination with sound thinking, this one included—that if Mormonism's not true, nothing is. Just because the Mormon god's scriptural teachings and church leaders contradict themselves over time, there is no physical evidence that the events of the Book of Mormon actually happened, the strongholds of the faith could have serious negative social consequences, and the Mormon god appears false, does it logically follow that no true God exists? One thing we had to consider was whether the Mormon god even represented or was the *same* god as the God of the Bible. If so, then the God of the Bible was not true either. But if they were not the same, then the biblical God could be the real God. Rather than believe what could be another untrue conclusion, why not investigate?

Why not, like the gentleman who read *Unveiling Grace*, investigate the possibility that all gods are not like the Mormon one and there may be a real one? Have we considered and tested more than the Mormon god?

This particular faulty thinking is a logical fallacy called a "false dilemma," created by the LDS teaching, If Mormonism is not true, nothing is. A false dilemma allows only two options, when in reality more are available. The first truth claim is not true because more options are available than Mormonism and nothing. Therefore, given the first false truth claim, the subsequent conclusion does not make a logically sound argument.

1. If Mormonism is not true, nothing is.
2. Mormonism is not true.
3. Therefore, nothing is.

This next logical fallacy is similar to the first.

If the Mormon God Does Not Exist, No God Does

Some who leave decide that since they now believe the LDS god is man-made and impotent, then it follows for them that there is no real God who exists. All faiths sporting God-belief must be man-made, impotent, and silly. But is this a sound argument or a logical fallacy? Are the truth claims accurate? Does the conclusion flow logically from each premise?

1. The Mormon god is not true.
2. Other gods are just like the Mormon god.
3. Therefore, none of the other gods can be true.

This is a logical fallacy called a "hasty generalization." The thinker is making a generalization based on a small sample. This is like saying all churches are boring (if one has not tried going to more than just one) or all Muslims are terrorists or all Mexicans in the U.S. are illegal. With no experience with, or more intimate knowledge of, a larger sample of churches or Muslims or Mexicans, this is, of course, a logical fallacy. Indeed, premise 2 is inaccurate if one has not tested and known other gods (or Muslims or Mexicans).

Can 15 Million People Be Wrong?

The next is one of our favorites. We hear it often. We must smile when someone says this common LDS expression: Can 15 million people be wrong!? This is like the old adage your mom might have said to you: If everyone was jumping off a bridge, would you do it, too? In other words, because it is popular, it has to be a good idea, right? But, doesn't that argument from Mormonism defeat itself? Are 15 million people so many, really? There are *2.3 billion* Christians and *1.6 billion* Muslims! Can more than two billion people be wrong? Actually, yes, numbers make no difference to truth. Truth is truth even if no one believes it.

1. The greater the number of people who believe something, the likelier it is true.
2. Fifteen million people believe Mormonism.
3. Therefore, Mormonism must be true.

This is a logical fallacy known as "appeal to popularity." The one offering this argument is trying to convince others using an appeal to its popularity (or sometimes force, pity, or consequences). It's not sound thinking. Truth exists outside of human popularity.

You're an Apostate: Can't Trust You

You couldn't live the church standards, you were offended by someone, or you committed a big sin like drugs or adultery (by the way, no drugs, no affair here). Perhaps it's because as a woman you went to work that you are now reaping what you sowed. These are just a few of the reasons suggested why the Wilder family must have left Mormonism. Once, when speaking at Southern Utah University, a former LDS bishop took the mic during the Q&A to point inches from my nose and asked rhetorically, "I just want to know what *big sin* you committed that made you leave the LDS Church?" To which I wryly answered, "I'm too old to commit any really big sins." This logical fallacy is called an "ad hominem." An ad hominem fallacy attacks someone personally and tries to discredit them, making any idea they offer not credible because of their poor character. We see this in politics habitually. Someone is accused of wrongdoing or heartlessness; therefore nothing they say or do can be taken seriously.

1. You say the Bible is true.
2. You left Mormonism and must have been offended or sinned.
3. Anything you say as an apostate cannot be trusted.

If You Leave the One True Mormon Church, You Will Reap Bad Things

Picking up on one of the comments above, "you went to work and now you are now reaping what you sowed," is another example of a logical fallacy. This one is called a "slippery slope." The person accusing the other exaggerates that increasingly negative events will happen as a result of their actions. The argument here is that a woman who works cannot be an effective wife and mother and increasingly bad things will happen to her family.

Sometimes those leaving Mormonism opine to us, "What if it's true what they say, that bad things will happen to me if I leave Mormonism? If it's true, I'll go to outer darkness and never see my family again in the next life. What if I really do get cancer or lose my house or my job or my spouse if I leave the LDS Church?"

1. The LDS prophet told us not to read "anti-Mormon" materials.
2. I did and now I doubt Mormonism is true.
3. Increasingly bad things will happen to me and my family as a result.

This stronghold of fear wrought by the "slippery slope" has far-reaching and long-term emotional effects for many.

This next fallacy is utilized both by some former-LDS atheists and by former-LDS Christians.

Religion Causes Hateful Gender and Sexual Orientation Bias, Violence, and War

This logical fallacy is everyone's favorite, the "straw man" argument. This is the practice of making the other person's point of view worse and their argument weaker than it actually is in order to improve your own argument. We caution Christians not to do this. In the case of Mormonism, there is no need to exaggerate the teachings of Mormonism or even focus solely on teachings of former prophets. There is plenty of current legitimate LDS doctrine to use in comparisons that simply speaks for itself, like words of recent LDS prophets and current scriptures. This would be an atheist's example of a straw-man argument:

1. Religion teaches hate.
2. Hate leads to war and violence.
3. Religion causes war and violence.

Truthfully, more people have died from atheist leaders' violent actions in the last century than in all wars in all previous centuries combined. This argument contains false truth claims and a false conclusion. Investigating and clear thinking matter!

The aforementioned fallacies are examples of faulty thinking on the part of some former LDS. Some of these lead to rejection of faith in God altogether. However, the three greatest objections to faith, which are held by departing Mormons who are influenced by the New Atheism are presented in the following sections.

OBJECTION 1: THE PROBLEM OF EVIL

Many departing the LDS faith we talk with want to retain some semblance of theistic morality rather than embracing moral relativism. But that is a challenge unless they retain some form of theism. Far from being a reason to reject God, we want to use the problem of evil as evidence for the biblical God's existence (the biblical rather than the Mormon concept of God) rather than non-theism. The LDS Church demonstrates its awareness of critical scholars like Bart Ehrman (agnostic) and his efforts to discredit the Bible. In some respects, the LDS Church probably embraces the criticisms in order to help promote Mormonism's "restoration" requirement of a living prophet (church went into a Great Apostasy, the Bible was corrupted, and the church had to be restored by its first prophet, Joseph Smith) by citing him on their website.[4] It is easy to see why. He's an ex-evangelical who has written several *New York Times* best-sellers as a New Testament (NT) historian. Many who read his works are shocked, however, to discover that what led him to become an agnostic and severe Bible critic is, by his own admission, not problems with the Bible but the problem of evil. He says, "The big issue that drove me to agnosticism has to do not with the Bible, but with the pain and suffering in the world. . . . I don't know how we can say that God exists given the senseless pain and suffering in this world."[5] Indeed, even the famous conversion of the most notorious atheist philosopher to theism was stillborn en route to his becoming a Christian because of the problem of evil, even while admitting that the most reasonable and evidential faith is the Christian faith.[6]

We believe that God's existence makes sense of the existence of evil better than competing worldviews. Nonetheless, few questions have so vexed the Christian faith and penetrated so deeply into the hearts and minds of people as the problem of evil, pain, and suffering. How many have not asked the question, If a good God exists, then why is there so much evil, pain, and suffering in this world? For our purposes, we will simply refer to this as "the problem of evil," inclusive of pain and suffering. The problem of evil is certainly a problem intellectually and emotionally, but it is a far greater problem for the non-theist than for the theist (a believer in an omnipotent Being that grounds morality). Evil is actually a reason to affirm the existence of the Christian God, not to deny it. What makes evil problematic for the Christian theist is certain background assumptions theists hold about the nature and character of God; assumptions that hold, of course, only if God exists. God is taken to be all-powerful (omnipotent) and all-loving or all-good (omnibenevolent). Even compared with the two other dominant Western theistic religions, Judaism and Islam, Christianity has the most robust conception of the love of God not just in word but also in deed given the doctrine of the incarnation where God in Christ enters into humanity. It is this colorful picture that creates what is initially a problem for the Christian.

Here is one version of an intellectual problem of evil known as the logical problem of evil:

1. If God exists, then there is no evil.
2. Evil exists.
3. Therefore, there is no God.

The issue normally doesn't concern whether evil exists. One has only to turn on the television or even look within one's own heart for evidence. The problem is with the first line which assumes that God is omnipotent and omnibenevolent. It seems that if God were all-powerful, he could stop all evil, pain, and suffering. If He were wholly good, he would want to stop it. Given that God doesn't stop it, then perhaps God is either impotent, malevolent, or both, which is to say the Christian all powerful, good God is nonexistent.

The first thing to notice is the fact that just because evil exists without being justly dealt with *now* is unproblematic. God's nature entails that one day all evil and injustice must be justly dealt with, leading to the idea that perhaps there are good reasons for permitting its existence now. If it can be shown that there is even a *possible* reason, then it does not follow that it is *impossible* for God and evil to co-exist, and the logical argument of evil is dead. This is easily accomplished and is why most atheist philosophers do not even argue the logical problem of evil anymore. For example, God created beings in his image who are free to respond to the divine-human relationship or not. God creates the use of freedom, but humans are responsible for the abuse of freedom. God cannot be blamed for moral evil caused by people, which accounts for most of the evil in the world. Perhaps there is no possible world where God could achieve his ends without allowing the risks that come along with free agents. Perhaps this is the greatest of all possible worlds wherein the maximal number of souls are saved and the minimal amount of suffering is allowed. Maybe the risk that comes with God lovingly creating beings who can use freedom for good or for evil is worth it in the end, even if it means allowing sin and its ugly consequences of suffering and pain. Freedom is a good thing. Finally, it is often contended that God permits evil with its consequences of pain and suffering to achieve a greater good (e.g., character, heaven, etc.).

It is thought that while some evil might be explained away by the value of free agency, a greater good, etc., clearly not all of the pointless evil can be explained by these. Maybe this is not so clear after all. Why think any evil is just pointless? The assumption behind it goes something like this: "So far as I can see, there is no good reason for allowing some particular evil; therefore, there is no good reason for allowing some particular evil." But it does not follow logically from this egocentrism that just because we do not *know* of a specific reason God allows some particular evil, there must not be a good reason for allowing it. Christians also hold that God is not indifferent to our experiences of pain and suffering. God allows human pain so that he can personally be involved in the great rescue operation. What better way for a Creator to persuade his creation to love him than to let them fall away of their own free choice, let them feel all the pain and misery that such defection and dysfunction brings, and then enter humanity via Christ to suffer and to save us as the Christian story goes. Resolved.

The problem of evil is a greater problem for the non-theist. Let us explain. If there is no God, then there really is no such thing as a problem of evil because there is no such thing as *evil*. But because we know evil exists, this is a formidable reason for thinking that God exists.

1. If there is no God, then there are no objective moral values.
2. But there are objective moral values (e.g., the existence of real evil).
3. Therefore, God exists.

The very problem that allegedly makes for the atheist's greatest argument, the existence of real evil, is the undoing of atheism, agnosticism, and non-theism in general. There are some things that we cannot *not* know. We know that human sex trafficking is evil. We know that taking a bat and hitting a homosexual over the head just for fun is absolutely evil. We know that rape and murder are evil and unjust rather than mere preferences. We often confuse preference claims with moral claims. Consider two statements:

1. I like chocolate ice cream.
2. Human sex trafficking is wrong.

The first is a preference claim and is subjective. The second is a normative claim and is objective, a claim that is said to be true for all people at all times and in all places. The first claim is describing a preference one holds. The second is prescribing one that people ought to hold. A claim of preference tells us nothing about what one ought to think or do. It is this "oughtness" that is a distinguishing characteristic of moral truths in contrast to empirical or mathematical truths. The statement "I do not like sex trafficking" would tell us nothing about the rightness or wrongness in the nature of the case. It is a preference claim. It tells you something about me, but not about the world. The second claim, however, tells us about the world and has little if anything to do with what one likes or dislikes. One ought not traffic humans for slavery, much less sex slavery, because these things are absolutely wrong and everyone knows it. The argument from evil for God's nonexistence typically assumes evil in an objective sense.

But to reject God on account of evil merely multiplies one's problems. It is very difficult to ground any notion of objective good or evil apart from

God's existence. Consider the perspectives of non-theist thinkers. Pantheistic religions (Hinduism, Buddhism, etc.) regard evil as ultimately unreal. Human suffering is simply a product of spiritual ignorance, a state brought about from previous lives into this one in accordance with karma. But non-theism in general is deficient as a set of worldviews at being able to account for evil. In *The Atheists Guide to Reality: Enjoying Life without Illusions*, philosopher of science Alex Rosenberg admits that in atheism there is no fundamental difference in moral categories of good and evil. He asks, "What is the difference between right and wrong, good and bad? There is no moral difference between them. Why should I be moral? Because it makes you feel better than being immoral."[7] Further, "In a universe headed for its own heat death, there is no cosmic value to human life, your own or anyone else's."[8] Rosenberg is a moral nihilist; in other words, he believes that there are no ultimate objective values. He writes, "Nihilism rejects the distinction between acts that are morally permitted, morally forbidden, and morally required," and goes on to claim that this does not commit atheists to moral relativism where anything goes, or to moral skepticism where we cannot figure out the more productive things to do, because evolution produces in us a sense of survival and cooperation.[9] The famous biologist and ardent atheist, Richard Dawkins, says:

> If the universe were just electrons and selfish genes, meaningless tragedies . . . are exactly what we should expect, along with equally meaningless good fortune. Such a universe would be neither evil nor good in intention. . . . The universe we observe has precisely the properties we should expect if there is, at bottom, no design, no purpose, no evil and no good, nothing but blind pitiless indifference. DNA neither knows nor cares. DNA just is. And we dance to its music.[10]

How can there even be a "problem" of evil if there is no objective evil? If good and evil are not objective but are rather relative and subjective much like personal preferences over ice cream, then it amounts to nothing more than emoting one's preference. Second, there is no objective notion of "good" on this atheistic account. There is only what works for survival in accordance with natural selection. At worst, this amounts to a kill-or-be-killed sort of jungle morality or, at best, a mere "good" for the sake of furthering the species.

Rosenberg, like others, might appeal to a universal moral code that virtually everyone recognizes. But even the idea of a near universal moral code is something that for him "nature just seduced us into thinking is right. It did that because that made core morality work better—our believing in its truth increases our individual genetic fitness."[11] Ironically, the subtitle of his book contradicts his view on morality since, according to him, morality is an illusion. He admits that there is ample evidence that natural selection is not very good at picking out true beliefs about reality including ethical beliefs.

> There are lots of moral values and ethical norms that enlightened people reject but which Mother Nature has strongly selected for. Racism and xenophobia are optimally adapted to maximize the representation of your genes in the next generation, instead of some stranger's genes . . . : male competition for access to females selects for the biggest, strongest males and so makes the males on average bigger than females. . . . [Natural selection] sometimes selects for norms we reject as morally wrong. Therefore, it can't be a process that's reliable for providing us with what we consider correct moral beliefs.[12]

Leading sociobiological evolutionary ethicist Michael Ruse demonstrates his agreement in this memorable classic piece:

> The position of the modern evolutionist . . . is that humans have an awareness of morality . . . because such an awareness is of biological worth. Morality is a biological adaptation no less than are hands and feet and teeth. . . . Considered as a rationally justifiable set of claims about an objective something, ethics is illusory. I appreciate that when somebody says "Love thy neighbor as thyself," they think they are referring above and beyond themselves . . . Nevertheless. . . . such reference is truly without foundation. Morality is just an aid to survival and reproduction, . . . and any deeper meaning is illusory.[13]

In contrast, the theist has a good explanation for why we can all recognize core moral beliefs across cultures. God created man in His image with a moral law embedded. But the non-theist picture is weak in terms of accounting for an objective morality that it seems open to justifying something like rape in evolutionary terms. Indeed, two evolutionary biologists, Randy Thornhill and Craig Palmer, have claimed that rape can be explained biologically—naturalistically. A man is driven by the subconscious drive to survive and reproduce to force himself upon a female. The strongest male in a species seeks to spread his seed by penetrating as many females as possible in order to perpetuate his DNA. It boils down to this: penetrate in order to perpetuate. In a radio interview, Thornhill said that rape "is a natural phenomenon that is a product of the human evolutionary heritage" comparable to "the leopard's spots and the giraffe's elongated neck."[14]

So either things like rape and sex trafficking are not evil and there is no problem of evil with respect to God's existence, or objective evil exists and reveals something profound about the universe.

Historically, this has been taken to be the most formidable argument used by non-theists and indeed it was used by C. S. Lewis prior to his conversion:

> My argument against God was that the universe seemed so cruel and unjust. But how had I got this idea of just and unjust? A man does not call a line crooked unless he has some idea of a straight line. What was I comparing this universe with when I called it unjust?[15]

Lewis came to see evil is a departure from the way things "ought" to be. This assumed a kind of design plan. After all, if nature is all there is, then why must there be any "ought" at all? If there is at the foundation no evil, then our pursuit of justice makes no sense. We just dance to our DNA.

There is no more reason to deny the objective reality of moral values than the objective reality of the physical world. The fact is we do apprehend objective values, and we all know it. Actions like rape, child abuse, human sex trafficking, and beating a homosexual just for fun, are all obvious injustices rather than simply socially unacceptable behavior. People who fail to see this are morally blind, and there is no reason to allow their impaired vision to call into question what we see clearly. The existence of objective moral values points to the existence of God.

Evil is a departure from the way things ought to be. This tells us two things. One, there is a way things ought to be. Good is basic and evil is parasitical. Second, this is fitting in theism, a worldview in which good is basic because it is grounded in the goodness of God. But this is not fitting as a recalcitrant anomaly of non-theism.

For those who do not want to bite the bullet and become moral relativists, who think there are moral facts apart from God's existence, let's consider this. Absolute justice simply existing seems incomprehensible. We don't know what it means to say that justice simply exists. Where? What does it taste like? Does it have a smell? How much does it weigh? If not sense perceptible, then perhaps it is a timeless, spaceless, universal moral principle. But we still do not know what that even means. Is justice simply "floating" around in some timeless, spaceless existence? We understand what it is for a person to be just, but are completely baffled, if there are no such things as persons, about how justice might simply exist. No. Moral properties like this one are properties of persons, not abstractions devoid of persons. The universe is fundamentally moral. Non-theism cannot adequately ground the nature of moral properties and our obligations. But Christianity can easily ground it in the person of God who is essentially good and where God's commands are for us our moral obligations.

Let us consider the nature of moral obligation. Why ought we be moral? What or who imposes moral duties upon us? Why is it that we ought to do certain things and ought not to do other things? Where does this notion of "ought" come from? Traditionally, our moral obligations were thought to be laid upon us by God's moral commands. But if we deny God's existence, then it is difficult to make sense of moral duty or right and wrong.

A duty is something that is owed. But something can only be owed to a person or persons. There is no such thing as duty in isolation. The concept of moral obligation is really unintelligible apart from the notion of God. The words are present, but their meaning is gone.

If Mormons leaving Mormonism do so for non-theism, then they have no rational justification for maintaining their desired theistic morality. The famous atheist philosopher Friedrich Nietzsche insisted, "When one gives up the Christian faith, one pulls the right to Christian morality out from under one's feet."[16]

The problem of evil is now shown not to be a serious threat—at least not for Christians. There is a final thought. Perhaps you no longer consider the mythological "problem of evil" as a general problem for theists even if severe for non-theists. This doesn't mean that you cannot invoke what I, Corey, call "the biblical problem of evil," calling into question not God per se but the Christian God in particular. It is not uncommon these days to see critics referencing biblical passages in their efforts to show that the God of the Bible is a moral monster. Neo-atheists completely misrepresent the Bible in doing so. Nonetheless, we should provide responses to troubling passages.

Troubling Bible Passages

While it is certain that the Old Testament contains what might be denoted as slavery, misogyny, and, most saliently, genocide, all of this has been met with formidable and satisfying responses for anyone genuinely interested in truth rather than propaganda. Slavery in the Bible, for example, is not at all like the antebellum South around the time of the American Civil War. Rather, it is more like being an indentured servant. Indentured servanthood helped the poor by giving them a place to live and work, not harming them by giving them handouts or enslaving them. Forced slavery was punishable by death. So it is with most of these objections ripped from their contexts by neo-atheists to subvert Christianity. Given a lack of space here, I (Corey) will tell you what I tell all of my philosophy students who bring up such an objection in their papers, namely, that they are irresponsible if they claim to undermine Christianity by using a straw-man argument that utterly misunderstands or misrepresents the Christian position. There is plenty of good, scholarly, recent literature unpacking the biblical texts and cultural background in response to the claim that the evil found in the Bible is a moral problem for the veracity of the Christian God. If you do not at least look at this literature and you reject the Bible and its God on account of the objection, you are irresponsible and to be pitied.[17]

We have shown that the non-theist can be moral (from a purely human viewpoint), but without God there would be no grounding of morality. And we are about to see that the non-theist can be rational, but without God there would be no grounding of rationality.

OBJECTION 2: THE BIBLE, RATIONALITY, AND MODERN SCIENCE

The assumption is often made that modern science is grounded in the realm of reason and the Bible (and its attending claims and miracles) is in the realm of faith. But this is problematic for several reasons. First, modern science and the university institution viewed as the center of rational enquiry are historically products of a Judeo-Christian worldview. This is no accident. This is just a matter of historical fact. Knowledge is prized in Christianity because the ultimate goal concerns knowledge, the knowledge of God (John 17:3).

While many think that Christianity is not fitting for the mind since it is thought by some to be untrue and irrational, in fact, the modern university owes its existence to the Judeo-Christian worldview. Mercenaries and merchants in the European expansion do not educate. Education is a Christian missionary enterprise. At its core, Christianity is rooted in thought. John 1:1 begins, "In the beginning was the Word, and the Word was with God, and the Word was God." The term *word* in Greek is *logos,* from which we derive our term *logic.* The medieval philosophical/theological tradition in Europe was largely a project in *fides quaerens intellectum,* "faith seeking understanding." The monasteries kept education alive through the Dark Ages. The first universities in Europe were Christian, and the study of philosophy was considered of central importance to the health and vitality of the university and the Christian life. Theology, it was said, is the queen of the sciences (*scientia* in Latin was more broadly construed back then to cover all of the knowledge disciplines), and philosophy is its handmaiden. Hence, we have the notion of the university grounded in the unity of truth within the diversity of disciplines. Think of it as a bicycle wheel whose hub is theology, whose spokes are the individual academic fields, and whose connection between the two is philosophy. This is why every professor who possesses a Ph.D. today possesses a doctorate of philosophy in their field regardless of whether they have ever taken philosophy. This same emphasis led to the American universities, where 90–95 percent of the original universities were Christian in orientation (including Harvard, Yale, and Princeton, which were centers of training for missionaries and ministers). This training influenced the spread of universities via Christian influence to places in the Far East like India and Korea.

This Christian academic foundation led to the modern era of scientific discovery where Francis Bacon spoke of God's two books—the book of nature and book of Scripture. There can be no contradiction because the same author is author of both. If there is an alleged discrepancy, it is not between the facts themselves, nature or Scripture, but the interpretation of the facts by science or theology.

The universe was designed by an intelligent Designer who created man in his image with the capacity to discover, to be rational, and to know. This explains why so many of the founders of the subdisciplines of modern science were Christians whose disciplines were inspired and informed by the content of their faith (Mendel in genetics, Pasteur in bacteriology, Linnaeus in taxonomy, Kepler in astronomy, Boyle in chemistry, Newton in physics, James Clerk Maxwell in bringing the second great unification of physics after Newton, etc.). It is no accident that the history of science developed in a Christian context and conviction rather than in the Far East (pantheism) or in Western atheism.

A pair of scissors is said to be a good pair of scissors when it cuts well, when it functions properly according to the way it was designed. This notion of design is the root idea of proper function or working properly. According to theism, human beings have been designed. Theism has an easy answer to the relevant set of questions: What is proper functioning? What is it for my cognitive faculties to be working properly? What is cognitive dysfunction? What is it to function naturally? My cognitive faculties are functioning naturally when they are functioning in the way God designed them to function. Theism provides a superior explanation of our rationality as humans.

The naturalist, however, has a fatal problem here. Darwin's dangerous idea is really two ideas combined: philosophical naturalism together with the claim that our cognitive faculties have originated by way of natural selection working on some form of genetic variation. That is, evolutionary naturalism. According to evolutionary naturalism, the purpose or proper function of those faculties (if they have one) is to enable or promote survival, as in survival of the fittest. The naturalistic philosopher Patricia Churchland explains the function of human beings viewed (as she does) as brains and central nervous systems.

> Boiled down to essentials, a nervous system enables the organism to succeed in the four F's: feeding, fleeing, fighting, and reproducing. The principle chore of nervous systems is to get the body parts where they should be in order that the organism may survive. . . . so long as it is geared to the organism's way of life and enhances the organism's chances of survival. Truth, whatever that is, definitely takes the hindmost.[18]

In other words, if naturalism is true, then evolution guarantees that we behave in certain ways to promote survival, reproductive success, as the end goal. The goal is not truth (true beliefs), but survival. Naturalistic evolution gives reason to doubt that human cognitive faculties produce for the most part true beliefs, including the belief in evolutionary naturalism.

Furthermore, the probability that our cognitive faculties are reliable (i.e., furnish us with a preponderance of true beliefs) is either low or impossible to estimate in Darwin's theory. Rosenberg comments that there is "lots of evidence that natural selection is not very good at picking out true beliefs, especially scientific ones."[19] Yet, he places his trust there, for "the methods of science are the only reliable ways to secure knowledge of anything."[20] But this gives the devotee of evolutionary naturalism a defeater for the proposition that his cognitive faculties are reliable, a reason for doubting, giving up, rejecting that natural belief. If so, then it also gives a reason for doubting any beliefs produced by those faculties. This includes, of course, the belief in science itself. Evolutionary naturalism, therefore, provides the one who accepts it with a defeater for scientific beliefs, a reason for doubting that science does in fact get us to the truth, or close to the truth. Indeed, in providing one who accepts it with a defeater for anything that a person believes, it also provides a defeater for itself; evolutionary naturalism is therefore self-defeating.

It is difficult, then, to press such a view into service as a foundation for rationality. Evolutionary theism is more rationally plausible than evolutionary naturalism. Unguided evolution is as hard to conceive of as a universe coming to be without a cause. Darwin himself may have seen this problem at the heart of evolutionary naturalism: "With me," says Darwin, "the horrid doubt always arises whether the convictions of man's mind, which has been developed from the mind of the lower animals, are of any value or at all trustworthy. Would any one trust in the convictions of a monkey's mind, if there are any convictions in such a mind?"[21]

Does this mean that an atheist cannot be rational? No, it does not. A non-theist can be rational, but without God there would be no rationality. The non-theist simply has no foundation to support the fact of rationality, whereas the theist does. Modern science was conceived, born, and flourished in the matrix of Judeo-Christian theism. One of the world's leading philosophers, Alvin Plantinga, concludes that "there is a superficial conflict but deep concord between science and theistic religion, but superficial concord and deep conflict between science and naturalism."[22]

The Relationship between Science and Religion

This brings us to our next point. There is a terrible misunderstanding about the nature of the relationship between science and religion. The relationship between science and religion is a philosophical relationship. There are three fundamentally different ways to look at this. First, the Bible and modern science conflict. Some people ignore the science and go with the statements of Scripture, whereas others ignore the Bible and go with modern science. Both are dogmatists. It may represent the popular cultural war of faith and science, but it is fallacious. Here is one dogmatic example.

> If we're going to be scientistic, then we have to attain our view of reality from what physics tells us about it. Actually, we'll have to do more than that: we'll have to embrace physics as the whole truth about reality. Why buy the picture of reality that physics paints? Well, it's simple, really. We trust science as the only way to acquire knowledge. That is why we are so confident about atheism.[23]

This is not a view of science, but a philosophy of science called "scientism." Scientism is like religious dogmatism. It hardly allows free thinking. Some of what is thought to be science is actually philosophy and goes unnoticed by the average person. Scientism is the view that only what can be known by science via the five senses or is quantifiable and empirically tested is true and rational. Far from being the disciplinary authority it is often claimed and believed to be, it is in fact dependent on other disciplines like philosophy (or even theology for that matter). Philosophy takes primacy over science in many respects.

Not only does scientism assume that naturalism is true, but it is self-defeating since it fails to satisfy its own criteria of being quantified and empirically verifiable via the five senses. I cannot taste, touch, smell, hear, or feel this verification principle. Real science is concerned with things internal to its discipline like measuring things, observing data, looking for repeatable events, and so forth. Answering the question "What is science?" is itself not a statement of science, but a philosophical statement about science, thereby appealing to philosophy.

Many assume that when a scientist puts on a white lab coat and begins to work with her measurements that she is merely objectively observing data about the world in order to deliver the facts and nothing but the facts. This is not the whole picture. Aside from limitations inside science, science is limited by several underlying philosophical presuppositions, only a few of which will be mentioned.

First, the scientific enterprise assumes that nature exists. The existence of the external world, assumed to be distinct from the observer, is believed to be mind-independent. That is, the world is what it is apart from you and me. However, this is taken for granted. One must engage in philosophical discourse about such views before a scientist can even begin to do his work. For example, some hold that knowledge is nothing but a social construction of reality. Second, science assumes that nature has a discoverable, intelligible order rather than a chaotic state of affairs. Third, it assumes the laws of logic exist, entities at the core of rational thought. But these are categories of philosophy, not of science. Further, these laws seem to be invariant, abstract entities that are true for all people at all times and all places. They are prior to science, are assumed by science, and we can be certain of their existence without sensibly perceiving them. Fourth, science typically assumes the reliability of our senses and their relationship to our minds, to deliver truths about the world. But one cannot prove this to the perception schematic without some circular reasoning, a track record sort of an argument. For all we know, we might be in a dream state. Again, these are all philosophical considerations that take place prior to science. They all fit nicely within a theistic world view, but are dubious within a non-theistic worldview.

But conflicting views are not the only views held. There are two views which do not see science and religion necessarily at war. One non-conflicting view sometimes goes by the name NOMA (non-overlapping magisteria). This view assumes that religion and science operate in completely independent realms of truth so that there is never conflict because there is never overlap. Science deals with the objective realm of empirically verifiable facts which is, in principle, publicly accessible. Religion deals with the subjective realm of values, beauty, and religion, which is privately owned. Science tells us about the age of rocks; religion tells us about the rock of ages. Science tells how the heavens go; religion tells us how to go to heaven. They are oil and water, apples and oranges, so to speak. Asserters of this view believe that there is no real connection between religion and the belief in supernatural events of any sort. But this is problematic because there are clear areas of intersection like creation, alleged miracles, etc., ones that are the very centerpiece of a religion like the resurrection of Jesus to Christianity which had publicly available evidence.[24] Those to whom Jesus appeared talked with, touched, saw, and perhaps even smelled Jesus. He was seen over a dozen times and to 500 people at once (see 1 Cor. 15:6).

If there are good, independent reasons favoring God's existence and for the claims of the Bible as historically accurate, then the better approach is one of integration. Theology and science are integrated and compatible in a unity of truth. All truth is God's truth. Science and theology share a common epistemology (theory of knowledge), both being rational enterprises seeking to make statements of truth about reality. The assumption that all truth is united is plausible, but one ought not to infer from this that there is a unity of interpretation.

The Mutual Compatibility and Integrity of Science and Theology

One of the greatest misunderstandings in pop culture and among academics is the proper relationship between science and religion/theology. Part of the role of philosophy is to clarify concepts, as well as to pursue truth and a coherent understanding of reality. In the disciplines of science and theology, similarity in method implies the possibility of integration between these two fields of inquiry. The methodology of science (i.e., the way we move from the data of science to theory and back again) and the methodology of theology (i.e., the way we move from the data of theology to certain doctrinal formulations and back to interpreting the data again), share a common epistemology and provide much overlap so as to count toward an integrated approach in developing a more robust and coherent worldview.

Theology and science are examples of the human mind thinking theoretically as it was designed to do. It is legitimate to differentiate these fields based on the types of questions being asked or the conclusions that they are trying to arrive at, and the types of data they are willing to accept. So while it may be legitimate to differentiate science and theology, this does not mean that we isolate them from each other. Neither science nor theology ought to subsume the other. They are largely different enterprises, but they can interact in a robust way. And they confront similar epistemological problems, while asking different sorts of questions. Together, they can help formulate a coherent view of the world, that broader view of the world than naturalism alone provides.

Certain things count as "data" for scientific input in terms of formulating scientific theories. These are the kinds of things that we generally think of when we think about science. These are such things as experimental lab results, observations, measurements, and background theories. But doing science does not take place in a vacuum without a set of assumptions. Likewise, certain things count as data for theological doctrinal formulation. These include personal experience (individually and communally), Scripture, church councils and creeds, and general revelation (including science).

Theology, quite far from an intellectually fluffy discipline, can be quite rational. Indeed, theology is the logos about the theos, or reasoning about God, where Scripture plays the central role since it is considered to be the ultimate epistemological authority as the revelation of God. But this is not contradictory to reason; it involves reason and invites reason as a check on possible contrary interpretations which might then rule out either one or both conclusions. Additionally, we do not start in a vacuum. We carry certain assumptions including the authoritative nature of the Bible itself (discernible and defensible on independent grounds) and certain beliefs that are consonant with church creedal traditions in guiding our exploration of theological truths. We interpret in communities now, as well as communities past, with a set of background theological and doctrinal assumptions shared through tradition. Finally, experience also plays a vital role in interpretation. We expect our experiences of the world to cohere rationally with the way things are portrayed to be in Scripture. When we find our experiences of the world in conflict with Scripture, we cannot accept incoherence, so we must question our interpretation either of our experience or of Scripture.

It is a grave mistake to equate interpretation with revelation as well as to take the Bible as a technical scientific treatise rather than a theological treatise as it was intended, along with its vast literary diversity in terms of genres, styles, and forms. It is also a grave mistake to equate science, a set of tools for developing a model to represent nature, with nature itself. Since all truth is God's truth and we have independent reasons for thinking that God exists, then the book of nature and the book of revelation cannot contradict. The word of God and the work of God are blueprints of the total harmony. Legitimate interpretive options in Genesis on the creation of the world, the earth, and man are prime examples over which interpretation differs, and the best overall interpretations should emerge triumphant.

Within both science and theology we need to recognize that there are certain beliefs that offer more or less certainty than others. Truth comes in degrees of verisimilitude. In Christian theology, the deity of Christ is a high mark of relative certainty. Similarly, in science the second law of thermodynamics is a high mark about which we can be relatively certain. Both scientists and theologians need to recognize that theories and doctrines are interpretive abstractions which cannot be confused with the data itself. Perhaps our interpretation of the data does express the truth, perhaps only in a verisimilitude way, or perhaps we misinterpret the data altogether. Theories and doctrines constantly need to be re-examined with the emergence of new data, which helps confirm, or disconfirm, the theories and doctrines, which in turn helps us to discover more data and understand it better.

In science we use structure, categories, explanation, evaluation, and repeatability or predictability to get from data to theories. We structure or systematize the data trying to perceive order. We assume that nature is orderly, and that such order is not a mere projection in our minds but is really there, and that our minds correspond to the reality in a verisimilar way. In categorizing, we postulate a new theoretical entity to explain something. When certain data seems anomalous to most the other data being explained and evaluated, it is often initially set aside or ignored. We then continue to test our theory for repeatable and predictable success as a means of consistency. As a whole, we use conceptual models, or pictures, in this process of formulating theories. Models have a key role in analyzing the data and synthesizing a theory.

In theology we use coherence, categories, explanation, evaluation, and replicability. We apply structure, or coherence, to a particular set of data. We also systematically categorize such data and seek to explain how it fits the model, as well as to explain possible anomalies that do not fit. We evaluate Scripture in light of Scripture and have certain hermeneutical rules that guide us in the process (e.g., interpreting unclear passages in the light of clear ones). Similar to science, we seek confirmation and consistency in repeatability, replicability, or predictive success. In doing this, we never build a doctrine on one obscure verse not attested to elsewhere in Scripture. We may even test it to see if it is attested elsewhere in the history of Christian doctrine. Unlike science, we are not looking for lawlike regularities, but coherence and confirmation.

Models in theology are used (e.g., various doctrines of the atonement), just as models in science are used (e.g., various theories of the atom). Models are analogues used to describe something else. Analogical predication exists in both scientific and theological reasoning. Similar criteria are involved in both types of reasoning, and are applied in formulating a scientific theory based upon the scientific data and in formulating doctrine based on theological data.

Given similar criteria involved in examining data for scientific and theological models in formulating theories and doctrines, both are rational enterprises, seeking to explain the way the world is as it relates to our experience, and how it is confirmed by our processes and communities. Both show analogical and approximately true reasoning taking place in the process which are communicated afresh with new data and with contemporary understanding.

The model of integration that we are advocating affirms both the "unity of truth" thesis wherein all truth is commensurable and that the God of the Bible is real, such that any alleged conflict cannot be at the level of the facts themselves—nature and Scripture—but at the level of the interpretation of the facts—science and theology.

OBJECTION 3: THE PROBLEM OF THE HISTORICAL TRUSTWORTHINESS OF THE BIBLE

As previously mentioned, LDS people are raised believing that the Bible is fraught with problems. Because of this, doubt about the Bible may keep them from investigating what it says once they leave the comfort of Mormonism. But this previous assumption does not need to interfere with exploring whether the Bible is God's Word. Rather, assuming it to be minimally a historical record, first ask, is the Bible an accurate record of history? The gap between the actual events and the time in which they were written down is an important clue in light of skeptical claims of legendary development or outright agnosticism about the Jesus of history. To begin, the biographies of Jesus are the primary source documents and they are early, multiple, independent, and come from both friendly and sometimes hostile witnesses. Matthew and John were eyewitnesses to the life of Jesus. Mark (according to the first-century bishop, Papias, who was a disciple of John) wrote the eyewitness account of the apostle Peter. Luke wrote his own historical and corroborative investigation of the eyewitnesses and was an associate of the apostle Paul. Some of Jesus's own family members like James and Jude, originally skeptical, wrote of him. And Paul, a Rabbi, scholar, and persecutor of Christians, is considered a hostile convert.

The evidence indicates that the Gospels are, indeed, early enough to have been written by eyewitnesses. For various reasons, many scholars recognize the early dating of the writing of the New Testament. Here is one line of thought for this claim. Certain omissions in the Gospel records and in the book of Acts are strong evidence for an early dating of these writings. The biographies of Jesus and especially the book of Acts omit certain information that otherwise would have served key apologetic purposes if written after the events occurred. One would expect the recording of these events in the Bible if the documents were written late (e.g., after A.D. 70).

Acts is the record of the development of the early church and contains discussions of minor persecutions, deaths of certain Christians, the Jew-Gentile controversy, and even names certain political leaders in its discussion of church and the state. Yet, missing is any mention of the major persecution of Christians by Emperor Nero (A.D. 64), the siege of Jerusalem (A.D. 67–70), and the utter destruction of the Jewish temple (A.D. 70). These items are of great interest for establishing Christianity to be true and God's judgment on Israel for their rejection of the Messiah. Later Christians certainly did not fail to point this out. Why did the biblical authors not report these major events if they already occurred? Indeed, it would have been perfect timing to mention the destruction of the temple given Jesus's prediction of its destruction (in Matt. 24:1–3 and Luke 21:5–6). But no gospel account records the destruction of the temple, and it is not in Acts or anywhere in the NT. Acts records nothing about the deaths of James (A.D. 62), Paul (A.D. 64), or Peter (A.D. 65) even though Luke mentions them prominently in the book, and yet far less significant Christian deaths are covered such as those of Stephen (Acts 7:54–60) and James, the brother of John (Acts 12:1–2). At the end of the book of Acts, Paul was still alive and under house arrest. The best explanation for why none of this gets any mention whatsoever in any of the NT, especially in the book of Acts, is because these writings happened *before* the events themselves. This is profound because the dates of the events are so well-established, ensuring our confidence that the NT documents were written early.

Paul appears to be aware of Luke's gospel when he wrote to Timothy in A.D. 62–64 saying, "The elders who direct the affairs of the church well are worthy of double honor, especially those whose work is preaching and teaching. For Scripture says, 'Do not muzzle an ox while it is treading out the grain,' and 'The worker deserves his wages'" (1 Tim. 5:17–18). Paul quoted two passages as "Scripture" here. "Do not muzzle an ox while it is treading out the grain" refers to Deuteronomy 25:4. But "the worker deserves his wages" refers to Luke 10:7, so clearly Luke's gospel was already common knowledge and accepted as Scripture by the time of Paul's letter to Timothy. Luke quoted Mark (and Matthew) repeatedly and most believe that Luke relied, in part, on Mark's gospel. He admitted that he was not an eyewitness to the life and ministry of Jesus. Luke described himself as a historian, carefully investigating and collecting the statements from the eyewitnesses who were present at the time (Luke 1:1–4). Based on these facts and others, an early dating timeline can be established: Mark (45–55); Luke (55–59); Luke writes Acts (59–61); deaths of James, Paul, and Peter (62, 64, 65); Nero's persecution (64); siege of Jerusalem (67–70); temple destroyed (70).

The historical evidence suggests early authorship of the primary source documents for the life of Christ. This makes them very credible. If the Gospels were written so early and in the region of the events recorded, it would have been difficult for them to include obvious lies or legends, given that they would have been written to people who were alive during the events recorded and the people would have been available to contradict the NT writings if they contained fallacious information. Christianity, a persecuted minority until the fourth century, emerged in a hostile environment. Its claims could have been easily debunked if invented.

Accuracy of Transmission

Given that we have good reasons for thinking that the history was accurately recorded, was it accurately transmitted throughout history? For various reasons, virtually no original writings from the ancient world have survived, including those of the New Testament. All we have are manuscript copies. Since the NT record is nearly twenty centuries old and has been copied several times throughout history, many skeptics conclude that it is not possible that the text we have today is an accurate portrayal of what was originally written.

The skeptic Bart Ehrman makes an alarming statement that would seem to subvert any confidence in the transmission of the record: "Some say there are 200,000 variants known, some say 300,000, some say 400,000 or more! . . . There are more variations among our manuscripts than there are words in the New Testament."[25]

One would think that from this and like statements that there is no way we can have confidence in any word in the entire NT. First, let us take a clue from the OT. Although the Dead Sea Scrolls discovered in 1947 were determined to be one thousand years older than our oldest existing OT manuscript at the time, they were nearly identical to our previously ancient manuscripts. This shows clearly that textual preservation is possible. Now, for the NT. Although no two manuscripts are completely identical, the vast quantity and quality of manuscripts available allow scholars to compensate for unintentional, and sometimes even intentional, scribal mistakes in copying. Through the process of textual criticism (the standard tool used also in non-NT literature), and modern computer aids, scholars are able to virtually reconstruct the original text to about 99+ percent accuracy, showing the faithfulness of the transmission of the text as it has come down to us through the centuries. While there are still a relatively small number of questions remaining, comparatively speaking, no Christian doctrine hangs upon a debatable text.

What Ehrman does not tell you is that all of those variants are spread across twenty-five thousand manuscripts. NT scholar Craig Blomberg points out that this is an average of only sixteen variants per manuscript. Furthermore, the variants tend to cluster such that only 6 percent of the New Testament contains most of it.[26] We know where the variations are, and, moreover, given the science of textual criticism, we know how to reproduce the text from these many variants that are largely due to misspellings, duplicating a letter or line, etc. Ehrman presents nothing new. Anyone with a Greek text can see where all of the variant manuscripts are for each particular variation in every manuscript. The only disputed passages involving two or more verses are Mark 16:9–20 and John 7:53–8:11, both of which are flagged in English Bibles. As Blomberg points out, "It cannot be emphasized strongly enough that no orthodox doctrines or ethical practice of Christianity depends solely on any disputed wording."[27] Furthermore, Ehrman himself concedes this, notably hidden in the appendix to the paperback edition: "Essential Christian beliefs are not affected by textual variants in the manuscript tradition of the New Testament."[28] Here is an example of the typical variations in manuscripts. Can anyone really say that they don't know what the original was intended to be?

Congratulations! You're just won $100,000.00.
Congratulations! You've just one $100,000.00.
Congratulations? You've just one $10,000.00.

It is obvious to anyone that the corruption found in all three statements can easily be used to reconstruct the original even when all three contain error.

One of the great manuscript scholars of this century points to what he calls the "embarrassment of wealth" in terms of the large number of manuscripts we possess to render the large number of variants as the key rather than a problem to reconstructing the originals. He says, "Precisely because we have hundreds of thousands of variants and hundreds of early manuscripts, we are in an excellent position for recovering the wording of the original."[29]

The evidence used in the reconstruction of the NT includes all of the Greek manuscripts, versions or translations into various languages, and citations by early Christian writers. The earliest of these NT manuscripts were written much closer to the date of the original writing than is the case for almost any other piece of ancient literature. In relation to the time interval between manuscript copies from the original writing, the oldest known manuscripts of any Greek classical authors are dated about a thousand years or more after the author's death. The NT manuscript copies reach back to within a remarkable fifty years.

AUTHOR	BOOK	DATE WRITTEN	EARLIEST COPIES	TIME GAP	NO. OF COPIES
Homer	*Iliad*	800–B.C.	c. 400 B.C.	c. 400 yrs.	2,200
Herodotus	*History*	480–425 B.C.	c. A.D. 900	c. 1,350	109
Caesar	*Gallic Wars*	100–44 B.C.	c. A.D. 900	c. 1,000	210
Tacitus	*Annals*	A.D. 100	c. A.D. 1100	c. 1,000	20
Pliny	*Natural History*	A.D. 61–113	c. A.D. 850	c. 750	200
New Testament		A.D. 50–100	c. A.D. 114 (John fragment) c. A.D. 200 (books) c. A.D. 250 (most OT/NT) c. A.D. 325 (complete)	c. +50 c. 100 c. 150 c. 225	5,856 (plus 20,000 in different languages)

The Greek manuscripts and ancient versions alone consist of nearly twenty-five thousand manuscripts. Further, if all of the NT manuscripts were destroyed, the NT could still be reconstructed merely by the thirty-two thousand citations from early second- and third-century church fathers, who quote from all but eleven verses of the NT. It is widely known among scholars in the field that the manuscript evidence of the NT is proven to be more numerous, earlier, more widely distributed, better copied, and written by more people who were closer to the events than for any other piece of ancient history, which provides scholars the opportunity for virtual reconstruction of the original text. To reject the NT is to reject all of ancient history by comparison. While similar evidence can be adduced for the Old Testament (e.g., Dead Sea Scrolls, Masoretic Text, LXX, etc.), for brevity and importance surrounding the life of Jesus, we are focusing on the NT.[30] In conclusion, the Bible that we have today is essentially the same as what they had in the generation that walked with Jesus.

While the NT documents are the primary source of our knowledge about Jesus Christ of Nazareth, and while there are very good arguments to sustain their reliability as superior to that of any other ancient literature, such documents are not alone in their witness about ancient history and the life of Christ in particular. The reliability of the NT documents is confirmed through external sources such as archaeology and ancient history. Although these secondary, non-biblical, external sources do not teach us much more than we already know through the NT, they do offer corroborative testimonial evidence which confirms the NT reliability, especially when such corroborative testimony is from multiple, and sometimes even very hostile, sources. These sources are largely from Roman, Jewish, Greek, Syrian, and Samaritan historians who were contemporaries with chronology of the biblical history. These external sources provide quite a detailed list about the historical Jesus, consistent with that found in the NT, which helps establish the credibility of the primary witnesses.

Here is but one example. Flavius Josephus (A.D. 37–100), the notable Jewish (non-Christian) historian, was a contemporary of the apostle Paul. Among other things corroborating the NT, he spoke of James the brother of Jesus, John the Baptist, and Herod. Most important is one statement that is often referenced of which only the more controversial portion will be given here:

> Now there was about this time Jesus, a wise man, if it be lawful to call him a man. For he was one who wrought surprising feats. . . . He was [the] Christ . . . he appeared to them alive again the third day, as the divine prophets had foretold these and ten thousand other wonderful things concerning him.[31]

Most scholars rightly point out that Josephus was a Jew who, according to Origen, never believed Jesus was the Messiah.[32] So then it is unlikely that Josephus would have mentioned Jesus in this way (e.g., "if it be lawful to call him a man," and "he was the Christ.") Some of it is probably later Christian interpolation, but not all of it. Therefore, most scholars affirm with good evidence that perhaps the core of what was said is authentically Josephus, as depicted in the Arabic manuscript of the statement:

> At this time there was a wise man who was called Jesus. His conduct was good and (he) was known to be virtuous. And many people from among the Jews and the other nations became his disciples. Pilate condemned him to be crucified and to die. But those who had become his disciples did not abandon his discipleship. They reported that he had appeared to them three days after his crucifixion, and that he was alive; accordingly, he was perhaps the Messiah, concerning whom the prophets have recounted wonders.[33]

From this quote alone we learn: (1) Jesus was known as a wise and virtuous man, (2) he had many Jewish and Gentile disciples, (3) he was condemned to be executed by Pilate, (4) and with crucifixion as the mode. (5) His disciples believed him to be resurrected from the dead (6) and to have appeared to them on the third day following. (7) Consequently, they continued his teachings. (8) Jesus was perhaps the Messiah.

In 2006, additional evidence for the Bible's reliability was uncovered. Focusing on the most common Jewish male names from Palestine 2,000 years ago (out of three thousand researched), these top nine names were found to occur in secular sources of the time 41 percent of the time. The NT first five books uses these same nine names 40 percent of the time. Also, when one of the top Jewish names was used in the Bible, it was followed with an identifier, like Matthew the tax collector or James the son of Alphaeus or James the son of Zebedee, consistent with secular sources. When a less common name was mentioned, like Thomas (not in the top one hundred names), there was no additional identifier.[34]

In sum, there are over forty-five outside sources that convey over 129 independent facts like these about the life, death and resurrection of Christ. This does not even begin to include all the empirical data from the relatively young science of archaeology.[35] This phenomenon of corroborative ancient history serves to confirm the historicity of the NT. Where the NT has been checked with outside sources, it has been found extremely reliable. Not only does ancient historical evidence not contradict the core historicity of the NT primary witnesses of the life and teaching of Jesus, but it shows positive evidence confirming it. We conclude that the historicity of the NT as it was recorded and transmitted to us is a reliable record of history. From this historical record, while it would take more work, we can show that Jesus viewed the OT as the inspired Word of God and appointed the NT authors for the inspiration of the NT as the Word of God.

Given these three atheist objections to belief in God, we have argued that: (1) the problem of evil is a bigger problem for non-theists than for theists and even turns in favor of theism once properly understood, (2) far from biblical theism being anti-science or anti-reason, it actually provides the grounding for science and rationality itself, whereas naturalism fails to provide grounding for any confidence in the deliverances of reason including belief in naturalism, and (3) the Bible we possess today is deemed historically reliable when assessing the evidence. Upon close examination, atheist arguments are not sound after all

WHY BELIEVE IN GOD?

Mormons and former Mormons may not want to entertain the idea that the real God could be found in biblical Christianity or that his teachings in the Bible come from a reliable source, because Mormonism teaches its members it is an improvement on traditional Christianity and the Bible, being both an expansion and a correction. This idea, too, may be stuck in the thinking of former LDS without their realizing it. We were taught that the Bible is mistranslated and can't be trusted, but the Book of Mormon and other books of LDS scripture are trustworthy. The God of the Bible failed twice to establish his church, once in Jerusalem and once in the Americas, but Joseph Smith's church will stand forever. Although Matthew 16:18 quotes Jesus saying that he will establish his church and the gates of hell will not prevail against it, Mormonism teaches the gates of hell *did* prevail against Jesus's church twice. Jesus's church purportedly failed once in the Middle East/Asia/Europe when the apostles died, and once in the Americas after the resurrection. Supposedly, Native Americans are descendants of Book of Mormon people in the Americas, and, supposedly, Jesus visited them and established his church. But who ever heard of Native Americans who have been Christians in the Americas for the last 2,000 years? No one. If Jesus came to the Americas and established his church, there would be some evidence like there is in archeological sites and historical documents around the Middle East. That's an impotent Jesus who can't keep his church together when he says he can. Who wants to follow someone like that? Over and over as LDS we were taught that the traditional Christian church falls short of the Mormon Church, it needs more of the truth (from Joseph Smith) added to corrupt, incomplete, and inferior teachings from the Bible, and the original traditional church is inadequate to offer eternal life, so why consider it? In the spirit of re-examining every idea: What if this teaching, too, is a lie and Jesus *did* establish his church in the Middle East like he promised and it didn't fail to stay alive? And, what if God *is* able to keep his Word together and the Bible is its reliable source?

Truth and Worldviews

The word *truth* is said to exist in every known language. Humans, it appears, consider it to be decidedly significant. Even Pilate, given an audience with Jesus, took the opportunity to ask, "What is truth?" (John 18:38). When one asks a question, states an opinion, or investigates a notion, that person presupposes there is a "true" answer at the end of the quest. Doesn't the physicist generate theories based on assumed universal and consistent physical laws, the forensic investigator seek hard evidence to solve a murder, the police investigator gather proof to substantiate a theory, and the auditor follow money trails to catch a thief? What if someone rear-ends your car? Don't you want them to admit to the officer and the insurance agent they rear-ended you instead of lying that you backed into them? These are all examples of efforts to verify that something did indeed happen and that there is a systematic, rational way to accurately describe that reality of facts that impartial, logically-minded humans, like those selected for a jury, can understand and judge judiciously. They seek to determine if the truth claims are linked together in a logical way that leads to a sound conclusion. Assuming there is an objective, reasonable truth, these lawyers, investigators, forensic examiners, auditors, drivers, and juries are expected to use unambiguous premises that accurately reflect the facts and then apply valid logic to determine their conclusions. Worldviews differ on a reliable source for this truth.

Worldviews are composites of sets of beliefs, not all of which pass the three tests for truth.[36] First, a set must not contradict itself. Mormonism is notorious for having contradictory teachings, even within Scripture (God is spirit, God has a body; polygamy is an abomination, polygamy is an eternal principle; etc). The Bible is not saddled with such doctrinal contradictions. Second, a worldview will be consistent with the facts. Mormonism has been shown in this book and elsewhere to be inconsistent with historical, archeological, geographical (there's no river running into the Red Sea), linguistic (what is reformed Egyptian?), medical (could Shiz from the Book of Mormon really raise up after he was beheaded?), and zoological (there were no horses in the Americas in the fifth century A.D.) facts. And third, it must have viability, sustainability. We create our own personal worldview through which we see the world and make judgments. Everyone has standards of truth and morality. Just say something one thinks is false (that's ridiculous—no one believes that in the twenty-first century) or do something to them one considers to be immoral (how dare you . . .). One's worldview will become apparent.

There are two prevalent, competing worldviews in academia today. (1) All that matters is observable and measurable and nothing else, such as miracles, can be real. This worldview is represented by naturalists. (2) Everything is relative and knowledge and experience are self-constructed. This worldview is represented by postmodernists. We have addressed the naturalist worldview of the hard sciences and now discuss the postmodern worldview of the social sciences. Postmodernism is also a worldview espoused by many former Mormons. Is there truth? Postmodernists would argue no, objective truth does not exist. In the hard sciences, some naturalists argue yes it does, but only what can be measured in the natural world, nothing more.

Postmodernism

Postmodernism is characterized by one word—*relativism (*i.e., socially constructed reality) whether in metaphysics, epistemology, or ethics. Basically, relativism means there are no absolutes, different things are true or real for different people given their culture, experience, and a million other factors. In other words, each human socially constructs his or her own reality. The key word is "relativism."

Where did postmodernity come from? Modernity (Modernism/Enlightenment, 1650–1800) is generally seen as the period beginning with Rene Descartes (theist French philosopher and mathematician; "I think, therefore, I am") who opened the period of the Enlightenment with a shift from reality (metaphysics) to knowledge (epistemology), initially doubting everything in order to see what remained through fire so as to expose items of certain knowledge. This became the age of reason (rationalism) and age of science (empiricism), but the emphasis was on human reason with the project being the pursuit of knowledge in terms of absolute certainty. Descartes, the father of analytical geometry, thought that all disciplines were subject to the same veritable standards of mathematics and logic (fields where certainty exists). He was wrong, and we say that Descartes "got de cart before de horse"). The Enlightenment project, a failed project, ended with Immanuel Kant (the father of agnosticism). Because it ended with agnosticism even though its project was focused on knowledge—certain knowledge—postmodernism is a reaction to modernism, ergo the "post" before the "modern." Once the seedbed of agnosticism was set, relativism was a foregone conclusion. So one might see postmodernism as nothing more than hyper-modernism.

Modernism then emphasized knowledge by sense perception alone as the empiricist philosophers won the day and scientism (a radical form of empiricism) emerged as the epistemological victor over rationalism. Postmodernism went a step further and taught that one can't even trust the sciences and sense perception. Knowledge is, for postmodernists (and now most of the humanities and social sciences), nothing but a social construction of reality. Many see the German philosopher, Nietzsche (1844–1900), as the first postmodern philosopher who coined the expression "God is dead."

John Dewey, the father of modern public school education in the U.S., promoted secular humanism and disavowed moral absolutes in the 1930s. After WWII, psychologist Abraham Maslow published his famed hierarchy of human needs, claiming the greatest human need was the need for self-actualization, not absolute truth. The search for meaning turned inward. Maslow's concept of self-actualization, finding oneself, encouraged humans to be their own gods, find their own version of truth; in other words, to socially construct their own reality. Social sciences in the U.S. embraced this thinking wholeheartedly, including the field of multiculturalism where my scholarly publications (Lynn) argue the need for a moral multiculturalism where worldviews are judged by standards and not all are accepted as equally ethical. The social constructivism and self-actualization principles of Dewey and Maslow run contrary to the idea of absolute truth once embedded in American schools. Postmodern relativism runs contrary to the truth propounded by naturalists in the sciences, yet even some scientists accept relativism.

Some would say as a cultural phenomenon, postmodernism began in the 1960s in the U.S., but note that the U.S. has been trailing Europe by decades. Perhaps it is true that it began with Nietzsche in Europe and bled to America later, certainly to the social sciences before the '60s. Today, there is a battle in the academy between the alliance of scientific naturalism (in the sciences) and postmodern anti-realism (in the humanities/ social sciences). Together, they are skeptical of religious or ethical claims of "knowledge."

Far too many professors in academia we have encountered in our years in higher education are atheists, or at least agnostics, and many further believe that faith in God is a harmful teaching. Famous atheist Christopher Hitchens asks, "How can we ever know how many children had their psychological and physical lives irreparably maimed by the compulsory inculcation of faith?"[37] Not all postmodernists are atheists, but many are since the ideas run contrary to an idea of a standard of absolute truth and morality. Everything is relative. Postmodernism supports the notion of numerous but different culturally constructed truths based on one's subjective experiences and how one feels about them. So one can cling to any perception that feels good, is self-serving, or seems to protect. But is it *true*? This is what we implore readers to probe.

To strict postmodernists, it may not matter. Humans are invited to disengage from arguments about truth and morality because all things are relative to the individual's own socially constructed worldview. Some avoid arguments about these topics, ignoring them as irrelevant since many believe there is no objective, discernible truth and therefore knowledge is "the social construction of reality."[38] "I'm comfortable with that" or "I'm not comfortable with that" replaces "that's true" or "that's wrong." Obviously, most individuals believe they have *some* moral yardstick based on personal views to determine which is which. If they, individually or collectively, determine a right and a wrong, then intentional attacks on others based on their "moral" interpretations can be justified. If there is *no* discernible right and wrong morality as some postmodernists assert, any willful attacks on others are groundless. Yet, we do attack and we think we know . . . .

So You Still Want to Be Your Own God Yet Reject God?

If we reject God, then, we turn to the sources of other humans or to ourselves to determine a true reality. Isn't this in a sense like being our own "God" or our own arbiter of truth? Leaving Mormonism, we had to ask, Am I a law unto myself? Are my own ideas always best? Certainly, we use human reasoning in faith, but ultimately Christians turn to a higher source than themselves for truth, not by ignoring reasoning but by using it. After reading the Bible, the first thing we had to decide was whether there exists a God more powerful and knowledgeable than we are. If so, then the next thing we needed to know was whether there was a reliable truth source for His teachings.

If this all-knowing God really does exist and the Bible is a reliable truth source, we have the basis for an argument for the existence of absolute truth. If there is no standard of truth set by an omniscient and moral God who knows better than humans, then all things are relative and each person decides on their own what to believe, what is true. As the ancient philosopher Protagoras once said, "Man is the measure of all things," that is, man is the arbiter of what is true. But the problem is that no one knows which man. It is all relative. Many former LDS embrace postmodern relativism after the rigidity of Mormonism.

While LDS, we were working our way to be clever enough to become a knowledgeable god. From Doctrines and Covenants 93:36: "The glory of God is intelligence, or, in other words, light and truth." Consider this—how is striving for godhood through this life and the next any different from acting as your own arbiter god of truth here on earth? In both cases, we rely on our own intelligence and effort, not some higher standard of right and wrong, true and not true from a source *more* intelligent than ourselves.

Many who leave the Mormon church say they spin their wheels. Is this true? Is that true? Is there a God who knows what is true? One former Mormon described the journey like this: "When LDS, I saw the world through the lens of one turn of a kaleidoscope. I thought that's all there was. Then the kaleidoscope turns and I see other possibilities for truth, then others, and others. All can't be true, but which, if any, is? Uncertainty is both a blessing and a burden." For us, acknowledging that there is a higher power with perfect advice, however, does not allow us to leave our brain at the door but requires that we use it efficiently. One could spend a lifetime in research and never touch truth. However, there is enough truth in the Bible to last a lifetime of digging it out, analyzing it, observing, testing, and learning.

The Bible is written in two modes: descriptive and prescriptive. Much of what non-theists point to in the Bible is descriptive of what flawed people *did* (war, polygamy), not prescriptive of what God approved or required. Even so, reconciling Scripture with Scripture by examining all Scripture throughout the Bible on a particular topic clarifies many things that are unclear from one passage or verse. Many biblical Christians disagree that science and the Bible clash. Accepting God and the Bible makes one a member of a 2.3 billion-person body of Christ, the Christian church. Every member espouses a set of core beliefs that are taught in the Bible and adopted universally. Less important beliefs can differ from Christian to Christian or from one Christian organization to the next. Mormon doctrine is incompatible with core Christian premises and, therefore, is reasonably placed outside of the body of Christ.

One reason for post-Mormons to enjoy the traditional Christian church is that it is very different from the top down, theocratic LDS organization named the Church of Jesus Christ of Latter-day Saints. In fact, they are nothing alike. The biblical church is not even an organization, not the Catholic church, not the Greek or Eastern Orthodox churches, not Protestant churches; not a "religious organization" at all. The traditional Christian church is a ragtag body of Christ-followers, a family of believers from all over the world who know an omniscient God they trust knows more than they do and accept that His teachings are contained in a reliable historical document, the Bible.

Outside of math, logic, and introspective philosophy, we are hard-pressed to find certainty. But that fact does not compel us to be unreasonable. Christianity is like Noah's ark. If it weren't for the great peril on the outside of the ark, people would want to jump ship because of the stench on the inside of the ark. More than just looking for land, Noah was probably peering out the window for a breath of fresh air. Being candid, some existential and intellectual hard questions remain for us as Christians. But no worldview is immune from this and those questions that remain are minimal compared to other worldviews. Christianity best explains our comprehensive human experience, and Jesus is the author of the world's largest and greatest movement in human history for a reason. Is it really rational to jump ship and exchange, say, five hard questions for fifty? Historical, traditional, biblical Christianity is more logically coherent, empirically adequate, existentially viable, and practically livable than any other competing worldview. Trusting in Jesus is most plausible and satisfying.

NOTES

1. C. S. Lewis, *God in the Dock: Essays on Theology and Ethics* (Grand Rapids: Eerdmans, 1970), 108–109.
2. Richard Dawkins, *The God Delusion* (New York, NY: Houghton-Mifflin Company, 2006), 308.
3. Tom Price, "Thinking Well: Logical Fallacies," RZIM Academy, http://courses.rzimacademy.org/lms/index.php?r=player&course_id=732&coming_from=lp&id_plan=59#training.
4. https://www.lds.org/topics/christians.
5. Bart Ehrman, *Misquoting Jesus: The Story Behind Who Changed the Bible and Why* (NY: HarperCollins, 2005), 248.
6. Antony Flew, *There is a God: How the Most Notorious Atheist Changed His Mind* (NY: HarperCollins, 2007).
7. Alex Rosenberg, *The Atheist's Guide to Reality: Enjoying Life without Illusions* (New York: Norton, 2011), 3.
8. Ibid., 95.

9. Ibid., 97.
10. Richard Dawkins, *River Out of Eden: A Darwinian View of Life* (New York: Basic Books/Harper-Collins, 1995), 132–33.
11. Rosenberg, *The Atheist's Guide,* 109.
12. Ibid., 110–12.
13. Michael Ruse, "Evolutionary Theory and Christian Ethics," in *The Darwinian Paradigm: Essays on Its History, Philosophy, and Religious Implications* (London: Routledge, 1989), 262, 268–69.
14. Randy Thornhill and Craig Palmer, *A Natural History of Rape: Biological Bases of Sexual Coercion* (Cambridge, MA: MIT Press, 2000), 20–28; Randy Thornhill, "Controversial New Theory of Rape in Terms of Evolution and Nature," National Public Radio, 26 January 2000.
15. C.S. Lewis, *Mere Christianity* (New York: Macmillan, 1952), 45–46.
16. Frederick Nietzsche, "Twilight of the Idols" in *The Portable Nietzsche,* ed. Walter Kaufman (New York: Penguin Books, 1976), 515.
17. Paul Copan and Matthew Flannagan, *Did God Really Command Genocide? Coming to Terms with the Justice of God* (Grand Rapids: Baker, 2014); *Is God a Moral Monster? Making Sense of the Old Testament God* (Grand Rapids: Baker, 2011); Clay Jones, "We Don't Hate Sin So We Don't Understand What Happened to the Canaanites: An Addendum to 'Divine Genocide' Arguments," *Philosophia Christi*, (Spring 2009): 53–72; *Why Does God Allow Evil? Compelling Answers for Life's Toughest Questions,* Harvest House (forthcoming); "Why Did God Let that Child Die?" *Christian Research Journal,* (February, 2015): 10–15.
18. Patricia Churchland, "Epistemology in the Age of Neuroscience," *Journal of Philosophy* 84 (October 1987): 548.
19. Rosenberg, *The Atheist's Guide,* 110.
20. Ibid., 6.
21. See Letter to William Graham (Down, July 3rd, 1881), in *The Life and Letters of Charles Darwin*, ed. Francis Darwin (London: John Murray, 1887), 1:315–16.
22. Alvin Plantinga, *Where the Conflict Really Lies: Science, Religion, and Naturalism* (Oxford: Oxford University Press, 2011), ix.
23. Rosenberg, *The Atheist's Guide,* 20.
24. Although the evidence is not considered here, the famous atheist philosopher Antony Flew, who changed his mind on God's existence a few years prior to his death, said, "*The evidence for the resurrection is better than for claimed miracles in any other religion. It's outstandingly different in quality and quantity, I think, from the evidence offered for the occurrence of most other supposedly miraculous events.*" See his interview in "My Pilgrimage from Atheism to Theism: A Discussion between Antony Flew and Gary R. Habermas," *Philosophia Christi* 6, no. 2 (2004): 209.
25. Ehrman, *Misquoting Jesus*, 89–90.
26. Craig Blomberg, *Can We Still Believe the Bible? An Evangelical Engagement with Contemporary Questions* (Grand Rapids: Brazos, 2014), 17.
27. Ibid., 27.
28. Ehrman, *Misquoting Jesus*, 252.
29. Daniel B. Wallace, "Has the New Testament Text Been Hopelessly Corrupted?" in *In Defense of the Bible: A Comprehensive Apologetic for the Authority of Scripture*, ed. Steven Cowan and Terry Wilder (Nashville: B&H, 2013), 151.
30. K. A. Kitchen, *On the Reliability of the Old Testament* (Grand Rapids: Eerdmans, 2003).
31. Josephus, *Antiquities*, 18:3, *The Works of Josephus*, trans. William Whiston (Nashville: Thomas Nelson Publishers, 1998).

32. Origen, *Contra Celsus*, 1:47, in *The Ante-Nicene Fathers*, ed. Alexander Roberts and James Donaldson (Grand Rapids: Eerdmans, 1989); quoted in Gary R. Habermas, *The Historical Jesus: Ancient Evidence for the Life of Christ* (Joplin, Missouri: College Press, 1996), 192.
33. James H. Charlesworth, *Jesus within Judaism* (New York: Doubleday, 1988), 95; quoted in Habermas, *The Historical Jesus*, 193–94.
34. Richard Bauckham, *Jesus and the Eyewitnesses: The Gospels as Eyewitness Testimony* (Grand Rapids, MI: Eerdmans, 2006).
35. Eric M. Meyers and Mark A. Chancey, *Alexander to Constantine: Archaeology of the Land of the Bible* (New Haven: Yale University Press, 2012).
36. Ravi Zacharias' Academy, RZIM Core Module, 2016, http://www.rzimacademy.org/courses/core-module/.
37. Christopher Hitchens, *God is Not Great: How Religion Poisons Everything* (New York: Hachette Book Group, Inc., 2007), 217.
38. Peter L. Berger, *The Social Construction of Reality* (New York: Penguin Books, 1966).

AUTHOR INDEX

SUBJECT INDEX

J

K

L

M

N

P

R

S

T